Highlights in the History of the
AMERICAN PRESS

HIGHLIGHTS IN THE
HISTORY OF THE
AMERICAN
PRESS

A BOOK OF READINGS edited by
EDWIN H. FORD and EDWIN EMERY

University of Minnesota Press MINNEAPOLIS

Library of Congress Catalog Card Number: 54-5606

PUBLISHED IN GREAT BRITAIN, INDIA, AND PAKISTAN BY
GEOFFREY CUMBERLEGE: OXFORD UNIVERSITY PRESS, LONDON, BOMBAY, AND KARACHI

FOREWORD

THE story of the American newspaper is a mosaic of myriad fragments: of newspapers themselves, of records and documents, of excerpts from general histories, of histories dealing specifically with journalism at large, of accounts of the development of single newspapers, of biographies and memoirs, and of articles from a wide assortment of periodicals, treating many phases and many periods of newspaper history.

In an attempt to present the most authentic and readable articles published in a variety of periodicals during the course of more than a century, a mimeographed collection of such articles was brought out by Edwin Ford in 1939. Interest in this limited edition, financed by a special University of Minnesota grant, was sufficient to justify the assumption that a revised edition issued in greater numbers and in more permanent form would be favorably received by scholars in related fields and by all those interested in newspapers and the men who make them as well as by students and teachers in journalism. Publication of this volume, with Edwin Ford and Edwin Emery as co-editors of a reorganized and augmented collection of articles, is the result.

The volume will, we hope, prove interesting to many types of readers. For those who wish to use it as a supplement to established histories of journalism, a word about the selections may be in order. The number of periodicals and writers here represented makes possible a catholicity in point of view toward the development of the newspaper which scarcely could be achieved by the author of a textbook, no matter how excellent a volume he might produce. On the other hand, few collections have the continuity, the singleness of purpose evident in the work of one writer.

In order as far as possible to present the articles so that they will give to the reader a sense of the continuity of newspaper development, they have been grouped with reference to six historical periods, the limits of which have been arbitrarily set with full realization that political, economic, and social trends and movements can be confined only approximately within the boundaries imposed by dates. Whenever limitations of space have forced a choice between excellent articles, we have sought to include those which best help to tell the story of the American newspaper in the most significant periods of its development, keeping also in mind the aim of preserving in book form the most rewarding of relatively inaccessible periodical articles about newspapers and newspapermen.

The completeness of a collection of *articles* on newspaper history is limited, it might be noted also, by the fact that much significant material is to be found only in books. Some journalists, some newspapers, some trends have engaged the attention of competent writers of articles far more than have others. So the factor of availability, as well as that of editorial choice, explains the absence of full-length studies of a few familiar journalistic personalities. Essays which introduce the six groups of articles are designed, therefore, both to put the individual studies into proper historical perspective and to examine briefly those journalistic events not covered in detail.

The seven articles which make up Sections I and II quite naturally deal mainly with general trends. The two great men of early English and American colonial journalism, Daniel Defoe and Benjamin Franklin, can be presented in some detail, but otherwise the journalism of their times was not sufficiently advanced to provide studies of individual editors or printers. The process of cleavage set up by the Revolution sharpened editorial pens and created issues which were to develop the professional approach to newspapering. Printers came closer to being editors after 1776, and a shift in emphasis to delineate the personalities of such stalwarts as Tom Paine and William Cobbett therefore logically follows.

With the onset of the popular press in the Jacksonian era there began to emerge more and more journalists capable of being cited as representative of their newspapers, their communities, their periods. Thus it is not surprising that the selections comprising the last two thirds of this volume deal with editors and publishers who have played a tremendous part in shaping the destiny of American newspapers from the days when the editorial thunder of Jackson's *Washington Globe* rolled across the nation to the days of giant metropolitan dailies.

The 27 articles presented here are selected from the files of 17 periodicals, representing a variety of publishing endeavors. Four contributions come from once-great but no longer published magazines: the *Galaxy, Independent,* and *Scribner's.* Eleven others come from general magazines: the *American Mercury, Atlantic Monthly, Collier's, New Republic,* and *Time.* Ten articles were first published in scholarly journals: the *Journalism Quarterly, Mississippi Valley Historical Review, New England Quarterly, Pennsylvania Magazine, PMLA, Quarterly Review,* and *South Atlantic Quarterly.* The final two come from magazines in the journalism field: *Editor & Publisher* and the *Nieman Reports.* Thanks are due to the several magazine editors for permission to republish the selected articles in this volume.

We wish also to acknowledge with gratitude the permissions granted by the authors of the articles, or by those speaking for them. Specifically we thank for their cooperation in copyright matters Arundell Esdaile, John Dos Passos, Robert L. Duffus, Henry F. Pringle, Kenneth Stewart, John Tebbel, Mrs. Gamaliel Bradford, Mrs. Will Irwin, Mrs. George P. West, and W. L. White.

Finally, there are those at the University of Minnesota whose aid has helped to make this book possible. Some of the research work was financed by a Graduate School grant. Colleagues in the School of Journalism have been helpful. And above all, members of the staff of the University of Minnesota Press contributed greatly to whatever success this publication may enjoy.

EDWIN H. FORD
EDWIN EMERY

Minneapolis, Minnesota
October 1953

TABLE OF CONTENTS

ix

TABLE OF CONTENTS

Highlights in the History of the
AMERICAN PRESS

I

THE RISE OF AN ENGLISH PRESS

BEFORE *any socially significant method of news dissemination had been adopted in England, there were sporadic attempts in Germany, Holland, France, Italy, and portions of the Orient to present news by means of ink and paper. Since, however, it is with English modifications of the early pattern that the history of American journalism is most closely associated, the story of the American newspaper, for all practical purposes, may be said to begin in England.*

The well-nigh universal desire for knowledge of what was happening beyond the boundaries of English villages and shires was very early satisfied in limited degree by ballad singers, later by writers of newsletters, and still later by printers of ballad sheets, news sheets, and news books. Not long after the advent of the seventeenth century, sheets of foreign news, called corantos, *were introduced in England and prepared the way for the printing of domestic news, an important source of partisan propaganda during the struggle between Charles I and Parliament which brought on the Civil War. Star Chamber decrees and licensing regulations imposed by monarchs fearful of the growing power of the printed word served only to retard for a brief period the progress of early English journalism.*

The decline of monarchial influence and the rise of political parties made England fertile ground for partisan journalism during the eighteenth century. Particularly in London, journals of news and opinion multiplied rapidly, most of them serving a party cause or group. While the effusions of Grub Street hack writers were being devoured by the half-illiterate outer fringe of coffeehouse circles, the more influential Englishmen were reading Defoe, Addison, Steele,

3

Swift, Dr. Johnson, Walpole, Burke, and Wilkes — men who were to leave their impress upon American literary and polemic writing.

It is not without design that Defoe's name heads this list. The brilliant coterie of writers who so effectively used the pamphlet and the newspaper for discussion, sober and satiric, of political and social questions during the 1700s had within its ranks no more typical journalist than Defoe. The pattern of his writing career anticipated that of thousands of English and American journalists who were to follow him. Starting as a pamphleteer — the eighteenth-century counterpart of the modern free-lancer — he later attached himself to a variety of newspapers and emerged finally as a novelist of power. He has rightly been termed by scholars "the progenitor of the modern journalist."

To what extent Addison and Steele may have learned from Defoe is largely a matter of speculation, but their Spectator *achieved, within the narrow limits of the Queen Anne period, greater acclaim than was given to Defoe's* Review. *The essay-journalism of Addison and Steele provided London with social commentary such as it had seldom met with in the pages of a periodical.*

John Wilkes' fiery opposition to the policies of Lord Bute, prime minister to George III, an opposition carried on in the columns of Wilkes' North Briton, *so aroused popular feeling that "Wilkes and Liberty" became a rallying cry in America as well as in England.*

The articles included in Part I of this volume have been selected to illustrate the manner in which the newspaper evolved in England from the time of its earliest beginnings until it emerged under these leaders as an instrument of political and social power in the eighteenth century. By that time the transition to colonial America had begun.

Arundell Esdaile in his article on the ballad journalism of the sixteenth century reminds his readers that these ballads were "mainly topical and inspired by current events of more or less public interest." The modern student of journalism can profitably compare the topics of the sixteenth-century ballad makers with the news selection of twentieth-century editors. Wars, fires, crimes, executions, miracles, obituaries, cataclysms of nature, material dealing with political and religious matters: the early news pattern is basically little different from that of today's newspaper.

The addition of a partisan journalism to the informational and entertaining type supplied by the news ballads is taken up in Elbert N. S.

4

Thompson's discussion of the part played by the press in England's Civil War. News books and pamphlets, he points out, were extensively used by Roundheads and Cavaliers in attempts to enlist public support for their causes. Limited though literacy was in the England of the 1640s, the printed word was beginning to be used for purposes of propaganda.

Englishmen were not slow to realize the partisan power of the newspaper, as William T. Laprade demonstrates in pointing out the significance of the English press in the eighteenth century. Of that period he writes, "The transition from a society in which newspapers were unimportant and almost unknown to one in which they were accepted as a matter of course and as almost essential if existing conditions were not to be radically changed, occurred in England in that century."

Out of the welter of controversy and progress which characterized eighteenth-century English journalism came Daniel Defoe, pamphleteer, editor, novelist. His chief journalistic service was performed very early in the century and he was, as John Dos Passos says, subject to the vicissitudes of a stormy political period, but his thinking was in many respects modern, and his instincts were those of the present-day publicist. In his footsteps followed Benjamin Franklin, who can be said to have been chiefly significant in the history of the American newspaper for carrying over into colonial life and vitalizing with his own personality the English journalistic tradition.

I

Autolycus' Pack: The Ballad Journalism of the Sixteenth Century

by ARUNDELL ESDAILE

ARUNDELL ESDAILE is both an authority on bibliography and a poet. Long-time secretary of the British Museum, he was made a Commander, Order of the British Empire, in 1952. His article on ballad journalism in the April 1913 *Quarterly Review* was later published in *Autolycus' Pack and Other Light Wares: Being Essays, Addresses and Verses* (Grafton & Co., 1940).

THE girl sitting opposite me in my suburban train of a morning, gravely studying her halfpenny illustrated daily paper, has perhaps not read "The Winter's Tale" — at least since she left school; and, if she were to read it, would not recognize herself in Mopsa, who "loves a ballad in print, for then we are sure it is true," nor her favourite paper as the direct descendant and representative of the ballads with which Autolycus' pack was so richly furnished. Yet this is the egg from which that full-fledged and loud-voiced bird, our modern journalism, has been hatched.

The first English periodicals were the newly-discovered series of "Courants" printed at Amsterdam in 1620–21. A predecessor to these, dated 1588 and reporting the defeat of the Armada, was ingeniously forged by the Earl of Hardwicke in 1743–44 in the form of three numbers ("50," "51" and "54") of "The English Mercurie. Published by Authoritie, for the Prevention of false Reportes." This, no doubt, he found much more amusing than the large history of the Armada which he gave up for it. He planned his forgery well, but it was very imperfectly executed; and, after a much longer success than it deserved, it at last met the eye of a bibliographer, Thomas Watts, of the British Museum Library, who promptly exposed it.

No doubt, before these regular — in dates of appearance often irregular — journals, there was a mass of catchpenny news-quartos; many of these bear title-pages of the most full-blooded and sensational kind, often so lengthy as to render the reading of the book itself quite unnecessary, even if one had any temptation to do so. Examples from the library of Worcester College, Oxford, catalogued in a little book printed by Canon Daniel at his private press, show plainly that the deviser of headlines and placards is not the son of later times, but an old and grey-headed disturber of the public peace. Earlier than these again, earliest of all, the first answer of the printing-press, at least in England, to that natural and universal desire of humanity to hear some new thing and then to tell it to someone else, was the ballad or "ballet." By this name we, of course, do not mean the "ballads" commonly so-called — that large and far more celebrated class of poems, the dramatic ballads of the Scottish border and elsewhere, first restored to favour by Percy, and now collected in Prof. Child's monumental volumes. Poems like "Binnorie" or "Lord Rendal" seem never to have been printed till comparatively recent times.* Perhaps they flourished most at a distance from the great cities; perhaps their singers, the wandering minstrels, kept them locked jealously in their own memories. Nor are we to speak of the duller narrative ballads, that arose about 1590, it seems, and flourished throughout the seventeenth century, such as "Patient Grissell" or "The Merchant's Daughter of Bristow." These are far commoner, and abound in the Roxburghe, Haigh Hall, Pepys and similar collections.

The sixteenth century "ballet" was different from either of these and, as has already been suggested, was mainly topical and inspired by current events of more or less public interest. Of these, about two hundred, out of the multitude that the Register of the Stationers' Company shows to have been poured forth by the Elizabethan presses, are known to exist to-day — all but two or three in single copies. About a third of these scanty survivors are now and have long been in safe keeping in the library of the Society of Antiquaries at Burlington House.† The remaining two-thirds have had a curious history. They were first heard of early in the nineteenth century, as a loose bundle in a sheep-skin wrapper, in the hands of the housekeeper at Helmingham Hall in Suffolk, who sold or gave them (with an absolute right

* "Chevy Chase" was printed as a chap book in the 17th century.
† They were well catalogued for the Society by Robert Lemon so long ago as 1866, but they still await reprinting.

7

to do so as far as any evidence goes, though it has been needlessly doubted) to a Mr. Fitch, postmaster at Ipswich. He knew something of their value, and sold them either to a dealer or direct to George Daniel of Canonbury, who, it is believed, gave the then fair price of 50 £ for them. Later in his life Daniel, perhaps following the practice of wise collectors whose funds are not unlimited, of selling or exchanging earlier acquisitions as their tastes alter, disposed of about half of his ballads to Thorpe, the dealer in Shakespeariana. Thorpe, who was the Bernard Quaritch of his day, and knew the tastes of all the collectors and was trusted by them, wrote to the omnivorous Richard Heber about his purchase, with the result that he sold it to him for 200 £. Heber's enormous collection of books, filling no fewer than eight houses, instead of being left to the nation, was dispersed at a series of sales in 1834–35; and the ballads, except a few based on classical authors which are now lost, passed with much else into the library at Britwell Court, then being formed by Mr. W. H. Miller, who, from his passion for the margin and condition of his books, was nicknamed "Measure Miller." There they have remained, a treasure among treasures; and a reprint of them was presented last year by their owner, Mr. Sydney Christie Miller, to the members of the Roxburghe Club.

There is such a thing as parentage in libraries; and, while the Britwell collection is the child of the "Bibliotheca Heberians," the Daniel library gave birth to the Huth. The one half of Daniel's "sleeping beauties" — as Heber called them — having been sold, as we have seen, to Thorpe, the other half remained with Daniel till his death in 1864. They were then secured by Mr. Henry Huth for the then remarkably high price of 750 £, to which Miller probably ran him up with the intention of reuniting what had been put asunder; and in Huth's library and that of his son they remained till last year, when the latter, crowning his and his father's long tradition of generosity, bequeathed to the British Museum its choice of any fifty of his books, and this volume passed into the national library as one of them.*

So much for the vicissitudes of these waifs of literature on their way to their final home; it is of more consequence to understand what they are and what sort of men produced them. These poems vary greatly, but one point nearly all had in common. The name "ballet" may re-

* In 1867 Henry Huth presented a reprint of them to the Philobiblon Society; this was reprinted by Joseph Lilly in the same year. Many of the quotations below are from the latter.

mind us that they were intended to be sung — as the Clown put it, "a very pleasant thing and sung lamentably." Often no doubt the wandering pedlar sang them himself; but that would not be so much to earn pence, like the minstrels, as by singing to show the quality of his wares. Occasionally the printed broadside bears the music; but more often the words were written to some familiar air, such as "Row well, ye mariners," "The Black Almaine," or someone or other's "Galliard." Sometimes the words are appropriate to the sprightly Galliard music, and the "ballet" is in fact a dance. Take this, of 1569:

> Good fellowes must go learne to daunce,
>   The brydeall is full nere a;
> There is a brall * come out of France;
>   The tryxt † ye harde ‡ this yeare a;
> For I must leape, and thou must hoppe,
>   And we must turne all three a;
> The fourth must bounce it like a toppe,
>   And so we shall agree a.
> I praye thee, mynstrell, make no stoppe,
>   For we will merye be a . . .
>
> A bande of belles, in bauderycke wyse,
>   Woulde decke us in our kynde a;
> A shurte after the Moryce guyse,
>   To flounce it in the wynde a.
> A wiffler § for to make the waye,
>   And maye brought in withall a,
> Is braver than the sunne, Iasaye,
>   And passeth round or brall a;
> For we will trype so tricke and gaye,
>   That we wyll passe them all a.
>
> Drawe to dauncing, neighbours all,
>   Good fellowshyppe is best a;
> It skylles not yf we take a fall,
>   In honoringe this feste a.
> The bryde wyll thanke us for our glee,
>   The worlde wyll us beholde a;
> O where shall all this dauncinge be,
>   In kent or at Cotsolde a?
> Oure Lorde doth knowe, then axe not mee,
>   And so my tale is tolde a.

* Brall, a dance.
† Tryxt, trickest, i.e. neatest.
‡ Harde, heard.
§ Wiffler, whiffler, a wand-bearing official at solemnities.

9

Others, if not dances, are essentially songs, such as "Adewe, sweete harte, adewe," and, in a less lyrical vein, "The Maid that would marry with a serving man," or "As pleasant a dittie as your hart can wish, Shewing what unkindness befell by a kisse." Such were the ballads with which Sir Toby Belch kept his kinswoman's household awake; some, too, are not without the "scurrilous words" that Perdita deprecated. But more are pious or moral or both. Several of these expound the Bible — that is, the Old Testament only; and these are perhaps the worst verse produced in the mid-sixteenth century, the driest desert that English poetry has had to pass through. One of the nine stanzas of John Symon's "Pleasant Poesie, or sweete Nosegay of fragrant smellyng Flowers gathered in the Garden of heavenly Pleasure, the holy and blessed Bible, to the tune of the Black Almayne," will show us the pathetic spectacle of the pious versifier endeavouring "not to let the devil have all the best tunes."

> Good Abraham, that faithful man,
>   In God dyd trust alway:
> He dyd not feare, nor once dispayre
>   His only son to slay;
> Isacke was no weede,
> Nor Jacob in very deede;
>   Joseph was a flower of price,
>   God dyd hym save from cruell device;
> Also Moses eke we fynd;
> And Aaron lykewyse up we bynd,
>   Josua is not out of mynd.

Even in the secular ballads the conclusion must be pious or loyal or both; a reference to the Queen is often introduced like a doxology at the end of a modern hymn. One balladist, John Saparton, was hard put to it to end

> Saparton's Alarum to all such as do beare
> The name of true soldiers in England or elsewheare,

and was reduced to this:

> So thus my leave I take;
>   O souldier, now farewell:
> No more to do now will I make,
>   But God preserve Queen EL.

This piece lies on the border of another substantial class, the satires and moral exhortations, for which the Elizabethan public seem to have had an almost insatiable appetite. It is, then, as ever, the age of iron; "neybourhed, love, and trew dealyng is gone"; the landlords "double the rent, to poore men's payne"; in the words of one ballad, which sarcastically (in no fewer than twenty-three stanzas) paints the world as perfect,

> O marvelous tydynges, both wonders old and new,
> The Devyll is endited, yf many men's wordes be true;

"The prisons be empty, there bee but iiij score and ten in Kynges Benche," and of them

>   som be tyed with clogges,
> Som gnaw broun crustes of bred, som burnish boones
>   like doggs;
> Som wysh to fyll thyr gutts with catts, ratts, myse,
>   or froggs —

an example which causes those outside to "abhorre Clinkerum" ("clink" or prison) to such an extent that

> A man may goo now over Fynsbery fylde
> Without sweard and buckler, without speare or shylde,
> With an houndred poundes.

These exhortations are often only half serious. For instance, we have "A proper new balade expressynge the fames Concerning a warning to all London dames." But the least poetical and the most illuminating to the student are the "occasional" poems, the true journalism. These are not so various as the contents of a modern newspaper; but there is nevertheless a considerable diversity. The obituary is represented by memorial poems on several nobles, just dead. One is on the Earl of Southampton, the father of Shakespeare's patron, and dates from 1581. The Earl of Huntingdon, too, who died in 1595, was celebrated in a set of verses, from which we learn his virtues as President of the Council in the North and also as a landlord:

> His tennants, that daylie repairde to his house,
> Was fed with his bacon, his beefe and his souse;
> Their rents were not raised, their fines were but small,
> And manie poore tennants paide nothing at all;

and as a patron of scholars (he was part-founder of Emmanuel College, Cambridge),

He built up no pallace nor purchaste no towne,
But gave it to schollers to get him renowne,
As Oxford and Cambridge can rightly declare
How many poore schollers maintained are there.

The correspondence column, too, was not absent. Indeed, the earliest unofficial broadsides were contributions to a controversy between the old and new religion. Towards the end of Henry VIII's reign it was thought worth while to issue a proclamation against these ballad-sheets, so the vogue must have risen quickly; and it is significant of the Protestantism of London that, whereas fresh proclamations were issued by Mary, under Edward VI and Elizabeth the balladists were left undisturbed. These controversies, ballad answering ballad, were not infrequent later, and probably, like similar controversies between well-known journalists of to-day, were primarily intended to keep their authors' names before the public.

A favourite form of the news-ballad was the description of monstrous births, now relegated by a more delicate public taste to an obscurity only occasionally broken by low-class showmen. By an Elizabethan popular audience these were received with avidity. We have accounts of a shark caught in 1569,* which recalls Autolycus' "ballad of a fish, that appeared upon the coast, on Wednesday, the fourscore of April, 40,000 fathom above water, and sung this ballad against the hard hearts of maids"; or Trinculo's exclamations at sight of Caliban: "A strange fish! Were I in England (as once I was), and had but this fish painted, not a holiday fool there but would give a piece of silver; there would this monster make a man; any strange beast there makes a man: when they will not give a doit to relieve a lame beggar, they will lay out ten to see a dead Indian."

These sheets are adorned — or disfigured — by crude woodcuts and generally consist, first of an account in prose of the creature, often containing an announcement that it is on show at such and such a place; and secondly of a set of verses pointing out that this is a warning from God for the sins of the age. However, where a human child is in question, the author is generally careful to observe that the par-

---

* This gives curious evidence of the origin of the word "shark" as applied to the fish. It is derived from the Old French "cherquier," to prowl, and originally meant a prowler or greedy fellow generally; but on this sheet of 1569 the description of the "marveilous straunge fishe" ends with the words, "There is no proper name for it that I knowe, but that sertayne men of Captayne Haukinses doth call it a sharke."

ents are respectable people; and so, it is implied, the warning is not
to be taken as confined to sinners. Some lines, taken from one of the
silliest of these poems, "A mervaylous straunge deformed Swyne," by
a well-known writer, John Phillip, will show the professional moral-
iser's attitude:

> Come neere, good Christians all,
>   Beholde a monster rare,
> Whose monstrous shape, no doubt, fortels,
>   God's wrath we should beware . . .
>
> For if you do way well ech poynt,
>   His nature and his shape,
> I feare, resembles some of those
>   As on the same do gape;
>
> For why, most swinish are our lives,

and so forth, elaborating the analogies in detail. Piety is the common
feature; a seventeenth-century account of two "Siamese twins" by
Martin Parker is even headed by the words "Admire the Creator in
His creatures." But it need not be supposed that these tales were all
true. The time was one of change; men could not know as we know,
looking back, that they were at the beginning of a long and secure
reign; the memory of a single life-time could recall all the changes, the
strife, the fears abroad and at home, which the country had passed
through since the early years of Henry VIII's reign; nor could men
know that worse was not to come. Hence their passionate devotion
to Elizabeth, who stood, in her earlier years at least, for a comparatively sane and tolerant rule; and hence also this readiness to swallow
any portent that they heard of, especially if it had the authority of
print: "I love a ballad in print o' life; for then we are sure they are
true. Is it true, think you?" says Mopsa; and Autolycus reassures her,
"Very true, and but a month old." Yet the author of Martin Mar-
Sixtus (1592) is probably nearer the facts when he tells us that "scarce
a cat can look out of a gutter, but out starts a halfpenny chronicler
and presently a proper new ballet of a strange sight is indited."

All was, as it still is, grist for the "halfpenny chronicler's" mill —
"quidquid agunt" (still more "quidquid dicunt") "homines." "Alas!"
Webster makes one of his characters say (blending Venice strangely
with London),

> Alas! I make but repetition
> Of what is ordinary and Rialto talk,
> And ballated, and would be played o' the stage.

Tarlton, the celebrated comic actor, began his career with a journalistic poem, which is only unconsciously humorous, on "the fierce Floods which lately flowed in Bedfordshire, in Lincolnshire, and in many other places, the 5 of October, 1570." So fierce were they that "The arke of father Noye Was had in mind as than." The author, in the true spirit of the reporter, records a conversation with certain Lincoln men:

> What countrey men they were
> I did request to knowe;
> They said of Lincolnshire,
> The certen truth is so.
>
> Quod they, your losse is small,
> But one hath lost her life:
> He askt whose dame she was?
> I said one Spencer's wife.
>
> In Lincolnshire (he said)
> We have sustained great losse
> Our stomacks are decaide,
> That late so frolick was.

Observe how each contends for the losses of his own county. In the peroration morality and loyalty have to be served, as usual:

> In us therefore for shame
> Let vice no more be seen.
> And eke our selves to frame
> To serve aright our Queen.

Far less was written on the defeat of the Armada than might have been expected; and of what was written scarcely anything survives. Among the most popular sensations—at least as popular an event as the Armada itself—was the execution of seven Catholics. Executions and fires, indeed, were always well written up; they rarely lacked what must serve for their *vates sacer*. In 1586 the Babington conspiracy failed, and there was a bath of executions; among those who paid the penalty figured Chidiock Tichborne (one of the well-known Catholic family names which recurred in every plot or rising), and it may be not uninstructive to see by a comparison of his well-known poem, written on

his last night before execution,* with the stanza devoted to him by
Deloney, how poetry, like the herbs Euphues mentions, "which the
more they are crushed the sweeter they smell," flourishes in "lost
causes" and withers in success. The last stanza of the three of which
Tichborne's poem consists runs thus:

> I sought my death, and found it in my wombe,
>   I lookt for life, and saw it was a shade:
> I trod the earth, and knew it was my Tombe,
>   And now I die, and now I was but made.
> My glasse is full, and now my glasse is runne.
> And now I live, and now my life is done.

Compare Deloney:

> O Techborne, what bewitched thee
>   To have such hate in store
> Against our good and gratious Queene
>   That thou must die therefore? . . .

Of another of the seven victims, who are dealt with in turn, we are
told:

> So likewise Jones did much complaine
>   Of his detested pride,
> And shewed how lewdly he did live
>   Before the time he died.

"What cause," exclaims Deloney in conclusion,

> But that the Devill inticed them
>   Such wicked words to render,
> For which these seven did suffer death
>   The twentith of September?

But what we may call the political news-ballad may be best studied
at a far less dangerous moment than that of the Babington conspiracy
or the Armada, in the month following the failure of the futile and
tragic "Rising in the North," in 1569–70. The Earls of Northumberland
and Westmoreland had collected a small force, and made a raid southward, with the intention of releasing Mary, Queen of Scots, and marrying her to the Duke of Norfolk, who, like herself, was destined to
perish on the block, but, unlike her, after no long interval. But Sussex,

* Published with one T. K.'s "Hendecasyllabon in cygneam cantionem Chidiocki
Tychborne," in "Verses of Prayse and Joye," 1586. T. K.'s poem is one of those
line-for-line and phrase-for-phrase replies which the century apparently found
so witty.

President of the Council in the North, was not caught napping; Mary was quickly moved to Coventry, out of the way of the rebels. Their untrained force speedily disbanded; the leaders, with the horse, fled northward through Durham and Hexhamshire, and up the dale of the North Tyne into the borderland known as the "Bateable," a wild, barren country of moors and gorges, dotted with peel towers, and lawless long after this date. The winter was now coming on, and the weather was "extreme of frost and snow." The horses of the Countess of Northumberland and her ladies were stolen, and they themselves were left in squalor at the mean house of a borderer, whose name survives in the lines

> He is weil kend, Johne of the Syde,
> A greater thief did never ryde.

Westmoreland only escaped by changing his sword and "cote of plate" with this John of the Side. The poet of the Northcountrymen tells an heroic legend how Westmoreland took ship with his companions, and, meeting with Don John of Austria, won for himself great glory and state in the service of the Queen of Sicily, fulfilling a prophecy "in the book of Mable" (whatever that may be) that "Charles Neville, with a child's voice," should come over the sea to be her deliverer from the Soldan. But this was the dream of a mind that sought escape from the miserable truth. The commonalty implicated in the rising were executed in numbers, the men of rank attainted. Westmoreland and the other leaders escaped to the Continent, to drag out years of dependence as poor pensioners on Philip of Spain; and often must they have thought with longing of their home, like Swinburne's exile of 1746,

> O lordly flow the Loire and Seine,
> And loud the dark Durance;
> But bonnier shine the braes of Tyne
> Than a' the fields of France,

and have envied Northumberland, who was betrayed by the Scots and executed in 1572, or the two sons of old Norton, whose limbs were already in 1570 (in the balladists' consecrated phrase) "wavering in the wind." As in 1586, the losing cause was compensated by its poetical superiority. The ballad of "The Rising in the North," in Percy's folio, opens with these dramatic, if unhistorical, lines:

Earl Percy is into his garden gone
    And after walks his awn ladie:
"I hear a bird sing in my ear,
    That I must either fight or flee."

"God forbid," she said, "good my Lord,
    That ever so that it shall be;
But go to London to the court,
    And fair fall truth and honestie!"

Well would it have been for him if he had!

Till the result of the rising was known, London was full first of alarm, then of flying reports of victory. Thomas Bette, in his "Ballad against Rebellious and false Rumours," says:

Some longeth to hear tell
Of those that dyd rebell,
And whether they be fled or take,
Thus still enquirie they do make;
Some sayth to Scotland they be goe,
And others sayth it is not so.

The small minority of Londoners with Romanist leanings minimised the rumours of the Earls' flight as long as it was possible. But it was not possible for long. The truth became known; and London, which now for more than a generation had been Protestant to the core, burst into an ecstasy of triumph. It must be allowed that sympathy for an opponent who, of the two great loyalties, to faith and to country, chooses the former, was a virtue yet unknown; but Protestantism in the day of prosperity, and still more in the very hour of victory, is perhaps as ugly, as insolent, and as unspiritual a thing as ever called itself religion. The songs of victory were not elevated productions; but some have spirit — the spirit of mockery. William Elderton (of whom more below) wrote two at least of the best,

A Ballad intituled a newe Well a daye,
As playne, maister Papist, as Donstable waye,

which ironically laments the failure of the rising and the hanging of Plumtre, the rebels' chaplain-general, for celebrating mass in the Cathedral at Durham, to the refrain

Well a daye, well a daye, well a daye, woe is mee,
Syr Thomas Plomtre is hanged on a tree,

and "Newes from Northumberland," in which he addresses the mortified Catholics of London as follows:

> You whisperinge fellowes that walke every wheare,
> Now clau your old elbowes, and skratch up your heaer,
> I will tell you for troth what newes I heare,
> The Bull * of the North is afrayd of the Beare.*
> *This geare goethe well, and better it shall,*
> *For triall will tell the treason of Ball.*†
>
> The moone * and the star are fallen so at stryfe,
> I never knewe warre so strange in my lyfe;
> And all is longe of a Babylon beaste
> That hath a thowsand heddes at the leaste,
> *This geare goethe well, etc.*
>
> Why walke ye not by three and three
> In Polles, ‡ as ye were wonte to bee,
> And say, as you were wont to do,
> I hold you a crowne it is not true,
> *This geare goethe well, etc.*

In the same style, among others, is Kirkham's

> Ballad rejoysinge the sodaine fall
> Of Rebels that thought to devower us all,

from which we learn that the rebels

> steadfastly did hope
> God's flocke cleane to destroy,
>
> And then set up within this land
> In every churche and towne
> Their idols on roode loftes to stand,
> Like gods of great renowne,
>
> Their aulters and tradicions olde,
> With painted stocke and stone,
> Pardons and masses to be sold,
> With Kyrieleyson.
>
> Friers shoulde weare their olde graye gownes,
> And maides to shrift should com,
> Then priestes should singe with shaven crownes,
> Dominus vobiscum.

* The crests of Westmoreland, Sussex and Northumberland respectively.
† I.e. Baal, easily identified by good Protestants with Rome.
‡ St. Paul's Cathedral.

18

Early in the next year, when the sensation of the rising was settling down, came the publication of Pius V's Bull, excommunicating Queen Elizabeth. This is "*the* Bull" of common parlance — that which has meant most to modern England. It was published in London by a devoted and foolhardy Catholic gentleman, John Felton, who, with little concealment, fastened a copy to the Bishop of London's gate. He was promptly taken, and after a short trial executed with the usual barbarities. This incident, it may be supposed, was a heaven-sent opportunity for the journalists; and the obvious pun on the word Bull was not allowed to rest unworked. There survives a prose pamphlet, with the title, "A Disclosing of the great Bull, and of sundry calves that he hath gotten, and especially of the monster Bull that roared at my Lord Bishop's gate." Ballads were numerous. Steven Peele, a professional balladist, wrote

> A Letter to Rome to declare to the Pope
> John Felton, his freend, is hanged in a rope,

to the popular tune of "Row well, ye mariners." It is jubilant, defiant:

> Wherefore, Sir Pope,
> In England you have lost your hope.
> Curse on, spare not,
> Your knights are like to go to pot;

and ends with a defiance:

> Now do I end,
> I came to show you as a friend:
> Whether blesse or curse
> You send to me, I am not the worse.

To the same tune and in the same style is

> A Lamentation from Rome how the Pope doth bewayle
> That Rebelles in England can not prevayle,

by Thomas Preston, the author of Cambyses, who should have known better than to produce this "scurrill ballate"; it is put into the mouth of a special correspondent in Rome, who has had exceptional opportunities.

> All you that newes would heare
> Give eare to me, poor Fabyn flye.
> At Rome I was, this yere,
> And in the Pope his nose did lye.

> But there I could not long abide,
> He blew me out of every side;
> For furst when he had harde the newes
> That Rebelles dyd their Prince misuse,
>   Then he with joye
> Did sporte him selfe with many a toye;
>   He then so stout
> That from his nose he blew me out.

Of the professional ballad-writers, those denizens of an earlier Grub Street, very little is known. They are spoken of with universal contempt by the Elizabethan men of letters. Anthony Munday, who calls himself "one of the Queen's servants," was a fertile translator of foreign romances; Thomas Deloney and Richard Johnson were the authors of "The Gentle Craft" and "The Seven Champions of Christendom" respectively; and all these three found it worth while to collect some of their sheets into the more permanent form of volumes, with fanciful titles, such as "The Crown Garland of Golden Roses." But for many years the Coryphaeus of the band was William Elderton, to whom references abound in the literature of the period. He is not a dignified figure. Few allusions to him omit mention of his red nose and its too notorious cause; and indeed he wrote an extremely bibulous tract in verse, with the pleasing title

> New mery newes,
>   As mery as can bee,
> From Italy, Barbary,
>   Turkie and Candee,

which concludes with a ribald drinking song, having for refrain the famous

> Hey jolly Jenkin!
> I see * a knave a-drinking!

There remains to us a fragment of a controversy between Elderton and a less notable balladist, William Fulwood, whose favourite subject was monsters, about one Leach, a hosier; Fulwood jeers at Elderton thus:

> It was no doubt unhomely done
>   To challenge in such case
> So fyne a fellow as Eldertonne
>   That hath so fayre a face.

* "See," not "spy," in Elderton. But the refrain may of course be older.

20

> And him methinks you should not blame
>> That can well shape a hose,
> For he may likewise cut and frame
>> A case for your rich nose.

In Elderton may be studied the "man in the street" of the sixteenth century; and it must be said that the study is enlivened for the student by Elderton's command of rhythm. It is elementary sing-song, of course; but he never, like so many of his fellows, "treads a foul, lumbering, boisterous, wallowing measure," floundering on from line to line, living for the next rhyme, with hardly a thought of the rhythm on the way to it or of the sense beyond it. These virtues and defects of Elderton are amusingly shown in a ballad of 1578, an account of one of Elizabeth's narrow escapes. It is called "A Newe Ballade, declaryng the dangerous Shooting of the Gunne at the Courte. To the tune of Siche and Siche." Its stanzas are far too numerous to quote; and these will more than suffice:

> The seventeene daie of Julie last, at evenyng toward night,
> Our noble Queene Elizabeth took barge for her delight:
> And bad the waterman to row, her pleasure she might take,
> About the river to and fro, as much as thei could make.
>> *Weepe, weepe, still I weepe, and shall doe till I dye,*
>> *To think upon the gonne was shot at court so daungerouslie.*

> But all this while upon the Thames, in Schuller's boat unknown.
> A wretched felloe got a gun, that was none of his owne,
> And shot a bullet twoo or three at random all about,
> And gave no greate regard to see what time the Queene went out.
>> *Weepe, weepe, etc.*

One of the bullets struck a waterman in the Queen's barge through both his arms.

>> His gushyng blood could not abashe her noble
>>> courage then,
>> But she was readier to give help than all
>>> the noble men.

This is probably true, for Elizabeth is known to have fairly earned the reputation for courage, which is so easily granted to crowned heads.

The offender, Thomas Appletree, "of courte a serving man," was quickly arrested.

>> He was committed to the gaile, at counsellors
>>> grave regarde,

> That thei might judge what vilest death were fit
>   for his reward.

He reaches the gibbet, and the populace weep to think of their narrow escape from losing the Queen.

> They tolde againe, if that mishap had happened
>   on her Grace,
> The staie of true religion, how perlous were the case.

The Queen pardons the rash young man; all kneel and say a prayer for her long life; the sky resounds with acclamations, and "explicit valde feliciter."

In 1584, as an old man, Elderton

> came thorow the North countrye
> The fashions of the world to see,

and passed through York, witnessing an archery match there, on which he wrote a laudatory ballad, "A new Yorkshyre Song," with the refrain

> Yorke, Yorke, for my monie,
> Of all the Cities that ever I see,
> For mery pastime and companie,
> Except the Cittie of London.

The following stanza from it has some interest, as showing that there was a direct connexion between the authors and the singers or hawkers of ballads; perhaps, too, it succeeded in impressing the men of York with Elderton's importance in the south.

> Farewell, good Cittie of Yorke to thee,
> Tell Alderman Maltbie this from mee,
> In print shall this good shooting bee,
>   As soone as I come at London.
> And many a Song will I bestowe
> On all the Musitions that I knowe,
> To singe the praises where they goe,
>   Of the Cittie of Yorke, in London.
>   *Yorke, Yorke, for my monie, etc.*

But let us part from Elderton with an example that will force us to admit that he had both poetry and humour in him — a memorial poem to "My Ladie Marques," * "whose Death is bewailed to the Tune of New lusty gallant":

* She may have been Elizabeth, Marchioness of Northampton, to whose funeral in 1565, as well as to her debts, there are many references in the State Papers.

Ladies, I think you marvell that
  I writ no mery report to you,
And what is the cause I court it not
  So merye as I was wont to doe;
Alas, I let you understand,
  It is no newes for me to show;
The fairest flower of my garland
  Was caught from Court a great while agoe.

For, under the roufe of sweete Saint Paull
  There lyeth my Ladie buried in claye,
Where I make memory for her soule
  With weepinge eyes once evere daye;
All other sights I have forgot
  That ever in court I joyed to see;
And that is the cause I court it not
  So mery as I was wont to be . . .

But sure I am, ther liveth yet
  In court a dearer frinde to mee,
Whome I to sarve am so unfit,
  I am sure the like will never bee;
For I with all that I can dooe,
  Unworthie most maie seeme to bee,
To undoo the latchet of her shooe;
  Yet will I come to courte and see.

Then have amongste ye once againe;
  Faint harts faire ladies never win;
I trust ye will consider my payne
  When any good venison cometh in.

The moralists were more severe than the men of letters on the ballads. Most condemned them altogether; yet one wrote himself a homoeopathic antidote in the shape of a ballad "Against filthy writing and such like delighting"; and popular ballads were sometimes "moralised," or parodied for pious purposes, with lamentable results. Moreover, good advice for the balladist and his printer was provided in "an Exhortation to such as write in metres" by an unknown R. B.

To such as write in metres I write
  Of small matters an exhortation,
By readyng of which men may delite
  In such as be worthy commendation . . .

Your balades of love, not worth a beane,
  A number there be, although not all,

Some be pithie, some weake, some leane,
　Some doe runne as round as a ball . . .

But now, lest ye thinke me to use excesse,
　I wyll to an end myself prepare,
Wyshyng all them that wyll adresse
　Their pen to metres, let them not spare
　To follow Chawcer, a man very rare,
Lidgate, Wager, Barclay and Bale,
　With many other that excellent are,
In these our dayes, extant to sale.

The printer should

Pourge chaff from corne, to avoyde offence,
　And not for lucre, under pretence
Of newes, to print what commeth to hand,
　But that which is meete to bring in pence
Let him print, the matter well scand.

Excellent good advice! The conclusion is

Let writers not covet the bottom or dale,
　If they may come to the hyll or brinke;
And, when they have written their learned tale,
　The printer must use good paper and inke,
　Or els the reader may sometime shrinke,
When faulte by inke or paper is seene;
　And thus every day, before we drinke,
Let us pray God to save our Queene.

The motto at the head of this piece is perhaps the best utterance of the whole ballad literature of that generation, and will make a fitting close:

When we have doen al that ever we can,
　Let us never seke prayse at the mouth of man.

REFERENCES

Catalogue of the Fifty Manuscripts and Printed Books bequeathed to the British Museum by Alfred H. Huth. Printed for the Trustees. 1912.

Ancient Ballads and Broadsides published in England in the Sixteenth Century, chiefly in the earlier years of the reign of Queen Elizabeth. Reprinted from the unique original copies, mostly in the Black Letter, preserved in the library of Henry Huth, Esq. [Philobiblon Society.] London: Whittingham, 1867.

Ballads and Broadsides, chiefly of the Elizabethan Period . . . now in the Library at Britwell Court, Buckinghamshire. Oxford: printed for presentation to the members of the Roxburghe Club, 1912.

Catalogue of a Collection of Printed Broadsides in the possession of the Society of Antiquaries. Compiled by Robert Lemon, Esq., F.S.A. Published by the Society of Antiquaries of London, 1866.

2.

War Journalism Three Hundred Years Ago

by ELBERT N. S. THOMPSON

ELBERT N. S. THOMPSON, professor of English at the State University of Iowa, published this article about early English newspapers and their war journalism in 1920 in *PMLA*. It is reprinted here in a slightly condensed form by permission of the Modern Language Association of America.

IT IS interesting to turn from the metropolitan daily of to-day, with its columns of cable dispatches, its reports of special war correspondents, its maps and profusely illustrated weekly supplements, to the small, five- or six-inch news-books that served the needs of the seventeenth century. They were virtually books rather than papers or sheets, for they were cut and printed like the other pamphlets of the day. And how strange the titles now sound, devised, as they were, not simply for identification but for information as well. *A continuation of certain speciall and remarkable passages informed to both houses of Parliament and otherwise from divers parts of this kingdome; A perfect diurnall of the passages in Parliament more fully and exactly taken than by any other printed copies, as you will finde upon comparing; Oxford diurnall: communicating the intelligence, and affaires of the court, to the rest of the kingdome; The Kingdomes weekly intelligencer: sent abroad to prevent mis-information.* Surely, the men and women who cried such titles on the streets of London were strong of lung.

Copies of these old papers are to be found still in some of the large libraries of this country, their pages yellowed with age and frayed by use. Under the title one looks in vain for the large type of our day; a single headline from one of the current dailies would have filled almost a whole issue of *Mercurius Britanicus*. One of the papers, *A Perfect Diurnall of the Passages in Parliament*, was adorned often with a cut, arranged about three sides of the title, representing a group of shovel-

hatted Puritan statesmen seated at the council table. In other issues of
this news-book the initial letter was printed in the middle of a little
picture representing a vessel out at sea under full sail. But in the main
the printer used, and quite arbitrarily, only two fonts of type, a small
Roman and italics, though he was always free to drop from a large to
a small type if he found himself pressed for space in the setting. Yet
the little, six- or eight-page news-books must have seemed to the
citizens of Milton's London the acme of perfection, and, supplemented
as they often were by the manuscript additions of the first purchaser,
they really gave the news that the people craved.

The student, therefore, familiar with the history of the time, will
look in vain for the "featuring" of important news. The items are
customarily introduced by the news-writer in such phrases as these: "a
true relation," "a true and exact relation," "there came letters from
Northampton on Monday last," "Wednesday a Hat-full of Letters
being intercepted," "it is informed that Lord Gray," and "the last
newes from the West is very variously reported." Occasionally, the
index finger of a printed hand called attention to an item of importance.
For example, in *A Perfect Diurnall of the Passages in Parliament* (No.
45, Apr. 10, 1643) such a device points toward the marginal comment:
"Note, herein is a true relation of another great victory attained by
Sir William Waller (not inferiour to any of the rest) against P.
Maurice, & his taking Tewxbury and the Magazine there." But ordinarily even such vital news as the battle at Newbury was not especially
stressed.

The *Kingdomes Weekly Intelligencer* (No. 10) in March, 1643,
announced in its ordinary style that "the sad newes came to towne on
Saturday last of the death of the Lord Brooke, who was shot dead with
a Musket Bullet as hee was looking out a window, after he had entred
the Town of Lichfield by Assault, and offered quarter to the Earle of
Chesterfield." Other papers gave a fuller account of the treacherous
shooting; but this journal simply added as an editorial judgment: "no
Englishman had more devoted himselfe and his fortunes as a sacrifice
to the cause in hand, then his Lordship had done," and recorded that
"the Common-Souldiers as soone as he was slaine, were so enraged,
that they vowed to give no quarter to the Earle of Chesterfield, nor any
of the Forces of the Colledge."

The common formulae for introducing the various items of each week's news are proof of the accidental means of obtaining it. Rumor and surmise were still the journalist's chief recourses. And there were times when even such news was wanting. The Puritan editor of *Speciall Passages and Certain Informations from severall Places, collected for the Use of all that desire to be truely informed,* was simply more frank than other writers when he admitted, "so little of action hath been this last weeke in the Armies, that much cannot be here expected." Naturally, then, the regularity of these weeklies was often interrupted. *A Continuation* begins in one issue (No. 52) with this explanation: "some occasions more than ordinary, hath caused an intermission of the Diurnall these two weekes past, for which I must Apologize my Excuse, and promise a more constant and elaborate continuation for the time comming." Such good intentions often came to nought; one paper, in fact, expired with its promise of greater regularity in the future.

The news-books appeared professedly once a week, at first on Mondays to catch the single mail sent each week from London to the country, and later on Thursdays or Fridays, when a second post-day was arranged for. The royalist journal at Oxford had the hardihood to come forth on Saturday evening; but Puritan scruples over the Sabbath discountenanced the act, and Tuesdays remained the commonest day for the dissemination of news. Consequently, from week to week, as news came slowly in, the rival weeklies had varying fortunes in getting possession first of important news. And repetition, of course, was common, since no one editor could afford to neglect a story just printed by a competitor. According to an item in the *Continuation* (No. 30), a trunk was "intercepted upon the Thames neare London . . . wherein was found a Packett of letters comming from the Queene and some others in Holland, which for the present are not to be reviled, there was also a great Pye found in the Trunck, but it is thought there will be found to be but unsavory meat in it when it is cutt up." This same story, with its innuendo, was repeated a few days later in *A Perfect Diurnall.* Such repetition must be where there is no general distributing agency for news, and where papers do not appear each day.

Just as necessarily the various papers were full of contradictory reports, and charges were frequently made of falsification and misrepresentation. The *Continuation* in 1643 reported the defeat of a royalist force (No. 26): "It is certainly informed that the Glocestershire Forces fell upon Sir John Byron in his quarters at a town called Burford (which is adjoyning upon Glocestershire) on Newyeares Eve, and killed about seven of his men, wounded the said Sir John, hurt many of his souldiers, and tooke twenty horse in one stable, and had it not been so late at night, that it was so dark they could not pursue them, they had given him a very great overthrow, and taken a brave booty." A quite different account of the fray was published in the *Oxford Diurnall*. On the thirtieth of December, according to this royalist authority, Sir John was ordered to lead his detachment to Burford. There he was attacked by five hundred rebels, who had been stationed at Cirencester. Sir John drove the attacking party "to the farther end of the lane where the Inn standeth, into which they ran, and into which he entring pell mell with them, received a blow on the face with a Pole-axe, or halbard." The building by that time was crowded with rebel muskateers, and Sir John was on horseback unarmed. Accordingly, he returned to the market cross, re-formed his troopers, and, storming the inn, drove the rebels out by the back door. The victors pursued the fleeing Roundheads six miles, but "being the night was wondrous darke and the Moone not risen, few of them could be overtaken." Only one of Sir John's troopers was killed and four injured.

After this fashion the news was selected or manipulated to suit the cause, and each party accused the other of deceit. "If they fight and are beaten," a royalist journal complained, "then either they deny it, and give thanks for a victory; or else confess some small losse, which God sent to them by his speciall Providence to draw the Cavaleirs into further destruction."[1] Another royalist paper, *Mercurius Aulicus*, asserted (No. 4): "it doth passe for currant in the streets of London . . . that the Kings forces have the worst in all their enterprises . . . and to beguile the people with the greater artifice, prisoners are led in triumph through the city, as if they had beene taken in those severall actions. Were it not that they did apply such Cordials, to keepe up the dejected spirits of their broken party, the cause had long ago beene subject unto fainting fits." Since the old Stuart days party enmity has not greatly changed its character.

The Puritan papers of London plainly reflected the enthusiasm of the city, and until 1647 even the sale of royalist papers was hardly tolerated on the streets. When the King asked for a conference over the difficulties at Brentford, Parliament decided "to spend no more time in making replyes to his Maiestie concerning the treaty," for the royalists aimed simply "to spin out time, whereby they may weary us out and spend the stock of the Kingdome, untill such time as they shall receive their supplyes from Holland, which they daily expect, and so much brag of." The soldiers under Essex, with as much determination, declared "that many dayes shall not passe them before they will give the Kingdom a sufficient token of their forwardnesse." And this promise "so farr enlivened the Citizens of London, that they are resolved to assist the Parliament with their lives and fortunes." Accordingly, they brought "money and plate into Guild-Hall with extraordinary freenesse"; forwarded "great store of bread and cheese, meat, tobacco and other things to the Army"; and resolved that Essex "shall not want moneys so long as their estates last." For these "large disbursements" Parliament thanked the city and promised restitution from the malignants' estates.[2]

Other Puritan news-books, however, compel us to discount somewhat this estimate of the city's generosity. Only a few days later *A Perfect Diurnall* (No. 26) reported that several parishes in London had not subscribed their quotas "for pay money for souldiers and Arms." At once church wardens and constables were ordered to assemble the delinquents and "to deale effectually with them to subscribe for the furthering of Arms and money for payment of Souldiers." The officials were further authorized to "repaire to the houses and places of aboad of such as shall not appeare at such meeting as well free men as others, and take their subscriptions for the purposes aforesaid and that they keepe a booke or roll for that purpose." As an additional source of revenue the Commons also agreed on an "Excise upon Wine Beare Tobacco, and severall other unnecessary commodities," and the saving of "a meales meat once a week" was even proposed as "a good way to raise a stock of moneys for the army" (No. 30). Assuredly, there is nothing new under the sun. When opposition was raised against such levies, compulsion was resorted to. The assessors, it is said, "this day made distraine in divers places in London, and tooke away the wares and goods of two woolen drapers in Paules Church-yard in London, and some others that refused to pay their assessments, and carried the same to Guild-hall to be sould to pay the same" (No. 33).

Prices apparently rose with the taxes. There is record, for example (No. 34), of "a complaint made to the Commons this day of the inhancing of the price of Coales, that since the restraint of the ships going to Newcastle, the price of Coales is raysed from 22 shillings a Chaldron, to 34 shillings." Consequently, the House agreed on "setting of a certaine price upon Coales." Still the opposition to the war increased, it seems, as the burdens pressed more heavily, and (No. 26) "many of the City malignants which hath hitherto stood as Newters" framed a petition for an immediate peace. The author complains that these people were ready to sacrifice "our Religion, our Lawes and liberties with all that we may prosperously call ours," in their desire "that all things shall be concluded in peace, & things reduced to the ancient custome when they lived in prosperity." We recognize these pacifists from their descendants. "They came up and down the Citie to draw on others to be of their faction," and when the Lord Mayor ordered them to desist, they "insolently pressed the same." They even attempted to hold a public meeting in the Guild-Hall, into which they forced their way. But (No. 26) Captain Harvey rode up with his troopers, and "at the sound of his trumpet they were all scared away . . . and escaped apprehending at this time." The news-writer, however, declared that "many of the chiefe Ringleaders are knowne whose names are certified to the L. Mayor, who will take a speedy course with them." In less than two weeks no less representative a citizen than Sir Paul Pindar was forced to confess his share in the agitation (No. 28).

Such discontents as these were eagerly seized by the royalists and possibly exaggerated. *Mercurius Aulicus* reported in January, 1643, that the army of Essex "was behind no lesse than five weekes pay," and that Parliament had emptied the treasury and "contrary to all rules of housewiferie, left not an egge in the nest for the henne to sit on." A little later it predicted mutiny in the city as a result of Parliament's arbitrary assessments. Several instances of such tyrannical exactions are given with due amount of gloating (No. 8): "A poorer widow, having a charge of five children, and her estate not worth above 200 l. . . . being not able to make present payment, was plundered of her Jack, Spits, and leaden Cistern, which was all the distresse [in the legal sense] that could be found in the house." Again, it is said that on a certain Sunday, following the afternoon service, the soldiers, "accompanied with Daniel the preaching Cobbler of Grub-street, whom the people call the prophet Daniel," went to the vestry of Saint Giles by Cripplegate and took the poor-money from the box. Finally, this wholesale depredation is recorded: "Cloath to a good vallue had been taken from one Price a Draper; 10. chests of Sugar from one Grimes a Grocer; and 900 l. of other mens money from a Scrivener: besides which violent taxations and intollerable pressures there were some every day imployed in going from house to house to know what men would give of their owne accord towards the maintenance of the Warre."

In London, where this one royalist journal could not be sold safely on the streets, less notice was given to these confiscations. Possibly the spectacular phases of warfare suited better the public taste than these prosaic means of maintenance. After the King's approach on London in 1642, which Milton commemorated in his half-defiant sonnet, the streets were fortified against a similar danger in the future. In various sources accounts of these preparations are to be found. In May, 1643, *A Perfect Diurnall* announced, what the citizens must have known, that "the Intrenching of the Citty round goes on with wonderous great speed, many thousands going out dayly to the Worke" (No. 30). Each day, one infers, certain trades or guilds assumed the responsi-bility; for the news continues: "On Tuesday last there went about 5000 Feltmakers and Cappers, neare upon three Thousand Porters, besides other great Companies of men, women and children," with "divers other Companies of the Trayned Bands and new Militia that goe out dayly to the Workes with their Drumms and Coullors in the usual way." While these activities were at their height, William Lith-gow, the adventurous Scot, was in the city, and found everywhere "new barrocaded posts . . . strongly girded with great chaines of yron." [8] He saw the builders of the defences "marching to the fields and out works . . . with great alacritie, carrying on their shoulders yron mattocks and wooden shovels; with roaring drummes, flying colours, and girded swords." On one day the tailors went out, with forty-six colors and eight thousand "lusty men." On another day "a thousand oyster wives advanced from Billingsgate through Cheapside to Crabtree field, all alone, with drummes and flying collours." Fear and what is now called the psychology of the crowd gave impetus to these "daily musters" that Lithgow found "wondrous commendable";

but even he noticed, too, that the city was filled with "a general muttering that money is hard to come by."

Reports of the distant movements of the armies, of battles and sieges, were not so easily secured by the authors as these stories of London's unrest, and for that reason they must have been still more eagerly read. The stories printed of such engagements disclose to the modern world, which is now learning so many new lessons, what military science was like in the seventeenth century.

In 1643 Prince Rupert attacked Chichester. "Whilst his Ordnance," we learn (*Diurnall*, No. 35), "was playing against one end of the Towne, he with a party of horse went to the other end, and made assault against it, shooting Grenadoes to set fire of the Barnes and Thatched houses that were at that end." Elsewhere, a fuller picture is given, in Cromwell's own words, of the Puritans' skirmish near Newark in 1643. His official report ran (*ibid.*, May 29, 1643):

God hath given us this evening a glorious victory over our enemies, they were as we are enformed one and twentie Colours of horse troops and three or foure of dragoones; it is late in the evening when we drew out, they came and faced us within two miles of the town, so soon as we had the alarum we drew out our forces consisting of about twelve troops, whereof some of them so poore and broken that you shall seldome seen worse; with this handfull it pleased God to cast the scale, for after we had stood a little above musket shot the one body from the other, and the Dragooners having fired on both sides for the space of halfe an hour or more, they not advancing towards we agreed to charge them, and advancing the body after many shots on both sides, came with our Troopes a pretty round trot, they standing firme to receive us, and our men charging fiercely upon them, they were immediately routed and ran all away, and wee had the execution of them two or three miles.

When this communication was penned, Cromwell must have been still hot from the combat, with no more care for the elegancies of style than Hotspur had. But for that reason the picture he gives of the open battles of that day, when the cavalry played the decisive part, is to be taken as typical of all.

The next year Rupert was at Newark, and another story was to be told. The city was besieged by a Puritan force, consisting of four thousand foot soldiers and two thousand horse. The King's nephew was ordered to ride to its relief. With his small detachment he was able to slip up unobserved within eight miles of the town. The next morning at nine the Prince himself led the charge, and the fight "grew sturdy," for the rebel army "disputed it toughly." Rupert himself, "having pierced deep into the Enemies, and being observed for his Valour, was dangerously at once assaulted by three sturdy Rebells, whereof one fell by his Highnesses own sword, a second being pistolled by M. Mortaine one of his own Gentlemen; the third now ready to lay hand on the Princes Coller had it almost chopt by Sir William Neale." In the end the Puritans surrendered, and Rupert took as booty three thousand muskets, eleven brass cannon, one of them four yards in length, and a great quantity of pikes and muskets.

Although the Civil War in England was much less barbarous than the conflict in Ireland, charges of atrocity were freely brought against both Puritans and Royalists. Prince Rupert was apparently the most dreaded of the Cavaliers, and items like this are frequent in the newsbooks: "There came Letters from Northampton on Monday last, by which it was certainly informed that Prince Rupert with at least 2000 horse is in that County, and makes great spoyle there, having plundered many places thereabouts.⁴ And again at Chichester, Prince Rupert was reported to have taken as booty "two thousand horse, with which he made his footmen Troopers, six hundred head of Cattell, and about sixty Cart-loade of plunder." His soldiers also "tooke pure Holland Sheets, and foulded them up under their Saddles, with which when they tooke up their lodgins they covered their horses withall instead of Horse-cloathes," and, having entered the town, "laid about them in that inhumaine manner it would grieue a Jew to heare the Relation." In another place, "much enraged at their losses, they put all to the sword they met withall both men women and children, and in a barbarous manner murthered three Ministers our godly and religious men."

So persistent were these charges that the royal trooper was forced to publish his defense. His spirited "Declaration" began with an apology for his appearance as an author, his "known disposition being so contrary to this scribling age." But the charges of barbarity forced him to declare: "I take that man to be no Souldier or Gentleman, that will strike (much lesse kill) a woman or a child." He defied his accusers to name the persons inhumanely treated by him, or the places where such atrocities had been committed. Finally, in retaliation, he reminded his readers of the sacking of the Earl of Northampton's house by the

Roundheads, their destruction of churches, and the imprisonment of innocent persons. He pledged his word, too, that, if Charles were received in London peacefully, no citizen need fear plunder, and closed with the knightly words: "And so, whether peace or warre, the Lord prosper the worke of their hands who stand for God and King Charles."

The royalist press in general supported the charges that Rupert here brought against the Puritan soldiery. In May, 1643, appeared the first number of a paper amply entitled, *Mercurius Rusticus, or the Countries complaint of the Murthers, robberies, plundrings, and other outrages committed by the Rebells on his Majesties faithfull subjects*. It told in full of the sacking of Sir John Lucas's house, and the outrages on its inmates. Another paper, *Mercurius Aulicus,* found an even more barbarous story to tell.

The Rebels speed so ill at downright fighting, that now they practise a new way of Murther, for we are certainly advertised from Dennington Castle, that when the Rebells close besieged that place, they hired a Souldier to poyson their Well. . . . This Souldier having informed the Rebells, that the Well was most necessary for supportation of that Garrison, received his 20 shillings . . . and in the night time conveyed the Poyson downe the Well. But next morning their Commander (toucht it seems with the horror of the fact) sent a Drum with a Letter to Sir John Boys to give notice what was done. . . . After which time, he kept the Well in despight of the Rebels, and to make tryall whether or no the Well were truly poysoned, he tryed the experiment upon a Horse, which having drank of it, swelld and dyed within 24 houres.

One of the last pieces of important news that these journals had to communicate before their suppression, was the execution of the King in 1649. *The Moderate Intelligencer* followed most fully the proceedings against Charles. Like the rest, it was a paper about five by six and a half inches in size. In it the news from England was as a rule printed first; then letters from the Continent were given; and often at the very end the notice of a new book was added, such as "A Continuation of Mr. John-Amos-Comenius School-Endeavours, or a summary Delineation of Doctor Cyprian Kinner Silesian his Thoughts concerning Education, Way and Method of Teaching, comes forth tomorrow."

In the issue of *The Moderate Intelligencer* for the week ending January 4, 1649, appeared the item: "An Ordinance was this day brought in, which is in way of Commission, in which certaine persons about 100 in number, Lords, Commons, Citizens, & others are qualified, with power to try the Kings Majesty." This bill having been read a second time the next day was referred to the committee for the insertion of "the names of such as were to be Commissioners therein." The King himself felt little concern at this step, if the editor was truly informed, for the report continues: "The King is merry, discourses upon subjects purporting a life of many dayes here, doubts not but within six moneths to see peace in England." Yet the plans for the trial went on, and "the Commons understanding how unanimously the Lords had gone against the Commission for tryall of the King, agreed to proceed themselves."

In the next issue of the paper the author discussed the three possible forms of government, whether by king, by Lords and Commons, or by the Commons alone, "which," he added "de facto it's now comming to." He explained that the word king, "as they that understood the Saxon Language say, signifies no more but cunning." In an unlimited monarchy, therefore, "a cunning or wise man is set over the people by their consent, because cunning, to see to their preservation." This line of argument seems to be leading to the conclusions soon to be propounded by Milton in *Tenure of Kings and Magistrates*. But here the author halted. Even were it necessary, he felt, for a king to be deposed, the divine rule is not to visit the sins of the fathers upon the children "unlesse they walke in the steps of their Fathers." Hence the line of succession should hardly be changed. In this article and the next the author appears plainly in the capacity of a modern editor to influence the judgment of his readers.

Soon, however, the editor resigned this function and dropped back into the role of news-writer to report the progress of events. Although the clergymen of Oxfordshire and others submitted petitions against a continuance of the prosecution, and although the Prince of Wales promised, if his father's life were spared, to see that Parliament's wishes were fulfilled, the proceedings went on. The House voted "that the King had exercised tyrannical government, was a tyrant, a Murtherer and Traitor" and agreed "to draw up the sentence of condemnation against him," ordering in advance that it should be counted "high treason for any person or persons to proclaim any King of England, without consent of Parliament."

On the 27th final sentence was accordingly pronounced. The King was brought before the Lord President and the sixty-seven commissioners present. They forbade his speaking "against the jurisdiction of the Court," but allowed him to plead in his own defense. So Charles began: "I must tell you, that this many a day all things have been taken away from mee, that I call dearer to me than my life, which is my Conscience and my Honor." His aim, he declared, in speaking was not to save his life, but to insure peace to the country. With that end only in view, he asked to "be heard in the Painted Chamber before the Lords and Commons." This request was denied, on the ground that Charles sought only delay, of which there had been too much already, and that "Judges are no more to delay then they are to deny Justice." The king still urged his plea, arguing that "a little delay of a day or two farther may give peace, whereas an hasty judgement may bring on that trouble and perpetuall inconvenience to the kingdome, that the childe that is unborn may repent." But the Lord President remained obdurate, arguing, as Milton did, that the oath at coronation was proof of a contract between king and people, and that Charles had violated the contract. The clerk then read the sentence, ending with the words: "For all which Treasons and Crimes this Court doth adjudge, That he the said Charles Stuart, as a Tyrant, Traytor, Murtherer, and a publike Enemy, shall be put to death, by the severing of his Head from his Body."

Since the measures against royalist papers were then very strict, the author had to give these facts without comment of his own. Some sympathy for the royal martyr seems to lie beneath the few facts that are given to conclude the story. The author reviewed the troubled reign of Charles, attributing the evil done chiefly to the Catholic marriage. He mentioned next a few of the touching incidents from the last hours of the king — the sending away of his dogs and his last words to his children. Then he told how Charles walked through the park to the scaffold and spoke there, behind the black-draped railing, to the small group of persons gathered to witness his end, before he finally gave a few of his personal belongings to his faithful friends and laid his head upon the block. It "was at one blow struck off by one in disguise, and taken up by another in disguise." The author then concluded with this expressive comment: "Thus have you from first to last of this Tragoedie, such particulars as could be got from severall hands. Many have said, and possible true, wilfulnesse hath chiefly occasioned what hath befallen."

The execution of King Charles brings one close to the end of this first flourishing period of English journalism. As early as 1647 the strictest measures were taken by the Puritans in control toward the suppression of the royalist papers in London. The old women who hawked them about the streets were whipped by the constables if they were caught. Then in 1651 Milton himself, the author of the grandest plea for the freedom of the press, became a sort of licensing editor of *Mercurius Politicus*. The Restoration led at once to the complete suppression of all papers but the one licensed by the new king's servant and to the establishment of the *Gazette*. Nevertheless, the progress of English journalism during Puritan days had been rapid, though short. The editors, or authors, as they were usually called, had learned to gather the news and get it before the people; they had learned, too, that the press is a potent factor in the influencing of public opinion. The history of English journalism had begun.

NOTES

[1] *The Round-heads Remembrancer*, May 16, 1643.
[2] *A Continuation*, No. 21, Dec. 1, 1642.
[3] *The Present Surveigh of London.* In Somers Tracts, vol. iv, pp. 534–545.
[4] *A Continuation*, No. 30, Feb. 2, 1643.

3

The Power of the English Press in the Eighteenth Century

by WILLIAM T. LAPRADE

An authority on eighteenth-century England, WILLIAM T. LAPRADE
has been a history professor at Duke University since 1909. He is also editor of
the *South Atlantic Quarterly* (published by Duke University Press), in which
this article appeared in October 1928.

IN THE past generation or two, students have begun habitually to use
newspapers as sources for the history of the time in which they were
published. The assumption seems to be that the papers were recorders
of facts or reflectors of opinion and so yield information, though often
of doubtful reliability, concerning the subjects reported in their columns. There is an element of truth in this assumption. But it is doubtful
whether newspapers can be used to much advantage as sources of information until they receive more attention as being themselves part of
the fabric of society. Newspapers are more in the nature of relics than
chronicles of their times. They have not served identical functions at
all stages in their history. In late years they have become media through
which important individuals and groups communicate with each other
and with the public at large, thus constituting a sort of cement for
holding society together, without which it is difficult to see how it
could exist in its present form. Thus newspapers have grown with the
society of which they are so vital a part. Their evolution from small
beginnings to their present impressive importance is not only a fascinating subject for study; it is a necessary one, if we are to understand
either the contents of the newspapers of a given time or the character
of the society in which they flourished.

Of no time and place is this more true than eighteenth-century England, the country and the period in which newspapers as we know

them were largely evolved. The transition from a society in which newspapers were unimportant and almost unknown to one in which they were accepted as a matter of course and as almost essential if existing conditions were not to be radically changed, occurred in England in that century. There were embryonic newspapers in 1700, to be sure. But the papers in which the subjects of George III read accounts of Napoleon's campaigns were more like those of today than like the insignificant sheets which brought to their grandfathers tidings of Marlborough's victories. In that interval occurred a world of experiment and struggle, sometimes against odds, which had much to do with forming the character of English newspapers — and also of English society as later generations know it.

From the beginning, English newspapers were primarily intended to mould opinion; that is, they carried facts (or assertions) and arguments designed to create in readers a state of mind favorable to the purposes of those sponsoring the several journals. Consequently, they need to be studied in close correlation with other information about the persons and causes they were meant to serve. Just as history written without reference to the newspapers (as is the case with much that has been written in the past) lacks an essential flavor and content necessary to give it verisimilitude, so quotations from papers apart from their setting in time and circumstance reveal very little of what was going on. The activities of the politicians and of the writers for the press must be considered together if we are to understand either.

This is not surprising when we reflect that most of the important statesmen of the eighteenth century inspired or even wrote for the press, and almost every writer of note contributed to it. From Harley and Bolingbroke to Canning and the younger Pitt, from Defoe, Swift, Addison, and Steele to Burke and Johnson — unless we bear in mind the relations of notable eighteenth-century Englishmen with the newspapers, we are in danger of overlooking a vital aspect of their lives. From Defoe's *Review*, conducted to support in Harley's interest toleration and the union of England and Scotland, and the *Examiner* of Swift and Bolingbroke, in which they made war on their political rivals, to the *True Briton*, inspired by Pitt to arouse the country against France, and Canning's *Anti-Jacobin*, intended to stimulate conservative fears of foreign radicalism to support a lagging war, scarcely a year was without its cause, and never a cause without its support in the press. Many persons remembered for other things achieved a large part of their reputation as writers for newspapers. Among them were Horace Walpole (in his father's time), Fielding, Smollett, Arthur Murphy, Wilkes, and Burke. Others who deserve to be remembered have been largely forgotten because their best work appeared in these passing records of the day. Such men were John Trenchard, Thomas Gordon, Nicholas Amhurst, James Ralph, John Campbell, William Guthrie, John Almon. All of these and a host of others deserve to live in history because of their part in giving tone and quality to the society of their times and because they lent a hand in shaping the character of newspapers in their infancy and lusty youth.

Like most institutions of importance, the newspaper grew without much taking of thought or premeditated planning. Many of the more significant journals were started to support the cause of the day and were suspended when that work was done. John Tutchin's *Observator* and Charles Leslie's *Rehearsal* were on opposite sides of questions relating to claims of the monarchy and the national Church at a time when passions on these subjects ran so high as to threaten the peace of the country. Thomas Gordon, succeeding John Trenchard, labored with Walpole, Hoadly, and other statesmen and Churchmen of the time in a campaign in favor of religious toleration, the importance of which is not appreciated in later generations largely because they did their work so successfully that people forgot that the previous conditions ever existed. The questions at issue in their day cannot be understood without reference to the *Independent Whig*, "Cato's Letters" to the *London Journal*, and similar contemporary writings.

When Bolingbroke and Pulteney joined forces in 1725 in a campaign to drive Walpole from office, almost their first step was to establish the *Craftsman*. In doing this, they but followed the example of Swift and Bolingbroke in 1709, of their opponents in the late months of Anne's reign, and of Walpole and Steele in 1717, when the ministry of the day threatened to change the character of the House of Lords. The *Craftsman* was opposed by as able, though some of them less well known, writers on the side of the ministers. In 1735 these writers in Walpole's behalf discontinued several of their weeklies and joined in alternate contributions to the *Daily Gazetteer*, which was then established as the first paper on record to purvey essays of this type as a part of its daily offering. Before its work was done, the *Craftsman* was joined by *Common Sense*, inspired and in part written by Lyttleton of the Cobham cousinhood, and by the *Champion*, one of Fielding's several ventures in the field of political journalism. The agitation that attended the actual defeat of Walpole gave birth to the *Westminster Journal*. In their fight against Carteret, Chesterfield and his associates used *Old England*, or the *Constitutional Journal*, later the *Broadbottom Journal*, for which Guthrie and Chesterfield himself wrote.

In the time of Pelham, propaganda was confined largely to the daily vehicles of news. But the preliminaries to the Seven Years' War saw Henry Fox and the elder Pitt striving against each other in the *Test* and the *Con-Test*, conducted by Arthur Murphy and Owen Ruffhead respectively, with William Beckford's *Monitor*, conducted by John Entick, speaking for the City groups who were interested in the war. The aftermath of the war gave birth to Smollett's *Briton*, Wilkes's *North Briton*, and Murphy's *Auditor* among the papers that arose to keep the surviving *Monitor* company. Though the essays of propaganda were soon to take a different form, the story of the rise of papers to serve causes of the moment might be continued to the end of the century.

The method of these political writers was to hark back to general shibboleths or principles, while they provided facts and arguments suited to the needs of the hour. Pursuing what Dicey called the "astounding method of retrogressive progress," almost without exception they appealed to history both to support their assertions and to obtain analogies for making covertly and indirectly points it was not expedient to make directly. Needing better, or at any rate different history from that they had at hand, many writers for the press became historians also, themselves helping to supply the material of which they felt the lack. Gordon, Ralph Campbell, Guthrie, Smollett, and Entick, to mention only a few, all wrote history or historical essays of a respectable character. Bolingbroke's pieces on the subject are well known, at least by reputation. Even Wilkes advertised and began a history, actually receiving subscriptions for the work, though he never found time to finish it. Needless to say, the works of all of these writers, like most histories in most times, need to be studied in relation to the questions of the day in which they were written in order to be understood or appreciated.

The appeal of these newspapers was not limited to the narrow circle of their readers. In fact, the earlier papers were not primarily intended for circulation to individual subscribers. They were "taken in" by the coffee-houses and other public places where men congregated. Often some one person read the essay of the week to groups seated about a table or gathered in front of the fire. The more fetching points became texts for discussions that frequently developed into heated arguments. Feeling aroused in these groups spread by oral communication to interested persons in every station in society. Both the printers of the papers and the promoters of causes were interested in the encouragement of such discussion, the printers in order to increase their profits from sales, the promoters of causes to accomplish their purposes. Therefore runners were frequently employed to visit the coffee-houses and take the initiative when discussion lagged, whispering now and then information, as likely to be fictitious as correct, about the identity of the author of a piece and communicating facts or allegations which it was impolitic to print.

These early journals were not intended primarily to influence voters in the exercise of the suffrage. They were rather designed to create an atmosphere which by a kind of intimidation would inhibit or promote action by statesmen and members of parliament. If we bear in mind the inadequacy of the London police throughout the eighteenth century and the keen prejudice against a large army and against the use of the forces which existed for the suppression of domestic disorders, the threat of a mob as an inspirer or deterrent of action is apparent. Later generations have tended to lose sight of the surging crowds in the yard of St. Stephen's Chapel which awaited and in a measure determined the decision of parliament on critical questions. The defeat of the excise in 1733, the beginning of the war with Spain in 1739, the repeal of the Stamp Act in 1766, and the Gordon riots in 1780 are but better known examples of mob influence that was more nearly habitual than historians have led us to think. The mob was ever a powerful, though a somewhat hazardous weapon in political warfare, and the newspapers were effective, as they were intended to be, in creating an atmosphere productive of mobs.

There is no better evidence of the effectiveness of the press in playing this role than the steps meditated and actually taken by almost every statesman of the century who remained long in office for its suppression or at least the restriction of its activities. Bolingbroke and

Harley sought by taxation to make opposition papers impossible. While Walpole was constantly urged to more positive action, he never did more than harry the publishers of papers opposed to him by prosecutions for seditious libel. In his time Hardwicke began to use the method of reserving to the courts the decision of whether matter was libellous, leaving to the jury only the question of publication. After the orgy of popular agitation from 1760 to the close of the war, Grenville and his associates seem to have seriously set about the task of restricting within very narrow limits political propaganda appearing in newspapers. For nearly a decade printers conducted their business in peril of ruinous fines and imprisonment.

That this campaign did not in the end accomplish its purpose was in part due to the fact that the press had by this time become a vested interest involving property in a considerable amount, and in part because people had come to depend upon the papers for certain services they could not obtain elsewhere. Moreover, on second thought, none of the opponents of the press ever went quite as far as he was tempted to go while in office, because he reflected that he might in time be again out of power himself. In that case, he did not wish to be deprived of the most effective weapon available for political warfare. This thought invariably disposed those in office to a greater tenderness in dealing with objectionable writers for newspapers than they would otherwise have shown.

The result was that by the close of the Seven Years' War the power of the press, or rather of those who knew how to use it and to supplement it with other appeals to the emotions of the day, became so great as to obstruct seriously the orderly conduct of the government. It was this fact in part which led the ministry to prosecute Entick, Wilkes, and others. Pitt, as the outstanding heroic figure of the time, and Bute, as its chief political villain, were largely creations of the press; neither owed his reputation to his real character and accomplishment. It was this reputation based on fiction rather than character and achievements that statesmen of the day had to consider in their efforts to govern the kingdom.

A part of the ease with which a fictitious reputation could thus be attached inseparably to political leaders was due to the mystery that concealed the proceedings in parliament. At no time in the eighteenth century was less known out of doors of what went on in the halls of the legislature. The debates were nowhere published. Even the monthly magazines ceased carrying, after the question was disposed of, their sketchy and fragmentary reports.

But this proved to be the darkest hour before dawn. Grenville himself, probably recognizing the unfortunate effects of some of the efforts to restrict the press, came to feel that it would be wiser to have the proceedings of parliament frankly reported in the papers as news. This was done increasingly after 1770. The way was opened for it in the following year by a contest between the House of Commons and the City over the publication of a fragment of a debate in a paper printed in London by one of its citizens. In the course of the dispute the Lord Mayor and one of his fellow magistrates were sent to the Tower. But they stood their ground. While nothing was decided formally, newspapers thereafter exercised more freedom in publishing the proceedings of parliament, and the houses felt it prudent not to do anything about it.

This implicit admission that the doings in parliament were legitimate news proved to be almost as revolutionary a step in the development of government as the rise of the newspapers themselves. The most noticeable effect was the decline in the direct power of the journals. The essays of the political writers were removed from the position of importance on the front page which they had been wont to occupy to make room for the sayings and doings of political leaders. In fact, the political writing that was carried by the papers came in time to consist largely of comments on the actions of these leaders or suggestions to them. Thus the newspaper tended to become more largely a mere medium of communication, a reporter of news. It had previously been a more dangerous political weapon, frequently in hands unknown except to the initiated. The lucubrations of Junius were among the last important examples of political writing of the older type. The struggle for publication of the parliamentary debates took place while Junius was still appearing.

Whether the contents of the newspapers were in the form of open comment on public questions and parliamentary discussion freely published, or appeals to feeling by indirect or covert allusion, no student of the history of England in the eighteenth century can afford to neglect them. But, to repeat, if he goes to the papers as mere records of the events of the time, he will usually find very little that is worth while, even of information. Eighteenth-century newspapers (whatever may be true of those in later times) were not simply reflectors of the atmosphere in which events occurred. They were among the most effective instruments used by leaders in imparting tone and quality to that atmosphere; frequently they were means of shaping the course of events. In short, they came to be themselves a vital part of the machinery of government.

That the cabinet as it is familiar in later generations largely took shape in the eighteenth century is well known. The cabinet, in an important sense, is a group of leaders united for the purpose of obtaining support for themselves from parliament and from the public at large in order that they may have power to carry on the government. It is scarcely conceivable that a cabinet in that sense could have come into existence or could have functioned without the aid of the press to make known the plans of the leaders and to create a favorable attitude towards them. Furthermore, had such a group obtained power, without the press it would have been almost impossible to unhorse it as long as it remained united in itself. That could only be done by circulating criticism and arousing in the discontented a community of feeling sufficient to lead to common action. On that very account, while men in office might meditate the suppression of the press and might actually attempt to restrict its activities, there was never an opposition in the century but advocated its freedom. The subject was dwelt upon so constantly by all writers against ministers that it became in the highest degree hackneyed, without becoming unimportant.

Thus English newspapers grew from small beginnings until they were accepted as a necessary part of the fabric of society. We take them so entirely for granted that we do not always appreciate the difficulty involved when we try to imagine life in a society where they did not exist. Perhaps it is almost as difficult for us to imagine what conditions were when newspapers were in the stage of their first rapid growth, changing their character from time to time, frequently with almost startling suddenness. The student of the history of England in the eighteenth century must cultivate this difficult capacity for imagination in himself before he can describe or reflect upon events of that time with much insight.

4

Daniel Defoe

by JOHN DOS PASSOS

JOHN DOS PASSOS, interpreter of the American scene, here turns to study a famous Englishman. The article appeared in the *New Republic*, November 18, 1940, and later was included in a chapter of *The Ground We Stand On* (Harcourt Brace, 1941; now published by Houghton Mifflin), pages 187–205. Copyright 1941 by John Dos Passos; reprinted by permission.

DANIEL DEFOE came from the class of dissenting small shopkeepers and artisans. He was the son of a Baptist tallow-chandler named Foe who rose in due time to the more respectable occupation of butcher. Daniel Foe was born in the heart of London in the parish of St. Giles, Cripplegate, about the year of the restoration of Charles Second. He grew up during the period of greatest repression of nonconformists, learned to read on the Bible, as a child piously copied out large sections of it in shorthand, when a rumor went around that the High Churchmen were going to confiscate the dissenters' scriptures, and being deemed a likely youngster by his family, was sent to the academy at Newington Green, under a divine named Morton (who moved to America later and became a vicepresident of Harvard College), to study for the ministry. Young Daniel's bent turned out rather for this world than for the next, so he was taken out of the academy and apprenticed to a wine-merchant. In connection with the business he traveled in Spain and Portugal and probably in the Low Countries, rose rapidly in the world, got caught in the speculative fever of the time, and became such a successful man of business that he failed before he was thirty for the sum of £17,000. Meanwhile, his non-conformism had taken political form. He had written Whig pamphlets and "ridden out" with Monmouth's premature and shortlived rebellion against the last Stuart, and on the great day of William of Orange's entry into London, had been seen, wearing a new wig and the gaudiest outfit money could buy, riding a fine horse in the protestant monarch's train.

But the England that emerged from under the courtly brilliance and the bloodshed of eighteen years of Stuart reaction was no longer the rapidly evolving fluid society of Elizabeth and the Commonwealth. It was the "tight little island" of highly stratified castes that continued almost to our own day. At the bottom was the great mass of laborers and tenants, disfranchised, illiterate and helpless, a prey to pressgangs and recruiting sergeants and laws against change of residence or association, under the direct, often paternal, but always absolute rule of the magistrates and country squires. In the early years of the eighteenth century, a period of rising prosperity, wages tended, it is true, to rise in relation to the price of wheat, so that the working class was possibly in better shape economically than in the century before, but opportunity for a working man to improve his station in the world was almost nil.

Immediately above the working class came the stratum that Defoe came from, the dissenting tradesmen and artisans, the undestroyed remnant of the defeated Commonwealth. They were barred by law from holding office, and separated from the rest of the community by differences in social and religious habits. Above them came the landowning gentry, who governed the country districts through the assizes as justices of the peace, whose sons went to the universities and made up the personnel of the great institutions of the Law and the Established Church. These county families were already allying themselves with the rich bankers and merchants and shipowners of the towns, with the commercial interest that gradually grew in importance until eventually it swallowed everything else.

At the very top there remained in ermine and coronets the remnants of the old nobility, a class that had lost its feudal and military prerogatives but kept its power through its great entailed estates and through the prestige of the House of Lords. But the House of Lords itself was coming, through the influence of the bishops and the creation of new peers for political purposes by whatever party happened to be in power, to represent the great institutions as such, rather than hereditary power. Feudalism in the continental sense had been broken up under the Tudors. The ladders of ascent to the upper levels of society, as the eighteenth century opened, were already pretty much established as the universities, the church, the acquisition of land: for a dissenting tradesman like Daniel Foe there was little hope of reaching even the foot of any of these ladders.

After his bankruptcy Defoe had to hide out for a while, first in the sanctuary round the Mint and later in Bristol, where, as bailiffs and process servers only operated on weekdays, he was able to come out for a walk on Sundays and, noticeable on account of his elegant dress and fashionable manner, was known to the townspeople as the "Sunday Gentleman." Eventually he managed to satisfy his creditors and to get back to London.

He already had taken up the habit of picking up a little money by writing when business got bad. He caught the attention of his adored King William by the satirical poem *The True Born Englishman* taking off the perennial prejudice against foreigners, and was rewarded for his faithfulness to the constitutional monarchy by a couple of small positions, that of director of a lottery and collector of a tax on glass works, and, so he tells us, by the personal friendship of the subtle Hollander himself. It was possibly under William that he started the sort of backstairs information bureau for the Government which he conducted during several subsequent reigns. In spite of his bankruptcy, he was very much the prosperous merchant at this time, with a mistress and a country house at Tilbury and a small yacht of his own on the Thames Estuary.

Defoe was forging boldly ahead as one of the leaders of the King's party, when the King's horse stumbled and threw him while he was riding in the park. All over England Tories and Jacobites drank the health of the horse; only the dissenters were really devoted to the House of Orange. William was already in bad health and never recovered from his injuries. After the death of his royal idol, nothing ever went completely well with Daniel *De Foe*. Somewhere during his rise in fortune he had managed to get the French particle into his name. He clung to it through good times and bad. It was the only respectable acquisition he never lost.

The reign of Queen Anne came in like a lion. The Queen was a sickly, rather querulous creature very much under the thumb of her women friends and of the highflying tory divines. Her one passion was for the Church, for Laud's High Church of England that taught passive obedience to the monarchy and touching for the king's evil. The Jacobite reactionaries felt that her reign was a chance to restore

48

the Stuart line and the good old times. The Roman Catholics encouraged by her highchurchiness were raising their heads hopefully. The country gentlemen of the tory Parliament felt that the time had come to squelch the nonconformists who had been getting too uppety under the last reign.

Defoe jumped flatfootedly into the row by publishing a pamphlet called *A Short Way With Dissenters* which anticipated the ironic method of Swift's *Modest Proposal* for solving the Irish question by selling steaks off Irish babies, by proposing a series of measures against dissenters so tough that Defoe thought they'd seem funny. The highflying divines fell into the trap and took the recommendations of the pamphlet seriously. The dissenters themselves were too scared by the fire and brimstone being breathed out against them to appreciate the joke and Defoe found himself in hot water indeed. In spite of abject apologies and his very characteristic offer to raise a regiment of horse and go fight for the Queen in the Low Countries, he was arrested and sentenced to the pillory and to imprisonment at the Queen's pleasure.

There followed one of those explosions of popular feeling that have made and kept England a free country throughout the centuries in spite of despotic laws, a rigid caste system and the dominance of the property interest. Defoe's exposure in the pillory turned into an ovation. Instead of emptying chamber-pots on his head and throwing rotten vegetables at him, the townspeople of London drank his health in mugs of ale, and brought him nosegays. Hawkers did a landoffice business selling copies of his *Hymn to Pillory* and, the last day he was brought out, the pillory itself was wreathed in greenery and flowers. The joke was turned back on the highflyers and the tory divines around the Queen.

In the excitement there was a cabinet shakeup and a moderately whiggish country gentleman from Devonshire named Robert Harley got into the saddle. Harley came from a puritan family. He had been Speaker of the House of Commons when Defoe was riding to prominence at the head of the friends of good King William at the time of the Kentish petition. While Defoe was in jail, strings were being pulled in his behalf by William Penn and other highly placed friends of toleration, and Harley, who understood the power of the press, got the idea that Defoe's writing might be useful to him. After much devious negotiation, Defoe emerged from prison the editor of *The Review* and Harley's backstairs confidant.

Meanwhile Defoe's latest commercial venture, a tile factory, had gone to smash and with it his hopes of a really respectable business career. Swift, too, was to work for Harley, but he went in to see the minister by the front door, as befitted a learned churchman, while Defoe had to use the tradesmen's entrance. Swift wrote for the court and the universities and the literate gentry. Defoe wrote for the business men and artisans and apprentices of London. In the end Swift pulled a deanery out of his work: all Defoe got for infinitely greater service was a wavering subsidy and a furtive career under continual threat from bailiffs and magistrates.

During the years of Harley's administration it was Defoe's job to explain his policies to the commercial interest in *The Review*. He traveled continually about the country looking into the state of public opinion and feeling out the electoral inclinations of the dissenters in the small towns. While Harley was engineering the Act of Union he transferred his activities to Scotland. When Harley turned his coat from moderate Whig to moderate Tory, Defoe and his publications turned with him. Meanwhile he went in for endless speculations on the side, each time sure that this time he'd be in the money, and published, for small change, occasional narratives of current happenings like *Some Account of the Late Storm* and the magnificently written *Apparition of Mrs. Veal*. Defoe was the first writer to understand and to appreciate the possibilities of that great gold mine of journalism, the middle-class public, just as Robert Harley was the first statesman to appreciate its political importance. The fortunes of the two men became inseparable. When Harley went into eclipse Defoe's income suffered, though he managed haltingly to carry on his various and devious activities under Harley's associate, Godolphin. When Queen Anne died and Harley was sent to the Tower, Defoe immediately found himself haled into court.

The wind of the new dynasty filled the sails of the Whigs. Like his patron Defoe had managed to get in wrong with both parties, but especially with the Whigs who felt he had ratted on them. The long administration of Robert Walpole initiated the rule of the whig squirarchy and Defoe's journalistic and political career came to a close. His business speculations had been pretty generally failures. To support his family in the suburban retirement of Stoke Newington, he turned altogether to writing and published volume after volume of educational and improving reading for the middle class. His *Family Instructor*, as well as being used by every butcher, baker and candlestick maker in the country, was used by the House of Hanover for the edification of the royal children. The period of the great leveling of the mind through journalism had begun.

Defoe was already a man in his late fifties when he started on the series of sturdy narratives, which, starting with *Robinson Crusoe* in 1720, expressed so perfectly the ethics, the aspirations, and the daily realities of the life of the rising commercial class. The books were enormously read, but Defoe himself remained the not quite respectable speculator, the flybynight journalist, the backstairs intelligence agent. He never gave up the gambler's hope for the golden throw that would make him rich and respected and raise his family into a higher sphere. But his ship never came in. He lived on far into the century, a miserable peevish old man continually rowing about money matters with his relatives, full of sure secret schemes and combinations for moneymaking that grew more and more fantastic as his mind weakened; and finally in the last year of his life, he ran away from home, frightened by some fancied or real threat of blackmail or of seizure for debt, and died hiding out alone in a London lodginghouse.

II

A COLONIAL PRESS IN THE ENGLISH PATTERN

~~~~~~

IMPORTANT *as were the contributions to American journalism of eighteenth-century colonial editors, the New World counterparts of Daniel Defoe, it is well to remember that for close to half a century before the first newspaper appeared in America a journalism of news and opinion had existed in the form of sporadic news sheets, tracts, and pamphlets. In concluding his "Forerunners of the Newspaper in America," Matthias A. Shaaber says, "it is evident that journalism—the printing and sale of news for the information of the public or for the profit of the publisher or for both reasons—is older in America than the newspaper by nearly forty years at least." And in discussing the opinion journalism of this pre-newspaper era, Edwin Ford, in his "Colonial Pamphleteers," emphasizes the significance of the public-minded pamphleteers and tract writers who spoke out courageously in behalf of charter rights and humanitarian causes.*

Thus tracts, pamphlets, and occasional news sheets came early from colonial presses, but it was not until John Campbell began his long-lived but dull Boston News-Letter *in 1704 that the colonists had a newspaper of continuous publication.*

Campbell, postmaster in Boston, began the colonial postmaster-editor tradition which lasted well into the Revolutionary period. Older and more substantial than the relationship of the postmaster to newspaper publishing, however, was the practice by printers of putting out news sheets and, later, newspapers. Both James Franklin and his brother Benjamin were printers, as were the Bradfords, the Greens, and other colonial families. Many of the capable colonial printers learned their trade in England. And from that country they brought back consid-

53

erably more than the mere mechanics of their craft. Benjamin Frank-lin's Autobiography *gives some idea of what an alert young apprentice could encounter in early eighteenth-century London.*

Good printers were important in the colonial economy, but it is the courageous, independent-minded editors of the period to whom the student of newspaper history looks for inspiration as well as enlightenment. In this group Benjamin Harris, John Peter Zenger, and James and Benjamin Franklin are outstanding.

Harris is perhaps the only publisher in the history of American journalism who has achieved fame on the basis of one issue of a newspaper. Modest though that fame may be, it has endured because of the principle involved. Bookseller-publisher Harris had paid for his independence of spirit in England by fine, pillory, and imprisonment. Coming to Boston in the 1680s, he started cautiously as a bookseller, but was evidently unwilling to live in a community without a newspaper and brought out the first, and only, issue of Publick Occurrences *on September 25, 1690. His editorial comment on the manner in which Indian allies of the British had treated French captives was branded by the governor and council of Massachusetts colony as "Reflections of a very high nature," and* Publick Occurrences *was suppressed.*

Four decades later John Peter Zenger was more successful in the battle for press freedom. By book, periodical, radio, and television the story of Zenger's trial on a charge of seditious libel has been given the public. His New York Weekly Journal, *backed by leaders of the faction opposed to the tyrannical policies of Governor Cosby, was the center of the now famous 1735 case. Andrew Hamilton's brilliant plea to the jury and the freeing of Zenger by that body are highlights in what has become an epic of American journalistic history. This one episode in Zenger's life raised a competent but ordinary printer-editor into a place of everlasting fame.*

Overshadowed by his famous brother, James Franklin has remained relatively obscure in the annals of American journalism. When James started the New-England Courant *in 1721 Boston had several other papers, the editors of which had readier access to the news than had the publisher of the* Courant. *Franklin wisely decided to overcome this handicap by the use of sprightly comment and entertaining matter presented with a literary twist. Backed by an unofficial editorial board made up of educated, liberal-minded Bostonians, the* Courant *pro-*

54

ceeded to challenge the authority and influence of the Puritan group, led by Increase and Cotton Mather. That the Courant *was wrong in opposing the recently introduced practice of inoculation against smallpox is of less importance, historically speaking, than is the fact that the smallpox crusade was the manifestation of an editorial policy which dared to defy the authoritarian dictates of clergy and government.*

Pre-eminent among colonial printers and editors was of course Benjamin Franklin, about whom more has been written than about any other publisher of his time. From his training in London he brought back to Boston and Philadelphia unusual understanding and appreciation of the lively, informative journalism which was developing in the English capital during the first half of the eighteenth century. His Pennsylvania Gazette *was probably the best printed and most ably edited newspaper of the American colonial group. Franklin was, as Albert Henry Smyth says in "Franklin as a Printer," "learned in paper, types and ink"; he was moreover "the largest all-around man that has yet been produced upon this continent."*

Printer-editors like Harris, Zenger, and the Franklins provided the leadership for an American press that was to become increasingly nationalistic as the colonies drew closer together in defense of common grievances against England.

5

Forerunners of the Newspaper in America

by MATTHIAS A. SHAABER

Students of the newspaper know MATTHIAS A. SHAABER for his *Some Forerunners of the Newspaper in England, 1476–1622*. His study of colonial fore-runners is reprinted here from the *Journalism Quarterly*, December 1934. The author is a professor of English at the University of Pennsylvania.

ALL our histories of journalism in America begin with Benjamin Harris's attempt to start a newspaper at Boston in 1690. So far as anybody knows, this was undoubtedly the first attempt to print a newspaper in English on this side of the Atlantic, but it was not necessarily the first attempt to print news. News does not altogether depend upon newspapers, as we are prone to think in these days when we are so plentifully served with them; it springs up everywhere, at all times, under all conditions. Once a settlement had been planted in America, there was plenty of news and there were plenty of people eager to hear it; and it was, of course, spread by hearsay and by letter. Therefore, one would say, *a priori*, that as soon as facilities for printing were available it might easily occur to somebody to put some of this news into print, either to serve some cause he was interested in or, if he was a printer or bookseller, for his own profit. He might well understand that the time was not ripe to start a newspaper published at regular intervals, but he could readily use some more primitive form of news-publication, such as other men had used in all the nations of Europe before the newspaper had evolved there. An examination of the issues of the earliest American presses shows that this is precisely what happened. Before there were newspapers there were pamphlets and broadsides of news — cruder methods of attaining the same purpose. These publications of news which preceded the newspaper deserve, I think, some notice; they belong, as a footnote, to the history of the beginnings of American journalism.

The number of separate newsbooks and broadsides which I have found is not large, but this fact is explained in part by conditions in the printing trade. It must be remembered that the first American press was not a commercial, or even an independent, enterprise. Although for more than twenty years the only press in the colonies, it was the property of Harvard College and was used primarily for academic and official work. The second press in America was sent over by the Society for the Propagation of the Gospel in New England, remained the society's property for some time, and then also passed into the control of Harvard College. There was no real commercial printing office until Marmaduke Johnson brought over, seemingly, a new press to Cambridge in 1665; but even so he seems to have spent much of his time after this date in assisting Green, the official printer. In 1674 Johnson moved to Boston, but he died there before he could open his shop. Consequently, it could be argued that John Foster, who acquired Johnson's equipment and commenced printing in 1675, was the first commercial printer in the colonies. It is evident, then, that only fifteen years separate Harris's *Publick Occurrences* from the opening of Foster's shop in Boston and only twenty-five years from Johnson's semi-independent start at Cambridge.

Consequently, as one would expect, very little news was published before 1665, and all of that was issued by the official printers at the order of the government. It consists of official statements which the authorities, to serve their own ends, saw fit to give publicity. The earliest appears to be *A declaration of former passages and proceedings betwixt the English and the Narrowgansets, with their confederates, Wherein the grounds and iustice of the ensuing warre are opened and cleared. Published, by order of the Commissioners for the united Colonies: At Boston the 11 of the sixth month 1645*, a pamphlet of seven pages, which was printed on the college press at Cambridge the same year. In 1659 the General Court of Massachusetts colony published a manifesto justifying itself in ordering the execution of two refractory Quakers, whose fate had excited an outcry of sympathy.[1] In 1660 it made public in the same way the text of the address which it had presented to King Charles II on his assuming the crown, petitioning him, from his *"Brittish* Israel," to "cast a favorable eye upon your poor *Mephibosheths* now . . . we mean *New-England.*"[2] Again, the council of the Massachusetts colony published a broadside, dated 7 December 1765, addressed "To our Brethren and Friends, the Inhabitants of the Colony of Massachusetts," which recites the history of the recent war with the Indians, in the tone of self-justification, and calls upon every citizen to do his duty.[3] The best-known document of this kind is the broadside entitled *The Present State of the New-English Affairs.*[4] This is a letter from the Rev. Increase Mather in London to Governor Bradstreet at Boston reporting what progress he has made in his negotiations with the London government as the Massachusetts council's agent; labeled "This is Published to prevent False Report," it obviously appeared with the indulgence of the authorities, who, at that very moment, were busy suppressing objectionable information, if not by their direction.

Some readers of my book on early journalism in England[5] have demurred to giving the name of news to governmental publications of this kind on the ground that they are really propaganda. Propaganda they certainly are, but in exactly the same sense a public address by President Roosevelt defending his program or a statement by the French representative at Geneva explaining why France cannot disarm is also propaganda, though nobody is surprised by our newspapers' printing it as news. In the seventeenth century, it seems to me, when the concept of news was much more naive than it is today and printed news was much scarcer, we must allow the title of news to any reasonably fresh information not previously available in print, regardless of the motives actuating those who published it.

As a clear case in point, I would cite the tract published by the opponents of Governor Leisler in New York in 1690.[6] Bitter as its animus against the governor is, it lives up pretty well to its own professions:

The Reader is hereby advertised, That the Matters contained in the following Declaration and Narration, were intended to have been presented to the Mayor's Court in New-York, the 21th of January last past, but that the Fury and Rage of this Insolent man Leysler, was grown to that highth, that the day before, by his order, several Persons of Note were violently seized, and divers Houses broken open, so as it was not thought safe to proceed in such Method. For which reason its thought well to publish the same, for information of all into whose hands it may come, but more especially for the benefit of our fellow Inhabitants, who are abused by the false Pretentions of this common Violator of our Laws and Liberties, as by the following Narrative will plainly appear, Wherein, the Courteous Peruser is desired to take notice, it hath been our great Care to relate nothing but Matters of Fact, of which we have substantial Credible Evidences.

This tract is undoubtedly propaganda, but is narrative, not argumentative or polemical, and therefore I think it deserves to be called news. Biased as it may have been, it very probably gave the people of New York and certainly the inhabitants of the other colonies a more comprehensive idea of the troubles with Governor Leisler than they could have got from any other source. I should also include in this category the tract called *The people's right to election Or alteration of government in Connecticott*,[7] although it is made up of argument and opinion as well as information. This consists chiefly of a letter by the Rev. Gershom Bulkeley of Hartford; but it seems in reality to be a manifesto on behalf of Governor Andros, of Massachusetts, then at loggerheads with most of the citizens of the colony. As the latter had the upper hand, the tract was necessarily printed at Philadelphia by the assigns of William Bradford. The addenda contain some information about recent events in Boston, including copies of several documents.

The remainder of the publications which I have to describe consist of news pure and simple. A good part of them relate foreign news. This was probably the easiest kind to get and perhaps the safest to publish. Most of these publications are simply reprints of newspapers and other news-reports printed at London. The earliest I have found [8] is an account of the eruption of Mt. Etna in 1669 reprinted at Cambridge by Green and Johnson from a pamphlet printed at London earlier in the same year.[9] Similarly there is a reprint of the *London Gazette* of 9 February 1685 announcing the death of Charles II and the accession of James II; [10] another of some documents relating to the invitation given the Prince of Orange to assume the crown of England in 1688;[11] another of more documents embodying the prince's acceptance; [12] a copy of the petition for clemency addressed by the bitterly hated Lord Chancellor Jeffreys to the king in 1689; [13] a copy of a letter from Admiral Russell relating his defeat of the French fleet in 1692;[14] a report of another earthquake at Naples in 1694;[15] a reprint of Ichabod Dawks's newsletter of 27 September 1697 with news of the wars on the continent.[16] All of these except the first-mentioned are broadsides; many of them were published by Boston booksellers who did not own a press and who therefore must have regarded them as vendible merchandise.

Of domestic news there is less to mention. The principal events of the years between 1665 and 1704 in the colonies, such as King Philip's War and the difficulties of the colonists with various of their governors, do not seem to have brought forth much printed news — as far as political events such as the latter are concerned, for obvious reasons. The definition of news, however, might be stretched a little to include the narratives of the Rev. Increase Mather[17] and the Rev. William Hubbard[18] relating the Indian wars. Although they would ordinarily be called historical treatises, as they were both published immediately after the end of the train of events which they describe and emphasize their timeliness on their title pages, they must have been just as good as printed news to our ancestors in 1676.

These two pamphlets were probably published on the initiative of their authors; but the three pieces which remain to be mentioned are evidently due to the enterprise of printers and booksellers, i.e., they are strictly journalistic publications. The oldest is a broadside entitled *A relation of Captain Bull, Concerning the Mohavvks At Fort-Albany. May, 1689.* This gives an account of the proceedings of Captain Jonathan Bull of Connecticut, who was sent with a company of soldiers to Fort Albany to help defend it against the Indians whom the French were exciting to violence in consequence of the outbreak of war in Europe. It also records the ousting of Major Jervas Baxter from the fort as a "papist" and the friendly overtures of the neighboring Indians.[19] The second is a four-page single-sheet published by Benjamin Harris in 1689 which records the endorsement by a meeting of the citizens of Boston and vicinity of the revolution which had just been accomplished in England.[20] The last, a pamphlet of twenty pages called *Blood will out*[21] printed at Philadelphia by William Bradford in 1692, is actually the story of a trial for murder, told chiefly in the form of a transcript of the testimony authenticated by the clerk of the court.

Thus it is evident that journalism — the printing and sale of news for the information of the public or for the profit of the publisher or for both reasons — is older in America than the newspaper by nearly forty years at least. If comparatively little news was printed before 1704, the reasons were rather that presses were few, the authorities strict, and publishers unenterprising than that there was no way of making news public in print. Indeed, news was still sometimes published separately even after newspapers appeared. In July, 1704, at

Boston, Nicholas Boone published, and presumably sold, a broadside (printed on both sides) entitled *An Account of the Behaviour and last Dying speeches Of the Six Pirates, that were Executed on Charles River, Boston side, on Fryday June 30th. 1704. Viz. Capt. John Quelch, John Lambert, Christopher Scudamore, John Miller, Erasmus Peterson and Peter Roach*, in spite of the fact that the *Boston News-Letter* had furnished its readers with an account of the incident.[22] In 1721, at Philadelphia, Andrew Bradford printed a broadside setting forth a treaty just concluded with the Indians: his newspaper, the *American Weekly Mercury*, on 6 July, announced the governor's departure to treat with the Indians, but made no mention of the treaty itself except in an advertisement of the broadside aforesaid on 27 July. The story of the forerunners of the newspaper in America and of their lingering survival after the emergence of periodicals of news follows exactly the same pattern as in the nations of Europe.

NOTES

[1] *A declaration of the General Court of the Massachusetts holden at Boston in New-England. October 18. 1659. Concerning The execution of two Quakers.* [Cambridge: Samuel Green, 1659.] Reprinted as *A true Relation of the Proceedings against certain Quakers, at the generall Court of the Massachusetts holden at Boston in New-England October 18. 1659. London Printed by A. W. 1660.*

[2] *The Humble petition and address Of the General Court sitting at Boston in New-England, unto The High and Mighty prince Charles the second. And presented to His Most Gracious Majesty Feb. 11. 1660. Printed in the Year 1660* [at Cambridge by Samuel Green].

[3] This broadside is apparently known only from the copy of it printed in *A Continuation of the state of New England* (London: Printed by T. M. for Dorman Newman, at the Kings Armes in the Poultry, 1676), which states that it had been printed at Boston. See *The Old Indian Chronicle . . . Introduction and Notes, by Samuel G. Drake* (Boston, 1867), pp. 187–92.

[4] Boston, Printed and Sold by Samuel Green, 1689.

[5] *Some Forerunners of the Newspaper in England, 1476–1622.* (Philadelphia, 1929.)

[6] *A Modest and Impartial narrative Of several Grievances and Great Oppressions That the Peacable and most Considerable Inhabitants of Their Majesties Province of New-York in America Lie Under, By the Extravagant and Arbitrary Proceedings of Jacob Leysler and his Accomplices.* [Philadelphia: William Bradford, 1690.]

[7] *The people's right to election Or alteration of government in Connecticott, argued in a letter; by Gershom Bulkeley Esq; one of their Majesties Justices of the peace In the County of Hartford. Together with a Letter to the said Bulkeley, from a Friend of his in the Bay. To which it is added, The Writing delivered to James Russell of Charlestown Esq; warning him and others concerned, not to meet to Hold a Court at Cambridge, within the county of Middlesex. By Thomas Greaves Esq; Judge of their Majesties Inferior Court of Pleas and one of their Majesties Justices of the peace within the said County And also his answer to*

Mr. Broadstreete and the Gentlemen mett at the Town-house in Boston concerning the same. Published for the Information & Satisfaction of their Majesties loyall (but abused) Subjects in New-England. (1689)

[8] Although the title-page of *Gods terrible voice in the City of London Wherein you have the Narration of the Two late Dreadful Judgements of Plague and Fire, Inflicted by the Lord upon that city; The former in the Year 1665. the latter in the Year 1666. By T[homas]. V[incent]. To which is added, The Generall Bill of Mortality, Shewing the Number of Persons which died in every Parish of all Diseases, and of the Plague, in the year abovesaid. Cambridge: Printed by Marmaduke Johnson 1668.* would seem to promise news, and the bill of mortality appended to it must have had a real interest as news, it is actually a theological tract written by a clergyman.

[9] *A True and Exact relation Of the Late Prodigious Earthquake & Eruption of Mount Ætna, Or, Monte-Gibello; As it came In a Letter written to His Majesty from Naples By the Right Honourable The Earl of VVinchilsea, His Majesties late Ambassador at Constantinople, who in his Return from thence, Visiting Catania in the Island of Sicily, was an Ey-witness of that dreadful Spectacle. Together with a more particular Narrative of the same, as it is Collected out of several Relations sent from Catania. Published by authority. Cambridge: Printed by S. G. and M. J. 1669.*

[10] *The London Gazette; Published by Authority. From Thursday February 5th. to Monday February 9th. 1684. Printed by Thomas Newcomb in the Savoy, 1684. And Reprinted at Boston in New-England by Samuel Green, 1685.*

[11] *Declaration Of the Nobility, Gentry, and Commonalty at the Rendezvous at Nottingham, November 22. 1688, Reprinted and Sold by Samuel Green of Boston, 1689.* This includes *The Declaration of the Lords Spiritual and Temporall . . . at Guildhall, 11th Decemb. 1688.*

[12] *His Highness the Prince of Orange, His letter to the lords Spiritual and Temporal Assembled at Westminister, In this present Convention. Boston, Printed by S. G. for S. Phillips at the Town-House 1689.* This includes *The address Of the Lords Spiritual and Temporal, and Commons. Assembled at Westminster, in this present Convention. Jan. 22. 1689.*

[13] *To His Highness William Henrick, Prince of Orange, The most Humble Petition of George Lord Chancellor Jeffries, Boston, Printed by S. G. for Samuel Phillips at the West end of the Town-House, 1689.*

[14] *Admiral Russel's letter to the Earl of Nottingham: Containing an Exact and Particular Relation of the Late Happy Victory and Success against The French Fleet. Published by Authority. Boston Printed, and Sold by Benjamin Harris, at the Landon-Coffee-House. 1692.* This includes a note on the celebration at Boston.

[15] *The Earthquake Naples; September, 21. 1694. Boston, N. E. Reprinted by B. Green. February 21. 1694,5.*

[16] *London Septemb. 27. Yesterday Morning arrived Three Holland Mails, which bring the following Advices. London, Printed by I. Dawks, Reprinted at Boston in N. E. by B. Green & J. Allen. 1697.*

[17] *A brief history of the vvarr With the Indians in Nevv-England, (From June 24, 1675. when the first English-man was murdered by the Indians, to August 12. 1676. when Philip, alias Metacomet, the principal Author and Beginner of the Warr, was slain.) Wherein the Grounds, Beginning, and Progress of the Warr, it summarily expressed. Together with a serious exhortation to the Inhabitants of that Land, by Increase Mather, Teacher of a Church of Christ, in Boston in New-England. Boston, Printed and Sold by John Foster over against the Sign of the Dove. 1676.*

[18] *A narrative of the troubles with the Indians in New-England, from the first planting thereof in the year 1607. to this present year 1677. But chiefly of the late Troubles in the last two years, 1675. and 1676. To which is added a Discourse*

about the Warre with the Pequods In the year 1637. By W. Hubbard, Minister of Ipswich. . . . Published by Authority. Boston; Printed by John Foster, in the year 1677.

[19] As this sheet bears no imprint, one cannot be certain that it was published by a bookseller for his own profit. It may have been an informal official announcement, though it does not read like something of that kind. It was doubtless published at Boston and was possibly singled out for the honor of being printed because the events it records probably gave great satisfaction to the opponents of Governor Andros.

[20] *The Declaration, Of the Gentlemen, Merchants, and Inhabitants of Boston, and the Countrey Adjacent. April 18th. 1689. Boston Printed by Samuel Green, and Sold by Benjamin Harris at the London Coffee-House. 1689.*

[21] *Blood will out, or, an Example of Justice in the Tryal, Condemnation, Confession and execution of Thomas Lutherland, Who Barbarously Murthered the Body of John Clark of Philadelphia, And was Executed at Salem in VVest-Jarsey the 23d of February, 1692. Philadelphia; Printed and Sold by Will. Bradford, 1692.*

[22] This sheet also advertises a forthcoming pamphlet recounting the trial of the same pirates.

6

Colonial Pamphleteers

by EDWIN H. FORD

EDWIN H. FORD has been a journalism professor at the University of Minnesota since 1929, specializing in journalism history and the literary aspects of journalism. His study of the early colonial pamphleteers appeared in the *Journalism Quarterly*, March 1936.

In the study of the development of public opinion in the United States, particularly with reference to the work of the editorial writer, the early Colonial pamphlet has had relatively little attention. Buried in libraries, sought only by scholars delving into the lore of special periods, this trenchant form of early American editorial expression has enjoyed a dignified obscurity. Yet it has played no small part in the American pre-newspaper era by establishing the precedent of sound, intelligent comment on public affairs by men who were leaders in national and civic life.

For at least fifty years before Benjamin Harris attempted to express his opinions in the first and last issue of *Publick Occurrences*, Colonial writers had been having their say, in tracts and pamphlets, on matters pertaining to human rights and conduct. Harris' indiscretion in daring to question the omniscience of the Colonial governors had an earlier counterpart in the unfortunate foray of Thomas Lechford into the field of ecclesiastical controversy when, in 1641, Lechford, a clergyman, returned to England from Massachusetts Colony, leaving the following noncommittal paragraph in the colonial records: "Mr. Thomas Lechford acknowledging he had overshot himself, and is sorry for it, promising to attend his calling and not to meddle with controversies, was dismissed." Lechford, however, was not through shooting, for upon his return to England he relieved his mind concerning affairs in New England in his *Plain Dealing*, a treatise intended to convey strongly the impression that those in authority in New England were making grave mistakes.

In the era between Lechford and the rise of Colonial newspapers, pamphlets played an important part in providing a background of public opinion upon matters which were later to engage the attention of newspaper editors. If, as Mr. Neal has pointed out, editorials frequently have for their subject "themes of perennial interest to mankind, needing no extraneous fact to give them appeal — themes that are always timely, such as the rights of man, problems of life and conduct," [1] then the pamphlets of such writers as Increase and Cotton Mather, Samuel Sewall, John Woolman, Nathaniel Ward, and James Swan may reasonably be considered the Colonial progenitors of the modern American editorial.

Such men were close to the religious and political turmoil of seventeenth-century England, out of which had emerged issues that were to be taken up in a new world. Writers like L'Estrange and Defoe had set a precedent which colonial pamphleteers were not slow to follow. How men were to be governed, how they were to worship, how they were to treat one another, had become matters for intelligent discussion rather than despotic edict. First because there were no newspapers available, and later because strict censorship made dangerous the publishing of opinion in newspapers, the pamphlet and broadside were the most effective media for disseminating ideas during the period preceding the establishment of the newspapers as a recognized repository of opinion.

Even after newspapers had become fairly numerous in the colonies the pamphlet habit persisted. The knack of brevity, of compressed statement had still to be acquired. The man who had opinions on public affairs in Colonial America needed plenty of space in which to air his views; his manner was leisurely and dignified, his argument logical and complete, his invective sweeping. Lack of space, then, and to a certain extent lack of prestige on the part of the newspaper, kept the pamphleteer off the newspaper page, restricted his audience accordingly but enabled him to write with freedom and individuality.

Such restrictions handicapped the pamphlet as an organ of wide appeal. It was an aristocrat where the lusty young newspaper was a democrat. One writer on journalism,[2] Frederic Hudson, has gone so far as to attribute the establishment of newspapers in the Colonies to a war of pamphlets arising out of a published treatise by Increase Mather. The pamphlet referred to was called *The Order of the Gospel Professed and Practised by the Churches of Christ in New England Justified*, and was printed by Bartholomew Green in 1700. Soon after, says Hudson, there was printed in New York a pamphlet entitled, *Gospel Order Revived, being an Answer to a Book lately set forth by the Rev. Mr. Increase Mather — by sundry Ministers of the Gospel in New England.* The following explanation accompanied it: "The Reader is desired to take Notice that the Press in Boston is so much under the aw of the Reverend Author whom we answer, and his Friends, that we could not obtain of the Printer there to Print the following sheets . . ." Printer Green immediately vindicated himself in a handbill with a preface by Cotton Mather; other pamphlets were issued in answer to the answer and the battle waxed hotly.

Whatever significance with regard to the development of newspapers in the colonies the above incident may or may not have, it serves to illustrate the power of Increase and Cotton Mather in Colonial affairs, temporal as well as spiritual. Both were prolific writers and delivered themselves of frequent polemics having to do with a variety of subjects. In a number of tracts, the contents of which were first delivered as lectures, Cotton Mather admonishes his hearers and readers concerning their duties in town government, in business, and in general conduct. In his concern with the affairs of his community and the forthrightness of his utterances, he is a kind of seventeenth-century William Allen White. The genial warmth of the Emporia editor's point of view is missing, however, in the exhortations of the Boston clergyman.

The Boston Ebenezer [3] contains a section devoted to the godly administration of civic affairs. Says Cotton Mather:

Let all that bear public office in the town contribute all the help they can, that may continue the help of God unto us. Truly there is cause to make that cry, Men of Boston, Help! For ignorance and prophaness and bad living, and the worst things in the world are breaking in upon us. And now will the Justices of the town set themselves to consider how they may suppress all growing vices among us? There are those who have the eye of the town so much upon them that the very name of Towns-man is that by which they are distinguished. Sirs, will you also consider how to help the affairs of the town, so that all things may go well among us? Moreover, may not the schoolmasters do much to instill principles of religion and civility, as well as other points of good education, unto the children of the town? Only let the town encourage its well-deserving school-masters.

In *A Testimony Against Evil Customs*, published in Boston in 1719, Cotton Mather was one of a group of ministers, an ecclesiastical editorial board, if you will, who expressed themselves sedately but emphatically on the conduct of the people of Boston and vicinity.

The following are extracts from the *Testimony:*

"It is to be wished that the innocent mirth of weddings may not be polluted with such riotous or immodest irregularities."

"It is to be wished that lectures were more generally attended."

"It is to be wished that the Huskings wherein the Joy of Harvest arrives unto us, may not be turned into revels."

"But for dancing schools we cannot commend the time and cost so often thrown away upon them."

The horrible consequences of debt are considered in Cotton Mather's *Fair Dealing Between Debtor and Creditor*. What would the sturdy old Puritan have thought of the modern method of doing business on a credit basis? That he considers the subject a timely one is shown by his assertion that "There are some circumstances of the day which may render a discourse on this point of morality, singularly seasonable. But indeed, it were never out of season."

After defining debt he proceeds to discuss the following maxims:

First: a man that is going into debt should keep the eye of prudence upon every step that is before him. Second: a man that would not be sinfully in debt ought to have a spirit reconciled unto a low and mean condition in the world, if this be what the Glorious God shall call him to. Third: for a man to run into debt, when he has no prospect, and perhaps no purpose of ever getting out, this is a dishonesty by no means to be countenanced. Fourth: Men ought often and nicely to examine the state of their business, if they would not find themselves irrevocably plunged into debt before they are aware, but it comes in unexpectedly like a traveller upon them; and then holds them like an armed man. Fifth: The man that is got into debt, ought to get out of it, and as if it were for his life. Sixth: If a man be so far brought into debt as to become insolvent, there is a behavior agreeable to our holy religion, both by God and man to be expected of him. Seventh: A wholesome antidote against the mischief of debt, it would be for a man to consider seriously what he does when he wrongs other men by lying in debt unto them.

When Cotton Mather calls the French "Gallic Bloodhounds" in his *The Present State of New England*, we are reminded of the vituperative writing of the early British journalists. Perhaps it was because he was younger when he wrote the tract (1690) and had not learned the cooler method of later years. But the emergency was very great, or so it seemed to the author, with "the news of an invasion by bloody Indians and Frenchmen begun upon us" still ringing in his ears, and he wastes no words in stating that the trouble has come upon the people of New England as a result of their sins and abominations. He calls for an awakening of public spirit and advises that "a Sally" be made upon the French territory. "Alas for the divisions of New England," cries the zealous writer, and he proceeds to warn those who presume to positions they do not merit, to "mind the business of your own station; pull the ropes, ply the oars and sails as you are commanded, but leave the helm where 'tis managed by those that can have no other interests but what is yours."

At approximately the same time that Cotton Mather was raising his voice against the depredations of the French, he and his father, Increase Mather, were taking a leading part in the Andros controversy and were aiding Massachusetts in every way possible in her fight to retain her charter. Autocrats though they were, they were tremendously jealous of the rights of the people in their colony. Increase Mather, representing the province in England, and Cotton Mather, laboring in its behalf at home, both brought their industry and eloquence to bear upon the loss of privilege suffered by a revocation of the charter.

Hutchinson, in his *History of Massachusetts*, referring to *The Declaration of the Gentlemen and Inhabitants of Boston and Country adjacent*, written in 1689 in connection with the charter fight, says, "There would be room to doubt whether the declaration was not a work of time and prepared beforehand, if it did not appear, by the style and language to have been the performance of one of the ministers of Boston (Cotton Mather) who had a remarkable talent for very quick and sudden composures." Here we have an editorial-writing qualification in its most modern sense, fulfilled as early as 1689.

"To get us within reach of the desolation desired for us," states the *Declaration*, "it was no improper thing that we should have our charter vacated and the hedge which kept us from the wild beasts of the field effectually broken down. The Commission [4] was as illegal for the form

68

of it, as the way of obtaining it was malicious and unreasonable. In little more than half a year we saw this commission superseded by another, yet more absolute and arbitrary, with which Sir Edmond Andros arrived as our governor." [5]

Increase Mather, in *A Vindication of New England*, written during the controversy, thus commiserates with his unhappy country: "Poor New England! Thou hast always been the eyesore of squinting malignity; the Butt of many envenomed arrows, which from time to time have been shot at thy tranquility; but of none more wickedly designed than those late addresses which have (after their fashion) endeavored to alienate their Majesties affections from thee. However, let it be known, thou hast friends in England who sufficiently know thy circumstances to wipe off the dust now cast upon thee, and give thee a better and more faithful character." [6]

Another pamphlet writer who took part in the charter controversy was Samuel Sewall, the honest, admirable "Samuel Pepys of American Colonial history," whose diary sheds so much light upon Colonial life as well as upon Sewall himself. Together with Edward Rawson, Sewall wrote *The Revolution in New England Justified*, the style of which is as much to the point as the most ardent patriot could desire. "The doctrine of passive obedience and non-resistance," affirm the writers, "which a sort of men did of late, when they thought the world would never change, cry up as divine truth, is by reason of the happy revolution in these nations, exploded, and the assertors of it become ridiculous."

An instance of forceful editorial expression having to do with Colonial charters is Jeremiah Dummer's *A Defense of the New England Charters*. It was written in 1728 at a time when the House of Commons was contemplating the passage of a bill annulling the charters of the New England colonies, and was republished in London in 1765 on account of its bearing on the state of affairs in the colonies at that time. The introduction is concerned with a brief history of the Andros controversy and the charter difficulties of the colonies generally. Dummer then makes four points: First, "That the Charter Governments have a good and undoubted Right to their respective Charters"; second, "That these Governments have by no Misbehavior forfeited their charters"; third, "That it is not the interest of the crown to resume the charters if forfeited"; and fourth, "That it seems inconsistent with justice to disenfranchise the charter colonies by an act of parliament." These writers were the forerunners of Isaiah Thomas, Samuel Adams and other patriot editors who later fought staunchly for Colonial rights.

Certainly not for the breadth of his views, but rather for the raciness of his wit and his astonishing manipulation of phraseology is Nathaniel Ward, writer of *The Simple Cobler of Aggawam*, remembered among Colonial pamphleteers. Ward was a graduate of Cambridge, was a lawyer as well as a minister, and had traveled extensively. He served as minister at Ipswich, Massachusetts, then known as Aggawam, from 1634 to 1636. The *Cobler* was written during Ward's residence of more than ten years in America, but was published in England. It has the robust, slashing style of H. L. Mencken in days when Mencken was creating his own sulphurous vocabulary for use against "the Bible Belt" and the professors. In terse, expressive language this lawyer-minister voices his dislike of religious toleration, the vanities of both feminine and masculine fashion, and the civil strife in England. Tyler calls the book "a tremendous partisan pamphlet, intensely vital even yet, full of fire, wit, whim, eloquence, sarcasm, invective, patriotism, bigotry." [7]

Of toleration Ward wrote in the *Cobler*: "It is said that Men ought to have Liberty of their Conscience, and that it is a persecution to debarre them of it: I can rather stand amazed than reply to this: it is an astonishment to think that the brains of men should be parboyl'd in such impious ignorance: Let all the wits under the Heavens lay their heads together and finde an assertion worse this (one excepted) I will Petition to be chosen the universal idiot of the world." On women's fashions he indulges in the following diatribe: "When I hear a nigiper-ous gentle-dame inquire what dresse the Queen is in this week: what the nidinstertion fashion of the Court; I meane the very newest: with egge to be in it with all haste, whatever it be; I look at her as the very gizzard of a trifle, the product of a quarter of a cipher, the epitome of nothing, fitter to be kicked, if she were a kickable substance than either honor'd or humor'd." And of the practice among men of wear-ing long hair, he says pithily, "A short promise is a far safer guard than a long lock." [8] It is interesting to observe in this seventeenth-century writer, the same qualities of exaggeration that have come to be regarded as characteristic of American humor.

While Colonial writers were setting down their opinions on matters of religion, government, and the rights of enfranchised humanity, there was developing in America a humanitarian group — writers who contemplated the problems of human relationship with an ennobling sense of justice. Payne declares that men like Cotton Mather "never dreamed that humanity could be led to reverence the Diety through the simple processes of Eternal Law unfolding and unraveling man's liberty, equality, and happiness." [9] Not only did these advocates of the humanitarian idea dream of such an accomplishment, but they employed their pens with vigor and clarity to the end that the ideal of "liberty, equality, and happiness" might be more quickly realized. A century before Greeley, humanitarian principles were being inculcated by the pamphleteers. The most universal theme in this group is slavery. With it, but subsidiary to it, is that of the welfare of the Indian.

Samuel Sewall, John Woolman and Benjamin Franklin were among Colonial writers who considered the lot of the Indian. Of Sewall, Tyler says that "the Indians of Massachusetts had no wiser or more generous friend than he." Woolman denounced the selling of rum to the Indians and Franklin spoke out courageously in his *Narrative of the Late Massacre* which denounced the killing of a group of Indians who were under government protection, by a band of Pennsylvania frontiersmen.

The frontiersmen surprised an Indian village in Lancaster County, Pennsylvania, in 1764, and massacred six of the natives, all who were in the village at the time of the attack. As the Indians were under the protection of the Colonial government, the remainder of them, who had been absent when their tribesmen were killed, were shut up in the workhouse at Lancaster for protection. Shortly after, this building was broken into by unknown persons and the remaining fourteen Indians were killed.

In his *Narrative* Franklin condemns the perpetrators of the deed in vigorous fashion, and brands the attacks not only as grave breaches of trust, but as bloodthirsty outrages of the worst sort. With his usual sagacity the writer foresees the danger that may result if any of the powerful Six Nations are antagonized, but it must be said in fairness to Franklin that in writing as he did, he undoubtedly made many enemies among that part of the population which believed the attacks absolutely justified. The Indian tribes along the Ohio and Susquehanna rivers were at that time engaged in war with the whites and feeling in Pennsylvania ran high.

Franklin handles the subject with his characteristic coolness and

71

common sense. "Because the members of one tribe murder a white man, should the white man's kinsmen go out and murder any Indian they see, no matter what his tribe or his guilt may be, as reprisal?" he asks. And with his usual penchant for homely and telling comparisons he enquires, "If a red-haired man should kill my wife, or one of my children, am I justified in slaying every red-haired person I meet thereafter?" And with reference to Will Soc, one of the murdered Indians, who was said to have been guilty of various crimes, Franklin says, "But if he was [guilty] ought he not have been fairly tried? He lived under our laws and was subject to them; he was in our hands and might easily have been prosecuted; was it English justice to condemn and execute him unheard?" These words, with but one alteration, might go, and probably have gone, into editorials denouncing instances of lynch law today.

Sewall's tract on slavery, *The Selling of Joseph*, written in 1700, is probably the first expression of opinion on the subject in Colonial America. More than half a century later, in 1754, John Woolman published his *Some Considerations on the Keeping of Negroes* in which he sums up with his gentle persuasion and deadly logic, the points against slavery. Here is no thundering denunciation, but the broad reflections of a mystic. Woolman can see no justifiable reason why one group of men should dominate another. Two of his eloquent arguments follow:

It appears by Experience that where children are educated in fulness, Ease and Idleness, evil Habits are more prevalent, than is common among such who are prudently employed in the necessary affairs of Life: And if children are not only educated in the Way of so great Temptation, but have also the Opportunity of lording it over their fellow creatures, and being masters of men in their childhood, how can we hope otherwise than that their tender minds will be Possessed with Thoughts too high for them.

Man is born to labour, and Experience abundantly showeth that it is for our Good: But where the Powerful lay the Burden on the Inferior, without affording a Christian Education, and suitable opportunity of improving the mind, and a treatment which we, in their Case, should approve, that ourselves may live at Ease and fare sumptuously, and lay up Riches for their Posterity, this seems to contradict the Design of Providence, and I doubt, if sometimes the Effect of a Perverted Mind: for while the Life of one is made grievous by the Rigour of another, it entails misery on both.

In 1762 Woolman brought out the second part of his *Considerations on Keeping Negroes*, and in the same year appeared a pamphlet of some eighty pages, usually ascribed to Anthony Benezet, entitled *A Short Account of that Part of Africa Inhabited by Negroes*. The title page further states that the material is "Extracted from divers Authors, in order to show the Iniquity of that Trade, and the Falsity of the arguments usually advanced in its Vindication." The same writer, in 1771, published a tract on the *Historical Account of Guinea with an Inquiry into the Rise and Progress of Slave Trade*.

Two years later Benjamin Rush and Richard Nisbet engaged in verbal combat over the question of slave-keeping, the former advancing arguments against the practice in *An Address to the Inhabitants of the British Settlements on the Slavery of the Negroes in America*, and the latter upholding the viewpoint of the slave owners in a treatise that bore the following title: *Slavery not Forbidden by Scripture, or a Defense of the West Indian Planters from the Aspersions thrown out against them*. Nisbet points out numerous instances where slavery and bondage are spoken of among the Hebrews. He states that there are "above four-hundred thousand Negroes in the British Islands," and asks where as many whites may be obtained to take their place. The tract is an attempt to show that under the climatic conditions of the West Indies, and with the plantation system organized in the interests of increased sugar production, slave labor is practically indispensable. The controversy grew hot and in his *Vindication* or answer to Nisbet's answer, Rush concludes, "I have avoided as much as possible every Thing through the whole of this Vindication, that would draw me from my subject to the author of the Defense. I shall not give him the Pain of repeating here the many unkind Insinuations and Reflections he has thrown out against me. He was perhaps warm when he wrote them — When he cools, I am persuaded he will be 'sorry for his ungenerous abuse of a man who never injured him,' or any other man born in the West Indies." The last words refer to the concluding line of Nisbet's *Defense*.

James Swan's dedication for his *A Dissuasion to Great Britain and the Colonies from the Slave-Trade to Africa* was written in the spirit of the modern crusading editorial, for in the dedication to the governor and the Council of the Province of Massachusetts Bay, Swan declares he is impelled to address them "by hearing that your Excellency and a majority of both houses are inclined to relieve in one degree or another the most dejected part of our species, from a slavery that is really odious in the eyes of every true British subject." And in concluding the dedication he charges the Governor and Council with the following responsibility: "at the ensuing Session I expect at least a finishing of what was begun in the last, of stopping a further importation of Negroes into this province. And you may do as much more for the relief of those that are here as you in your great wisdom, shall see meet. — Think that they are men possessed of reasonable souls; that we are all upon a level in the beginning, and what right have we to keep them in their present situation, — then I am pretty well satisfied you will give them the relief they want, and which I most ardently wish for." There is little difference between this exhortation and the challenge of the modern editorial writer to the legislature of his state.

But even as Nisbet and Rush were writing their tracts a new nation was rising in Colonial America, a nation that was to be too engrossed in the problems of government and commercial prosperity to consider for more than half a century the status of the Negro. New conditions were to bring the era of the newspaper and the magazine. The day of the pamphleteer had passed, but the tradition of independent and fearless expression of opinion which he had handed down was to set the pattern for generations of future American editors.

NOTES

[1] Robert Wilson Neal, *Editorials and Editorial-Writing* (Springfield, Mass.: The Home Correspondence School, 1921), p. 17.

[2] Frederic Hudson, *Journalism in the United States from 1690 to 1872* (New York: Harper and Brothers, 1873), p. 51.

[3] Old South Leaflets, Vol. III, No. 67 (Boston, 1896).

[4] Appointed by the King to govern Massachusetts.

[5] *Andros Tracts*, Prince Society, Vol. I, p. 12.

[6] *Ibid.*, Vol. II, p. 21.

[7] Moses Coit Tyler, *A History of American Literature During the Colonial Time* (New York: G. P. Putnam's Sons, 1880), Vol. I, p. 230.

[8] *The Simple Cobler of Aggawam in America*, edited by David Pulsifer (Boston: J. Munroe and Company, 1843), p. 32.

[9] George Henry Payne, *History of Journalism in the United States* (New York: D. Appleton and Company, 1926), p. 11.

Franklin as a Printer

by ALBERT HENRY SMYTH

Internationally known at the century's turn as a scholar and lecturer, ALBERT HENRY SMYTH was selected to edit the definitive ten-volume publication of the *Writings of Benjamin Franklin*. This article, about one facet of Franklin's career, appeared in the famous old *Independent* on January 11, 1906.

WHEN Franklin wrote his will he began with the words, "I, Benjamin Franklin, *printer*." Thruout his life he was chiefly interested in the art of printing, and his dearest friends and most intimate companions were members of that craft. He was learned in paper, types and ink. He printed his bagatelles upon his private press at Passy with types cast by his household servants. He was proud of the glossy blackness of his ink, and he furnished Pierres (Imp^r Ord^{re} du Roi) with the special paper upon which he printed his *Manuel d'Epictete en Grec*. His most esteemed correspondent in England was William Strahan, the King's printer, and among the chief of his French intimates was Fournier the younger, the celebrated printer and type founder at Paris in the second half of the eighteenth century.

It was, he says, his bookish inclination that determined his father to make him a printer, tho he had already one son of that profession. He was but twelve years old when he signed the indentures that bound him to his brother, James Franklin. He was to serve as an apprentice till he was twenty-one years of age, only he was to be allowed journeyman's wages during the last year. His brother began in 1721 to print the *New-England Courant*, the fourth newspaper that appeared in America. It was for this paper that Benjamin Franklin wrote the Dogood papers. He commenced his literary career with the first of these anonymous articles, stealthily written and timidly thrust under the door of his brother's printing office. American literature may almost be said to date from these anonymous productions of an ambitious lad of sixteen.

The *Courant* was conducted in such a reckless manner that the Boston Council declared that the tendency of the paper was to mock religion and to disturb the peace and good order of the province. James Franklin was therefore forbidden "to print or publish the *New-England Courant* or any other pamphlet or paper of the like nature, except it be first supervised by the secretary of the province."

To circumvent the Council and to avoid "carrying the manuscripts and public news to be supervised by the secretary," it was determined at a meeting of the "Couranteers," as the contributers to the *Courant* were called, that James Franklin should appear to abandon the publication and that Benjamin Franklin should appear as the sole publisher. His apprenticeship indentures were canceled and new indentures were signed and concealed. His editorial preface appeared February 11th, 1723, and it was stated that the *Courant* was "printed and sold by Benjamin Franklin in Queen street, where advertisements are taken in." The style of the youthful publisher's introductory preface showed that the *Courant* had sustained no loss by its change of management. He wrote:

Long has the Press groaned in bringing forth an hateful, but numerous Brood of Party Pamphlets, malicious Scribbles, and Billingsgate Ribaldry. The Rancour and bitterness it has unhappily infused into Men's minds, and to what a Degree it has sowed and leaven'd the Tempers of Persons formerly esteemed some of the most sweet and affable, is too well known here, to need further Proof or Representation of the Matter.

No generous and impartial Person then can blame the present Undertaking, which is designed purely for the Diversion and Merriment of the Reader. Pieces of Pleasancy and Mirth have a secret Charm in them to allay the Heats and Tumours of our Spirits, and to make a Man forget his restless Resentments. They have a strange Power to tune the harsh Disorders of the Soul, and reduce us to a serene and placid State of Mind.

Few stories in literary history are more widely known or more frequently repeated than that which relates to Franklin's quarrel with his brother and his subsequent flight to New York and Philadelphia. Every one has read in the "Autobiography" how he was nearly drowned in New York Bay; how he walked from Perth Amboy to Burlington, fifty miles, thru ever-during rain; how he took boat at Burlington on an October evening, and landed at the foot of Market street in Philadelphia on the following Sunday morning; how he walked the quiet streets, a ridiculous figure, munching his roll; how he found shelter the first night in the strange city at the Crooked Billet in Water street. He had offered his services in New York to old William Bradford, who had been the first printer in Pennsylvania, but removed from thence upon the quarrel of George Keith. "My son at Philadelphia," said Bradford, "has lately lost his principal hand, Aquila Rose, by death; if you go thither I believe he may employ you." Andrew Bradford received him civilly, gave him a breakfast and referred him to another printer named Keimer, whom Franklin found in a printing house consisting of an old shattered press and one small, worn out font of English, composing elegiac verses on Aquila Rose, "composing them in the types directly out of his head."

Franklin worked for Keimer and for Bradford in Philadelphia and for Palmer and for Watts in London, when he went thither a victim of the pitiful tricks of Governor Keith. When Keimer sold his printing house and removed to Barbados his newspaper passed into Franklin's hands, and with No. 40 (October 2d, 1729), the *Pennsylvania Gazette* began a new existence. It became the leading newspaper of the day, with a large circulation and advertising patronage. Franklin was the sole editor and proprietor for nearly twenty years, and for eighteen more he was jointly so with David Hall, who had been recommended to him by William Strahan. His printing house was the source of all his wealth, accumulated by industry and frugality, for his political services were an expense to him, and he declined to secure patents for his inventions or copyrights for his publications, saying "That as we enjoy great advantages from the inventions of others we should be glad of an opportunity to serve others by an invention of ours; and this we should do freely and generously." Le Roy said to him, "Like Charles XII and other conquerors, you only seize empires to give them to others."

Two productions of Franklin's press can never be forgotten. First in fame is "Poor Richard's Almanac," begun in 1732 and continued for a quarter of a century. It contained much delightful and memorable writing and has had extraordinary and almost unexampled popularity. "Father Abraham's Speech to the American People at an

Auction," which appeared in Poor Richard for 1758, was reprinted as "The Way to Wealth," was copied into all the newspapers of the continent and was circulated in Great Britain as a broadside. Paul Leicester Ford said of it: "Seventy editions of it have been printed in English, fifty-six in French, eleven in German and nine in Italian. It has been translated into Spanish, Danish, Swedish, Welsh, Polish, Gaelic, Russian, Bohemian, Dutch, Catalan, Chinese, modern Greek and Phonetic writing. It has been printed at least four hundred times, and is today as popular as ever!"

The other noteworthy product of Franklin's press was an edition of "Cato Major," translated by James Logan. [M. T. Cicero's "Cato Major," or his Discourse of Old Age: with Explanatory Notes. Philadelphia: Printed and sold by B. Franklin, 1744.] Franklin's preface to this beautifully printed volume concluded with this statement: "I shall add to these few lines my hearty wish that this first translation of a classic in this western world may be followed with many others performed with equal judgment and success; and be a happy omen, that Philadelphia shall become the seat of the American muses."

It was not the first American translation of a classic, but it was the first made *and published* in America.

In Franklin's vast correspondence with men of note everywhere over the world there are many letters of interest addressed to and received from type founders and printers. He early recognized the genius of Baskerville, and subscribed to his editions of Milton and Virgil. Prejudices existed against Baskerville's work which Franklin labored to combat. A gentleman told him that Baskerville would be a means of blinding all the readers in the nation, for the strokes of his letters, being too thin and narrow, hurt the eye, and he could never read a line of them without pain. "I thought," said Franklin, "you were going to complain of the gloss of the paper, some object to." "No, no," was the reply. "I have heard that mentioned, but it is not that; it is in the form and cut of the letters themselves; they have not that hight and thickness of the stroke which make the common printing so much the more comfortable to the eye." How he tried this *connoisseur's* judgment Franklin amusingly told in a letter to Baskerville in 1760:

Yesterday he called to visit me, when, mischievously bent to try his judgment, I stepped into my closet, tore off the top of Mr. Caslon's specimen, and produced it to him as yours, brought with me from

Birmingham, saying I had been examining it, since he spoke to me, and could not for my life perceive the disproportion he mentioned, desiring him to point it out to me. He readily undertook it, and went over the several fonts, showing me everywhere what he thought instances of that disproportion, and declared that he could not then read the specimen without feeling very strongly the pain he had mentioned to me. I spared him that time the confusion of being told that these were the types he had been reading all his life with so much ease to his eyes, the types his adored Newton is printed with, on which he has pored not a little; nay, the very types his own book is printed with (for he is himself an author), and yet never discovered this painful disproportion in them till he thought they were yours.

Thus at a time when Baskerville could not, in his own words, "get even bread" by his art, and when he was unable to get from the London booksellers a single job, Franklin had testified to the superiority of his types over those of Caslon, "the English Elzevir." They were purchased four years after Baskerville's death by a literary society in Paris, and were used in printing Beaumarchais's edition of Voltaire.

Early in life Franklin corresponded with Cadwallader Colden concerning a proposal of the latter which had some resemblance to the early attempts at stereotype printing. In France forty years later we find him instructing the celebrated Didot, and giving him his first notions of stereotyping. It was always the paramount interest of his life. Only three months before his death he wrote at great length to Noah Webster acknowledging the receipt of a copy of "Dissertations on the English Language," and taking occasion to criticise the methods of latter-day publishers. He lamented that the method in vogue between the Restoration and the accession of George II of beginning all substantives with a capital had, by the fancy of printers, been laid aside, from an idea that suppressing the capitals shows the character to greater advantage, "those letters prominent above the line disturbing its even, regular appearance."

Among other "improvements *backward*" he mentioned the "modern fancy that gray printing is more beautiful than black; hence the English new books are printed in so dim a character as to be read with difficulty by old eyes, unless in a very strong light and with good glasses." He censured the printers who used the "short round *s* instead of the long one, which formerly served well to distinguish a word readily by its varied appearance." "Certainly," he said, "the omitting this prominent letter makes the line appear more even, but renders it less immediately legible; as the paring all men's noses might smooth and level their faces, but would render their physiognomies less distinguishable." He was convinced that it was an error to place the "point called an interrogation" at the end of a question, "so that the reader does not discover it till he finds he has wrongly modulated his voice, and is therefore obliged to begin again the sentence." The Spanish printers, he observed, placed an interrogation at the beginning as well as at the end of a question. Upon these matters he had positive opinions, and when he sent Woodfall a contribution for his paper he begged him to take care that the compositor observed strictly "the Italicking, Capitalling and Pointing." Failure to observe such directions when his "Edict of the King of Prussia" was reprinted in the *London Chronicle* caused him to write regretfully to his son: "Printing such a piece all in one even small character seems to me like repeating one of Whitefield's sermons in the monotony of a school boy."

It is a fact I fancy little known that Franklin encouraged the establishment of the *Times*. John Walter was deeply interested in the *logographic* method of printing, or printing with words entire instead of single letters. At great expense and with much enthusiasm and labor he brought the process to completion, and solicited the favor and the judgment of Franklin. He wrote to him (May, 1784):

You will excuse my being very minute in description of the arrangement, on which the facility of the work depends, because I mean to offer a font of it to the Court of France, as I have already to that of Russia, by the Ambassador of that Court, who did me the honor to view it with the Duke of Richmond on Saturday last. Thus far I may venture to inform you that the whole English language (except technical and obsolete words) are comprised in eight cases of 3 feet 3 inches by 1 foot 7 inches each, which takes up an extent of only 6 feet 6 inches, because two pair cases are in front and one pair on either side, making a triangular box, so that the compositor, by the method of placing, has no more than 4½ feet to range in. One case contains all particles, pronouns and auxiliary verbs, likewise words of all figures; six cases contain the rest of the language as simple words, with and without the concluding letters where they admit of a compound, and one case has every termination, so that, for instance, if the word *converse* is wanted, *convers* admits of *ation, ing, ed, ible,* etc. etc.

Franklin approved the ingenuity of the reduction of the number of pieces by the roots of words and their different terminations. He liked much also "the idea of cementing the letters instead of casting words of syllables, which I formerly attempted, and succeeded in having invented a mold and method by which I could in a few minutes form a matrix and adjust it, of any word in any font at pleasure, and proceed to cast from it."

In consequence of Franklin's encouragement John Walter proceeded with his herculean task. He printed logographically an octavo edition of "Robinson Crusoe" and another of "Butler's Analogy," and at Franklin's suggestion founded a newspaper to be printed by the new method. It is a singular episode of history that "the Thunderer" should thus have originated from the suggestion of the chief of political insurgents.

Nor is this all. In a hitherto unpublished letter to Franklin (July 18th, 1789), John Walter made the following interesting and remarkable disclosure:

This undertaking has been most perilous both to my fortune and sensibility. It happens in the course of human events that you, tho innocently, have been the cause of this undertaking being on the decline. I have sent you a brief relation of many circumstances which have attended it, but how will you be astonished when I relate that from some authority I understand you were a stumbling block from the name of whom Majesty shrunk — certain it is the King was pleased with the plan, that his librarian appeared to forward it, that he promised to get the King's name to the head of my subscription, and after I had sent him a list of the subscribers he shrunk back and from the civility of a courtier he dwindled down to the rudeness of a sycophant. All the applications I have made to the Treasury during five years, tho flattering, are so much time spent in vain.

One of the seemingly indestructible misconceptions concerning Franklin is the very prevalent notion that the famous letter written by him to William Strahan:

You are a member of Parliament and one of that majority which has doomed my country to destruction. You have begun to burn our towns and murder our people. Look upon your hands; they are stained with the blood of your relations. You and I were long friends; you are now my enemy, and I am, yours, B. Franklin,

was seriously meant and actually sent. It was merely a *jeu d'esprit*, without any serious intention. No estrangement ever took place between these two friends, who grew old together in undiminished loyalty and affection. They lived to the end without a moment of coldness or fretfulness. After the war was over Franklin wrote to Strahan — "Dear Straney," as he called him —

I remember your observing once to me as we sat together in the House of Commons, that no two journeymen printers, within your knowledge, had met with such success in the world as ourselves. You were then at the head of your profession, and soon afterwards became a member of Parliament. I was an agent for a few provinces, and now act for them all. But we have risen by different modes. I, as a republican printer, always liked a form well *planed down*; being averse to those *overbearing* letters that hold their heads so *high* as to hinder their neighbors from appearing. You, as a monarchist, chose to work upon *crown* paper, and found it profitable; while I worked upon *pro patria* (often, indeed, called *foolscap*), with no less advantage. Both our *heaps hold out* very well, and we seem likely to make a pretty good day's work of it. With regard to public affairs (to continue in the same style), it seems to me that the compositors in your chapel do not *cast off their copy* well, nor perfectly understand *imposing*; their *forms*, too, are continually pestered by the *outs* and *doubles*, that are not easy to be corrected. And I think they were wrong in laying aside some *faces*, and particularly certain *head-pieces*, that would have been both useful and ornamental. But, courage! The business *may* still flourish with good management, and the master become as rich as any of the company.

The world is coming in these days, two hundred years after the birth of this great and extraordinary versatile character, to recognize that Benjamin Franklin was, all things considered, the largest all-around man that has yet been produced upon this continent. He may be studied in countless ways, but above all as the philosopher, the politician and the printer. Proud of his success in a worthy calling, he did much to improve the art of typography upon both sides of the sea. He had printing houses in five different colonies, and he advised with unerring wisdom the younger members of the craft. He foresaw that "the rapid growth and extension of the English language in America must become greatly advantageous to the booksellers and holders of copyrights in England." The vast audience that was assembling in America for English authors was clearly in his eye. Even as a printer working at the press he heard the tread of the coming generations and saw in prophetic vision the swift expansion of the English race and the marvelous extension of the English language in the New World for whose welfare he planned so wisely.

III

THE REVOLUTION AND NEW REPUBLIC:
A NATIONALISTIC PRESS

~~~~~~

COLONIAL *newspapers took an increasingly important part in the discussion of Anglo-American affairs after 1765, especially discussion of such widely unpopular measures as the Stamp Act. The journalistic literature of protest changed to one of denunciation and challenge as Americans faced the issues involved in the impending separation from England. Samuel Adams, writing for Edes and Gill's* Boston Gazette, *was particularly effective in espousing the American cause. John Dickinson, Philip Freneau, John Holt, Isaiah Thomas, Benjamin Franklin, and Thomas Paine were among the able writers and printers who performed significant service in uniting colonial Americans in a common cause against England, and in circumventing the counterefforts of such capable Loyalist editors as James Rivington.*

John Dickinson, though neither printer nor editor, served the colonial cause as a contributor to newspapers. His Letters from a Pennsylvania Farmer, *which set forth and analyzed the American grievances against Great Britain, were widely circulated by newspaper publication before they were set up in pamphlet form. John Holt and Isaiah Thomas were printer-patriots whose newspapers were typical examples of the Revolutionary press.*

If the story is true that colonial agent Benjamin Franklin induced Tom Paine to interest himself in American independence, it is further evidence of Franklin's shrewd appraisal of men, for Paine turned out to be one of the most forceful writers of the Revolution. His great pamphlet Common Sense, *published in 1776, roused the colonies to the need for decision, and his* Crisis *papers were a brilliant, fiery series of wartime editorials which did much to uphold military and civilian morale during the trying days of America's first war. With particular reference to works like* Common Sense, *the anonymous writer of the article "Tom Paine's First Appearance in America" gives Paine credit for founding "a new school of pamphleteering," and says, "He was the first who wrote politics for the million."*

Pamphlets served effectively to focus the attention of Americans upon crucial issues, and to rouse them to action, but the outbreak of a shooting war brought the need to tell colonial readers what was being done as well as what was being thought. How that need was met is described, in part at least, by Frank Luther Mott's article on "The Newspaper Coverage of Lexington and Concord."

With her military problems settled, at least temporarily, by the surrender of Cornwallis at Yorktown, America faced a period of civil crisis and conflict. The two great political opponents of this period, Alexander Hamilton and Thomas Jefferson, through their use of newspapers to expound the principles for which their parties stood, greatly influenced the course of American journalism during the years between the close of the Revolution and the election of Madison.

As soon as the new constitution had been ratified by the states, which action was given considerable impetus by publication of the Federalist *papers in the* New York Independent Journal, *the struggle between the Federalist and Anti-Federalist parties began in earnest. Leading the Federalists, made up largely of eastern merchants and professional men who favored the English system of government control in the hands of a relatively small group of financial and intellectual aristocrats, was Hamilton. At the head of the Anti-Federalists, whose ranks comprised chiefly the laborers of the East and the farmers and frontiersmen of the West who were in sympathy with the doctrines of the French Republic, was Jefferson. During the height of the struggle, Jefferson's* National Gazette, *with Philip Freneau in the editor's chair, and Hamilton's* Gazette of the United States, *edited by John Fenno, fought out the issues of the period with extreme bitterness.*

Early in the life of the new republic William Cobbett came over from England and stayed to wage stout combat for the Federalists with his paper, Porcupine's Gazette. *His chief journalistic antagonist in Philadelphia was Benjamin Franklin Bache, educated on the Continent and inheritor of his grandfather Benjamin Franklin's liberal cast of thought. Bache stubbornly opposed the cause of the Federalists and brought down nation-wide opprobrium on his head by attacking President George Washington, who, he felt sure, was being made a tool by unscrupulous Federalist politicians.*

Cobbett's combative personality, his forceful writing style, and his unique place in American and English partisan journalism have brought him more attention from historians than has been accorded Bache. William Reitzel's appraisal of Cobbett's significance in American journalism is so thorough and inclusive as to provide illuminating background for the entire American journalistic scene between 1793 and 1800. Philadelphia set the pattern for the bitter political journalism of the period. His experiences in that city may be said to have provided Cobbett with his niche as a writer, to have given him his start as a pamphleteer and political journalist. When the decline of the Federalist party deprived him of an American audience, Cobbett took his journalistic weapons to England, where he used them to good effect in his Political Register.

Among other notable Federalist editors were Benjamin Russell, Noah Webster, and William Coleman, the last-named having been Hamilton's choice for the founding editor of the New York Evening Post, *established to bolster the declining fortunes of the Federalist party. When failing health caused Coleman to turn over editorial responsibility to his assistant, William Cullen Bryant, Federalism was all but dead and the more liberal policies introduced by Bryant were representative of the steadily developing democracy of the 1820s, a broadening concept of the place of the common American citizen in public affairs. The election of Jackson in 1828 was the first politically nationwide manifestation of that concept.*

8

The Newspaper Coverage of Lexington and Concord

by FRANK LUTHER MOTT

FRANK LUTHER MOTT, dean of American journalism historians, Pulitzer-prize-winning magazine historian, and dean emeritus of the University of Missouri School of Journalism, wrote this article on 1776 battle coverage for the *New England Quarterly*, December 1944.

T HE commencement of actual hostilities between the English troops who had been quartered in Boston and the American militia who had been arming to defend their rights was a major "news-break" of the eighteenth century. The men of 1775 did not need the perspective of history to realize its importance; they understood at once that by this event they were plunged into "all the horrors of a civil war." It was big news by any standard, and everyone knew it was big news.

How, then, did the newspapers of the American colonies cover this great event? Did they all have their correspondents on the scene, ready to rush off hourly reports to be hurried on the streets in the columns of extras? Not at all; their coverage was conditioned by the primitive techniques of eighteenth-century news-gathering, by such facilities of communication as existed, and by the stage of development at which the newspaper had arrived. Perhaps as good a way as can be devised to study the American newspaper of these times is to see it in action in the coverage of this important event.

On April 19, 1775, thirty-seven newspapers were in course of publication in the thirteen colonies which were later to form the United States. All were weeklies except the *Pennsylvania Evening Post* (later to become the first American daily), which was then being published three times a week. They varied in page-size from 12 x 19 inches to 8 x 13; nearly all were four-page papers, though some of the more prosperous often added two or even four pages as a supplement to accommodate large advertising patronage.

None of them had even part-time correspondents in any of the news centers, if by "correspondent" one means a reporter who might be depended upon to cover important news with regularity. The nearest approach to a correspondent that any of them had was a postmaster-friend, or a friend in the shipping trade, who would write occasionally to send routine items, mainly of the sailings of ships, the weather, or the movements of the governor. Means of news-gathering were three: other newspapers, from England, the Continent, and the other colonies; letters of friendship, of business, or of official or semi-official affairs; and word of mouth by ship-captains, travelers, or newly arrived visitors.

The system may be said to have been founded upon the method of exchange of news by the newspapers themselves. In default of correspondents and news-gathering agencies, the papers by common agreement relied upon whichever one of their number was nearest to the scene of a "news-break" to cover that event; and then all the others helped themselves to the story as published in that paper, commonly without credit. Of course, if some letter with this news came to hand, or if some traveler or official courier brought in something about the event before the printed paper was received, the editor might take advantage of the windfall. But the newspapers mainly depended on one another for the more important news. Though home news was greatly slighted in general, local events which were considered really important must be covered, not only for the paper's own readers but for the other papers at a distance. This made the exchange system among newspapers extremely important, and a paper which did not keep up its exchange list was hated as an outlaw. Such a system also made the papers in such large and central towns as Boston, New York, and Philadelphia the most important "exchanges" on the lists of papers in the smaller towns.

Before we examine the sources of the news reports of Lexington and Concord, however, we shall find it interesting to see how the newspapers of that time "played the story" — where they placed it and how they headlined it. It would undoubtedly surprise anyone unacquainted with the colonial papers to know that only two of them — the *New-Hampshire Gazette* and the *Georgia Gazette* — put this really big news on the first page. We may be sure that this was not because the editors evaluated the news improperly; they fully realized its importance. The reason was that front pages were not then the bill-boards of the newspaper, on which to blazon the most sensational news. As in England, the front page was the most dignified and often the heaviest part of a very sober-sided newspaper, and was given over to the printing of some document, like an address to the King, or to the proceedings of a colonial assembly, or to some serial essay or disquisition on public affairs. The only surprising thing in the handling of the bloody business at Lexington is that two papers did place their report of it on the front page: here were two editors who were unconventional enough to "play" this sensational news on page one. News of the colonies — all local and domestic news — properly went on pages two and three, and that is where all the other editors put their accounts of the Lexington and Concord fights.

And how was the news headed? With but two exceptions it was headed only with the name of the town at which the story originated (the paper's home town if the story was derived from a letter received there), set merely in capitals of the body-type of the next size larger, with perhaps a line or two in italics telling how the information was received. This was, of course, no headline at all in the modern sense; it conveyed no intimation whatever of what was in the story. But it was again strictly in the tradition of English and colonial journalism. Indeed, there were some papers which did not even give the Lexington story the kind of head that has been described, but simply tucked it in following other news items from the same source. Of the two exceptions noted, one — the *Maryland Journal* — merely made a two-line head in pica caps of the salutation of the letter it printed: "TO ALL FRIENDS OF AMERICAN LIBERTY." The other was the *New-Hampshire Gazette*, one of the two papers which gave the news anything like a headline in the modern sense. This headline consisted of the two words "BLOODY NEWS" and was set modestly in pica caps. Daniel Fowle, editor of the paper which alone of all the colonial press gave both position and headline to the Lexington story, was, as we are told by Isaiah Thomas, who knew him well, "pacific in his disposition, agreeable in his manners, liberal in his sentiments, and attached to the cause of his country." He is most noteworthy as the founder of the *New-Hampshire Gazette*, which for many years before its suspension in 1943 was the oldest of American newspapers.

Let us turn now to matters of communication. How long did it take the great news to reach other towns and villages, and when was it published there? What with bad roads and slow sailing vessels, inter-colonial communication was slow; but in harmony with the old saw which tells us that bad news travels fast, the report of the fight at Lexington made surprising time. This was chiefly because the Patriot committees of New England saw how important it was that the other colonies should be fired simultaneously from the Massachusetts flame, and that to bring this about it was essential to get the news of the killing of the Patriot minutemen out over the whole country at once. With this object, they hurried the reports southward, sometimes dis-patching their own couriers, and other Committees of Correspondence cooperated by sending their messengers on to the next towns, and so the news went at top speed. John H. Scheide has told in detail[1] how the Palmer "Alarm" was rushed southward by expresses. Mails were, by official order, held up in New England, but the Patriot couriers sometimes carried newspapers containing the Lexington story, as well as the official Committee letters; so editors were not wholly deprived of the "exchanges" upon which they so much depended. The New Bern, North Carolina, Committee endorsement on the Wallingford message directed the next town on the route to "send all the bundle of papers forward as soon as possibly you can."[2]

But even though the news traveled fast, for those times at least, prompt publication was a different thing. These papers were weeklies, and publication of anything, however important, had to await the regular press-day. The advancement of the set time of printing was very rare indeed, and we are aware of only one such piece of irregu-larity in the handling of the Lexington story; this was an advancement of one day by the *Connecticut Journal* at New Haven, which had received its first news of the event by express three or four days earlier. The outstanding examples of enterprise were the issue of "handbills" by five colonial publishers between publication dates in order to give the Lexington news more promptly. Indeed, three of these publishers printed two each of the little extras, the first giving the initial news report (Palmer's "Alarm") and the second a more extended story.

89

These "handbills" were small sheets one or two columns wide; strictly speaking, they were not extras, since they did not bear the name of the paper. With these exceptions, the newspaper publishers stuck to regular issues, even under the impact of the news of the outbreak of war.

The first near-by paper, then, to have a press-day after the battles of Lexington and Concord on Wednesday, April 19, was the *Boston News-Letter*, oldest of colonial papers and thoroughly Tory in sympathies, which went to press on Thursdays. The *News-Letter*, frightened at the thought of what was likely soon to happen to Boston Tories, printed a paragraph of only twenty-six lines about the events of the day before, ending with this sentence:

The Reports concerning this unhappy Affair, and the Causes that concurred to bring on an Engagement, are so various, that we are not able to collect any Thing consistent or regular, and cannot therefore with certainty give our Readers any further Account of this shocking Introduction to all the Miseries of a Civil War.

The next day, Friday, April 21, was press-day for Ezekiel Russell's *Salem Gazette, or Newbury and Marblehead Advertiser*, published at Salem, some twenty miles from Boston and about the same distance from Lexington. Russell had gathered a much more comprehensive story, which he told briefly and straightforwardly, with estimates of the numbers engaged, killed, and wounded on each side. This story was included in the famous "coffin broadside" which Russell printed two or three weeks later under the black display heading "A BLOODY BUTCHERY BY THE BRITISH, OR THE RUNAWAY FIGHT OF THE REGULARS." Included also in the broadside was the story of its Salem rival, the *Essex Gazette*, with a list of killed and wounded, and "A Funeral Elegy to the Immortal Memory of Those Worthies Who Were Slain in the Battle of Concord," composed in the best style of contemporary bathos. Lined up at the top of this broadside were forty small coffin-shaped figures, each marked with the name of one of the minutemen who had been killed by the British. The whole sheet was dressed in typographical mourning by means of turned rules. This was the first of six editions of this famous broadside. Later issues showed two additional coffin cuts in honor of two minutemen who had died since the first was printed. It was designed for Patriots "either to frame and glass, or otherwise to preserve in their houses . . . as a perpetual memorial."

Friday the twenty-first was also the publication day of the *New-*

Hampshire Gazette, printed at Portsmouth, over forty miles north of Salem on the postroad, and the northernmost town in the colonies to have a newspaper. The news had come to Portsmouth early Thursday morning by an express of the Committee of Correspondence of Newburyport, dispatched the evening before. It has already been noted that this paper gave the news a headline and front-page position. First came the letter brought by the express, signed by James Hudson, which gave first a short, excited, and confused account and then an appeal for "the readiest and fullest assistance in your power." This was followed by a paragraph of details given by the express-rider by word of mouth, including an error in the date of the fight, which was given as the eighteenth. This was followed in turn by news brought by a second messenger from Newburyport, who arrived at one o'clock Thursday, and that by some details from a third messenger who got in at six o'clock. Thus Editor Fowle filled the whole of one column of Friday morning's paper with the "bloody news."

Saturday was the press-day of the *Providence Gazette and Country Journal.* Providence had received the first news of the fighting on Wednesday evening, in a message to a Patriot committee there. A general meeting, including militia officers, was immediately assembled; two expresses were dispatched to Lexington for further news, and others to towns to the westward to spread the alarm; and a thousand militia were mobilized on Thursday and were ready to march. The expresses sent to Lexington were back by Friday morning, and the body of the *Gazette*'s account consists of their report. Editor John Carter was himself a member of the Providence Committee of Correspondence, and was in the midst of all this activity. Three new elements enter the reports of the battles with the *Providence Gazette* story: first, the recital of British atrocities, such as killing all the enemy wounded and bayoneting the sick and aged in private houses (though setting fire to churches had already been mentioned in the *New-Hampshire Gazette* story; the killing of babes was to come later); second, the controversy about who fired first at Lexington — the British troops or the American minutemen; and third, the editorial appeal as a part of the news story. Carter's story ends:

Thus, through the sanguinary Measures of a wicked Ministry, and the Readiness of a standing Army to execute their Mandates, has commenced the American Civil War, which will hereafter fill an important

Page in History. That it may speedily terminate in a full Restoration of our Liberties, and the Confusion of all who have aimed at an Abridgement of them, should be the earnest Desire of every real Friend to Great-Britain and America.

The *Providence Gazette* story was the best that had thus far appeared, and it was reprinted in at least three later papers in other towns. It supplemented the account of the two Lexington expresses by that of "a Gentleman arrived from Concord" somewhat later, and by some rumors — among them one that the British troops were burning houses Friday night, a great light having been seen in the direction of Boston. This was later explained as a fire in the woods south of Boston.

Late on the same Saturday which saw the appearance of the *Providence Gazette* there appeared a broadside at Norwich, Connecticut, about fifty miles by road southwest of Providence, which contained most of Carter's story. That was fast work; and though the broadside is dated "10 o'Clock, P.M.," it was probably distributed considerably later in the night. The first news of the Lexington and Concord fights had reached Norwich Friday morning by an express sent from Pomfret, bearing a letter from Ebenezer Williams, who had the news from an express dispatched from Woodstock, who had, in turn, taken it "from the mouth of the Express that arrived there." All these expresses were part of the system organized by Patriot Committees of Correspondence with the purpose of arousing the country to face what seemed an imminent campaign of the British troops to subjugate all the New England villages. Added as a postscript to the Williams letter which was published in the broadside, or "handbill," were a few details reported by a Plainfield merchant who had just returned from Boston, and who had "conversed with an Express from Lexington."

Monday, April 24, was press-day for the *Boston Evening-Post*. The week before the outbreak of hostilities at Lexington and Concord, there had been no fewer than five papers published in the town of Boston. But the two strongly Patriot presses — those of the *Gazette* and the *Massachusetts Spy* — threatened with suppression by the royal government, or worse, fled the city shortly before the ill-fated nineteenth of April, the *Gazette* going up the river to Watertown, and the *Spy* across country to Worcester. The three Tory papers could certainly find no home in the rebellious country villages, while in Boston they faced the enmity of the people, even when protected by the troops. And so the *Post-Boy*, disheartened by this prospect, shut up shop during the confusion of the first hostilities, and was never again published. This left two papers — the *News-Letter*, whose publication day made it (as already noted) the earliest newspaper reporter of the battles, and the *Evening-Post*. The Fleet brothers, publishers of the latter paper, were quite as discouraged as the printers of the *Post-Boy* had been; but they got out one issue after the battles of Lexington and Concord, in which they announced the paper's suspension "till Matters are in a more settled State." It was never resumed. It was this last issue of the *Evening-Post* that was published on Monday, April 24. In it appeared the following three-line statement under the Boston heading: "The unhappy Transactions of last Week are so variously related that we shall not at present undertake to give any particular Account thereof." So the *Boston Evening-Post*, closing its eyes to perhaps the greatest "news-break" of the century, gave up the ghost. The *News-Letter* was left alone in Boston, where it persisted irregularly and unprosperously, until the British evacuation.

The *Newport Mercury* also printed on Mondays. The news of the Lexington bloodshed had come to Newport on Friday, whereupon an express was immediately sent to Providence for further details. The messenger returned Saturday evening with a copy of the *Gazette* published that morning; and the *Gazette* story, with an additional paragraph comprising some reports which the messenger had picked up in Providence, furnished the *Newport Mercury*'s account.

The news apparently reached Hartford either late Friday or early Saturday; it was published in the *Connecticut Courant* on Monday. The *Courant* story began like that of the *Boston News-Letter*, but it soon diverged into a much more detailed and colorful report of the engagement, evidently derived from several sources. This story was without any heading, only a paragraph break separating it from the preceding material.

The great news reached New York by sea from Newport about six o'clock on Sunday morning, interfering with the customary Sabbath worship of many of the Patriots. At noon an express, probably Israel Bissel, who had brought the Palmer "Alarm" all the way from Watertown, Massachusetts, since Wednesday morning, rode into town. To Palmer's message, which Bissel had brought to a dozen Connecticut villages and towns, had been added (at Fairfield) the Williams letter and its postscript. These reports furnished material for a "handbill" which was published in New York Sunday afternoon, probably by John Holt, of the *Journal*. That evening the Sons of Liberty took over certain stores of arms in the custody of the city, and on Monday they marched up and down the streets, beating a drum and enlisting volunteers for the American army.

Monday was the publication day of Hugh Gaine's *New-York Gazette and Mercury*. That paper stated that the early reports from Rhode Island and New London had been discredited, but that about noon on Sunday an express had arrived bringing reports which were evidently convincing even to Gaine, since he published them. These were the letters which had been published by broadside the day before.

An express had in the meantime been sent on to Philadelphia with the Palmer "Alarm" and the Williams letter. He arrived at five o'clock Monday evening, to find John Dunlap getting out a "Postscript" to the regular edition of his *Pennsylvania Packet* printed that morning. Dunlap made room for the news on the second page of his supplement; but the Bradfords, of the *Journal*, at the same time issued a single-column "handbill" with the identical material. The next day, Tuesday the twenty-fifth, the same matter appeared in Ben Towne's diminutive Philadelphia tri-weekly, the *Pennsylvania Evening Post*, and, in a German translation, in the *Philadelphische Staatsbote*.

Tuesday was also the press-day of the *Essex Gazette*, published in Salem, Massachusetts. Since Salem was close to the scene of action, and its editors had had five days to gather up the details, their story, with its list of killed and wounded on the Patriot side, is rather commonly regarded as the most satisfactory early account of the battles. That being the case, it will be interesting to give some attention to its form.

A present-day news story based upon the same set of facts might begin something like this:

Open war broke out last Wednesday between the British troops and the Massachusetts militia. The British were decisively defeated in their attempt to capture Patriot leaders and arms at Lexington and Concord, with the loss of 112 killed and 103 wounded, while the militia lost 40 killed and 20 wounded.

The *Essex Gazette* story began:

Last Wednesday, the 19th of April, the Troops of his *Brittanick*

94

Majesty commenced Hostilities upon the People of this Province, attended with Circumstances of Cruelty not less brutal than what our venerable Ancestors received from the vilest Savages of the Wilderness. The Particulars relative to this interesting Event, by which we are involved in all the Horrors of a civil War, we have endeavored to collect as well as the present confused State of Affairs will admit.

After this "lead," the story goes on to relate the events in strict chronological order, beginning with the embarkation of the troops "at the Bottom of the Common in Boston," their landing "a little Way up Charles River"; tracing their movements to Lexington, where they encountered a body of militia, and on to Concord; and then describing the retreat. The main story is followed by a paragraph detailing reported atrocities of the British, and that by the following paragraph:

We have the pleasure to say, that, notwithstanding the highest Provocations given by the Enemy, not one Instance of Cruelty, that we have heard of, was committed by our victorious Militia; but, listening to the merciful Dictates of the Christian Religion, they "breathed higher Sentiments of Humanity."

The account closes with a list of American killed, wounded, and missing, an estimate of the British casualties, and an expression of sympathy for "the Friends and Relations of our deceased Brethren, who gloriously sacrificed their lives in fighting for their Liberties and their Country."

The next day after this story was published, the *Essex Journal*, of Newburyport, reprinted it in full and with credit. This was just a week after the battles; but the *Journal*'s regular press-day was Wednesday, and the story waited.

On this day, Wednesday, April 26, a day earlier than its regular press-day, appeared the *Connecticut Journal*, of New Haven, which reprinted the story that its contemporary at Hartford, the *Connecticut Courant*, had published two days earlier. April 26 was the press-day of two more Philadelphia papers, the *Pennsylvania Gazette* and the *Pennsylvania Journal*, both of which reprinted the material of the *Journal*'s "handbill," with added paragraphs presenting parts of letters recently received from the North by Philadelphians.

The news appears not to have reached Baltimore until the twenty-sixth — probably early in the morning, since Mary Katherine Goddard got out a reprint of the Philadelphia "handbill" without waiting to print it in her *Maryland Journal*, regularly published that day. She used the same type in the paper that had been set for the broadside.

95

The next day, Thursday the twenty-seventh, the *Maryland Gazette*, in Annapolis, reprinted the Goddard handbill, saying it was "received yesterday." Thursday was also the press-day of Hugh Gaine's two competitors in New York — John Holt's *Journal* and Rivington's *New-York Gazetteer*. The *Journal* had a fuller account of the fighting than any other paper had contained up to this time: it ran to nearly three long and wide columns, and consisted of letters from various Massachusetts and Connecticut points. All were unsigned except one from the Committee at Wallingford, which had been brought by express through Fairfield, Norwalk, Stamford, Greenwich, and New Haven. Rivington's paper published the New York "handbill," the Wallingford communication, extracts from a letter from Boston "to a Merchant in this City," and the following editorial comment:

The late melancholy accounts from Boston have filled the minds of the good people of this city with the most anxious concern. It was the wish of every generous mind that the unhappy contest with the mother country would have been compromised without the shedding of blood; and the time when it would become necessary to enter into an unnatural civil war with those, with whom we are connected by the tenderest ties, has ever been deprecated as the most horrid calamity. May the Almighty interpose his gracious providence and avert the impending miseries, and may the blessings of peace be restored to this great continent upon the principles of liberty and the constitution!

Friday, April 28, was press-day for the *Connecticut Gazette*, of New London. Since the news from Lexington had reached New London on the preceding Friday at seven in the evening — too late to be printed in that week's *Gazette* — it had to be left over a full week. Even then, Editor Timothy Green had been so busy with "public affairs" that he had had time to get out only a "half-sheet paper" — that is, two pages. His account of the outbreak of war is his own forty-line summary. He apologized to his readers as follows:

The Printer requests his Customers to excuse the issuing only a half-sheet Paper this Week — the alarming and confused State of public Affairs, for some Days past, having made it difficult for him to execute his usual Business.

On this same Friday, the *Pennsylvania Mercury* published its first account of the troubles in the North. It reprinted the "handbill" — its fifth appearance in the Philadelphia papers — and the Wallingford communication, together with several letters from New England and New

York. One of them — from Boston — had come in by mail, so that we know the post was now riding again, at least between New York and Philadelphia. Altogether, the *Mercury* devoted four columns to the battles — more than any other colonial paper in its first account.

The next day, Saturday the twenty-ninth, the *Pennsylvania Ledger*, sixth and last of the Philadelphia papers to carry the news, was issued. Its story consisted of four letters from Boston and Hartford, three of which had appeared the day before in the *Mercury*.

Also on Saturday appeared the first Virginia paper to print the story. This was Dixon and Hunter's *Virginia Gazette*. The news had arrived in Williamsburg only the night before, and the *Gazette* printed the contents of the "handbill" on the third page of its Supplement. Purdie's rival *Virginia Gazette* would not be published until the next Thursday; so he issued the same matter in a broadside.

John Dunlap started a brand-new paper in Baltimore on Monday, May 2. In its first number he printed the Wallingford letter and extracts from two unofficial letters giving details of the fighting at Lexington and Concord.

On May 3, Isaiah Thomas, who had now got his press set up at Worcester, printed the first copy of the *Massachusetts Spy* to be issued in that town. His story of the battles in that issue is probably as well known as that of the *Essex Gazette* — possibly better. It begins:

AMERICANS! forever bear in mind the BATTLE OF LEXING-TON! — where British Troops, unmolested and unprovoked, wantonly, and in a most inhuman manner fired upon and killed a number of our countrymen, then robbed them of their provisions, ransacked, plundered and burnt their houses! nor could the tears of defenceless women, some of whom were in the pains of childbirth, and cries of helpless babes, nor the prayers of old age, confined to beds of sickness, appease their thirst for blood! — or divert them from their DESIGN OF MURDER and ROBBERY!

In his story of the fight, Thomas emphasized the claim that the British fired first upon the Continentals, who "did not even return the fire." He also recounted all the atrocity stories which had become current. Thomas had himself taken part in the running fight with the British troops, and by virtue of this story he has some title to be called the first of American war correspondents.

Rind's *Virginia Gazette*, Williamsburg, appeared on Wednesday, May 4, just two weeks after the battles. Its story consisted of the letters from Boston which had appeared in the *Pennsylvania Mercury*. The next day Purdie's *Virginia Gazette* appeared with precisely the same matter.

The big news reached North Carolina by sea. It arrived by a vessel which docked at New Bern on Wednesday, May 4, from Newport, Rhode Island, and was published in the *North-Carolina Gazette* the next day. The story was given in a letter from Newport, dated April 22, the day after the citizens of that town had first heard the news, and was based on the report of "a gentleman from Cambridge." Either the gentleman or the typesetter insisted on spelling the name of the Massachusetts village "Lixington."

The news came to Charleston, South Carolina, on Monday morning, May 9, "by the Brigantine, Industry, Captain Allen, who sailed the 25th ult. from Salem," thus striking the press-day of the *South-Carolina Gazette and Country Journal*. The account of the battles was in the form of the *Essex Gazette* story, supplemented by a few additional details from Captain Allen. Three days later, on Thursday, the twelfth, the *South-Carolina and American General Gazette*, also of Charleston, used the same story, but substituted for Captain Allen's remarks an extract from a letter received in Charleston from a British officer in Boston. This letter was far from rancorous; indeed, it praised the bravery of the "Provincials."

The southernmost newspaper in the colonies was the *Georgia Gazette*, at Savannah. Just when the news of Lexington and Concord was received in Savannah, and by what means, is not clear; but it came some time between May 24 and 31, probably by sea from New York. It was published on the thirty-first, just six weeks after the event. The main story was the one originally published in the *Providence Gazette*.

Thus we come to the end of the original or first newspaper stories of the Lexington-Concord engagement. Through the month of May, several of the papers which published the earliest reports printed supplementary accounts, lists of killed and wounded, and so on. An essay entitled "The Rural Heroes; or, the Battle of Concord" was published in the *Newport Mercury* May 8, and copied in the *New-Hampshire Gazette* and perhaps in other papers. At least five papers published General Gage's "Circumstantial Account of an Attack that Happened on the 19th of April, 1775, on His Majesty's Troops," some with interpolated comments and denials. At least as many printed the score or more of depositions made by members and groups of members of the American militia regarding the moot question of who fired first at Lexington and Concord; and many published the official statement of the Provincial Convention of Massachusetts Bay, giving the details of the action. Finally, some of the papers printed a series of "intercepted letters from the soldiery in Boston," apparently first published in the *Boston Gazette,* newly established at Watertown, on May 12. Many of these letters, written to relatives at home, gave details of the fight of April 19.

In one respect the coverage of this great news event was not typical of colonial journalism: letters and papers received by the post were comparatively unimportant in connection with it. The fact that the post had been "stopt" for the time, in New England at least, had something to do with this aberration; but the main reason was that the Committees of Correspondence mistrusted the government control of the post. It would have been too slow, anyway; the Patriot organization needed expresses who would ride at night as well as in daylight, despite dangers.

Consequently, the Committee expresses were the chief means of communication in the coverage of this news-break. Sailing ships in two or three instances were of major importance. Only three stories can be said to have been first-hand; all the others were made up of information from the following sources, listed in the order of their relative importance: (1) bulletins of the Committees of Correspondence (more than a third of the original newspaper accounts used Palmer's "Alarm" and the Williams letter), (2) reprints of the three first-hand stories, (3) letters received by obliging friends of the editor from gentlemen living near the scene of the trouble, and (4) word-of-mouth reports of travelers who had just come from that scene. Most of the stories, indeed, utilized more than one — some of them all — of these news sources. Finally, the time-lag between "news-break" and publication, due to faulty communication and the weekly issue of newspapers, varied from one day to six weeks.

NOTES

[1] *Proceedings* of the American Antiquarian Society, L (1940), 49–79.
[2] Scheide, 74.

9

Tom Paine's First Appearance in America

Tom Paine made a decisive contribution to the American Revolution
with his *Common Sense* and his *Crisis* series. This story of the great radical's
wartime journalistic accomplishments appeared as an unsigned contribution to the
Atlantic Monthly in November 1859.

W HEN Tom Paine came to America in 1774, he found the dispute
with England the all-absorbing topic. The atmosphere was heavy with
the approaching storm. The First Congress was in session in the autumn
of that year. On the 17th of September, John Adams felt certain that
the other Colonies would support Massachusetts. The Second Congress
met in May, 1775. During the winter and spring the quarrel had grown
rapidly. Lexington and Concord had become national watchwords; the
army was assembled about Boston; Washington was chosen commander-
in-chief. Then came Bunker's Hill, the siege of Boston, the attack upon
Quebec. There was open war between Great Britain and her Colonies.
The Americans had drawn the sword, but were unwilling to raise the
flag.

From the beginning of the troubles the Colonists had been consistent
in their acts. Public meetings, protests, burnings in effigy, tea-riots,
militia levies, congresses, skirmishes, war, followed each other in regular and logical succession — but theoretically they did not make out
so clear a case. They had fine-drawn distinctions, not easy to appreciate
at this day, between taxes levied for the purpose of raising revenue
and duties imposed for the regulation of trade. Parliament could lay a
duty on tobacco in a seaport, but might not make the weed excisable
on a plantation, could break down a loom in any part of British
America, could shut out all intercourse with foreign nations by the
Navigation Act, but had not the legal right to make the Colonial merchant write his contracts or draw his bills on stamped paper. As to
independence, very few desired it. "Independence," it was the fashion

to say, "would be ruin and loss of liberty forever." The Colonists insisted that they were the most loyal of subjects; but they had men and muskets ready, and were determined to resist the obnoxious acts of Parliament with both, if necessary. These arguments of our ancestors led them to an excellent conclusion, and so far are entitled to our respect; but logically we are afraid that King George had the best of it.

Before many months had passed, lagging theory was left so far in the rear by the rapid course of events that the Colonists felt it necessary to move up a new set of principles to the van, if they wished to present a fair front to the enemy. They had raised an army, and taken the field. Unless they declared themselves a nation, they were confessedly rebels. And yet almost all hesitated. There was a deep-seated prejudice in favor of the English government, and a strong personal liking for the people. Even when it was known that the second petition to the King — Dickinson's "measure of imbecility" — was disregarded, as it deserved to be, and that the Hessians were coming, and all reasonable men admitted that there was no hope for reconciliation, they still refused to abandon the pleasing delusion, and talked over the old plans for redress of grievances, and a constitutional union with the mother country. With little or no belief in the possibility of either, they stood shivering on the banks of the Rubicon, that mythical river of irretrievable self-committal, hesitating to enter its turbid waters. A few of the bolder "shepherds of the people" tried to urge them onward; but no one was bold enough to dash in first and lead them through. Paine seized the opportunity. He had a mind whose eye always saw a subject, when it could perceive it at all, in its naked truth, stripped of the non-material accessories which disturb the vision of common men. He saw that reconciliation was impossible, mere rebellion folly; and that, to succeed in the struggle, it was necessary to fight Great Britain as an equal, nation against nation. This course he recommended in *Common Sense*, published in January, 1776.

Paine told the Colonists in this pamphlet that the connection with the mother country was of no use to them, and was rapidly becoming an impossibility. "It is not in the power of England to do this continent justice. The business of it is too weighty and too intricate to be managed with any tolerable degree of convenience by a power so distant. *To be always running three or four thousand miles with a tale or a petition, waiting four or five months for an answer, which, when obtained, requires five or six more to explain it in, will in a few years be looked upon as folly and childishness.*" As to the protection of England, what is that but the privilege of contributing to her wars? "Our trade will always be a protection." "Neutrality is a safer convoy than a man-of-war." "It is the true interest of America to steer clear of European contentions, which she can never do while by her dependence on Britain she is made the make-weight in the scale of European politics."

According to *Common Sense*, not only was a separation necessary and unavoidable, but the present moment was the right time to establish it. "The time hath found us." The materials of war were abundant; the union of the Colonies complete. It might be difficult, if not impossible, to form the continent into a government half a century hence. Now the task is easy. The interest of all is the same. "There is no religious difficulty in the way." "I fully believe that it is the will of the Almighty that there should be a diversity of religious opinions among us. *I look upon the various denominations among us as children of the same family, differing only in what is called their Christian names.*" All things considered, "nothing can settle our affairs so expeditiously as an open and determined declaration of independence." "This proceeding may at first appear strange and difficult. A long habit of not thinking a wrong gives it a superficial appearance of being right"; but in a little time it will become familiar. "And until independence is declared, the continent will feel itself like a man who continues putting off some unpleasant business from day to day, yet knows it must be done; hates to set about it, wishes it over, and is continually haunted with the thoughts of its necessity." To this he thought it necessary to add a labored argument against kings from the Old Testament, which may possibly have had much weight with a people some of whose descendants still triumphantly quote the same holy book in favor of slavery.

The King's speech, "a piece of finished villany," in the eyes of true patriots, appeared in Philadelphia on the same day as *Common Sense*. Thus Paine was as lucky in his time of publication as in his choice of a subject. All contemporaries admit that the pamphlet produced a prodigious effect. Paine himself says, "The success it met with was beyond anything since the invention of printing. I gave the copyright up to every State in the Union, and the demand ran to not less than one hundred thousand copies." The authorship was attributed to Dr. Franklin, to Samuel Adams, and to John Adams.

It is hardly necessary to mention that the movement party, with General Washington at its head, considered Paine's "doctrines sound, and his reasoning unanswerable." Even in England, Liberals read and applauded. The pamphlet was translated into French. When John Adams went to France, he heard himself called *le fameux Adams,* author of *Common Sense.*

It soon became apparent that the people were charged with Independence doctrines, and, like an electrified Leyden jar, only waited for the touch of a skillful hand to produce the explosion. *Common Sense* drew the spark. The winged words flew over the country and produced so rapid a change of opinion, that, in most cases, conservatives judged it useless to publish the answers they had prepared. One or two appeared. None attracted attention. About five months later, Congress declared independence; "as soon," Paine wrote, "as *Common Sense* could spread through such an extensive country." In a few years Paine asserted and believed that, had it not been for him, the Colonial government would have continued, and the United States would never have become a nation.

If we countermarch and get into the rear of Time, to borrow an expression from *The Crisis,* and, placing ourselves in January, 1776, look at *Common Sense* from that date, we may understand without much difficulty why it produced so great an impression. Paine, as later, when he brought out the *Rights of Man,* caused a chord to vibrate in the popular mind which was already strung to the exact point of tension. The publication was not only timely — it was novel. Paine founded a new school of pamphleteering. He was the first who wrote politics for the million. The learned political dissertations of Junius Brutus, Publicus, or Philanglus were guarded in expression, semi-metaphysical in theory, and Johnsonian in style. They were relished by comparatively few readers; * but the shrewd illustrations of *Common Sense,* the homely force of its statements, and its concise and muscular English stirred the mind of every class. Even Paine's coarse epithets, "Common Ruffian," "Royal Brute of Britain," and the like,

* Compare, for instance, Judge Drayton's Independence Charge to the Grand Jury of Charleston, delivered April 23, 1776, with *Common Sense.*

which offended the taste of the leaders of the American party—for party-leaders were gentlemen in 1776—had as much weight with the rank-and-file as his arguments.

Paine became suddenly famous. General Charles Lee said "that he burst upon the world like Jove, in thunder." His acquaintance was sought by all who were of the true faith in Independence; and when, soon afterward, he visited New York, he carried with him letters from Dr. Franklin and John Adams, introducing him to the principal residents "as a citizen of the world, the celebrated author of *Common Sense*." Had he been a man of fortune or American-born, he might have reached a place in the foremost rank of the Fathers of the Country. But nativism was powerful, and position important at that time, as Lee and Gates and even Hamilton himself experienced. The signature *Common Sense*, Paine preserved through life. It became what our authorlings, who ought to know better, will persist in calling a *nom* * *de plume*—a Yankee affectation, unknown to French idioms.

In the autumn of 1776, Paine joined the army as volunteer aide-de-camp to General Greene, and served through the gloomy campaign which opened with the loss of New York in September. He remained in the field until the army went into winter-quarters after the battles of Trenton and Princeton. It was not as a combatant that Paine did the States good service. He played the part of Tyrtaeus in prose—an adaptation of the old Greek lyrist to the eighteenth century and to British America—and cheered the soldiers, not with songs, but with essays, continuations of *Common Sense*. The first was written on the retreat from Fort Lee, and published under the name of *The Crisis*, on the 23d of December, when misfortune and severe weather had cast down the stoutest hearts. It began with the well-known phrase, "These are the times that try men's souls." "The summer soldier and the sunshine patriot will in this crisis shrink from the service of his country; but he that stands it now deserves the love and thanks of man and woman. . . . But after all," he continues, "matters might be worse. Howe has done very little. Fort Washington and Fort Lee were no loss to us. The retreat was admirably planned and conducted. General Washington is the right man for the place, 'with a mind that can even flourish upon care'." He closes with a cheerful sketch of the spirit and

* They generally spell it *nomme*.

condition of the army, attacks the Tories, and appeals to the Colonies for union and contributions.

This *Crisis* produced the best effect at home; in England it had the honor of being burned by the hangman. The succeeding issues were brought out at irregular intervals, whenever the occasion seemed to demand Paine's attention; some of them not longer than a leader in a daily paper; others swollen to pamphlet dimensions. They were read by every corporal's guard in the army, and printed in every town of every State on brown or yellow paper; for white was rarely to be obtained. In their hours of despondency, the Colonists took consolation and courage from the *Crisis*. "Never," says a contemporary, "was a writer better calculated for the meridian under which he wrote, or who knew how to adapt himself more happily to every circumstance. . . . Even Cheetham admits, that to the army Paine's pen was an appendage almost as necessary and as formidable as its cannon."

The next campaign opened gloomily for the Colonies. The Tories felt certain of victory. In the political almanac of that party, 1777 was *"the year with* three gallows in it." The English held New York and ravaged the Jerseys on their way to Philadelphia. Howe issued a proclamation "commanding all congresses and committees to desist and cease from their treasonable doings," promising pardon to all who should come in and take the oath of allegiance. Paine met him with a *Crisis*. "By what means," he asked, "do you expect to conquer America? If you could not effect it in the summer, when our army was less than yours, nor in the winter, when we had none, how *are* you to do it? If you obtain possession of this city, [Philadelphia] you could do nothing with it but plunder it; it would be only an additional dead-weight on your hands. You have both an army and a country to contend with. You may march over the country, but you cannot hold it; if you attempt to garrison it, your army would be like a stream of water running to nothing. Even were our men to disperse, every man to his home, engaging to reassemble at some future day, you would be as much at a loss in that case as now. You would be afraid to send out your troops in detachments; when we returned, the work would be all to do." Paine then turns to those who, frightened by the proclamation, betrayed their country, and paints their folly and its punishment. In speaking of them, he calls upon the Pennsylvania Council of

Safety to take into serious consideration the case of the Quakers, whose published protest against breaking off the "happy connection" seemed to Paine of a treasonable nature. "They have voluntarily read themselves out of the Continental meeting," he adds, with a humor, doubtless, little relished by the Friends, "and cannot hope to be restored to it again, but by payment and penitence."

In April, Paine was elected, on motion of John Adams, Secretary to the Congressional Committee on Foreign Affairs, with a salary of seventy dollars a month. When Philadelphia surrendered, he accompanied Congress in the flight to Lancaster. The day after the affair at Brandywine, a short *Crisis* appeared, explaining the accidents which had caused the defeat of the Continentals, and insisting that the good cause was safe, and that Howe's victories were no better than defeats. Paine was right. The Americans were gaining more ground in Northern New York than they had lost in Pennsylvania. Burgoyne, who,

> Unconscious of impending fates,
> Could push through woods, but not through Gates

had capitulated. The news reached Philadelphia on the 18th of October.

This winter ought to have closed the war. The alliance with France, Burgoyne's capture, two campaigns without useful results, Washington's admirable patience and management at Valley Forge, with starvation and mutiny in the ranks and disaffection to his person in the officers of the Gates faction, ought to have convinced every Englishman in America that the attempt to reduce the Colonies was now hopeless. Paine was so indignant with the reckless obstinacy of the British government that he conceived the idea of carrying the war into England with pen and paper — weapons he began to think invincible in his hands.

"If I could get over to England," he wrote to his old chief, General Greene, "without being known, and only remain in safety until I could get out a proclamation, I could open the eyes of the country with respect to the madness and stupidity of its government." Greene had no confidence in the success of this appeal to the English people, and advised Paine not to attempt it.

In the meantime the French fleet had arrived, bringing M. Gérard, the first foreign minister to the United States, and with him trouble to Thomas Paine. It is well known that the French government employed

Beaumarchais, the author of the *Barber of Seville,* as their agent to furnish secret supplies to the American insurgents, and that Beaumarchais imagined a firm, Rodrigue Hortalez & Co., who shipped to the United Colonies munitions of war furnished by the King, and were to receive return cargoes of tobacco, to keep up mercantile appearances. Silas Deane, a member of Congress from Connecticut, represented the Americans in the business. In 1777, Congress, out of patience with Deane for his foolish contracts with foreign officers, recalled him. He returned, bringing with him a claim of Beaumarchais for the cargoes already shipped to the United States. As Deane could produce no vouchers, and Arthur Lee had cautioned Congress against his demands, the claim was laid on the table until the vouchers should be presented.

Deane, confiding in the support of his numerous friends, appealed to the public in a newspaper. Congress bore this indignity so amiably — refusing, indeed, by a small majority to take notice of it — that Henry Laurens, the president, who had laid Deane's appeal before them for their action, resigned in disgust, and was succeeded by John Jay. But Paine, whose position as Foreign Secretary enabled him to know that the supplies had come from the French government, and not from Beaumarchais, answered Deane in several newspaper articles, entitled "Common Sense to the Public on Mr. Deane's Affairs." In these he exposed the whole claim with his usual unmitigated directness. M. Gérard immediately announced officially that Paine's papers were false, and called upon Congress to declare them so and to pay the claim. Party feeling ran high on this question — a foreshadowing of the French and English factions fifteen years later. Congress passed a resolution in censure of Paine. Mr. Laurens moved that he be heard in his defense; the motion was lost, and Paine resigned his office. A motion from the Deane party to refuse his resignation and to discharge him was also lost, the Northern States voting generally in Paine's favor. His resignation was then accepted.

As the French government persisted in denying that the King had furnished any supplies, Congress admitted the debt, and in October, 1779, drew bills on Dr. Franklin in favor of Beaumarchais, for two millions and a half of francs, at three years' sight. Beaumarchais negotiated the bills, built a fine hotel, and lived *en prince.* But neither he nor Deane was satisfied. They still demanded another million.

We have no doubt that Paine was correct in his facts, however injudicious it may have been to use them in his position. Deane's best friends gave him up, before many years had passed. M. de Loménie, in his interesting sketch of Beaumarchais, has tried hard to show the justice of his demands on the United States, but without much success. He does not attempt to explain how Beaumarchais, notoriously penniless in 1775, should have had in 1777 a good claim for three millions' worth of goods furnished. The American public looked upon Paine as a victim to state policy, and his position with his friends did not suffer at all in consequence of his disclosures. Personally, he exulted in his conduct to the end of his life, and took pleasure in watching and recording Deane's disreputable career and miserable end. "As he rose, like a rocket, so he fell like a stick," a metaphor which has passed into a proverb, was imagined by Paine to meet Deane's case. The immediate consequence of Paine's resignation was to oblige him to hire himself out as clerk to an attorney in Philadelphia. In his office, Paine earned his daily bread by copying law-papers until he was appointed clerk to the Assembly of Pennsylvania.

Early in May, 1780, while the Assembly of Pennsylvania was receiving petitions from all parts of the State, praying for exemption from taxes, a letter was brought to the speaker from General Washington, and read to the House by Paine as clerk. It stated simply that the army was in the utmost distress from the want of every necessary which men could need and yet retain life; and that the symptoms of discontent and mutiny were so marked that the General dreaded the event of every hour. "When the letter was read," says Paine, "I observed a despairing silence in the House. Nobody spoke for a considerable time. At length a member, of whose fortitude I had a high opinion, rose. 'If,' said he, 'the account in that letter is true, and we are in the situation there represented, it appears to me in vain to contend the matter any longer. We may as well give up first as last.' A more cheerful member endeavored to dissipate the gloom of the House, and moved an adjournment, which was carried."

Paine, who knew that the Assembly had neither money nor credit, felt that the voluntary aid of individuals could alone be relied upon in this conjuncture. He accordingly wrote a letter to a friend in Philadelphia, a man of influence, explaining the urgency of affairs, and inclosed five hundred dollars, the amount of the salary due him as clerk, as his contribution towards a relief fund. The Philadelphian called a meeting at the coffee-house, read Paine's communication, and proposed a subscription, heading the list with two hundred pounds in good money. Mr. Robert Morris put his name down for the same sum. Three hundred thousand pounds, Pennsylvania currency, were raised; and it was resolved to establish a bank with the fund for the relief of the army. This plan was carried out with the best results. After Morris was appointed Superintendent of Finances, he developed it into the Bank of North America, which was incorporated both by act of Congress and by the State of Pennsylvania. Paine followed up his letter by a *Crisis Extraordinary*. Admitting that the war costs the Colonists a very large sum, he shows that it is trifling, compared with the burdens the English have to bear. For this reason it would be less expensive for the Americans to raise almost any amount to drive the English out than to submit to them and come under their system of taxation.

Our ancestors read the *Crisis Extraordinary*, and understood every word of it, we may be sure. Paine's lucidity of statement is never more remarkable than when he handles financial questions. But conviction did not work its way down to the pocket. Few men gave who could avoid it, and each State appeared more fearful of paying, by accident, a larger sum than its neighbor, than of the success of the British arms. Congress, finding it at last almost impossible to get money or even provisions at home, resolved to resort again to the financial expedient which has proved so often profitable to this country, namely, to borrow in Europe. Colonel Laurens, son of the late President of Congress, was appointed commissioner to negotiate an annual loan from France of a million sterling during the continuation of the war. Paine accompanied him at his request.

They sailed in February, 1781, and were graciously received by King Louis, who promised them six millions of livres as a present and ten millions as a loan. In little more than ten years, the American secretary, who stands respectfully and unnoticed in the presence of his Majesty of France, will sit as one of his judges in a trial for life! Is there anything more wonderful in the transmutations of fiction than this? Meanwhile, the future member of the Convention, as little dreaming of what was in store for him as the King, sailed for Boston with his principal. They carried with them two millions and a half in silver — a great help to Washington in the movement southward, which ended with the capitulation of Yorktown. While in Paris, Paine was again seized with the desire of invading England, incognito, with a pamphlet in his pocket, to open the eyes of the people. But Colonel Laurens thought no better of this scheme than General Greene, and brought his secretary safely home again.

Cornwallis had surrendered, and it was evident that the war could not last much longer. The danger past, the Colonial aversion to pay Union expenses and to obey the orders of Congress became daily stronger. The want of a *Crisis,* as a corrective medicine for the body politic, was so much felt, that Robert Morris, with the knowledge and approbation of Washington, requested Paine to take pen in hand again, offering him, if his private affairs made it necessary, a salary for his services. Paine consented. A *Crisis* appeared which produced a most salutary effect. This was followed a few days later by another, in which a passage occurs which may be quoted as a specimen of Paine's rhetorical powers. A rumor was abroad that England was treating with France for a separate peace. Paine finds it impossible to express his contempt for the baseness of the ministry who could attempt to sow dissension between such faithful allies. "We sometimes experience sensations to which language is not equal. The conception is too bulky to be born alive, and in the torture of thinking we stand dumb. Our feelings, imprisoned by their magnitude, find no way out; and in the struggle of expression every finger tries to be a tongue." It will be difficult to describe better the struggle of an indignant soul with an insufficient vocabulary.

When peace was proclaimed, Paine, the untiring advocate of independence, had a right to print his "Io Paean." The last *Crisis* announces "that the times that tried men's souls were over, and the greatest and completest revolution the world ever knew gloriously and happily accomplished." "America need never be ashamed to tell her birth, nor relate the stages by which she rose to empire." But it is to the future he bids her look, rather than to the past. "The remembrance of what is past, if it operates rightly, must inspire her with the most laudable of all ambition, that of adding to the fair fame she began with." "She is now descending to the scenes of quiet and domestic life, — not beneath the cypress shade of disappointment, but to enjoy in her own land and under her own vine the sweet of her labors and the reward of her toil. In this situation may she never forget that a fair national reputation is of as much importance as independence, — that it possesses a charm that wins upon the world, and makes even enemies civil, — that it gives a dignity which is often superior to power, and commands reverence where pomp and splendor fail." As indispensable to a future of prosperity and dignity, he warmly recommends the Union. "I ever feel myself hurt," he says, "when I hear the Union, that great Palladium of our liberty and safety, the least irreverently spoken of. It is the most sacred thing in the Constitution of America, and that which every man should be most proud and tender of." Thus he anticipated by seventy-five years our "Union-savers" of 1856, few of whom dreamed that their pet phrases, or something very like them, originated with Thomas Paine.

10

William Cobbett and Philadelphia Journalism, 1794–1800

by WILLIAM REITZEL

This analysis of the American sojourn of William Cobbett was written by WILLIAM REITZEL of Haverford College for the July 1935 issue of the *Pennsylvania Magazine*, published by the Historical Society of Pennsylvania. The author, now with Brookings Institution, has edited a volume of Cobbett's writings.

WILLIAM COBBETT's life in England after 1800 as editor of *Cobbett's Political Register* is reasonably well-known to readers of English history. His more amusing and adventurous activities as a soldier of the 54th regiment of foot in Nova Scotia and New Brunswick from 1784 to 1791 have been interestingly reported by Cobbett himself in various autobiographical passages.[1] But of his life in and near Philadelphia from 1793 to 1800, the record is confusing. It is true enough that Cobbett had much to say about it at a later date, but his memory then was busy with trying to make his career seem coherent. And, though the name of William Cobbett occurs in all works covering this decade of Philadelphia life, the statements are almost invariably careless, inadequate, or plainly wrong.

This period of Cobbett's life is an awkward one to present because his exact place in American life has never been described. Such contemporary accounts of him as one meets with are likely to be contradictory and misleading. He is an agent of William Pitt, engaged in subverting American judgment for a reward of British gold; he is the scurrilous opponent of the French patriots; he is the victim of a terrific whirlwind of violent pamphlets; he is the dear friend of honorable Quaker merchants like John Oldden; he is, this time in his own opinion, a virtuous and patriotic Englishman cast on a foreign shore and openly and honorably defending his country against the general malice of the

French Republicans and the particular slurs of the American democrats. So Cobbett, following Shakespeare's generalization about man, appears in Philadelphia as an actor playing many parts.

This article, although its purpose is to sketch Cobbett's place in Philadelphia journalism during the last decade of the eighteenth century, will also by implication at least make clear his more general position in the American scene. If his activities are analyzed with reference to the background of Philadelphia's political and cultural interests, it becomes plain that Cobbett was not creating his own audience or defying the foul fiend in a lonely and heroic way; but that he was fitting himself into a place that circumstances had made for him.

Cobbett returned to England from his service in Nova Scotia late in the year 1791. He obtained his discharge on December 19 and proceeded to London where he laid before the War Office certain charges of peculation against the officers of his former regiment. The skirmish thus begun dragged on until March 1792, when, just as the matter was at last being brought to trial, Cobbett left the country. His later explanation was that he "had been baffled in his attempts to obtain justice, only because [he] had neither money nor friends." [2] He went with his bride, Ann Reid, to France in order to learn the French language. In September, while on his way to Paris, he heard at Abbeville that the king had been dethroned and his guards murdered. Fearing arrest in France if England declared war, he turned aside to Havre de Grace and within a fortnight was embarked for America.

Cobbett speaks of himself as having been "touched by Republican Principles at this time." His mind was inflamed by his conflict with established authority at the War Office; he had moved from an interest in the common soldier by way of Thomas Paine to an interest in the common man; and he looked to America with some of that confused political nostalgia that was so common in the feelings of his contemporaries. More practically, he had secured for himself in France a letter of introduction to Thomas Jefferson. An American stationed at The Hague had written it at the request of "a gentleman in the family of the English Ambassador here and acquainted with Mr. Cobbett. . . ." [3] In this letter Cobbett is described as intending to settle in the United States.

After a dangerous passage of eight weeks, Cobbett and his wife landed at Wilmington. The fact is certain, but the account of the events leading to it are a little contradictory. The husband says that he had meant to go to Philadelphia but that the port was closed by the fever and he was forced to disembark down the river. The wife remembered that, while on board, her husband had "looked at a map and fixed upon Wilmington as the place where he would go and settle and keep school."[4] Mrs. Cobbett may have been remembering after the event, because her husband did settle in Wilmington and did take pupils.

But before he did this, he forwarded his letter of introduction and recommendation to Jefferson, covering it with a note of his own, dated November 2, 1792. In this accompanying letter he gives an explanation of his purpose in coming to America that is of some interest in view of his later activities there:

Ambitious to become a citizen of a free state, I have left my native country, England, for America. I bring with me, youth, a small family, a few useful literary talents, and that is all.

Should you have an opportunity of serving me, my conduct shall not show me ungrateful, or falsify the recommendation I now send you. Should that not be the case, I shall feel but little disappointment from it, not doubting but my industry and care will make me a happy and useful member in my adopted country.[5]

It should be remembered, in order to appreciate this letter to the fullest extent, that Jefferson, in 1792, was recognized in American political life as a professed admirer of the French and that this admiration was already being organized into the opposition party of American politics. It is impossible to say flatly that Cobbett was aware of the implications of offering himself to Jefferson, but it is safe to say that, given the republican tastes he describes himself as having, he was not averse to the connection nor unwilling to follow wherever it might lead. Jefferson's answer, however, put an end to this first effort to establish a contact in "a free state." He regretted that he could be of no service, for "Public Offices in our Government are so few, and of so little value, as to offer no resource to talents"; but he added that after Cobbett had settled himself and looked about he would be pleased to hear from him again.

So Cobbett turned to another aspect of the French interest in America, the émigrés from the West Indies. Wilmington, as a point of disembarkation, was filled with these people; and, as many of them apparently considered going into business in the United States, there was a brisk market for a teacher of English who knew French as well. To one of these pupils, James Mathieu, he became so attached that he took him as a boarder, and this led, after Mathieu's departure for Philadelphia, to a constant supply of recommended guests. Through this work and through the connections that resulted, Cobbett found himself kept in close contact with all the varieties of French opinion that came into the vicinity of Philadelphia. By January, 1794, the stream of his particular customers had shifted to Philadelphia and at the end of the same month he closed his Wilmington establishment and followed them. Mrs. Cobbett remembers this very clearly:

Mr. Mathew [Mathieu] was one of these French gentlemen, but he was so pleased with Papa's company that he would insist on living in his house, as well as being taught by him and they used to go on together . . . stealing each other's bread at supper and so on. . . . They continued to receive boarders for some months, but Mama found them disagreeable and got to dislike Wilmington, and Mr. Mathew thought Papa might do much better . . . in Philadelphia . . . so to Philadelphia they went. . . .⁶

Publicly, Cobbett said nothing of this period of his life; and, at least while he was active in Philadelphia, his silence was justified. When he did, in 1796, become somewhat of a public character, he so sharply identified himself with the Federalists and the Anti-French factions that he might well have found it hard to explain the circles in which he first moved and the connection he first sought. Even more difficult would it have been if any of his opponents had brought up against him the earliest occasion on which he had tried to exercise what both he and Thomas Jefferson had agreed to call "a talent." Sometime between November, 1792, and February, 1793, he translated from the French the following item: *Impeachment of Mr. La Fayette: containing his Accusation, (Stated in the Report of the Extraordinary Commission to the National Assembly, on the 8th of August, 1792) . . . with a Supplement, containing the Letters, and other authentic Pieces relative thereto.*⁷

This pamphlet, published in Philadelphia, has a preface addressed by William Cobbett "To the Citizens of the United States," dated from Wilmington, February 19, 1793. A single sentence shows plainly enough its political intention: "To do justice to La Fayette as well as to those who have persecuted him, in the minds of a people who feel

such a lively interest in every thing that concerns the honor and welfare of the French nation, I present the public with the following
pieces. . . ."

But Cobbett seems to have found it unsatisfactory to exercise his
talents for the republican school of thought. In a letter to James
Mathieu, written December 13, 1793, he lets off a blast that appears
to be a reference to the *Impeachment of Mr. La Fayette*. "For the
Pamphlets, I beg you to let them remain with Mr. Dobson, and to tell
him if he pleases to sell them as soon as he can, he will much oblige
me. — At any rate I shall be glad to have made a settlement with these
Gentlemen; and I'll be damned if I do not take care how they cheat
me again." [8] It is at least a good guess that Cobbett is referring to his
pamphlet, because the only other writing on which he is known to
have been engaged during 1793 was a work that combined practical
value with political neutrality, a work that when finally published in
1795 was called *Le Tuteur Anglais, ou Gramaire reguliére de la langue
anglaise, en deux parties*.[9] Even before this he describes with grim disapproval a quarrel between the factions in Wilmington, and gave Mathieu
a lecture on preserving himself "from the political pest" — advice that
he had not followed some months before.[10] By the end of 1793, he
has made up his mind: his work is that of a teacher of languages, and
he writes again to his friend in Philadelphia: "I am of opinion to go
to Philadelphia . . . for if the French go away, I shall have nothing
to do here. At P. there will always be resources for me as a maître de
langue . . . a small house and going out to teach French seems to me
the most reasonable plan. . . ." [11] And in another month, everything is
arranged and he writes to say what coach he is coming by.[12]

It is at this point that Cobbett came into touch with the realities of
American political life. Within a few months he threw his own advice
and his own resolutions to the winds and he was at it with ungloved
hands. That he should have bounded into the arena is not a matter for
surprise. He had very definitely a taste for violent political discussion;
he had also that capacity so necessary for a pamphleteer of seeing all
events, even the most trivial, in those precise unshaded colors black
and white. Given these qualities, he could scarcely have been other
than a political writer in the 1790's. What is surprising, however, is
that in 1794, after having tentatively sought the hand of Jefferson,
after having experimented with the republican interest, after having

rested in a spell of neutrality, he should have so wholeheartedly plumped for the opposing side. The simple fact that Dr. Priestly had come from Birmingham, had been feted in New York City, and had made a few speeches whose sentiments were quite justified by the Doctor's experiences with the King and Church mobs of Birmingham, could not explain the tone of Cobbett's pamphlet-greeting. To any honest unthinking man of the time Cobbett could only appear as a plain hireling, so clearly had he stepped from one camp to the other when he wrote what he called *The Tartuffe Detected* and what Bradford finally published as *Observations on Dr. Priestley's Emigration, to which is added, a Story of a Farmer's Bull.*

Of course, this is speaking from knowledge that Cobbett's contemporaries did not have. The pamphlet was issued anonymously and was not connected with Cobbett's name until he was long-established in the public mind as a writer on the English side. By then, his early ventures in the other direction were unknown or forgotten, or at least, if remembered, were by some chance never brought up against him. Cobbett himself was very discreet at first. In a letter written to an English friend, he talks in what can only be a cautiously dissembling way of an attack that some Englishman or other has just made on Dr. Priestly.[18] Next, he used the pseudonym of "Peter Porcupine," and so concealed himself behind this name that not until 1796 was it generally known, or did it become, as he puts it, "a matter of notoriety," that he "was the person who had assumed the name of Peter Porcupine."

But now it is necessary to wonder at the change that had taken place in Cobbett and the search for an explanation cannot be avoided. I have deliberately written "explanation" rather than "reasons" because the precise answer needed by the word "reason" cannot be found. If we restate the essential facts we can see in the sharpest way the thing to be explained. Cobbett reached America at the end of 1792. He called himself to Jefferson's attention. He moved in consistently French circles. He translated revolutionary documents and presented his work to the public in a way that leaves no doubt of where his stated interests lay. These efforts are far from establishing him in the United States. He becomes politically neutral and supports himself by teaching. This brings him, by the spring of 1794, to Philadelphia. By the middle of 1794, however, he has written a strong anti-revolutionary pamphlet anonymously; by January, 1795, as Peter Porcupine, he is definitely of the pro-British party;[14] by January, 1796, he enters vigorously into domestic politics on the Federal side with *A New Year's Gift to the Democrats*; and he is in full cry from then on until he sailed for Falmouth in June, 1800. The discrepancy is undeniably great; the partial resolution of it appears to depend on the character of the man and on the circumstances of Philadelphia life in which he found himself.

Cobbett was a man in whom instinctive habits of mind and unconscious forms of thought and feeling were always being overlaid by efforts at rational organized thinking. But, being a man to whom these rather complex processes were not natural and in whom they were produced by self-forcing, he was without that sort of intellectual consistency that formal education at its best gives to its pupils. He was constantly discovering, sometimes with too deep a pain, sometimes with too much enthusiasm, ideas and implications of ideas that for other men were so normal a part of thinking that they called for no particular consideration. This means that if one speaks of Cobbett as a thinker one cannot hope for a steadily growing line of thought. All one finds is a series of leaps and bounds. And it was exactly the spectacle of Cobbett jumping from rock to rock across the stream of time that so disconcerted his opponents: they never knew what rock he would next be on, and as they looked back on his track they could see that he had for a moment rested on stones that they themselves had used. The charges of inconsistency, of being a turncoat, of charlatanism that they brought amply express their confusion and their dismay at seeing all rational principles denied.[15] Cobbett devoted much space to explaining away these charges, giving circumstantial accounts of his life and feelings in which he vigorously tries to rationalize what simply cannot be made coherent by logical means. All that he says can be reduced to a few facts: he changed his mind, he saw more implications than he had at first seen, he discovered that what he had been thinking was not what he felt. To him, these were good reasons for altering his course; but they were not strong weapons to use in a political quarrel.

But if one studies the growth of Cobbett's feelings and forgets that he imagined he was thinking, all, or nearly all, is steady and sincere. Cobbett's feelings were fixed in the past, in a rural England, in a lovely agrarian utopia of the eighteenth-century countryside, in a neat world of cottages, gardens, rich pig-sties, buxom girls, flushed young men, solid belongings, huge hay ricks, beef-lined stomachs; and the more the present became unlike this memorable past, the more harshly Cobbett judged its divergence. It was a slow process, however, for an untrained mind to find this fixed basis for its opinion when it had to penetrate revolutionary confusions, industrial change, varied experience of life, the vainglorious sensations of the ploughboy who rose in the world. In the first forty years of his life, every word Cobbett wrote was the product of a mind in which thought and feeling were so interpenetrating that the principles on which that mind worked were as obscure to himself as to his contemporaries.

If Cobbett's own story of his entrance in American politics is read again in the light of what has been said above, the part played by his character in explaining his shift from the side of the pro-French democrats to the pro-English Federalists can be studied. Also the peculiar mixture of an emotional sincerity with a superficial disregard of facts can be seen. And then we can turn to the background of circumstances for still further explanation.

In 1804, in answering a series of attacks, Cobbett gave a long account of his early career. He was, of course, anxious to prove himself as good an Englishman as anyone else, and this desire colors the telling of the tale. He speaks of his work as the logical fruit of a sharply awakened patriotism; he calls his early republicanism the consequence of inexperience and of being "a perfect novice in politics"; age dismisses youth. In the sense that this is a record of feeling it is true; in the sense that it is record of fact, our knowledge of his earlier activities prevents our accepting it. This contradiction is the one that needs to be emphasized, and, if possible, one should be aware of it without seeing Cobbett as disparaged by it.

It was at the memorable epochs of Dr. Priestley's emigration to America . . . The manifestoes of the Doctor, upon his landing in that country, and the malicious attacks upon the monarchy and the monarch of England which certain societies in America thereupon issued from the press, would, had it not been for a circumstance purely accidental, have escaped . . . my knowledge of their existence.

One of my scholars . . . chose, for once, to read his newspaper by way of lesson; and, it happened to be the very paper which contained the addresses presented to Dr. Priestley at New York, together with his replies. My scholar, who was a sort of republican, or, at best, but half a monarchist, appeared delighted with the invectives against England. . . . Those Englishmen who have been abroad, particularly if they have had time to make a comparison between the country they are in and that which they have left, will know how difficult it is, upon occasions such as I have been describing, to refrain from expressing their indignation and resentment. . . . The dispute was as warm as might reasonably be expected between a Frenchman, uncommonly violent even for a Frenchman, and an Englishman not remarkable for *sang-froid*; and, the result was, a declared resolution on my part, to write and publish a pamphlet in defense of my own country. . . . Thus it was that, whether for good or otherwise, I entered on the career of political writing. . . .[16]

If one is content to overlook the fact that behind this story lies a change of heart and take it for what Cobbett honestly remembered it as being, the story of a heart's awakening, there then remains one more item to be brought into the account. What were the circumstances in which real feeling was for the first time called up, and called up so strongly as to cancel the petty details and the little theories of the past?

The essential factors of the situation, as they must have appeared to Cobbett's limited knowledge, can be stated roughly. It may be assumed that he knew nothing of the long historical process that had produced the federation of American states by 1790. He certainly did not understand the precise tangle of financial obligation, cultural inheritance, practical distrust, and theoretical enthusiasm that made up the American attitude towards the world in which the United States found themselves. But these confusions and historical vaguenesses were momentarily cleared in the last decade of the century by the fact of the French Revolution. Generally for all men, particularly for Cobbett, this event and its consequences provided an exact point of reference. For the first time in its long course, the eighteenth century had something large enough to force its citizens to take sides, and what was more, to force decisions in the light of all the possible motives on which human beings can act: reason, feeling, tradition, hope, and fear. Probably, up to this moment, a man like Cobbett had never been made to consider his full relation to the social order in which he freely moved. Now when he was asked to do so, he found himself responding without further consideration to the tradition in which he had been inconspicuously born. In making his choice Cobbett was doing no more than following crudely a line already marked out with greater refinement of feeling by Edmund Burke, and anticipating, again crudely, the steps by which the emotions of Wordsworth and Coleridge were to be stabilized.[17] Once this necessity of choosing is understood, one can look at the details of the situation without getting lost.

Around the new Federal government revolved, as an inheritance from its colonial past, one of the most fundamental antagonisms of which human society is capable. In its most general form this was a clash of interest between the groups whose activities were mercantile and those whose activities were agrarian. By 1790 this material for forming two political parties had begun to take shape, and their oppositions could already be described by such sectional, personal, or theoretical names and catch-terms as one chose to use. It was the mercantile, shipping, financial North against the planting, slave-holding, indebted South; it was Federalist against Republican democrat; it was Hamilton against Jefferson. It was, if one states it abstractly, the low Hobbesian view of human nature against the high hopefulness of Locke and the French physiocrats.[18]

However unsound in practice and politically vicious Hamiltonian finance seemed to the agricultural gentlemen of Virginia, it fitted the facts of life as understood by the merchants and financial men of Philadelphia, New York, and Boston. They knew from their ledgers the complete dependence of their section of society on a successful maintenance of credit in the English money-market; and they found it as easy to rationalize this fact into a conservative theory of government as their opponents to rationalize their own situation into a democratic theory.

The supporters of these rapidly sharpening alternatives had already settled themselves to the detailed maneuverings of political life when Cobbett arrived in America. The final restatement of their differences in the significant terms of foreign policy came in 1793 when the news belatedly arrived that the French Republic had declared war on Great Britain and Spain. In the year that followed the confused practical issues and the blurred outlines of theory became clear and precise for American minds, for there was at last a plain European pattern against which both doctrines and practice could be measured.

In the tumultuous year 1793 Americans gazed on the French Revolution as in a crystal ball, for an answer to their hopes and fears. Presently they looked up, satisfied, with a hearty "Yes!" or a thumping

"No!" . . . Thus the French Revolution seemed to some a clean-cut contest between monarchy and republicanism, oppression and liberty, autocracy and democracy; while to others it was a mere breaking out of the eternal strife between anarchy and order, atheism and religion, poverty and prosperity. The former joined the Republican Party; the latter the Federalist.[19]

It was just because the circumstances sharpened and clarified themselves in the way described, it was because events and the opinions they generated could finally be related to formulas like Republican-France, Federalist-Britain, that Cobbett found his feet in the American scene.

From Cobbett's character and out of the general situation in which he lived it should be possible to derive an explanation of his position and of why he took the position he did. The best procedure will be to state the factors, tangible and intangible, that must have influenced him, and to leave it to the reader to calculate their comparative weight. Cobbett had a family to support, and nothing to rely on beyond his own exertions. Whatever he did, his actions were conditioned by this necessity; throughout his long life he always thought of himself as simply and unquestionably accepting this as a primary obligation. His efforts to use what he felt to be his talents as a political writer had led him nowhere before 1794, and he had with good reason turned to a more neutral occupation. But, as an individual, he found his feelings again involved in 1794; he had in his own heart to take a stand; the movement of events denied the possibility of one of his temperament finding any more ease on a bed of neutral roses.

Under some immediate, though now probably undiscoverable compulsion, he found himself to be moved, more deeply than he had been moved by the writings of Thomas Paine, by the feelings of an Englishman, a member of the Church of England, a patriot of the mother-country. The *Observations on the Emigration of Dr. Priestley* has the unpremeditated violence of mind that flows naturally from a man who has suddenly discovered in himself unsuspected sources of feeling. But now comes the interesting fact that by the simple writing of this pamphlet Cobbett uncovered for himself an American career: what may have been the product of spontaneous emotion was converted into a livelihood, a consciously organized business, and a business that while it lasted offered both profit and a chance to exercise a talent.

Unwittingly Cobbett stumbled into a market for his wares, then his eyes opened and he began to develop his market; and finally he found himself linked in a thousand unexpected ways with one whole school of American feeling.

For if there was an opening for writers on the Republican-French side, there was bound to be an opening on the Federalist-British side. Circumstances of which Cobbett could not have been more than half aware had created a special demand for the special and apt services he could render not only as a writer of propaganda, but as an importer of English books, as a publisher who reprinted important English items, and finally as a journalist who could unite these various activities. His mind, stirred by patriotism, supported by conviction that grew with what it fed on, practically guided by the need of keeping a family, saw and exploited all the avenues of expansion the situation in Philadelphia offered. The rest of this article naturally becomes a record of this development; and if the account is read with all of the contributing factors in mind, it will be possible to understand Cobbett's place in American life.

During 1794 and 1795 Cobbett was the pamphleteer, "Peter Porcupine," and William Cobbett, *maître de la langue*. In the first capacity, he was reprinted in Birmingham and Liverpool and noticed by "Old Sylvanus" of *The Gentleman's Magazine* in a comment that elegantly blended polish and patriotism.[20] He further replied to a nasty piece of democratic propaganda called *The Political Progress of Britain*, with the slashing *Bone to Gnaw for the Democrats*.[21] As a teacher of language he translated Marten's *The Law of Nations* and got into print *Le Tuteur Anglais* on which he had been at work when he left Wilmington.

These two years must presumably have opened his eyes to the unthought of possibilities of his new profession. The interest he had aroused in England in anti-revolutionary circles proved to be worth cultivating, since it lead to commercial contacts with the London publishers and by degrees to the establishment of an export and import business. And, in Philadelphia, he found himself looked to as the popular writer on the Federalist side. He could estimate this position pretty accurately from the pains taken by his opponents, the whole democratic mob, to write him down. He was treated to *A Rub from Snub, A Twig of Birch for a Butting Calf, a Democratiad, A Little Innocent*

Porcupine's Hornet's Nest, A Roaster, a Pill for Porcupine, a Last Confession and Dying Speech, and to a wide range of miscellaneous insults. In return he gave, though not so copiously, as good as he got, commenting with malice on Mr. Randolph's susceptibility to French gold in *A New Year's Gift for the Democrats;* [22] and replying to the personal attacks with a masterly blend of autobiography and germane lies called *Life and Adventures of Peter Porcupine.* [23]

But these things were not the real task to which he settled: they were but incidental to his larger schemes. In the spring of 1796, as the bedrock of this plan, he took a house in Second Street opposite Christ's Church, and in July opened a publishing and book-selling business. He set himself frankly forward as an Englishman, as no friend to "democratic principles," as a man who with the cool remoteness of a stranger would give to the struggling young nation advice as to her proper course. In the circumstances, this plain statement of his position was a good stroke. It gave him the almost unique position of being free from direct American political influences, made him a focus for the pro-English party of the City, and made him seem to those in England who had their eyes on America an outpost of English sentiment. Its only danger was one that he was willing to face — broken shop windows and the charge that he was supported by "Pitt's Gold."

The use he made of his position is an interesting one. The direction in which his mind worked was made clear in one of the earliest productions of his new trade, *The Bloody Buoy, thrown out as Warning to the Political Pilots of America; barbarity of the French Revolution.* In this work he parallels in the United States the methods of the Anti-Revolutionists who had in England turned into propaganda the generalized materials of Burke's *Reflections.* The method was to turn on the French party by raising the terrible cry of barbarous anarchy. The details of the method were to produce horrid examples from revolutionary annals. By falling into this vein, Cobbett was identifying the anti-revolutionary parties of both England and America; and, in practice, he became a medium for the exchange of anti-revolutionary literature between the two countries. [24]

The greater part of Cobbett's work derived from the purposes indicated by this volume. He saw as one and the same, revolutionary sentiment in France and democratic sentiment in America: and it must be admitted that the language of the American democrats might easily have deceived him. From this point it will be more convenient to describe these activities under several heads: as a pamphlet writer, as a publisher introducing important English writings, as an importer of English books, and as a journalist in contact with politicians of the Federalist group.

First of all, as a pamphlet writer, he developed his attack on revolutionary principles in a series of works.[25] In this same line of duty, by treating many of the aspects of life in republican America as identical with life in republican France, he produced works that add to his catalogue of the consequences of "licentious politics." *The Democratic Judge*, an account of his prosecution before Thomas McKean, Chief-Justice of Pennsylvania, for a supposed libel on the King of Spain and his Ambassador, enabled him to draw valuable conclusions about the freedom of the press and the operations of justice in a society corrupted by dangerous political theory; and probably, under its English title of *The Republican Judge*, it was read with great satisfaction by English anti-Jacobins. It is not surprising to find Cobbett, after his return to England in 1800, reducing all that was unpleasant in his American adventure to a pamphlet, *The American Rush-Light; by the help of which, Wayward and Disaffected Britons may see a Complete Specimen of the Baseness, Dishonesty, Ingratitude, and Perfidy of Republicans, and of the Profligacy, Injustice, and Tyranny of Republican Governments.*

As a publisher and importer, Cobbett's work was entirely consistent with the principles shown in his writings. If he wrote to combat Jacobinism in its American forms, and if these writings were useful in the creation of anti-Jacobin sentiment in England, then the obvious corollary was to bring into America, to republish in America, and to distribute in America, such English works as would carry on the same principles. If we examine a list of Cobbett's reprints we see that this is exactly what he is doing. In every case he adds, in the character of "Peter Porcupine," a prefix or an appendix that will point the work in question at the situation in the United States.[26]

Following his activity as a writer and a publisher for a special market, Cobbett found himself rapidly engaged in pursuing the related possibilities that soon showed themselves. At first, he worked jointly with booksellers like Benjamin Davies; and his paper, *Porcupine's Gazette and Daily Advertiser*, was an obvious place for the advertisements of small dealers like Omrod, Humphreys, and Cruikshank the importer. But he seems, in time, to have overtopped these lesser men, for in following the advertisements we note how items that first appear in the shops of the other dealers gradually come into Cobbett's hands. There is no suggestion that Cobbett was a leader in this particular branch of Philadelphia book-selling; probably he did no more than draw to himself by superior activity the major portion of the trade in English items.

Although he dealt most particularly in the sort of English work that fitted the political and social interests of his clientele and his own announced purposes as a writer of propaganda, he did not disdain the milder reaches of English culture. He announces, as published, *Camilla*, ". . . by the admired Miss Burney"; [27] he introduces that splendid fruit of literary endeavour, *The Pursuits of Literature* by T. Mathias; [28] and he was proud of having reprinted in a fine style the *Baeviad* and *Maeviad* of the solidly satirical Mr. John Gifford. [29] His biggest bow in this direction is to be found in his letter to John Nichols, editor of *The Gentleman's Magazine:*

Few booksellers carry on that branch of business with more life than I do. If you choose, and can fall upon any arrangement, I will receive from you a few volumes of your magazine half-yearly? I could get 50, if not 100 subscribers to the work, and this would take off a good number of your surplus dead-stock . . . and please to communicate to me the mode in which I can be most useful to your excellent publication. [30]

Naturally, in this line he showed no discrimination. He had very little taste for polite literature, and his judgment for the most part was conditioned by the extent to which such writings could be made to fit political opinions. But quality is not the point in the present case; there is nothing involved beyond indicating the growing range of Cobbett's activities, and showing the fairly consistent intention that gave them coherence.

It is easy enough, as long as one is speaking of books and pamphlets, to speak of Cobbett as a simple sharer in the whole English movement against the French Revolution. But when we come to Cobbett the Philadelphia journalist, this clear definition needs modification. A journalist is driven by the demands of his trade to think entirely in terms of localized events and opinions; the only place for abstraction in his work comes when he sees an immediate event as an illustration of a general principle. Cobbett's journalism becomes part and parcel of his larger political interest if one reads it with the above limitation clearly in mind. It becomes a method for interpreting daily circumstances by means of a broad background of feeling and opinion. In this respect it is, of course, like all political journalism. If, in a pamphlet, Cobbett can provide illustrations of "democratic principles," so, in a daily paper, can he do the same; only, in the latter, he is more affected by the chopping and changing and confusion that follows the effort to find principles illustrated by the recurring flux of small happenings. But the complete run of *Porcupine's Gazette* is as much an illustration of republican behavior as were any of the more deliberate pamphlets.

Journalism, in addition, requires one other thing: a body of supporters, subscribers, people who want to have their opinions stated for them in this convenient form. A paper, unlike a pamphlet, demands that it be organized with reference to a group of actual or possible backers. For Cobbett to enter their field, therefore, meant that he had come to be a representative of a recognized and fairly coherent point of view. This is certain, even though the details of the matter cannot be produced. In Philadelphia political life there must have been men who encouraged, who found in Cobbett a mouthpiece, who suggested practical forms and supplied the daily food for his editorial digestion.[81]

A single piece of evidence will show what is meant by Cobbett's getting support from those men in American politics who appreciated the general point of view that he presented. Robert Goodloe Harper, a lawyer and a Member of Congress, was attached to the ranks of the Federalists. There was a long contact between him and Cobbett. Its beginnings are not known, but its course can be charted. Cobbett published in June, 1797, a pamphlet Harper had written presenting the Federalists' argument against France.[82] In 1800, after leaving Philadelphia, Cobbett sent Harper an itemized account covering the years 1797–1799. It shows that they worked together for a common cause. Harper had purchased a great many works of propaganda for distribution: 100 copies of *The Cannibal's Progress*, 121 of his own pamphlet; and, apparently for his own use, he imported volumes like Gifford's *French Revolution*, collections of unspecified English pamphlets, and the *Pursuits of Literature*![83] Finally, when Cobbett was brought to trial in Philadelphia for his libel against Dr. Rush, Harper acted as one of the lawyers for the defense. The significance of this brief record is that it indicates a direct link between Cobbett, a political writer, and a Federalist politician who was anxious to produce a given political result — turning public feeling from the revolutionary French to the stable English.[34]

Harper was not Cobbett's only connection with the feelings that expressed themselves through the Federalist party. His writings were used in various sections of the country apparently with effect. *Porcupine's Gazette* appeared in a Pennsylvania-German version at Reading, and in due course Cobbett was libelled in *Der Unpartheyische Readinger Adler.*[35] Daniel Clymer, a Reading lawyer and a Federalist politician, was instructed to bring suit.[36] There is also some sort of link with the same party at Boston through a series of business transactions with Jedidiah Morse, the famous gazetteer.[37]

Cobbett summarized these American activities in an article written in 1804, and the following passage can be used as an introduction to the conclusion of this paper:

> From the summer of 1794 to the year 1800 my labours were without intermission. During that space there were published from my pen about twenty different pamphlets, the whole number of which amounted to more than half-a-million copies. During the three last years, a daily paper, surpassing in extent of numbers, any ever known in America, was the vehicle of my efforts; and, by the year 1800, I might safely have asserted, that there was not in the whole country, one single family, in which some part or the other of my writings had not been read; and in which, generally speaking, they had not produced some degree of effect favourable to the interests of my country.
>
> The people of America, still sore from the wounds of their war against England . . . were so loud and enthusiastic in the cause of the French, that . . . everything seemed to indicate that the Government could be forced into a war with England in aid of the French. I took the English side; the force of my writings gave them effect; that effect was prodigious; it prevented that which both Governments greatly dreaded; peace between America and England was preserved. . . .[38]

Of course, this shows no more than the form of Cobbett's thoughts, but its exaggerations can be easily reduced. It overlooks, and Cobbett can be pardoned the omission, the fact that the work he was doing was only a single element in a much larger pattern of activity, a pattern that included Washington, Hamilton, John Adams, the merchants of Boston, New York and Philadelphia, and that whole complex of ideas — republican, mob, democracy, the best man of the community, Christian faith, atheism, barbarism, England, France, all men are created equal — that were disturbing poor human minds. Cobbett called his work serving "the interests of my country"; those in America to whom he was fitted, naturally ignore this description, and saw only a mind that in a rough and ready way moved vigorously along a common track.

This distinction is an important one because when Cobbett at last drew it plainly he lost his place in the American scheme, found his livelihood gone, and properly retired to his native land, where his fame as an ardent anti-Jacobin had preceded him. Cobbett must be seen as a writer whose work, following almost unconsciously a private bent, fell into the American puzzle only through the accidental working of events. As long as European affairs could be sharply stated for American minds in such precise antagonistic forms as English and French, Tradition and Revolt, God and the Devil, Cobbett, whose pen ran with faith and tradition, and who stood as a Britisher, had his listeners. But the feelings stirred and clarified by these contradictions soon found resolution in the practical compromises of political and social life. Yet by the time such compromises were making themselves felt, Cobbett's traditional manner of speaking had become fixed; and the inevitable consequence was that he found himself in an increasingly lonely position. He no longer fitted into the puzzle, and being what he was he could not analyze the change. He could only console himself by growing more defiantly patriotic, by looking more and more towards his own land; and finally he had to go.

The departure, comparatively speaking, was rapid. Near the end of 1798, Mr. Liston, British Envoy to the United States, informed Cobbett that the Government at home were aware of what they owed him, and were prepared to advance his interests. Cobbett insisted that he had rejected all such offers and called upon Lord Henry Stuart, a young attaché of the Embassy and later in England his friend, to confirm the denial.[39] The denial is acceptable on the basis of Cobbett's character, but the circumstances formed a natural basis for the charge of being a British agent that his opponents steadily brought against him. Truth was not the point, the effect gradually produced on the public mind was the heart of the matter, and Cobbett's enemies were quick to point him out as a fit object for attention under the Alien and

Sedition Acts of 1798. Cobbett himself thought that he had been marked for deportation by President Adams. There is no evidence that this was the case. What was happening was too large to fix its attention on one man; American politics were reverting to their more normal domestic forms, were being stated in local rather than international terms, and it was this that sank Cobbett rather than any specific act, for his audience melted away and the general themes he had so boisterously embroidered were turning into more practical questions, answerable by the less rugged phrases of professional diplomats.

Cobbett, of course, traced his collapse to specific conspiracy: his being brought to trial for his libel against Dr. Rush some two years after the charge had first been laid, the suit coming on just when it was clear that he had shifted his business to New York, the enormous damages awarded to Rush, the speed with which the sheriff sold his Philadelphia property, Chief Justice McKean's democratic disapproval of his political sentiments, the general malice of his foes. But this interpretation of events, even if taken at its face value, sacrifices the basis for the superficial. Cobbett's business, and the ends he had pursued, were brought to their natural conclusion even before Dr. Rush came on him. The significant fact to hold to is that he could not re-establish himself in an identical business in New York. He had no public left, the times wanted a new product, and this Cobbett could not supply. His mind had already shifted its attention to England, where Pitt was repressing the radicals, where acquaintances were happily engaged in exactly the sort of pamphleteering he so well knew, and where John Reeves, who admired him, was the indefatigable chairman of The Loyal Association against Republicans and Levellers.

So, at last, aware only of where his tastes and his talents led him; not knowing the imponderable forces that had brought him to the surface of American life and that were now pushing him under again; with the United States reduced in his mind to a formula illustrating the profligacy of all republican governments, he set sail for Falmouth in June, 1800. By August he turns up in the diary of that traditional gentleman, William Windham, as present at a Council dinner with Hammond, Frere, Canning, and Pitt.[40] He is a bookseller and publisher and journalist again, operating under an impressive sign of The Crown and Mitre in Pall-Mall, and engaged in the fitting and glorious task of preserving English traditions and English feelings against all foreign opinion, but most particularly against the barbarous subtlety of French ideas.

NOTES

[1] Reitzel, ed., *The Progress of a Ploughboy* (London, 1933), ch. ii–iv.

[2] *Political Register*, VIII, 522.

[3] Short to Jefferson, Aug. 6, 1792; printed in *To the Independent Electors of Pennsylvania* (Philadelphia, n.d.), 7–8; a copy is in the Historical Society of Pennsylvania (H.S.P.).

[4] Susan Cobbett to John Cobbett, Sept. 30, 1835; in *Progress of a Ploughboy*, 59–60.

[5] Original in the Morgan Library, New York City; printed with scornful comments in *To the Independent Electors of Pennsylvania*.

[6] *Supra*, note 4.

[7] There are two copies of this pamphlet in H.S.P.; one printed in Philadelphia in 1793 and the other in Hagerstown in 1794.

[8] Cobbett to Mathieu, Dec. 13, 1793; HM 22882. The Henry E. Huntington Library, San Marino, California, possesses twenty-two letters from Cobbett to Mathieu; the quotation above and those that follow are made with the kind permission of the Director of the Huntington Library.

[9] He mentions being engaged on this in two letters to Mathieu, Dec. 13 and 25, 1793; HM 22882, 22884.

[10] Cobbett to Mathieu, July 19, 1793; HM 22842.

[11] *Idem*. Dec. 25, 1793; HM 22884.

[12] *Idem*. Jan. 31, 1794; HM 22885.

[13] Cobbett to Rachel Smithers, July 6, 1794; Melville, *Life and Letters*, I., 85ff.

[14] Bradford published *A Bone to Gnaw for the Democrats*, parts I and II; and *A Little Plain English addressed to the People of the United States*.

[15] In England the favorite method of attacking Cobbett was to collect passages from his earlier writings and quote them in parallel against passages from his later writings: cf. *Elements of Opposition* (1803); *Political Sketches in 1805* (1805); *Cobbett Against Himself* (1807); *A Refutation of the Present Political Sentiments of Himself* (1808); *Blagdon's Political Register* (1809); *The Beauties of Cobbett* (1816); *Anti-Cobbett; or the Weekly Patriotic Register*, Nos. 1–8, Jan.–April, 1817; *Cobbett's Reflections on Religion* (1820); *The Book of Wonders* (1820); *Cobbett's Gridiron* (1882).

[16] *Political Register*, VI, 450.

[17] As a publisher and bookseller in Philadelphia, Cobbett took great pride in keeping the genius of Burke before the American people. He imported his works, he republished his anti-revolutionary speeches, he filled *Porcupine's Gazette* with references to the opinions of this admired leader.

[18] Compare the following passage from Hamilton's report of 1795 (*Works*, 1886, VII, 462): "One great error is that we suppose mankind more honest than they are. . . . All communities divide themselves into the few and the many. The first are the rich and the well-born; the other the mass of the people . . . turbulent and changing. . . . Give therefore to the first class a distinct, permanent share in the government," with the Jeffersonian phrases of the Declaration of Independence.

[19] S. E. Morison, *Oxford History of the United States*, I, 156. This section of my paper is so deeply indebted to this work that I can do no more than make a general acknowledgement of the able analysis that is given in it, pp. 114–76.

[20] *Gentleman's Magazine*, LXV, pt. i, 47.

[21] This pamphlet, issued in January, 1795, went through three editions in the year and ended up in London in 1797 with a preface by Humphrey Hedgehog —

John Gifford, editor of *The Anti-Jacobin Review*. After an interlude in February, 1795, entitled *A Kick for a Bite: or, Review upon Review, with a Critical Essay on the Works of Mrs. S. Rowson* . . . he added *Part II, A Bone to Gnaw for the Democrats*, in which he replied to a pamphlet recording the *Proceedings of the United Irishmen*. He finished the year with *A Little Plain English*, a work in which he lectured the people cf the United States and defended Jay's Treaty.

²² Published by Bradford, January, 1796.

²³ Published by Cobbett and sold at his own new shop, 1796.

²⁴ If one studies the career of a book like *The Bloody Buoy*, Cobbett's peculiar work can be more easily understood. In 1797 it was translated into Pennsylvania German, printed at Reading, and distributed by the Federalists of that area, under the title of *Die Blut-Fahne ausgestecket zur Warnung politischer Wegweiser in Amerika*. The same year John Wright of London, an associate of John Gifford, reprinted it, giving it a more universal title, *The Bloody Buoy, thrown out . . . to the Political Pilots of all Nations*. In 1797 also it fell into the hands of F. Hodsen, a bookseller of Cambridge, England, who reprinted it and gave it a really scarehead title, *The Annals of Elood . . . by an American*. Mr. Michel, Vice-Provost of King's College, presented it to the University Library, no doubt as a warning to undergraduates.

²⁵ *The Life of Thomas Paine (1797); Letter to the Infamous Thomas Paine (1797); Democratic Principles . . . Part the First (1798); Democratic Principles . . . Part the Second (1798)*; all of these were reprinted in London by John Wright, and the last is particularly to be noticed because it contains ". . . an Instructive Essay, tracing all the horrors of the French Revolution to their Real Causes: the licentious Politics, and Infidel Philosophy of the Present Age."

²⁶ I give here a list of the more striking of these items: *A Letter from Right Hon. Edmund Burke . . . [1796?]; The History of Jacobinism . . . by William Playfair. With an Appendix . . . Showing the close connection which has ever subsisted between the Jacobins of Paris and the Democrats of the United States of America (1796); An Answer to Paine's Rights of Man . . . By H. Mackenzie (1796); The Cannibal's Progress; or, the Dreadful Horrors of French Invasion (1798)*.

²⁷ *Porcupine's Gazette*, April 18, 1797.

²⁸ Cobbett to T. Mathias, Philadelphia, March 12, 1799; British Museum, Add. MSS. 22, 976, f. 212.

²⁹ Cobbett to John Wright, June 10, 1799; Bodleian Library, MSS. Montagu, d. 17: "I think this is the most valuable parcel I have ever received from you. The things you intend sending me by Mr. North, particularly the portrait of Burke, will be gratefully received. Oh! I had like to forgot to thank you kindly for the poetry of the Anti-Jacobin. It is a charming collection. I send you a copy of my edition of the Baeviad and Maeviad. . . . One Humphrey advertised the work as being in press; but, after he had done this he came to get a copy of me. But this I found he had none; but I knew he would get one from gentlemen who had purchased of me; and I resolved to get the start of him. He would have murdered the work in a shabby shilling pamphlet, and I was determined it should not be so disgraced."

³⁰ *Gentleman's Magazine*, N.S., IV, 246.

³¹ Cobbett rose to full fledged journalism slowly, and perhaps his tentative steps indicate the gathering of supporters. The first step was a monthly pamphlet, *A Prospect from the Congress Gallery, No. 1*, February, 1796. This came out with a pretence at nonpartisanship. With the second number, March, 1796, he dropped this pretence, changed the paper's name to *The Political Censor*, and proceeded to indulge his taste for controversy. With each number – there seems to have been eight more, coming out irregularly until March, 1797 – he exercised more and more of the journalist's prerogative. This led him directly to a daily paper,

Porcupine's Gazette, the first issue of which appeared on March 5, 1797; it ran through 778 issues until October 26, 1799.

[32] *Porcupine's Gazette*, June 26, 1797, advertised *Observations on the Dispute between the United States and France*, by Robert Goodloe Harper.

[33] This account is enclosed in a letter dated from New York, Jan. 20, 1800; in the possession of Mr. J. G. E. Hopkins of Brooklyn, who very kindly supplied me with a transcript.

[34] This relationship appears to have been a purely practical one, for when Harper spoke in Cobbett's defense he was careful to dissociate himself from his client: "That my client has overstepped the bounds of good manners and decorum, I have admitted . . . his conduct must meet with strong disapprobation, but agreeable to the rules of law . . . he merits your verdict. . . ." Cf. *Rush v. Cobbett* (Philadelphia, 1800). And among the Rush MSS., at the Ridgway Branch of the Library Company is a letter from Harper to Dr. Rush, Oct. 15, 1805, on which the Doctor's son James has noted: "This gentleman . . . a friend of Dr. R's, yet was the counsel for Cobbett . . . he said to Dr. R. after the trial, 'I was obliged to say something for him!'" Rush MSS. 21,100.

[35] No. 113, Feb. 26, 1799.

[36] *Readinger Zeitung*, March 27, 1799. On Aug. 15, 1800, Cobbett was writing from London to Clymer; his letter is extremely intimate in tone and gives the names of other members of the Federalist group at Reading, of whom Edward Tilghman is to be noticed for his having served as Cobbett's lawyer in the suit *Rush v. Cobbett*; H.S.P., Clymer Collection.

[37] Cobbett to Morse, Aug. 13, 1796; H.S.P., Gratz Collection. Cobbett to Morse, Feb. 28, 1798; New York Historical Society.

[38] *Political Register*, VI, 150–151.

[39] *Idem.*, VIII, 549.

[40] *Diary of Rt. Hon. William Windham* (London, 1866), 430.

IV

JACKSONIAN DEMOCRACY AND A POPULAR PRESS

THE *stream of emigration across the Alleghenies into the new West in the 1790s swelled to a vast tide during the early decades of the nineteenth century. In every community large enough to support it, a newspaper was started. Ohio, Kentucky, Indiana, and Illinois followed one another rapidly in acquiring settled communities and newspapers, and the newspapers, for the most part, voiced the rugged liberalism of pioneer living and thinking, a liberalism which was to characterize the West and to put a frontiersman, Andrew Jackson, in the White House by 1828.*

The election of Jackson indicated the decline of the eastern mercantile and conservative influence in politics and the ascendency of the West with its broader concept of democratic government. Although Jackson's spoils system included favors to newspapers which supported him, his desire for a strong administration press at the capital was caused not only by adherence to the old principles of party-endowed journalism but also by a realization of the importance of the newspaper in an informed democracy. No preceding president had been in such close touch with the press as was Jackson. His unofficial Kitchen Cabinet, upon which he relied for important counsel, contained a number of editors, most trusted of whom was the Kentuckian Francis P. Blair.

William E. Smith's article on Blair not only presents a picture of President Jackson's chief journalistic ally; it also acquaints the reader with the rugged partisan newspaper pattern of the 1830s. Blair was a product of Kentucky frontier journalism. At the head of each issue of the Globe, *the newspaper Jackson had brought him to Washington to publish, he carried, author Smith relates, "the Jeffersonian slogan which was an epitome of his frontier philosophy of government: 'The world is governed too much'."*

While the rough, dynamic journalism of the frontier continued its progress toward the Pacific, a new type of democratic newspaper made its appearance in the East. Following sporadic and unsuccessful attempts by progressive but inexperienced publishers to establish cheap popular newspapers for the masses, Benjamin Day, in 1833, started a penny paper, the New York Sun, *to be run as an adjunct of his printing business. The* Sun *prospered and was followed by James Gordon Bennett's* Herald *in 1835, Horace Greeley's* Tribune *in 1841, and Henry J. Raymond's* Times *in 1851. All of them were published in New York City and appealed to a larger group, with a lower income, than had any of their predecessors of the party press period. Their success was due to many factors, including the start of the American industrial revolution, the rise of a working class interested in labor organizations, the spread of general education, and marked progress in mechanical and transportation facilities. The introduction of the telegraph in 1844 was an event of tremendous significance in the development of news presentation.*

Although the credit for establishing the first successful penny paper in the United States goes to Day, the three most significant of the early publishers of popular newspapers are Bennett, Greeley, and Raymond. Of the three, Bennett and Greeley represent the extremes; Raymond the conservative, constructive center.

Bennett's friends regarded him as a genius; his foes called him a scoundrel. Paul Peebles, writing of him many years ago in the now almost forgotten Galaxy *magazine, was too close to Bennett's time for perspective. So Peebles chose the easy but readable method of letting Bennett scintillate for* Galaxy *readers. Greeley was perhaps as erratic as Bennett, but whereas Bennett put his faith in aggressive, comprehensive news coverage, the editorial pages of Greeley's* Tribune, *particularly the weekly edition, came to be a kind of political bible for northern Republicans. From among the many articles written about Greeley, Gamaliel Bradford's candid portrait is presented here as coming closest perhaps to showing the whole man.*

With the East developing its financial and industrial resources, the West opening new land for small farm holdings, and the South still depending upon its old system of extensive plantations worked by

136

Negro labor, the United States by the fifties had become strongly sectionalized. Newspapers reflected this trend; western and southern papers especially were largely sectional in the decade before the Civil War, only New York City and Springfield, Massachusetts — the home of the Bowles publishing family — having newspapers that might be called national in appeal.

As the free-soil controversy became more intense and the secession movement gained strength, the press of the country split sharply into advocates of the northern and southern causes. So great had become the influence abroad of Bennett's Herald *by 1860 that his inclination to favor the South played a part in the British sympathy for the Confederacy, outweighed only by the economic significance of England's need for southern cotton. It was not until Bennett realized war was inevitable that he swung wholeheartedly over to support of the North. Greeley was perhaps the unhappiest of the New York editors when Fort Sumter was fired on, for he hated equally slavery and war.*

The effect upon the American press of actual warfare was marked. Thousands of new readers scanned newspapers for word of relatives or friends in the armies. War correspondents, especially from the North, rode with the troops and enjoyed access to information which thrilled the public and discomfitted generals. The rapid succession of important events heightened the tempo of news and brought about consequent sharpening of the techniques of news gathering and presentation. Terseness in writing and speed and facility in getting material into print were demanded by news-hungry readers.

This middle third of the nineteenth century thus was a time of change for the American newspaper, from the party press era of the Blairs to the beginning of publication of a popular press by the Bennetts and the Greeleys. In the last third of the century others would build upon the foundations laid by Bennett and Greeley to continue a development of journalistic thinking and techniques in keeping with the changing characteristics of an American society in transition.

Francis P. Blair, Pen-Executive of Andrew Jackson

by WILLIAM E. SMITH

WILLIAM E. SMITH has authored a two-volume work on the Blair family as well as this article for the March 1931 *Mississippi Valley Historical Review*, reprinted with the opening section condensed. He is now graduate school dean and history professor at Miami University in Ohio.

SEND it to Bla-ar!" exclaimed President Andrew Jackson when he and his friends were puzzled with a baffling problem. His decision was as final in such matters as that of a dictator. And so it went to the greatest partisan journalist and defender of Jacksonian democracy, Francis P. Blair, formerly of Frankfort, Kentucky. The problems which confronted Jackson ranged from petty social scandals in and about the capital to those which concerned the existence of the Union. He was confronted with the avowed Democratic practice which was aptly expressed by the shrewd political tactician, William L. Marcy, who laconically said: "To the victors belong the spoils." It should be remembered, however, that, except in cases wherein civil examinations came to be required, the spoils principle has been followed more or less until today. Jackson rebelled only against those in power. He ruled for the people and appealed to them for support. His party journalist, who was of the people and had lasting faith in them, effectually convinced the multitudes of the good intents and purposes of his master. He was of the people, for some of the people, and believed in government by Democratic-Republicans.

The story of how Blair was called to Washington to found a loyal Jacksonian newspaper is variously told. Probably the truest version is that which is found in *Thirty Years' View*, the two-volume memoir which Thomas Hart Benton published in 1854 and 1856. Before this important historical source was published the author invited his bosom friend, Blair, to criticise and rewrite parts of it. The facts in some of the chapters were furnished by Blair; some parts of it were taken by Blair to Lindenwald where he and Martin Van Buren corrected them. It may be safely assumed, therefore, that Blair sanctioned the story therein of how he was called to Washington to establish the *Globe* to defend President Jackson's administrative policies.[1]

His call to Washington marked the beginning of his importance as a national character. It came after President Jackson had lost faith in the loyalty and ability of Duff Green as editor of the *United States Telegraph*. Benton and Blair said Green was intriguing in 1830 to seat Calhoun in the White House in 1833.[2] Green made his plans known to a job-printer, J. M. Duncanson of Washington. He was to have sent Duncanson to Frankfort, Kentucky, to undertake the editorship of the *Argus of Western America*, then owned by Amos Kendall and edited in part by Blair. It was planned to have the Democratic press of the country announce at a concerted moment its support of Calhoun for the presidency, subject to the voters in the election of 1832. Duncanson exposed Green, and the latter, a bosom friend of Calhoun, soon gained the lasting ill will of Andrew Jackson. The rupture between Jackson and Calhoun caused the former to seek an able editor for an administrative organ to be founded for the especial purpose of promoting the interests of the President and his official friends as well as of defending the principles for which he stood.

The story runs that a gentleman in public office showed the President a copy of the *Argus* "containing a powerful and spirited review of a certain nullification speech in Congress." The President, deeply impressed by the cogent argument of the author, inquired who he was, and being told, immediately "had him written to on the subject of taking charge of a paper in Washington."[3]

The truth of the matter is that Blair was known to Jackson before his controversy with Calhoun. He was a Kentucky politician of Scotch-Irish descent and notorious as a relief and "New Court" man. He had grown up from childhood amidst the stirring political scenes at Frankfort. His father served as state attorney-general of Kentucky for twenty years, beginning in 1796.[4] Young Blair borrowed money from his uncle, Governor Madison of Kentucky, to attend Transylvania University at Lexington. There he gained among the students some reputation as a linguist and penman. He was graduated with honors in 1811.

From his youth he was greatly interested in the politics of the day. He served as clerk of the New and Old Courts of his state and as president of the novel Bank of the Commonwealth of Kentucky. While acting clerk of the New Court, he nearly precipitated civil war in his state by unwisely and forcibly taking the records from the office of the Old Court, and then threatening the man with death who would dare take them from him until the legislature ordered him to return them. His scathing pamphlets on the Old Court party are excellent examples of frontier philosophy — philosophy written by men who were steeped in debt and who wanted as little governmental interference as possible. While he was deeply involved in these struggles, he joined his friend, Amos Kendall, as co-editor of that much hated newspaper, the *Patriot*. The Old Court party then founded the *Spirit of '76* to counteract the influence of Kendall and Blair. Each of these papers is another example of ephemeral journals of party factions that arose in frontier conditions. Blair, however, emerged from the relief struggles a well-known man in Kentucky. His friends and foes recognized his ability to analyze, his fearlessness, and his stinging pen.[5]

In the campaign of 1828 he acted as chairman of the Democratic central committee of Kentucky, whose object was to elect Jackson to the presidency and Major W. T. Barry to the office of governor of Kentucky. Barry and Blair carried Kentucky for Jackson but Barry was defeated by a few hundred votes. At the same time Blair assisted Kendall as editor of the *Argus*, and performed his duties as president of the Bank of the Commonwealth. After the election Kendall hurried to Washington where he secured an appointment in the treasury department. Blair was left to assume full responsibility for the *Argus*.

He immediately began to write severe strictures on Jackson's enemies. He denounced the nullifiers whom he accused of attempting to unite the South against the remainder of the country, and rejoiced in the fact that a strong man like Jackson was at Washington to defend the Constitution — a man whose motto was: "The Union, it must be preserved." [6] He declared that Congress had the power to levy a protective tariff, but that the existing tariff should be revised downward. He proposed legislative review of judicial decisions, the direct election of the President of the United States, and the abolition of imprisonment for debt.[7] He took up the cudgel for Peggy O'Neal Eaton and accused Clay's home paper of being the only organ in the West that carried on a "vile insidious warfare upon" the helpless sex.[8] His spirited editorials against the Bank of the United States must have informed the *Argus* readers of his implacable hatred for that institution. A study of his early editorials and letters convinces one that he believed he was a constitutionalist, a moderate states-rights man, and a thorough Jacksonian Democratic-Republican.

The *Argus* was read by Van Buren, Kendall, Barry, and others at Washington. Barry and Blair loved each other like brothers. During the early eighteen thirties Kendall had great respect for Blair's ability. It was only natural that the latter, who had previously corresponded with Jackson, should be called to establish the *Globe*.

The President took Blair into his confidence at once. He told him of the loss of his Rachel, of the Eaton scandal, and of his troubles with Green and Calhoun. He asked him to be on guard against the publication of articles written by Andrew J. Donelson, his private secretary and nephew. He urged the friends of the administration to subscribe in advance for the new paper. Blair's press was a gift from friends of the administration.[9] Departmental officials were informed in one way or another that their favors should be extended to the new editor.

Blair called his paper "The Globe," and printed his first issue in December, 1830. He said as far as he was concerned it was like the earth — "it was created out of nothing." At the head of each issue he carried the Jeffersonian slogan which was an epitome of his frontier philosophy of government: "The world is governed too much." His problems as an editor were no less than first to persuade the warring factions to re-elect Jackson in 1832; second, to defeat the nullifiers in their "damnable" plans; third, to blast Henry Clay's hopes for the presidency and to attempt to secure his utter destruction as a political leader in the West; fourth, to popularize any measures of the Jackson administration; and fifth, to destroy the Bank of the United States.

As the editor of the official organ, Blair was eminently successful during Jackson's administrations. The two men worked cooperatively. Blair was necessarily very often in the White House with the President. His visits were more and more frequent as the years passed until he became a daily visitor. There is a family story to the effect that he carried a pail of fresh milk to the President's kitchen every morning during the last years. Be that story true or not, the two worthies sat down by the kitchen fire to plan their work for the day. Afterwards the one performed his executive duties and the other hurried off to his newspaper to publish and to defend. Blair certainly belonged to the "Kitchen Cabinet." His influence with the President was undoubtedly great, but it is difficult to measure the strength of it. Few letters which passed between Jackson and Blair from 1831 to 1833 remain for the historian's use. It must not be forgotten that the Blairs talked rather than wrote when conversation was possible. Available letters from 1833 to 1837 and from 1837 to 1845 show that Jackson had unbounded confidence in Blair's integrity and ability to the day of his death.

The family friendships between Jackson, the Donelsons, and the Blairs were always of the best. Jackson's genteel manners in the presence of women were never better exemplified than in the presence of Mrs. Blair and young Elizabeth Blair, whom he called "Betty." Mrs. Blair returned his fatherly affection by knitting woolen socks for him and entertaining him in her home when he came to escape the arduous duties of office and to rest and to talk with her husband. For several months "Betty" Blair copied his letters for him. Her son relates that his mother often told him she had never heard Jackson say "By the Eternal!" nor did he smoke his beloved pipe in her presence. He was deeply interested in the Blair sons. He persuaded Montgomery Blair to leave Transylvania University and accept an appointment to West Point; he gave James Blair an office in the navy; and he lavished a part of his affection for children on young Frank Blair in whom he had great hopes for the future. The latter was trained by his father to be a "Young Hickory," as the elder Blair and Benton called him. Politics of the Jackson sort were dinned into his ears from the time he was a child until he became a lawyer and politician in St. Louis, Missouri.

Blair wielded a tremendous influence on his party through the *Globe*. He was aided by the general belief that politicians of the day could hang their "harps on the willows," to quote Van Buren, if they did not have an efficient party paper.[10] He lived in the heyday of powerful partisan newspapers, or of "official organs." His contemporaries were Isaac Hill of the *New Hampshire Patriot*, Edwin Croswell of the *Albany Argus*, Thomas Ritchie of the *Richmond Enquirer*, and Joseph Gales and William Seaton of the *National Intelligencer* — a powerful array of editors with whom to compete. With Jackson, Van Buren,

Benton, and Silas Wright at his back, Blair believed that he was next to invincible. Letters poured into the *Globe* office immediately upon its establishment from new subscribers who announced that the *Globe* was being substituted for Green's *Telegraph*.[11] Country correspondents informed him in forceful language that they were going "whole hog or none" for Jackson, and that if the *Globe* deviated a hair's breadth from pure Jacksonianism they would stop their subscriptions at once.[12]

Exchanges were quite freely made with the Democratic presses. Enthusiastic Jacksonians subscribed for copies for their friends. They insisted that the local editors become subscribers to the *Globe* and that they publish its pithy editorials in their own papers. Editors who refused this cooperation received stinging rebukes. Blair and Kendall sent articles on various subjects to local papers for publication in order to reprint them in the *Globe* as original excerpts and made it appear that the country as a whole applauded, demanded, or suggested, as the case might be. The iron hand was laid upon all Democrats who chose to differ with Jackson's policies. Persuasion was first used; that failing, warning was given, soon to be followed by the inevitable reading out of the party.

The *Globe* frequently attempted to wreck the political future of rebellious Democrats by omitting their names in its pages. Other papers took their cue from it. The editor flayed enemies of great influence with his biting sarcasm and bitter denunciation, while men of little influence were left to the tender mercies of his partner, John C. Rives. Blair delighted in agitating rivalries among the enemy into open quarrels. Calhoun, William C. Rives, George McDuffie, and many others came to despise him, his *Globe,* and the things for which he stood. Clay launched tirades from the floor of the Senate against him and the *Globe*; he pronounced the paper a dirty, filthy sheet that published the "Muckraking scum" of the earth. Many worthy editors feelingly called Blair an unprincipled liar, an ogre who attacked men in a "savage and ferocious" manner.[13] Had they but known it, they were doing just what he desired them to do, for on such occasions he played the role of a martyr in the cause of the people. He declared indiscriminate warfare on the aristocracy of wealth. As compared with Ritchie of the *Richmond Enquirer* he was radical. He was dogmatic, bold, and defiant in the face of opposition. He shaped the policy of the *Globe* to appeal to laborers, debtors, frontiersmen, and partisans.

He was poorest in defense, strongest in aggression. When there was one of his strong attacks on the enemy published in the *Globe* he sent a marked copy to the appreciative President.

Blair has been severely condemned by authors of reminiscences and autobiographies for his apparently unflinching policy of "shooting the deserters" and of "carrying the war into Africa." Years afterwards he made many apologies for his sledge-hammer policy. He said he pursued such a course for the sake of principle and the people. "Measures, not men" was his party battle cry. Rives asserts that Blair hesitated to attack a friend who disagreed with him politically, but he did it frequently to advance the interests of his party; his object was to whip those into line who threatened party defection, or to drive them from the party before they gained too many followers.[14] There were a few men of different political faith whom he refused to attack. Among them were Senator John J. Crittenden of Kentucky, who had been his early benefactor, and William W. Seaton, associate editor of the *National Intelligencer*, a man for whom he had much admiration.

The first to receive Blair's notice were Calhoun, Green, Clay, and the officials of the United States Bank. He had at first hoped that Calhoun might succeed Jackson in 1837, but a few weeks of experience in Washington caused him to regard Calhoun as a rascal and Van Buren as a man with "excellent judgment and prudence."[15] He had two major objections to Calhoun: namely, his desire to succeed Jackson in 1832 and his doctrine of nullification. The publication of Calhoun's pamphlet that announced to the country the break between its author and the President openly began the tremendous struggle between the Jackson–Van Buren and Calhoun factions. Blair replied that the pamphlet was a "firebrand wantonly thrown into the republican party."[16] He denounced it as one phase of the intrigues of Calhoun, Green, and congressmen who had leveled themselves to "club managers." Green angrily called Blair an "ungrateful hypocrite." Blair said Green was a liar. As a result of the explosion, Green's *Telegraph* withered away and died in 1837, and Calhoun fell to the level of a sectional leader. Blair's conduct during the struggle so won Jackson's admiration that the former wrote to his sister-in-law, Mrs. Gratz: "Where I am I can do nothing wrong. If Van Buren says, 'You are rash in this business, Mr. Blair,' the old hero says, 'You are right, Mr. Blair, I'll stand by you.' "[17] He shunned the Eaton scandal as long as he could, but once he perforce entered it, he accused Calhoun of being the prime mover in that. When the subject of nullification was being hotly debated, it was Blair's explanation of Jackson's proclamation that lessened the fears of the Virginians who were concerned about the principle of state rights. They were correct in their supposition that Jackson approved Blair's exposition of his proclamation on nullification. His approval, however, came after the publication of the exposition.

Blair was not a good fighter without a major issue. He labored best under a certain amount of excitement. At other times he was often disinclined to produce editorials; then Rives published his own editorials, or articles by Kendall and many others. If Blair was very busy in his office or garden, Mrs. Blair would scan the newspapers for important news. If she found an article that needed attention, she would either mark the selection, or stop Blair at his work, read the article to him, and under the impulse of the moment he would sit down and dash off an answer.[18] Sometimes he blundered, as in the case of Santa Anna and Texas, but he was usually right in Jackson's judgment, so thoroughly grounded was he in Jacksonianism.

The editor of the *Globe* was a constitutionalist and a chauvinist. He steadfastly believed in the delegated and reserved powers of the national and state governments respectively. He helped to spread the theory that the national government had no power to aid internal improvements within states. He opposed slavery, but he did not believe the northern abolitionists had any right to disturb the institution in the South. Each state must settle its own slavery question. From the beginning of his editorial career at Washington he accused the nullifiers of engendering hatred in southern breasts against abolitionists in order to unite the southern Democracy with Calhoun as its leader. He disliked England because of her attitude of superiority towards the United States, and he resented any reference to New England's superiority in culture and influence in this country. He was a Bentonian expansionist, a believer in "manifest destiny," and an Anglo-phobist.

Blair's fertile brain produced with ease a flow of lengthy editorials on nullification and on the Bank. From his youth he had opposed the Bank on constitutional grounds. Before he reached Washington he had come to hate it. As the president of the Bank of the Commonwealth he had been humiliated more than once by the Bank of the United States. He laid the hard times in the West in 1819–1820 to the monopolistic control of the supply of money exercised by the Bank of the United States. He had pledged security for friends to an amount in excess of $24,000 during those trying years in Kentucky. His friends had left him to pay their indebtedness, and as a consequence, a $20,000 debt hung over his head when he reached Washington in 1830. Furthermore he believed that the Bank was corrupt in its practices, a monopoly that threatened the principles of democracy. He and Kendall made a strong attempt to convince the country that the Bank participated in the election of 1828 to defeat Jackson. The latter came to believe it.

Blair was an entertaining conversationalist, well informed and keen in argument. He used his powers daily to convince his friends and Jackson that the Bank must be destroyed. The public found mild attacks on the institution in the *Globe* long before the question of rechartering the institution became a political issue. Gradually they became bitter and venomous. He suggested that probably the editors and the congressmen who supported the Bank were deeply obligated to it. Green and Gales and Seaton made light of such implications. Other editors who supported the Bank did likewise. Blair led them on until he was ready to publish his facts, then to a surprised country he proved that a number of the editors and congressmen owed large sums at the Bank or to its branches. The truth was damaging in the eyes of Jackson and his devoted supporters. Blair's sarcasm bit like vipers. Never was he happier than when he was fighting the Bank. He labored unceasingly against it. Often, says Rives, he wrote so fast before going to press that he kept two boys running with copy to the composing rooms. Just before Jackson vetoed the bill to recharter the Bank, Blair talked almost nothing else to his friends. And when Jackson was deciding to remove the deposits to give the Bank its final blow, he took the Blair family to the Rip Raps at his own expense on a vacation trip.

In passing it may be worthwhile to mention that Blair was one of the first to suggest and urge the appointment of Roger B. Taney as treasurer to remove the deposits. The destruction of the Bank was an injury and a blessing to the United States. It brought on a panic at a time when no other machinery existed to furnish sound money and credit, but it was a blow at monopoly early in the life of our government. Some years later, John C. Rives said Blair and Benton were most responsible for the defeat of the Bank — the one with his press and his influence with Jackson, the other with his influence in Congress.

Blair considered the *Congressional Globe* his greatest contribution to American history. He published his first volume of it in 1834. It appeared weekly at a cost to the subscriber of one dollar per copy each session, index included. Extra sheets were published when unusually strong speeches were made, or important events happened in Congress. In later years each congressman was furnished with twelve copies, bound and wrapped, which when franked, were sent to whomsoever he wished. This documentary publication was read in logging camps in the great Northwest, by men on the prairies, and by hundreds of Jacksonians of the North, South, and East. Supplemented with the *Globe*, it was Jackson's political Bible. Speeches by loyal Democrats in Congress made for political purposes were published at reduced rates and distributed by the thousands. Blair first reported the debates in the House, because he considered its deliberations most important, and Rives reported those of the Senate. Later reporters were employed and trained for that work to relieve the editors for other duties. Blair, nevertheless, visited the Senate frequently where he often sat with Benton. He gathered news for his own use and for editorials. Daily proceedings of Congress were published in the *Globe*, and the same set-type was preserved for the *Congressional Globe*. In case of a printer's or reporter's error congressmen were privileged to have changes made. Written speeches were generally supplied by congressmen for the *Congressional Globe*. They were often quite different from those actually delivered on the floor, but the editors courteously permitted the authors to change them to please their own tastes and the whims of their constituents. The *Congressional Globe* competed with the *Register of Debates*, published by Gales and Seaton until 1837, when the latter was discontinued for financial reasons. Blair retired from active work on the *Congressional Globe* in 1849.

Blair's influence waned rapidly after the close of Van Buren's administration. He was a devoted friend of Van Buren, but like thousands of Americans, he could never become enthusiastic about him. The *Globe*, consequently, mentions Van Buren little in campaigns, and devotes much space to lambasting the Whigs. Being a hero worshipper, Blair needed a hero to exalt before the people; Van Buren lacked heroic qualities. He, therefore, naturally utilized the magnetic influence of "Old Hickory" until the latter died. His unrelenting policy toward Tyler and Calhoun was one phase of extreme bitterness between party factions during the forties. Internal party conditions and the dying influence of Jackson in political circles led to the undoing of one of the ablest of the partisan editors. President Polk and his intriguers forced him to sell the *Globe* in 1845.

Blair was more vitriolic than Croswell, less learned, calm, and sedate than Gales, broader visioned and keener than Ritchie, more truthful and loyal than Green, less original than Horace Greeley, and not a nice political editor like Thurlow Weed. He was undoubtedly an experienced politician and journalist clothed with granted and assumed powers which were respected by friends and challenged by foes. When Jackson while President visited the Hermitage, he wrote to Blair and sent through him his greetings to his friends at Washington. That does not mean that Jackson wrote only to Blair, but presumably he wrote more often to him, because he regarded Blair as his chosen defender and pen-executive. As an ex-president he used Blair to forward messages to leaders like Van Buren and Benton. During the time that Kendall was writing his biography, and when Kendall and Blair, apparently, were unfriendly toward each other, he consigned his papers to Blair to defend his character and policies. Deeply in debt, he turned to Blair and Rives for a ten thousand dollar loan, and again for eight thousand dollars more. The principal was not paid until long after Jackson's death and the interest at six per cent is still unpaid. Van Buren claimed that Polk should have accepted Blair's services and advice as he and Jackson had done. John C. Rives, of unimpeachable character, maintained that after 1831 Blair had more influence with Jackson than any other man. It cannot be said positively that Rives was right, but Blair had far more influence with Jackson and Van Buren than is generally credited to him.

NOTES

[1] Blair to Martin Van Buren, August 5, 1855; Benton to Van Buren, August 16, 1855, Van Buren MSS; Francis P. Blair Jr. to Montgomery Blair, n.d., Blair MSS.
[2] Thomas H. Benton, *Thirty Years' View* (New York, 1854–56), I, Chap. 43.
[3] *Ibid.*
[4] Lewis Collins, *History of Kentucky* (Covington, 1874), I, 508.
[5] A. M. Stickles, "The Critical Court Struggles in Kentucky (1819–1829)" (Bowling Green, Kentucky, 1923); a doctoral thesis in manuscript submitted to the University of Indiana.

FRANCIS P. BLAIR

[6] *Argus*, August 18, 1830; *Globe*, September 3, 1833.
[7] *Argus, passim*; "Francis P. Blair," in *Dictionary of American Biography* (New York, 1928), II, 330–32.
[8] *Argus*, October 20, 1830.
[9] William L. Mackenzie, *The Lives and Opinions of Benjamin Franklin Butler and Jesse Hoyt* (Boston, 1845), 88.
[10] Edward M. Shepard, *Martin Van Buren* (New York, 1897), 163.
[11] Blair-Rives MSS.
[12] *Ibid.*
[13] *Globe*, June 23, 1856; *passim*.
[14] *Globe*, June 23, 1856. The *Globe* throughout is a proof of this statement.
[15] Thomas H. Clay, "Two Years with Old Hickory," in *Atlantic Monthly* (Boston), LX, 192; see early issues of the *Globe*.
[16] *National Intelligencer*, March 31, 1831.
[17] Clay, *op. cit.*, 193.
[18] Blair to Barker, May 20, 1831, Blair MSS; verified in conversations with Blair descendants.

12

James Gordon Bennett's Scintillations

by PAUL PEEBLES

When James Gordon Bennett, founder of the *New York Herald*, died in 1872, a writer for the now almost forgotten *Galaxy* magazine, PAUL PEEBLES, prepared this account of the reasons why the elder Bennett became a nationally known figure in the eyes of his contemporaries.

JAMES GORDON BENNETT, in the spring of 1835, threw out upon the sidewalks of New York a bundle of detonating fire-crackers, which he styled the *Herald*. Not the *New York Herald*, but a herald in a general way, heralding a new era of such remarkable character that the town stood agape in wonder, half-conscious that an unexpected revulsion had begun, and wholly uncertain as to the proper method of regarding the phenomenon. For Bennett's venture was absolutely phenomenal in every aspect. It was an innovation upon the old-time easygoing methods of American journalism; it was a startling revelation of the presence of an iconoclast, who had no respect for customs, traditions, or prejudices; it was a new Gospel, in short, for Society and the Church, and neither the Church nor Society knew in the least degree what to do with it. But Bennett knew. In his prime, at the age of forty, he had hit upon his true vocation, and the disappointments and disasters of his earlier years had ripened him into a full and hearty flavor—a flavor as strange to the New Yorker of that day as the pungent juices of tropical fruit to the palate of the dweller among the snows of Lapland. His shrewd Scottish sense, his indomitable energy, his unconquerable spirit of enterprise, and his inextinguishable thirst for novelty, combined to point the way to notoriety and to fortune. He discerned the greatest want of his time, and he was swift to supply that want. Before his day *news*papers did not exist. He determined that they should be brought forth. Before his day the world as represented in our public journals was lethargic, pretentious, pedantic. He resolved that it should become wide-awake, sensible, representative of the popular sentiment, and progressive. But one method to gain his end appeared feasible, and he adopted it without hesitation. The method was a novelty; and that consideration, outweighing all others, overriding all questions of money, influence, or support, and spurring him constantly onward, impelled him to undertake his extraordinary task.

Biographers who have sketched the career of Mr. Bennett have often failed to strike the key-note of his unquestioned success as journalist. It was not because he was a man of profound learning or of singular attractiveness of personal character that he won his triumphs, but rather that he was content to become the mouthpiece of the people among whom he dwelt. Appreciating the character of the citizens of New York, and foreseeing the grandeur to which the city would attain in the course of a generation, he adapted himself to the process of development which has made the American metropolis what it is. The younger men of 1835 had become weary of the inanities of the public journals, which excluded the news of the world and substituted therefor the dullest of political disquisitions. The city was expanding; great measures of public utility were contemplated; a new life was beginning; old things were passing away, and the new were beginning to struggle into existence. What wonder, then, that Bennett and his *Herald* gained an early foothold, and a strong one?

True, the paper was impudent. It could not have been otherwise and have lived. The secret of its first success lay in its incisiveness. It was incisive in everything — in its manner of presenting the current news, in its dealings with men and manners, in its warfare upon what Bennett contemptuously called "the old-fashioned sixpenny papers," and especially in its keen little paragraphs. These paragraphs were short, pointed, often witty, and they were read with delight by about one half of the population, and with horror by the other half; but it was impossible to resist the temptation to read them. We have called them "fire-crackers," and so they were — mischievous little explosives, conveying a world of meaning, creating a prodigious clatter, and, as the country had observed, "good things to get out of the way of." Here is one of them: "Newspaper abuse made Mr. Van Buren chief magistrate of this republic, and newspaper abuse will make me the chief editor of this country. Well, *be it so. I can't help it.*"

Another is of a personal character, in which Bennett, after throwing himself upon "the heavenly compassion" of his female readers for his persistence in the sin of celibacy, concludes thus: "I am so much engaged in building up the 'Herald' and reforming the age, that actually I have scarcely time to say 'How do ye do?'"

In another paragraph he smites the Roman Catholic clergy: "As a Catholic, we call upon the Catholic bishop and clergy of New York to come forth from the darkness, folly, and superstition of the tenth century. They live in the nineteenth. There can be no mistake about it; *they will be convinced of this fact if they look into the almanac.*"

Learning from the pages of the *Annual Register* that there were 1,492 rogues in the State prison in 1835, Bennett made use of that bit of statistical information by adding this comment: "But God only knows how many out of prison, preying upon the community, in the shape of gamblers, blacklegs, speculators, and politicians." The same volume of the *Register* also contained a return of the number of paupers receiving State aid, and Bennett cited the figures with the remark: "And double the number going there as fast as indolence and intemperance can carry them."

Consistent in his belief that the world was greatly given to lying, and that the cormorants of society were bent upon cheating the public, Mr. Bennett opened fire upon the "speculators" whenever he found an opportunity to hit or to hurt them. An amusing instance of his firecracker style occurs in one of the early numbers of the *Herald*. A communication in regard to the Morris Canal Bank having been sent to the *Herald* office, its receipt was acknowledged in a characteristic paragraph, as follows:

Here is, now, some fellow in Wall street who has a private object in view — the making of a few thousand dollars by speculation — and he asks us to help him to do so at our expense. If we refuse, he threatens to say, "You are bought up." We tell this patriot, and every other patriot, that we have no sort of objection to publish his communications on being paid for them, as for any other advertisements. If "M. Q." will transmit $15 (for the article will occupy thirty squares *), we shall publish them with as much fearlessness as we do "Loco-foco Matches," "Dancing Parties," "Dr. Moffat's Vegetable Life Pills," or "Dr. Brandreth's Vegetable Universal Pills."

* The *Herald*'s prices were lower then than now. Very many persons would be thankful for the privilege of paying $15 for the use of "thirty squares" in any issue of the *Herald* of our day.

But the best illustration of the character of Bennett's mind is to be found in his salutatory address to the readers of the *Herald* (May, 1835). In a few but well-chosen words, he declares his independence of party and avows his intention of making the *Herald* a piquant sheet:

In *débuts* of this kind many talk of principle — political principle, party principle — as a sort of steel-trap to catch the public. We mean to be perfectly understood on this point, and therefore *openly disclaim all steel-traps — all principle, as it is called, all party, all politics.* Our only guide shall be good, sound, practical common sense, applicable to the business and bosoms of men engaged in every-day life. We shall support no party, be the organ of no faction or coterie, and care nothing for any election or any candidate, from President down to constable. We shall endeavour to record facts on every public and proper subject, stripped of verbiage and coloring, with comments, when suitable, just, independent, fearless, and good-tempered. If the 'Herald' wants the mere expansion which many journals possess, we shall try to make it up in industry, good taste, brevity, variety, point, piquancy, and cheapness.

At a later period, reviewing his editorial career and replying to a personal attack, he writes:

Possessing personal industry and indefatigability, with some talent, for which I am thankful to God Almighty, *no one in this city can say aught against my private character.* I can venture to say that in all the relations of life it is without a stain. The benefit of this indefatigability was entirely directed to advance the interests of Webb for nearly three years. To me he is principally indebted for the success and establishment of his paper. I can prove it by documents in my possession. Enjoying for many years a friendly correspondence with several of the most distinguished men in the country, among whom were Martin Van Buren, Vice-President, and Nicholas Biddle, president of the United States Bank, my endeavors, during my connection with Webb, were to benefit his establishment as far as in my power, without compromising honor, reputation, and the decencies of life.

Always intensely personal, Mr. Bennett was as fond of writing about himself as of expressing his opinions concerning other men; and it is an interesting study in psychology to trace through years of paragraphs a series of allusions, which, if placed in proper order, would constitute an excellent autobiography. We transfer from early numbers of the *Herald* two passages that cannot now be read without a certain feeling of tenderness. In one of these Mr. Bennett replies to a taunt published by a political opponent, who declared that he had once followed the vocation of a peddler in the streets of Glasgow:

I am, and have been a peddler — and part of my name is Gordon. This I admit. From my youth up I have been a peddler, not of tapes and laces, but of thoughts, feeling, lofty principles, and intellectual truths. I am now a wholesale dealer in the same line of business, and people generally believe I have quite a run, and, what is better, no dread of suspension. I was educated and intended for a religious sect, but the Almighty, in his wisdom, meant me for truth and mankind, and I will fulfill my destiny in spite of all the opposition made to me either in the Old or New Hemisphere.

Yes, I have been a peddler, and am still a peddler of the thoughts and feelings and high imaginings of the past and present ages. I peddle my wares as Homer did his, as Shakespeare did his, as every great, intellectual, and mighty peddler of the past did; and *when I shall have finished my peddling in this world, I trust I shall be permitted to peddle in a better and happier region for ever and ever.*

I have been a wayward, self-dependent, resolute, self-thinking being, from my earliest days. Yet there were implanted in my burning soul those lofty principles of morals, honor, philosophy, and religion, that the contumely of the world cannot shake, or all the editors or bankers in Christendom intimidate. I feel myself, in this land, to be engaged in a great cause — the cause of truth, public faith and science, against falsehood, fraud and ignorance, I would not abandon it even to reach the glittering coronet of the extinct title of the Duke of Gordon.

In the following paragraphs amusing egotism and accurate insight are curiously intermingled:

I mean to make the "Herald" the great organ of social life, the prime element of civilization, the channel through which native talent, native genius, and native power may bubble up daily, as the pure sparkling liquid of the Congress fountain at Saratoga bubbles up from the centre of the earth till it meets the rosy lips of the fair. I shall mix together commerce and business, pure religion and morals, literature and poetry, the drama and dramatic purity, till the "Herald" shall outstrip everything in the conception of man. The age of trashy novels, of more trashy poems, of most trashy quarterly and weekly literature, is rapidly drawing to a close.

This is the age of the Daily Press, inspired with the accumulated wisdom of past ages, enriched with the spoils of history, and looking forward to a millennium of a thousand years, the happiest and most splendid ever yet known in the measured span of eternity!

My life has been one invariable series of efforts, useful to the world and honorable to myself — efforts to create an honorable reputation during life, and to leave something after my death for which posterity may honor my memory. *I am building up a newspaper establishment that will take the lead of all others that ever appeared in the world*, in virtue, in morals, in science, in knowledge, in industry, in taste, in power, in influence. No public reputation can be lasting unless it is built on private character and virtue. My whole private life has been one of virtue, integrity, and honorable effort, in every relation of society. Dissipation, extravagance, and fashionable follies never had any charms for me. . . . This has been the cause of the success attending the "Herald."

Civilization is yet defaced with traits of barbarism. We are only half-civilized. In our most polished communities, solitary outrages spring up that are a disgrace to the age — more the inroads of the desert than the manners of a civilized country. We have plenty of laws, but they are powerless and weak. The radical defect is in our social system. Moral courage is unknown and brutal outrage encouraged. Virtue is driven from society, and vice impudently occupies the seats of honor and of power. This state of public opinion and of social manners must be reformed. Honor and reputation must only be associated with virtue, truth, order, and cultivated minds. Now is the period to begin this great reform, and we are one of those cool, courageous spirits that will aid and assist it forward.

Among the new elements introduced into New York journalism by Mr. Bennett, the "Money Article" became one of the most popular and prominent. No daily paper is now published without a careful review of "the Street" and of all the operations in the markets, and the Money Editor has attained a position of power, which, if rumor does him no injustice, is made available for the making of his own fortune; but in 1835 neither Money Articles nor Money Editors were thought of until Mr. Bennett created them. The reader may be interested in seeing the first specimen of the Money Article, taken literally from the *Herald* of June 13, 1835:

COMMERCIAL.

Stocks yesterday maintained their prices during the session of the Board, several going up. Utica went up 2 per cent; the others stationary. Large quantities were sold. After the Board adjourned, and the news from France was talked over, the fancy stocks generally went down 1 to 1 1-2 per cent; other stocks quite firm. A rally was made by the bulls in the evening, *under the trees*, but it did not succeed. There will be a great fight in the Board to-day. The good people up town are anxious to know what the brokers think of Mr. Livingston. We shall find out, and let them know.

The cotton and flour markets rallied a little. The rise in cotton in Liverpool drove it up here a cent or so. The last shippers will make 2 1-2 per cent. Many are endeavoring to produce a belief that there will be a war. If the impression prevails, naval stores will go up a good deal. Every eye is outstretched for the Constitution. Hudson, of the Merchants' News Room, says he will hoist out the first flag. Gilpin, of the Exchange News Room, says he will have her name down in his room one hour before his competitor. The latter claims having beat Hudson yesterday by an hour and ten minutes in chasing the England.

Six years later Mr. Bennett announced his intention of publishing reports of the debates in Congress, "without asking a cent of the public treasury," and in June, 1841, he succeeded in enlisting the services of Henry Clay in his interest. At that time newspaper reporters were freely admitted into the House of Representatives, but in the Senate there was a rule excluding from the reporters' seats all persons not connected with the Washington press. Mr. Bennett wrote to Mr. Clay to request a modification of this rule, and announced that he had "organized a corps of reporters, at an expense of *nearly two hundred dollars per week*," to give daily reports of the debates in both Houses. The incident is worth recording, if for no other reason than its remarkable illustration of Mr. Bennett's enterprise. Thirty-one years ago, the sum of two hundred dollars per week was an enormous outlay for any single journal for the sole purpose of getting reports of Congressional debates. Yet the *Herald* was then but six years old, and it had been started in a cellar in Wall street!

The personal assaults to which Mr. Bennett was subjected were often the malicious acts of men whom he had mercilessly but deservedly rebuked. Yet, on the other hand, it must be admitted that he sometimes deserved the punishment he received. One of his bitterest antagonists was Mr. James Watson Webb, then the editor of the *Courier and Enquirer*, against whom the *Herald* directed its sharpest shafts. Mr. Webb finally attacked Mr. Bennett, and on the following day the *Herald* described the scene, with the following terse comment: "The fellow, no doubt, wanted to let out the never-failing supply of good humor and wit, which has created such a reputation for the 'Herald,' and appropriate the contents to supply the emptiness of his own thick skull. He did not succeed, however, in rifling me of my ideas. . . . My ideas, in a few days, will flow as fresh as ever, and he will find it so, to his cost."

The promise of the concluding phrase was kept to the letter. The *Herald* blazed with personal allusions to Mr. Webb, and the natural result was another personal encounter, which was also described by Mr. Bennett in a vein of humor which even now creates a smile. After recounting the circumstances of the attack Bennett writes: "My damage is a scratch, about three-quarters of an inch in length, on the third finger of the left hand, which I received from the iron railing I was forced against, and three buttons torn from my vest, which any tailor will re-instate for a six-pence. His loss is a rent from top to bottom of a very beautiful black coat, which cost the ruffian $40, and a blow in the face which may have knocked down his throat some of his infernal teeth, for anything I know. Balance in my favor, $39.94."

One more passage will serve to show the manner in which the *Herald* dealt with its early contemporaries:

OUR SMALL CONTEMPORARIES. — It gives us great pleasure to learn that the "Sun" and "Transcript" intend this day to make the last typographical improvements of which their appearance and dimensions are susceptible. The "Sun" enlarges a little, and the "Transcript," not being able to enlarge, contents itself with a new set of type. All these efforts the public view with perfect unconcern. The improvements most wanted in these two papers were of a more intellectual cast — not merely physical. Who cares, for instance, about the "Sun's" enlarging itself? It is the same low-bred, vulgar, licentious sheet of duplicity it was when it was called the "Free Enquirer," and openly advocated skepticism and Fanny Wright. As to the "Transcript," though it originated in the same source, it is too flat and insipid to deserve a remark.

It grieves us to tell these truths, but it was our duty to do so. Both papers having played their last trump card, it remains for the "Herald" hereafter to take up the line of march in the way of improvement. In a short time we shall begin. Many of our subscribers ask us not to enlarge till we shall complete the first volume, embracing six months, and we are not sure but the idea is worth consideration. Having now the position and the power to make the "Herald" one of the greatest papers in the country, we shall proceed in that enterprise, and before we close *we shall astonish some of these big-bellied journals that now affect to look down upon us, with scorn.*

In the same issue of the *Herald* in which this article appears is an announcement of the proposed enlargement of the paper. "It is yet," says Mr. Bennett, "hardly four months since the 'Herald' rose from the Ann street conflagration, with impaired means but undying energy of mind and spirit." The patronage of liberal advertisers is gratefully acknowledged, and with good reason, for the little sheet, containing but sixteen short columns all told, counts ten columns of business announcements.

To conclude: An extract from a letter written by Mr. Bennett while making a summer tour in August, 1842, is worthy of reproduction for more than one reason. It shows the play of his fancy in moments when he was relieved of the burden of daily drudgery, and it also leads us to the reflection that the world has undergone no radical changes in thirty years. His comments upon public affairs in 1842 might be applied with great exactness to the conditions of 1872. He writes:

The aspect of nature at this season is the very reverse of her ordinary appearance; and the moral atmosphere seems to keep pace with the natural. We have had more unnatural murders, horrid crimes, flagrant defalcations, infamous elopements, robberies of banks, *crim. cons.*, breaches of private trust, repudiations by brokers, violations of social confidence, abuses of immense magnitude by public officers, court-martials of big and little officers, scandalous conduct naval and military, disobedience to superiors, dreadful delinquencies in duty, and every conceivable shape and modification of human turpitude that could deface the surface of civilized life.

And yet we are prosperous as a people, blessed of Heaven, and happy. And why? *Because the politicians and their clique form but a miserable minority of the nation. The majority of the people of this country are honest, hard-working, patient, pious, persevering, talented, tenacious of their rights, and able at all times to maintain them.* With such a people, such a climate, and such a soil, we have resources within ourselves that enable us to correct every family error, rectify the balance of the world, and whip it into decency whenever it deserves it.

In this sketch we have chosen to let Mr. Bennett speak for himself, rather than to subject his early work to the test of a critical analysis. To the younger generation of readers, his quips, his innuendoes, his biting sarcasms, his skilful fencing with antagonists, the secrets of his wonderful success, are almost unknown; to older persons, the crackling paragraphs of the *Herald* are faded memories. Both these classes, therefore, may find in the passages we have quoted some amusement for a leisure moment. Mr. Bennett, with all his shortcomings, is at least entitled to the credit of having infused new life into the journalism of this country, and the stimulus which he imparted to the laborious avocation of news-gathering is still visible in the conduct of every great newspaper which appeals to the public for support. He originated the aggressive policy, and contrived to hold his own in spite of vigorous opposition, personal detraction, and outrageous assaults; and his promise to make the *Herald* the best known and most profitable of American newspapers was kept to the letter. Sinking all other considerations in the greater one of building up his journal, he struck a straight furrow through or over every intervening obstacle, and the desire of his heart was accomplished many years before he was called to lay down the burden of his life. The little sheet, with four short columns on the page, which amazed the town in 1835, has disappeared from public view so completely that any specimen of the first year's issue is now a rarity; but the ample twelve-page *Herald* of to-day, with its seventy-two columns of advertisements and news, is a living memento of the industry and talent of James Gordon Bennett.

13

Horace Greeley

by GAMALIEL BRADFORD

GAMALIEL BRADFORD wrote some two dozen books during his distinguished career, many of them biographical in nature. Horace Greeley was an obvious choice for an article by such an author and the study of Greeley reprinted here was published in the *American Mercury*, April 1924.

~~~~~~

Horace Greeley was all his life an intense and passionate worker. From his boyhood in the tens and twenties of the last century, until his death in 1872, it was work, work, work for him, and nothing else. As a child in school and on the farm he worked with his hands and with his brain. As a printer in New York he worked with his brain and with his hands. As editor of the *New Yorker* and the *New York Tribune* he worked with his brain, but still also with his busy fingers, till the fingers were weary and the brain worn to shreds and tatters.

Work was all of life that interested him. What would you do unless you worked? You worked all the time, except when you were asleep. He had a physique which, on the whole, admirably seconded all this intense activity. To be sure, his nerves were sensitive, played queer tricks with him, bothered him even as a child. But in general his body served him well, and he did not suffer from that physical drag which makes all work tormenting, if not impossible. Work, never tormenting to him, became such a habit that he could hardly conceive the attraction of idleness. He even extended his own passion to humanity in general, and could not believe that all men did not love to work as he did. "A lazy man, in my view," he said, "is always the pitiable victim of miseducation. Each human being, properly trained, works as freely and naturally as he eats; only the victims of parental neglect or misguidance prefer hunger and rags with idleness, to thrift won by industry and patient effort."

To men of that temperament work seems sufficient in itself, a reward and a delight, quite independent of any ulterior motive. They work from mere restless impulse, from the mechanical instinct of nerves and muscles craving to be used, almost regardless of any definite aim or object to be attained. At no time in his life was the earning of money in itself an incentive to Greeley's efforts. He earned and saved because that was the natural accompaniment of his excessive work, and because his foresight and far-sight felt the power of protection in such saving. But money meant little to him, for he lived sparely and hardly and had no taste for spending. His youth was the homely, rugged youth of the New England farmer's boy in the first half of the century. The bare necessaries were all that Horace was ever accustomed to and apparently all he ever wanted. In the poverty of those early years were established the oddities of dress which became so peculiarly associated with him that men rarely think of him today without them. As a boy, even when he began to earn, he would spend nothing on clothes. He went into New York with the crudest country garments and he had no disposition to shed them even under the pressure of ridicule. All his life he dressed roughly, uncouthly, ineptly, wore trailing coats and trailing trousers and clumsy boots, and his slouch hat and white overcoat were objects of everlasting caricature.

Even with a family and a city household of his own it appears that Greeley maintained the same Spartan regime that had taken possession of his spirit in youth. No doubt the wife and children had the necessaries of life and many of the comforts, but they were trained to consider luxury as superfluous, if not wicked, and to believe that only the idle needed to spend money in order to be happy. Yet Greeley was fond of his children, devoted to them, and spoke of them with singular tenderness. The boy Arthur, familiarly known as Pickie, who was such a favorite of Margaret Fuller's, is described at length in his father's autobiography with a pathetic, lingering fondness, and his death was for the time a prostrating blow.

II

More and more, as I study the lives of men of mark, or of any men, for that matter, I feel curiosity about their wives. It is evident that Greeley's wife played a considerable part in his career, though we can get at her only very indirectly and obscurely. Here and there comes a touch that makes her stand out. For instance, we are told that, when Greeley married her, she was a teacher and was "crazy for knowledge." How clearly you see the type! You begin to understand how she could put up with her husband's oddities; perhaps she had plenty of her own. Her rigid family discipline is drolly illustrated in an account of Governor Seward's attempt to smoke on the Greeley premises: "Now Mrs. Greeley happened to be ill in a room just over that in which the gentlemen were, and her husband knew that just so soon as the cigar-smoke made its way to her nostrils, through the flue of the chimney, she would descend upon them like an avalanche in whatever costume she happened just then to be." Wherefor Seward and his cigar were coaxed out into the street and kept promenading for an hour in astonished perplexity as to the cause of such inhospitable treatment. But, whatever Mrs. Greeley's oddities, she was a loyal and helpful wife, and the loss of her, just as her husband had failed in his last great political struggle, was too much to bear. "In the darkest hour my suffering wife left me, none too soon, for she had suffered too deeply and too long. I laid her in the ground with hard dry eyes." But the memory that lingers with one most is that she was "crazy for knowledge." What a profound and pitiable epitaph!

Work and the domestic affections — these seem to have been all of Greeley's life. It is remarkable how the other common interests of mankind were slighted or left out altogether. All the references to his boyhood agree that he had no taste for play, never cared to join in childish sports or amusements. He was fond of fishing, but, as his biographer remarks, he fished not for fun, but for fish. He did like to play checkers. Also, he played cards occasionally, though never for money and never on Sunday. But such things were a waste of time and rather to be frowned upon, and "he advised persons of sedentary habits to shun them because of the inevitable tendency to impair the digestion and incite headache." Beyond question the people of that generation took life seriously!

It was the same with all the more elaborate distractions which are supposed to divert maturer age. Travel? Oh, yes, the man traveled, but it is clear that he was always in a hurry, and always accumulating copy for the *Tribune*. Social life? If you got him with people whom he liked and let him have all the conversation, he would talk and talk well. But he had no taste for ordinary social gatherings, and avoided them, and did not appear to advantage in them. His dress was inappropriate, his manners were uncouth. Alcohol he never touched, and he discouraged others from touching it. As for tobacco, you can't say much more against it than this: "The chewing, smoking, or snuffing of tobacco has seemed to me, if not the most pernicious, certainly the vilest, most detestable abuse of his corrupted sensual appetites whereof depraved Man is capable." Whew!

What are usually considered more refined pleasures had little better luck with such an instinctive Puritan. He tolerated the fine arts and filled his house with pictures; but I doubt if he ever looked at them. Even nature, from the aesthetic point of view, meant little more to this ardent farmer than it does to most farmers: crops and bugs and manure always loomed larger than sunsets. The same was true of books. Greeley had been an enormous reader from childhood. He was always at a book or a newspaper, read in the woods, or on his way from school, or by the fireside at night. But while in youth he read anything that came handy, literature proper or anything else, his taste was wholly practical, and the practical was all he got from all he read. He wanted education to be practical, and preached that it should be so, wanted it to turn out farmers and artisans who should understand their business and like it. Colleges, which he had never frequented, seemed to him to be dangerous, or at least greatly in need of reform. "We must have seminaries which not merely provide work for their pupils, but require it inflexibly from all." Work, work, always work! No doubt work is an admirable thing; but when you pack life too full and solidly with it, something is bound to explode.

III

Yet the work in Greeley's case was certainly not for himself alone, nor, though it was eminently practical, was it by any means always material in its nature or aims. His mind was constantly busy, and often in abstract thinking, but always with a practical bearing and purpose. His intelligence was almost preternaturally quick and active, a swift sequence of skipping, frisking, cavorting thoughts, which kept both the inner and outer cosmos in a perpetual whirl. At the same time, the thinking was not always very logical or very deep. It was that of the self-made, self-taught man, who acquires knowledge readily and widely, but without much system or much exact training in its use.

Greeley did not gain control of his ideas; he lacked the capacity naturally, was erratic, easily led and misled, and duped by himself more often and more disastrously than he was ever duped by others.

In the more lofty regions of thought he counted for little or nothing. Religion did not trouble him much, or, in its higher emotional aspects, greatly concern him. When he was a child the darker phases of Calvinism repelled and distressed him. The old puzzle of an omnipotent God who made His creatures to suffer eternally would not let him rest. He finally solved the problem by adopting the comfortable doctrines of Universalism. The long and the short of it was that, as he said in later years, "I am so taken with the things of this world that I have too little time to spend on the affairs of the other." He was a faithful church-goer, but seemed to think that his bodily presence was the main essential, and allowed his mind to profit by the golden opportunity for sleep. "He generally stalked in rather early, the pockets of his long white coat filled with newspapers, and, immediately on taking his seat, went to sleep. As soon as the service began, he awoke, looked first to see how many vacant places were in the pew, and then, without a word, put out his long arm into the aisle and with one or two vigorous scoops, pulled in a sufficient number of strangers standing there to fill all the vacancies; then he slept again."

There you have the man: whatever benefits the church or anything else gave him must be shared with others, and the sharing was rather more important than the benefits. The side of religion that appealed to him was the practical, and the most fruitful field of labor for his vastly laborious spirit was work for others. His own personal benevolence was almost unlimited. He gave and especially he lent widely, freely — many persons thought, foolishly. Yet, if he was often duped, he was not fooled, that is, he fell into the trap with his eyes open, and knew that he was complying with Christian charity rather than with deserving need. And when a cause did not interest him or appeal to him, he could refuse with a decided petulance, and even with the curious coarse vigor of language which his wandering youth engrafted upon his age, as when he replied to the man who appealed for a subscription to "a cause which will prevent a thousand of our fellow-beings from going to hell," "I will not give you a cent. There don't half enough go there now."

IV

Greeley not only gave money, but advice, and in incredible measure. As a popular editor, the demands upon him in this regard were enormous, but he gladly spent his time and strength in meeting them. The advice was often roughly and broadly given, as in the celebrated "Go West, young man, go West!" or as in the more concrete story of the boy who had been living with his sister, had quarreled with her and left her, and came into the *Tribune* office to ask for assistance. Greeley kept on writing and did not even look up. "Is your sister married?" "Yes." "Is she respectable?" "Certainly, sir." "Go straight to your sister and tell her that you are ashamed of yourself, and ask her forgiveness. If she will take you, go back and live with her; and after this remember that if your own sister is not your friend, you will not be likely to find any friend in New York City." The boy went and Greeley kept on writing. He was too busy for gentleness, but his advice was sound and wholesome, and those who took it profited.

He was just as ready to advise the world at large, and his editorial employment gave him a magnificent opportunity for doing it. He had the essential qualities of the born reformer; the immense energy, the quick and ready, if superficial, sympathy, the unfailing enthusiasm, the limitless confidence in himself. Various reforms appealed to him — in fact, all reforms did, so long as they were practical and could be felt and touched. He wanted Prohibition, he wanted a reorganized education, he worked with tireless zeal for the abolition of slavery. But perhaps he was most constantly and consistently interested in improving the conditions of labor and the general status of the poor. It is curious to see him trumpeting all the nostrums and panaceas of our own day — and of a thousand years ago — in the middle of the last century, with the same familiar and eternal confidence and undying hope. It is true that he was in some respects moderate. He never urged any fundamental attack upon the rights of property. But he was fascinated by schemes of association, long and ardently advocated Fourierism, and believed that if men of all types and classes would only meet each other and work together in good faith the worst of human evils might be overcome. On the practical side it may at least be said that he anticipated much of the cooperative tendency under which social reform has actually made its most decided gains.

As he had the zeal of the born reformer, so he had the superb unfailing optimism. You can see it written in his face. The author of the "Essays of Elia" proposed to hire a stone-cutter to set up a monument engraved, "Here Charles Lamb loved his fellow men." Greeley needed no stone-cutter: he carried his monument with him, in those benignant features from which even thirty years of New York journalism could not erase the delightful rustic candor, in that fringe of sparse white whisker which always leaves one doubting between an inverted halo and a tonsorial negligence. He expressed his immense belief in the future and in humanity not only with his countenance but also with his pen: "I see no reason why the wildest dreams of the fanatical believer in Human Progress and Perfectibility may not ultimately be realized, and each child so trained as to shun every vice, aspire to every virtue, attain the highest practicable skill in Art and efficiency in Industry, loving and pursuing honest, untasked Labor for the health, vigor, and peace of mind thence resulting, as well as for its more palpable rewards, and joyfully recognizing in universal the only assurance of individual good." When a man carries such sentiments in his heart, he may surely be excused for wearing optimistic whiskers!

v

It was unavoidable that Greeley's philanthropy should draw him into practical politics, though it would have been far better for his reputation if this had not happened. On abstract political questions he always had a definite opinion and an energetic one. He early devoted himself to the extreme protectionist theory and worked for it to the end. His opposition to slavery in the fifties probably made him more friends than anything else, as well as more enemies, and in that earlier period he was a useful and effective agent. But when the Civil War broke out it was too much for him. He was distracted between humanity, love of the Union, hatred of slavery, hatred of war, and his general disposition to dictate to everybody in everything. First he was for letting the South go, then for prosecuting the war and emancipating the slaves; then, when the struggle dragged on, he was for making peace, by foreign mediation if necessary; then after it was all over, for forgiving everybody, especially Davis, whose bailbond he eagerly signed. Sometimes he pleaded with Lincoln, sometimes he bullied him, sometimes he rejected him as a poor creature. And always the *Tribune* was an enormous power in the country, which whirled millions after its vagaries, and forced the President to consider its editor, even when he could not agree with him. It is impossible not to contrast Greeley's flighty inconsistencies with Lincoln's deliberate and statesmanlike opportunism. Yet under all the inconsistencies we recognize the fundamental patriotic feeling and high-mindedness which Lincoln appraised when he wrote to Wilson, "I do not know how you estimate Greeley, but I consider him incapable of corruption or falsehood."

When it came to personal participation in political activity, Greeley was even less successful than in theorizing. It is clear that he was in no way adapted to direct political success. He had no magnetism at all, and it often seemed as if he had no manners. He irritated people and fretted them and rubbed them the wrong way. In those rough days this would often have resulted in personal conflict if he had been anything of a fighter. He was not. He had his courage, but it was of the passive order. When he was a boy, he would not stand up and fight. "When attacked, he would neither fight nor run away, but stand still and take it." And this was exactly what he did when he was attacked in Washington by a political enemy. He used his tongue savagely, without knowing it; he did not know how to use his fists, and did not care to.

Yet, with all these disqualifications, he was always eager for public office, always felt that he could be useful to his fellows there and always wanted the chance to prove it. His political desires and interests were much fostered by his association with Weed and Seward, the greatest political forces in the New York of that day. Weed early appreciated the value of Greeley's journalistic ability and made the most of it, but it soon became apparent that the qualities of a great editor were not necessarily those of a great administrator, and neither Weed nor his chief manifested any eagerness for getting their friend into office. Greeley resented this and finally broke off all relations in the well-known letter dissolving the partnership of Weed, Seward and Greeley; and his bitter opposition did as much as anything to prevent Seward from being nominated for the presidency in 1860. The episode as a whole did not make an agreeable phase of Greeley's career.

The only instance of his actually taking part in governmental work was when he was elected to fill an unexpired term in the House of

Representatives in 1848. His brief activity in Washington was bustling at any rate, if not glorious. He at once started a furious investigation of the mileage allowances for members of Congress, which was no doubt well intentioned and beneficial to the public service, but did not increase his personal popularity. In his congressional career, as in everything, you see his vigorous self-assertion, his genuine desire to do good to everybody, and his complete disregard for what happened to anybody's feelings in the process.

In 1872 Greeley was nominated for the presidency. Grant was the regular Republican candidate, but there had been much disapproval of his first term, and the discontented Republicans got together at Cincinnati and nominated Greeley, who was also later nominated by the Democrats. There was something so ludicrously inconsistent about this procedure that it made the campaign almost a farce, though a bitter one. Greeley had spent his life abusing the Southern slave-holders, and the absurdity and hollowness of their supporting him could hardly be veiled by any pretext of shaking hands across the bloody chasm. The contest was cruelly personal in many respects, and the savage efforts of the cartoonists, notably of Thomas Nast in opposition to Greeley, gave it a vivid grossness which has rarely been surpassed. Greeley was not only beaten, but overwhelmed. As he him-self expressed it, "I was the worst beaten man that ever ran for high office. And I have been assailed so bitterly that I hardly know whether I was running for the presidency or the penitentiary." The strain, the fatigue, and the fierceness of the struggle were too much for nerves already overworked, and within a month after his defeat Greeley was dead.

The element of ambition in his character has been a great deal dis-cussed and disputed. But it is evident that, like most of us, he wanted to succeed in whatever he undertook. He disclaimed political ambition, yet he felt that he had good ideas, great ideas, on governmental matters. The immense flattery that always waits upon popular editorship had to some extent turned his head, and he believed that he would make as good a President as another man, perhaps much better. What would have happened if he had been elected it is difficult to guess. High responsibility might have toned him down and made him practical and useful, but one has one's doubts. It is a familiar boast with our mothers that any American can get the presidency, and sometimes when one scans the long list of incumbents, one is tempted to think that any American *has* got it. Certainly many types have occupied the sacred chair, from genius to gentlemanly insignificance; but it is hard to think of any type, outside the State's prison, which is rather unfairly excluded, more incompatible with it than that of the fiery, versatile, garrulous, emotional, whimsical editor.

VI

All the same, he was a great editor. The cheap, popular newspaper came into prominence and power about the time he reached manhood, and he took to it naturally and completely. From childhood he wanted to be a printer, and he had a passion for reading the papers. As soon as he could get his elbows free from the fiercest necessity of self-support, he became an editor, first of the *New Yorker*, then of the political *Log Cabin*, then of the *Tribune*, which was the child of his effort and the mother of his reputation.

He grew as the paper grew, grew as journalism grew, grew as New York grew, developed daily and yearly in self-possession and self-assertion, if not in self-comprehension. On the merely business side of his undertaking he was not especially distinguished. I do not find his name associated with any of the mechanical discoveries which so greatly facilitated the dissemination of newspapers as the years went on, nor do I note that he was especially interested in them. Neither was he a great or successful financier. His magnificent thrift and self-control, his zealous and well-directed industry, enabled him to hold his own, even when unsupported. But the difficulties were enormous and almost overwhelmed him. He worked all day and nearly all night, drove everything and everybody about him. Yet even so, it was a struggle to keep the credit going and the bills paid. "I paid off everybody tonight, had $10 left, and $350 to raise on Monday. Borrowing places all sucked dry. I shall raise it, however." This, on a larger and larger scale, was the story, until McElrath came along and undertook the business management. It was the salvation of Greeley, and after that he had nothing to think of but his pen. The *Tribune* grew to be a vast investment, and its editor was always well provided for. True to his theories, he insisted on introducing cooperation, and the paper was early made into a stock company, with opportunity for all who worked for it to share in the ownership.

It does not appear that Greeley was particularly active in the advertising department, though he well understood the importance of it. What impressed him chiefly at the beginning was the danger of the advertising influence. Once allow yourself to be subsidized by rich and unscrupulous advertisers, what becomes of the independence of journalism? Godkin highly praises Greeley's earlier attitude: "He sacrificed everything, advertisers, subscribers, and all else, to what he considered principle." At a later date there came a change. The growth of business, the subtle and insinuating pressure of politics, forced Greeley to abandon his lofty position to some extent, never certainly in theory or in his own view, but distinctly in the unprejudiced opinion of others. His tolerance of the Tweed regime was as servile as that of the other papers, until the *Times* shook them all into unavoidable action. Here again, however, it is clear that Greeley was duped, partly by clever machinations, partly by his own ambition and enthusiasm.

The news in the paper was more in Greeley's province than the advertising. Here it is interesting to note his desire for and insistence upon accuracy. He was scrupulous as to form, emphasizing the importance of clear and readable English. He was scrupulous as to fact, at all times endeavoring to get a clear account of what really happened and then to stick to it. He condemned sensational journalism, even going so far as to say that the "violent hurt inflicted upon social order and individual happiness" by the lurid account of a murder involved greater guilt than that of the murderer himself, which is going pretty far, though perhaps not too far.

VII

But it was in the editorial columns that his main strength lay, and from the start he had an intense appreciation of the power that was just beginning to develop in the popular press and the future that lay before it. That power was completely a growth of the Nineteenth Century and it is doubtful whether anyone has yet analyzed its full nature and extent. To some persons its benefits and advantages must appear more questionable than they did to Greeley; there are certain evils which he was disposed to underrate or overlook. For instance, the American newspaper has been antireligious, not so much by direct attack, which is not usual, as in a subtle undermining of the influence of the church. Again, it is antisocial. Before it came, men got the news by word of mouth and had to find and meet each other to get it. Now you learn more by staying at home in quiet and silence: the newspaper unites communities, but separates individuals. Little drawbacks like these, however, were nothing in the enthusiasm which Greeley felt for the newspaper as a universal, democratic, educative force. When he was invited to go before an English parliamentary committee and discuss the subject of journalism, he told the committee that he considered the newspaper "worth all the schools in the country. I think it creates a taste for reading in every child's mind, and it increases his interest in his lessons."

Another proof of the man's indomitable optimism! But he at any rate did his best to make the editorial influence what he would have had it, to use it to develop and educate and bring out what was best and noblest in the American people, whom he labored in his way to serve with all his heart and all his energy. Listen to his summing up of editorial requisites: "An ear ever open to the plaints of the wronged and the suffering, though they can never repay advocacy, and those who mainly support newspapers will be annoyed and often exposed by it; a heart as sensitive to oppression and degradation in the next street as if they were practiced in Brazil or Japan; a pen as ready to expose and reprove the crimes whereby wealth is amassed and luxury enjoyed in our own country at this hour, as if they had only been committed by Turks or pagans in Asia some centuries ago." This is a high ideal for a journalist, and if Greeley did not always live up to it, he could hardly be expected to. He carried it in his heart, at any rate, which was something.

To be sure, his methods seem to us to have been singularly at variance, sometimes, with his standards. He had heard too much of a rough and brutal style of speech in his youth, and he never got over it. Coarse and ugly terms applied to adversaries with careless inconsideration never really help a cause, and Greeley was too prone to them. He used profanity in his private talk and the equivalent of profanity in his editorials. These things made hard feelings, sometimes even resulted in legal proceedings, as in the case of the celebrated Cooper libel suit. They were a disfigurement which cannot be overlooked.

At the same time, they came partly from the man's very qualities of power. Words were natural to him, and he poured them out almost unthinkingly, ugly as well as graceful, bitter as well as sweet. His style has been extravagantly praised by excellent judges, notably by Godkin. It seems to me diffuse and by no means of the highest literary quality; but it is certainly vivid and energetic. He had no humor, because he never had the humorous, detached view of life; everything was too intensely and immediately absorbing to him. But he had a quick apt wit in giving things a mocking or satirical turn, after the somewhat exaggerated fashion of Mark Twain. His intellectual powers, while they were, as we have seen, not profoundly penetrating, were quick and agile, and ready to turn at any moment to any subject. Above all, he was inexhaustible in fertility of argument, and had that splendid confidence in human reason, especially his own, which some of us are born without, but which seems to be almost indispensable to the successful editor. He liked to argue, actually enjoyed it, would argue about anything. He liked opposition, liked to have people differ from him: it gave him a chance to show and especially to feel his own power. And he was reluctant to give up an opinion; he hated above all things to own that he was wrong.

With these editorial qualities he endeared himself to the vast masses of the American people and became perhaps the most notable of all the great personal editors of the middle of the Nineteenth Century. The personal element in the handling of a paper seems now, for various reasons, largely to have passed away. Curiously enough, the personal was intimately bound up with the impersonal. Beyond question what gave the editorial columns their singular power was chiefly their anonymity. You might laugh at Jones's opinion, or Smith's; but the editor's — that was different! The large type and the lack of signature somehow seemed to compel respect. So, though you knew it was Horace Greeley, he of the white coat and old hat, who was writing, his editorial words seemed to get a larger significance. And the impersonality at once developed egotism and was benefited by it. You could not help feeling yourself a big man when you were swaying the minds of millions; and the bigger you felt yourself, the more you swayed.

VIII

Some such feeling of almost godlike consequence certainly informed and inspired the soul of Horace Greeley, and he carried round with him in later years the sense of personifying one of the greatest forces and achievements of his century. This is clearly seen in the striking passage in which he describes his relation to his journal: "Fame is a vapor; popularity an accident; riches take wings; the only earthly certainty is oblivion; no man can foresee what a day may bring forth; while those who cheer today will often curse tomorrow; and yet I cherish the hope that the journal I have projected and established will live and flourish long after I shall have mouldered into forgotten dust . . . and that the stone which covers my ashes may bear to future eyes the still intelligible inscription, 'Founder of the New York *Tribune*'."

It must be admitted, as Greeley himself admitted, that the glory belonging to his journalistic enterprise was of a somewhat ephemeral character; it was like that of the actor or the athlete, immense for the moment and immediately savored, but transitory and fast-fading as a dream. Yet when one looks about one at the enormous flood of literary production, and realizes how slight is the chance of any slow or careful work, or any hidden genius, ever making its way to permanence through such a throng of competitors, one wonders whether perhaps, after all, immediate renown, like Greeley's, is not better than the effort to create a masterpiece which posterity may or may not worship. Only most of us would rather cherish the hope of the masterpiece!

At any rate, Greeley made the *Tribune*, and swayed America, and passed away. In his solemn and impressive funeral all antagonisms were forgotten. The New York papers, which a month before had been ready to put him in jail, united in eulogy, and the President, the Vice-President, and the Vice-President-elect rode in one carriage behind the hearse. It was only fair that these honors should be extended to his end; for the poor man was dead before the breath was out of his body, utterly and finally dead. Shakespeare tells us that

> The evil that men do lives after them,
> The good is oft interred with their bones.

Greeley had done no evil, or none to speak of, and the good he did, extensive and indisputable as it was, was not of a character to outlive him very long.

V

POST CIVIL WAR: A PRESS IN TRANSITION

~~~~~~

BY THE *1870s the immediate issues of the Civil War had been settled, southern reconstruction was beginning to assume the intelligent, humanitarian aspect President Lincoln had desired, and the North and West were well started on a period of dynamic economic expansion. In the years between Appomattox and the turn of the century the developing forces of industrialization and mechanization transformed American society and welded a new nation. Railroads crossed the plains and broke up old frontier lines, millions of immigrants poured into the industrial centers and out onto the fertile acres of the Middle West, urban population mounted at the expense of the rural areas, and American inventive ability produced farm and factory machinery vital to the development of the national resources.*

While the United States was thus undergoing a transition from a largely agrarian economy to the era of "big business," its journalism was keeping pace in response to pressures of socio-economic change. Introduction of the Linotype and the typewriter, perfecting of printing by stereotype plates, and improvement in the speed and quality of presses were mechanical factors of great significance, making possible the production of mass-circulated newspapers which found increasing reader and advertiser support. Telegraph, telephone, and cable were utilized to speed and improve the gathering of news. More complete and more impartial news reporting, and growing independence of editorial opinion from partisan pressures, were journalistic trends in keeping with the times.

During the period when the established New York City newspapers were adapting themselves to the post Civil War era, new publishers and editors were appearing in that city. Greeley was followed on the

Tribune *by Whitelaw Reid; James Gordon Bennett, Jr., had succeeded his father on the* Herald; *Charles A. Dana had acquired the* Sun *and was beginning its rejuvenation. In 1881 Henry Villard, who had won fame as a correspondent in the Civil War, bought the* New York Evening Post *and entrusted its editorial direction to a triumvirate consisting of Carl Schurz, Edwin Lawrence Godkin, and Horace White.*

E. L. Godkin and a number of associates had earlier founded in New York one of America's most influential journals of opinion. That journal was the Nation. *Godkin sensed the need in the United States for a politically and economically independent periodical, one which would make its chief appeal to the intellectual readers of the country. The years Godkin spent guiding the* Nation *were an invaluable apprenticeship for the wider editorial leadership which he later enjoyed as editor of the* Post. *It is this latter aspect of Godkin's career that provides the subject matter for Henry Pringle's article, "Godkin of the* Post."

By looking at Godkin in New York, Samuel Bowles in Springfield, Massachusetts, Henry Watterson in Louisville, Henry W. Grady in Atlanta, and William Rockhill Nelson in Kansas City, it is possible to get a reasonably accurate cross section of America's able editorship during this period of transition.

Throughout its years of service to western Massachusetts and the country in general, the Springfield Republican *had no abler or more devoted editor than Samuel Bowles III. Founded in the 1820s as a weekly by the second Sam Bowles, the* Republican *was turned over to Sam III in 1844. During more than thirty years, years encompassing one of America's most tempestuous and crucial periods, Bowles directed the destiny of the* Republican. *"He was," writes Gamaliel Bradford in his article on Bowles, "a journalist who grew as his paper grew. . . . In 1844, at eighteen years of age, a country boy, he took hold of his father's weekly country paper, the* Springfield Republican, *and before he died, he made it one of the most intelligent and valuable dailies in the United States."*

It was a mark of journalistic distinction to have worked on the staff of the Springfield Republican; *it was equally noteworthy to have worked for Henry Watterson's* Louisville Courier-Journal. *"Marse Henry," as he was affectionately called by fellow Kentuckians and members of his profession, edited newspapers for more than half a century; too long thinks Henry Pringle, who writes at the beginning of his article on Watterson: "We shall not see his like again and it is just as well. For Marse Henry Watterson, although he ranted against Wall Street and the extreme reactionaries, was a conservative at heart and he would, I am afraid, have viewed modern America with explosive alarm and disgust." Perhaps Watterson's greatest service to his country as an editor was the influence he wielded in both North and South on behalf of sane, forward-looking reconstruction policies in the 1870s.*

Not so picturesque as Colonel Watterson but acknowledged to be one of the South's outstanding newspapermen was Henry W. Grady of the Atlanta Constitution. *His fame extended far beyond the borders of Georgia. With the aid of such able and beloved colleagues as Joel Chandler Harris, he used the columns of the* Constitution *with tremendous effect to turn the South in the direction of intellectual and economic rehabilitation. Not only was he an editor of note but, as Raymond B. Nixon points out, he was a great reporter. He was a man of ideas and an accomplished public speaker, but it was the wide and perceptive news coverage of the* Constitution *under his editorship which brought to that paper its country-wide fame. Fittingly, Mr. Nixon closes his article with one of Grady's last editorial utterances: "A good reporter who subsides into an able editor marks a loss to journalism."*

A happy blending of subject and writer is found in the article on William Rockhill Nelson written by William Allen White, shortly after death took the founder of the Kansas City Star. *White's warmth and felicity of style not only convey an eminently readable impression of Nelson, his friend of many years' standing, they also give considerable insight into the personality of White himself.*

Before the "transition" editors had bowed out, a new trend was emerging, the period of "the newspaper as Leviathan," as Frank Luther Mott has termed it. Coming to the front along with Grady and Nelson as pioneers of the new journalism were publishers like Pulitzer, Hearst, and Scripps, who would work for larger and more intensive circulations and who would become the press giants of a corporate journalism — press giants of a different type than the individualistic editors like Godkin, Bowles, Watterson, Grady, and Nelson, whose editorial voices had brought them fame.

14

Samuel Bowles

by GAMALIEL BRADFORD

The Bostonian author GAMALIEL BRADFORD was particularly interested in the influential figures of nineteenth-century America. This study of a great Massachusetts editor, Samuel Bowles III of *Springfield Republican* fame, appeared in the *Atlantic Monthly*, October 1915, as one of a series later collected in a book, *Union Portraits*.

IT SEEMS highly suitable to conclude a series of Union Portraits with a study of one of the great journalists who played so important a part during the war and the years preceding and following. Several of these men have wider reputations than Samuel Bowles, but perhaps hardly any was more singly and intensely identified with his work. Weed and Greeley had an active personal interest in politics. Dana was a valuable public servant as well as an editor. Garrison was something far different from a mere newspaper man. Bennett was confessedly a money-maker. Raymond was, indeed, a thorough journalist; and Godkin also, one of the highest type; but Godkin was, after all, not born an American, though perhaps of more use to us on that account. Then, I confess that what draws me chiefly to Bowles is that no other journalist — and few other men of his time — has left us so complete, vivid, and passionately human a record of himself.

He was a journalist who grew as his paper grew. He had little more education than that of simple New England home life. In 1844, at eighteen years of age, a country boy, he took hold of his father's weekly country paper, the *Springfield Republican*, and before he died, he made it one of the most intelligent and valuable dailies in the United States, "the most comprehensive paper," declared the *Nation*, at the time of his death, "we believe it is no exaggeration to say, in the country." And a good authority asserted: "No American journal during the last ten or twenty years has been more diligently studied by editors."

There was always, to be sure, about the paper, as about its editor, a certain spice of provincialism, or, as he would have put it, localism. But those who know the old-fashioned New England country towns will admit that their atmosphere may be far broader and less fundamentally provincial than that of larger centres. There was fifty years ago — perhaps there is to-day — some truth in this provincial editor's jibe at the metropolis of his state: "Always except Boston, of course, which has no more conception of what is going on in the world than the South Sea Islanders themselves."

Bowles's whole life, outside of his family affections, was in his paper, and he saw the world and mankind through his paper's eyes. Every department was always under his immediate supervision, and he interested himself as much in the advertising and business management as in the editorials.

When he began work, modern possibilities of news were just developing, and he seized upon them eagerly. In the early days he himself reported, with keen observation and that journalistic sense of what counts which is more than observation; and he was always on the lookout for capable reporters. "News," he said, "is the distinctive object of the *Republican,* to which all other things must bend." Some thought he was not over-particular about the news he printed or the means of obtaining it. Even his ardent biographer, Merriam, admits that he sometimes appeared to cater to an unhealthy curiosity; and the ill-natured review of Merriam in the *Nation,* said to be by W. P. Garrison, calls Bowles "a great gossip and by no means a safe confidant." Yet he would certainly not have subscribed without reserve to the rather generous principle of Dana: "I have always felt that whatever the Divine Providence permitted to occur I was not too proud to report" — just as Dana himself might have shrunk from some later developments of his own doctrine, though indeed the chief error of these is apt to consist in reporting what even the Divine Providence did not permit to occur.

But, however vast his appetite for news, Bowles would have been the first to recognize that the newspaper had another function besides mere reporting — that of commenting on news and shaping public opinion in regard to it. How important this function is can best be realized by reflecting that it did not exist at all a hundred years ago, and that even now it hardly exists elsewhere as it does in America. Up to the nineteenth century the pulpit did what the newspaper now does. The minister had the leading, because he had the reading, of the community. He commented on the world's doings in the light of the moral law, and men went away and saw God's finger in everything. Just how far the daily and Sunday papers have undermined the influence of the pulpit, who shall say? They have certainly taken the place of it, with some gain in universal information, but with enormous moral loss. "This country is not priest-ridden, but press-ridden," said Longfellow shrewdly. With the best will in the world — and I believe such will is seldom altogether wanting — the editor has many matters to consider besides moral elevation; and even if he wishes to furnish such a thing, he is not always competent to do so. When we read the words of Bowles, "The church organization seems to me a failure — at least that we have outgrown it, or are fast outgrowing it," and think, as he no doubt thought, of the newspaper as supplying the church's place, we should remember the weighty remark of Godkin in regard to the defects and dangers of journalism, "defects and dangers which nearly every one sees but editors, and which it would be well if editors saw oftener — the recklessness, haste, indifference to finish and accuracy and abstract justice which is apt to beget in the minds of those who pursue it, and especially of those who pursue it eagerly."

No one would have recognized these defects in general more heartily than Bowles. But no one was more earnest in insisting upon the power of the press as guide and leader. A *Republican* editorial, written during the war, which we may assume to be his, proclaims, "With all its failings, with all its prostitutions, the press is the great reliance and safeguard in a time like this, and with a government like ours. And we believe it mainly appreciates its opportunities and responsibilities and is earnest to fulfill them." He, at any rate, was earnest, and he did his very best to make a paper that should bring him an honest livelihood and should at the same time be a great and inspiring influence in public affairs, should consider the public good only, should be conservative with the radicals and progressive with the conservatives, should regard principles and not parties, measures and not men, and should follow truth without the slightest care for a merely formal consistency.

This is a high ideal for a newspaper or anything else in this imperfect world; and it is needless to say that the *Republican*, having an editor who was thoroughly human, did not always live up to it. It is a fine thing to avoid extremes, but in doing so you are sure to become obnoxious to all extremists. Hence the *Republican*, in its thirty years' development during Bowles's life, got plenty of shrewd knocks from all parties in succession. It is a fine thing to be independent. Unfortunately complete independence is impossible. There are so many cross twists and conflicting considerations to be taken into account, that at times independence may be taken for discretion; and Garrison could even go so far as to say of his able competitor that as a politician "he was essentially timid and time-serving." Again, it is a fine thing to scorn consistency. Emerson did, and why should not Sam Bowles? "It is no trouble at all to me," he says, "that the paper contradicts itself. My business is to tell what seems to me the truth and the news to-day. It's a daily journal. I am not to live to be as old as Methuselah, and brood in silence over a thing till, just before I die, I think I have it right." The excuse is fascinating certainly, but the practice is likely to have its difficulties.

These difficulties showed in nothing more than in the *Republican*'s — and its editor's — delusions as to men. One hero after another — Banks, Dawes, Colfax, Greeley, not to mention others — was set up and urged upon the public, till Time stowed them all neatly away in that vast wallet which contains his tribute to oblivion. Andrew, wrote Bowles, in 1861, "is conceited, dogmatic, and lacks breadth and tact for government"; Lincoln "is a 'simple Susan'." These are things that a man — or a newspaper — would rather not have said.

II

But such criticisms do not alter the fact that during all those trying, bitter, passionate years the *Republican* stood earnestly for the best, the highest things, and was in every way and at every point alive. If it was so, it was because Samuel Bowles was as thoroughly alive as any man who ever put pen to paper to describe the doings and sufferings of this intricate world. He had his faults and weaknesses; but sloth and inertia and indifference were not among them.

All his life, the man's whole soul, are reflected in the letters contained in his biography, which are much more significant than his formal books of travel, or even his editorials. It is a great pity that his correspondence has not been collected and published separately, for in my judgment no more telling, varied, human letters have been written upon this side of the Atlantic.

Dead letters do not mean dead souls. There are souls touched with the keenest intensity of living that either cannot or will not reveal themselves in correspondence with even their most intimate friends. Take as an instance the letters of Matthew Arnold. Here assuredly was a man of the widest thought and the subtlest spiritual experience. Yet he writes almost wholly of practical affairs, in a dull conventional strain, which has no claims to attention except those of undeniable simplicity and sincerity. But letters alive as those of Bowles must certainly indicate a burning heart behind them. Take the verve of a scrap from one of the earlier. "Croak, croak, croak! Why the devil can't Berkshire do something besides? Let those who are right go to work." Nor is it any way a matter of mere slang or expletives. These fly freely when they add force or color, but there is plenty of force and color without them. There is grace and sparkle in the adjectives; there is delicate suggestion in the sweep of the phrases; there is, above all, the cunning, instinctive use of rhythm to charm, to spur, to stimulate, which is perhaps the most effective instrument of the great prose writer. "I should chiefly regret Aiken of this lot. I have imbibed a good deal of respect for that man. Ben Butler says he is an exaggeration of the stage Yankee; but he is fresh and hearty, and keen and human, and says civil things about me — and of course I like him." When letters run on like that, through two stout volumes, we are bound to learn something of the man that writes them.

First, he was a man of the deepest, tenderest affection and devotion. He married very young a girl who was very young, and their attachment through early years of struggle and later years of illness is charming to study and appreciate. They had ten children, which naturally means care, especially for a worker of limited means and nervous temperament. The difference of sex gleams vividly in the father's casual remark concerning the death of one of these children at birth: "She [Mrs. Bowles] feels her loss terribly. Though a disappointment, it is a small matter to me, only as it affects her."

Yet the most watchful care and solicitude for both mother and children are everywhere apparent, a care that was duly and lovingly returned. The husband's full appreciation of all he received shows in this passage, referring to a journey proposed for his benefit: "Of course

Mrs. Bowles is always ready to say go; you know how she would give up any gratification, or endure any suffering, to give me a pleasure, or get me out of the way of a half-day of work. But that doesn't make it always right that I should take her at her word—by no means." While his constant anxiety for the welfare of the woman he adored appears characteristically and delightfully in a letter laying down a minute programme of what she should do for her health every hour in the day: the meals, the air, the exercise, the society. "Have somebody come to see you every day. Read newspapers more. Read light books more. Study things that make for fun and peace." And we know, and he knew, that nobody ever obeys such injunctions. But to give them eases the tired heart of love in solitude. As for his children, his care of them was guided by this exquisite precept, which would save a world of woe if it were written on every parent's heart: "It is not much that I can do for my children, but I never want to lose sight of myself at their ages—then the little I do can be done more intelligently."

Nor was his family affection all care and solicitude. As to his children, listen to this pretty rapture on one of the ten in infancy: "He is practicing on *Yes* and *Mamma*; but all his efforts at the latter melt sweetly into *Papa*—so ravishingly." And the following delicate discrimination proves the thoughtful study of enduring tenderness: "We are all pretty well; Ruth is a breeze from the northwest, and Dwight from the south, all the while; Bessie is dainty and shy and quiet and strange, and Charlie enterprising beyond his power."

As for the depth of conjugal devotion, it is shown so profoundly and so searchingly all through the book, that passages are difficult to choose. I select one not addressed to Mrs. Bowles, that, underneath its general analysis of emotion, implies personal experience of the deepest and most intimate character:

You must give if you expect to receive—give happiness, friendship, love, joy, and you will find them floating back to you. Sometimes you will give more than you receive. We all do that in some of our relations, but it is as true a pleasure often to give without return as life can afford us. We must not make bargains with the heart, as we would with the butcher for his meat. Our business is to give what we have to give—what we can get to give. The return we have nothing to do with. It will all come in due time—in this world or another.

As these words indicate, Bowles's sympathy and tenderness extended far beyond the family circle. Indeed they were as wide as the world. He has observation just as subtle and delicate on unselfishness and sacrifice as on positive affection. "We, unfortunately, know our failures, and, alas, how well we know them. And yet, out of our very selfishness, out of our very neglect, God buildeth us up; so that what we do perform for kindred and friends takes on larger power and gives deeper bliss than if in a narrow way we had given more hours and thought and service to the beloved. It is a shadowy, tender line between service to ourselves and service to others."

It is true that this is a newspaper man, who looked at life from the journalistic angle, which is not always strictly humanitarian. To be sure, even as an editor his keen, delightful sympathies often warm his impersonal comment, as when he writes of a deceased celebrity, "Years and invalid experience have unlocked for us some of the mysteries of his life; we know him better lately without seeing him at all." But it is also said that his zeal for news sometimes led to disastrous revelations, as when he stopped prize-fighting in Springfield by printing the names of respected citizens who had patronized it; while in other cases his methods were less justified by results.

In private life Bowles's kindness was by no means confined to theory or sentiment. There is clear record of many deeds of broad generosity and covert indication of many more. Perhaps the most touching is recorded in the last words written by him to his wife, before sailing for Europe in search of health, when money was none too abundant and other prospects were dreary enough: "———— has just come to say good-bye. He will write you. He accepts our offer. I am very glad of it. Now send him and ———— the money regularly, and tell nobody."

There are little kindnesses, little matters of thoughtfulness, which often mean more than money, and certainly endear more. In these Bowles was admirably proficient, because he had the instinct for them. And there is no occasion when such kindnesses are more needed, more appreciated, and more difficult than during travel. General Walker, an admirable judge, who was with Bowles for some months in England, testifies to his exceptional qualities in this direction. He was always thoughtful of others, enjoyed every minute of their pleasures, and was much more anxious to discover what his young companions wished to see, than to see anything himself.

In short, he was an eminently social being. This is evident from the

184

first page of his biography to the last. It is true that he had his times of reserve and repression, times when he did not seem to welcome even friends. Such times must come to every man who lives a busy, eager, crowded inner life. "Why," he said to one of his acquaintances, "why don't people clap me on the shoulder, with a 'How are you, old fellow?' as they do you?" "Because," was the answer, "you go along with a look that says, 'Keep away from me, d———n you!'" But the very pathos of the query shows a longing for human contact and fellowship and intimacy, and this pathetic longing is especially apparent in Bowles's exclamations of solitude and loneliness when he is traveling and among strangers. Busy as his thoughts were, they did not give him sufficient companionship. If he had a delightful experience, he wanted a friend to share it. If he had a bitter experience, he wanted a friend to take away the sting.

The intense human interest undoubtedly served him well in the business of his life. Nobody profits more by human contact than the journalist. To Bowles the wide world was, in a sense, fodder for his paper. He talked with men of all types and occupations, gathered ideas from the professor and the mechanic, from the farmer and the lawyer, from the fine lady and the ditchdigger in the street. He carried to perfection the delicate art of listening, and knew how to make his own speech serve to elicit the speech and the inmost thought of others.

At the same time, in doing this he was no hypocrite, did not seek men's company with any cold design of betraying their confidence, did not scoff at or deride them. If he mingled freely and widely with his fellows, it was first of all because he loved to do so, loved the touch of the human hand and the sound of the human voice. It was this spontaneous and constant humanity which made his presence so widely sought in all societies. Senator Dawes wrote, after Bowles's death, "I never knew a man who knew him who wouldn't rather have him at his table than any other man in the world."

Even in illness and decay, when most of us prefer to brood alone over disappointment and failure, this same charming social instinct found utterance in one of those delightful passages which are in themselves complete lyric poems. "I was sure you would have a pleasant summer with the Haskells. They are dreadful good fellows, both of them. But I couldn't have kept up with your gait. I am the chap for 'the bank where the wild thyme grows,' with one other fellow, male or female, lying in the sunshine, picking flowers to pieces and discoursing on the frivolity of things we cannot do."

The distinction, or indistinction, of sex in this passage is characteristic; for among Bowles's multitude of friends there were many women. His relations with them seem to have been wholly intellectual, and I see no reason to suppose that Mrs. Bowles had ever any cause for jealousy. But his quick, light, active spirit naturally responded to a woman's gaiety and sensitiveness, and he sought them, wanted them, missed them. At Baden-Baden he writes, "There are no women to chaff with, and to rub your mind out of its morbidity." None of his letters are more varied, more charming, more full of fresh and vivid interest than those he writes to Miss Whitney. At one moment he laughs with her over some trifle, some new fashion or folly, at the next he is discussing the future of democracy or the welfare of his soul.

It appears that with women he was always perfectly easy and natural; that he did not stand in awe of them or regard them as in any way different. Says one lady of his visits, "He used to come in for a few moments, on his way back and forth between his home and his office, and would perhaps sit with both legs hanging over the arm of a chair, his hat low down over his eyes, and talk *sarse*, as he called it." Also, he did not abstain from that affectionate criticism which one sex always feels privileged to bestow upon the other. "Women are fascinating creatures; yet it is treading upon eggs all the time to deal with them." And again, in his extraordinarily careless, vivid fashion, "Traveling with women sops up one's time awfully."

But we have the testimony of the most intelligent men and women both, that this ease and occasional apparent flippancy did not spring from indifference or contempt. "I hardly ever saw any one give just the sort of recognition to a woman that he did," says one male friend, "treating her as an equal, yet with a kind of chivalrous deference, suggested rather than expressed." And a woman has rarely paid finer tribute to a man than has Miss Brackett to him: "Of all the men I have ever known, he was the only one who never made a woman feel as if he were condescending in thought or word when he talked to her."

III

I have not meant to emphasize Bowles's social qualities at the expense of his intellectual, for it is the latter that make him most interesting now and that account for most of his achievement, though here also the social did its part. He was not a profound or elaborate thinker on abstract questions, did not pretend to be. In all matters of practical morals and the conduct of life he had very energetic and decided opinions and proclaimed them in his letters and in his paper, perhaps not always logically or consistently, but always with a manifest intention of promoting the good in the world. He liked to preach and believed that he did it better than a good many parsons, in which he was certainly right. "Nor do I see any other line of influence or noble effort in this world except in behalf of ideals." What could be more touching or more significant of a life passed with high aims than his last words to Dawes, "Drop on your knees, Dawes, and thank God that you have done a little good in the world, and ask his forgiveness that you have done no more."

Also, as time served, he liked to wrestle with great spiritual problems. "Without philosophy," he wrote, "there is vastly little of life but a passion and a struggle." The long letter written to Miss Whitney in January, 1862, is an intensely curious analysis of religious and speculative theories, the earnest effort of a mind not schooled by abstract thought to disentangle the complex web of human longing and passion and despair. Of almost equal interest is the letter to Mrs. Bowles expressing a humble desire to conform to her religious observances, even when he could not himself wholly enter into them.

Yet the attitude generally is one of groping, not a sad or morbid groping, but a willingness to leave to God the things that are God's, while working day and night at the task which God has set us to be done in this world. The whole nature of the man leaps out in one of those splendid phrases that he had the secret of coining: "It is comforting to *people with free and vagrant heads* to feel that there is a Christianity back of and without Christ, and to which he seems rather interpreter and disciple than founder." (The italics are mine.)

A free and vagrant head! That is what gives Bowles much of his charm, and he himself prized that freedom far above what any conventional education could have afforded him. For he had no academic discipline, and very little of school; he got what learning he possessed from the touch of human heads and hearts and the careful contemplation of his own. "His lack of early training was never compensated by self-culture or wise reflection," says Garrison, scornfully. This is far too severe. At the same time, it is curious to consider that a man who was all his life a guide to the public through written words should have been so little conversant with the written words of others. Bowles's reading was mainly newspapers; and newspapers, though good seasoning, are not very substantial diet for the intellect.

Bowles himself was keenly aware of his deficiencies. Indeed, as regards style and literary quality, he was far too humble. "The book made itself," he says of one of his volumes of travel; "it is a newspaper book; I am a newspaper writer, and not a book writer; and I do not aspire to be other than I am." Again: "I was afraid you would think it [an editorial] a little overwrought, and not low-toned enough for the subject. That is where I always err in my work; it gives it something of its power and charm with the mass of readers; it loses for it something of the impression on the select and superior few." And as he criticised his own writing, so he often lamented his lack of leisurely reading, of wide contact with the best thought and experience of humanity. When he traveled in Europe, art meant little to him, historical association meant little to him. He sighs for time and strength to think, to adjust himself to the larger current of the world, to get out of the mad, exhausting whirl of news, more news, which makes the passing passions of the hour seem out of all proportion to the permanent interests of life. Yet even in these longings, books, the distillation of human activity, do not take first place. "I would roam about the world, studying books some, nature a good deal, and people and institutions more."

For the man was above all a worker and liver. It was just the "free and vagrant head" that made his life so joyously abundant and his paper so forcible. His intelligence may not have been profound, but it was splendid in its vigor, its energy, its variety, its speed. How direct and frank it was, profiting by its very self-training to brush away old convention and the dry bones of formal futility! Has he to congratulate a friend on a congressional victory? "It is not statesmanship, and you know it. But it is all of statesmanship, I frankly admit, that the present Congress is up to." Do fools torment him with old saws about dead reputations? "I hate the '*Nil de mortuis,*' etc. What do men die for, except that posterity may impartially judge, and get the full benefit of their example?"

So in his business. He wanted no shirkers, no drivelers, no fuss, no make-believe. He exacted work — faithful, earnest, driving work. He was in a sense a severe task-master, having sharp reproof at his command, when necessary, not in stormy verbosity, but in just the word or two that find a joint and put a barb in it. He insisted upon exactness, nicety, finish, and set a high standard of mechanical production in days when there were fewer facilities than at present.

But he knew how to make work easy, so far as it ever can be. His office was systematized. Each man had his task, was taught how and when to do it and by whom it was to be controlled and criticised when done. And if the chief could reprove, he could also encourage. Sharp words were lightened by a touch of the quick, sympathetic humor that was natural to him. Words of praise were rare, but they meant something when they came, and power of achievement in any special line was quickly discerned and energetically supported.

Moreover, work was urged on by the most powerful stimulus of all, example. This was no man to set wheels a-going and then watch them whirl at his leisure. From his journeyman days to the last minute when work was possible, and longer, he labored with all that was in him. "What with forty-two hours' continuous work Tuesday and Wednesday and Thursday, without sleep, and getting over it, I had not time to write to you," is one of his casual, significant comments. Work was his life, writes one who knew him intimately. We have seen the depth of his domestic affection. Yet in a sense it would be just to say that for thirty years the *Springfield Republican* was wife and child and food and sleep to him. It certainly robbed him of any complete enjoyment of all these things, though it also made his enjoyment of them keener. Even his recreation had usually storm and fury in it. He liked a horse, but he cared nothing for looks or pedigree. What he wanted was speed. An acquaintance, who had studied this phase, said of him, "He was fonder of reckless driving than any man I ever knew." Then, though rarely, he would relax and drop into absolute quiescence. As he lay one afternoon on the piazza, with the apple-blossoms blowing over him, he murmured, "This, I guess, is as near heaven as we shall ever get in this life."

For, as you see, he was a mere bundle of nerves, the quintessence of our sun- and wind-driven New England temperament, whose life is work, whose death is work, whose heaven is work, whatsoever other heaven we may dream of. You can read it written on his spare, energetic figure, on his sensitive, strained, wistful forehead; above all, in his intense and eager eyes. It was the quick, responsive nerves that enabled him to do the work he did, that gave him passionate joys and passionate sorrows. Even when the nerves are disordered and tormenting, he recognizes their value with wonderfully subtle analysis. "There is a certain illumination with the disorder that is enchanting at times." He is determined that they shall be his servants, not his masters. Now he lays whip and spur to them, forces them to do and overdo, till a set task is accomplished. Again he restrains them, lives by rule and system, makes schedules of food, schedules of hours. These exuberant sensibilities are splendid things, so you control them. "Sympathies and passions are greater elements of power than he admits. All they want is to have judgment equal to and directing them. No matter how powerful, how acute they are — the more so the better. But sympathies and passions that run away with us are oftener a curse than a blessing." He thinks he has controlled them, declares he has. "You must remember I have necessarily schooled myself to coolness and philosophy, and to the look ahead. Otherwise my life would have killed me years ago."

But such control, especially when carried beyond the normal, is a wearing, exhausting process, and is sure in the end to bring a penalty. Bowles, with his "look ahead," knew this perfectly well and faced it always. When a friend warned him of what was inevitably coming, he answered with these striking words: "I know it just as well as you do. When my friends point out that I am working toward a breakdown, they seem to think that is to influence my action. Not at all! I have got the lines drawn, the current flowing, and by throwing my weight here now, I can count for something. If I make a long break or parenthesis, to get strong, I shall lose my chance. No man is living a life that is worth living, unless he is willing to die for somebody or something — at least to die a little!"

Admirable words, and perhaps wise, though not for all, nor at all times. Dying a little is not always conveniently managed at discretion, nor even dying a great deal. And Bowles's disregard and positive abuse of his nerves not only killed him at fifty-two, but caused him and all who loved him infinite distress and misery before that time. He perfectly understood the cause of his troubles. "My will has carried me for years beyond my mental and physical power; that has been the offending rock." Again, "Nobody knows how I have abused my brain but myself, and I therefore ought to be the most patient with its maladies."

But to know the cause and to find the cure, are far, far, different. Therefore, from a very early stage, his life was made up alternately of extravagant effort at home to do more than he or any one man could do, and then of forced change and travel to procure that renovation which could come only — or at any rate could come far better — from within by the acquired habit of repose.

Repose, peace, and the tranquil sleep that should go with them — these were the remedies, the blessings that Bowles sought far and wide, up and down, for thirty years. He told Mr. Howells in Venice that he was sleeping only one hour out of the twenty-four. Sometimes he slept more than that, but he never slept enough. Modern medical methods might have helped him a little. The advice he had was well meant, but now sounds strange. "Kill a horse, and it will do you good." He might have killed a dozen horses, but black care would none the less have buzzed and snarled about his ears.

Peace! Peace! Not Clarendon's Falkland could more longingly ingeminate the word. Perhaps Bowles knew so little about it that he overestimated its blessings. "I never saw in his face," said a friend, "the expression of repose — the look was always of fire or tire." But even Clarendon wrote few things more striking than this paragraph on peace in heaven, though the quality is not Clarendon's:

I wonder whether we shall have such weather in heaven! whether or no we go — whether or no such weather. But if the world lives much longer it will have abolished all these whims of its youth. The Unitarians came, and abolished hell; Parker came, Higginson stays, to abolish Christ; the next conceited set of upstarts to invent a new elixir of life, out of gin and juniper berries, will probably supersede heaven, or bring it down to earth. But that is what the rest of us dream of doing — but it can't be done so long as nerves thrill and stomachs labor. No elixir of love, or gin, can make heaven, with neuralgia playing on the fiddles of the orchestra, and dyspepsia groaning through the grim trombone. Give it up. I think I will stick to the original heaven as a thing more sure.

Nerves so thoroughly and constantly jangled could not fail to produce some unfortunate results in practical life. However perfect the control, there was irritability that would break out at times. Bowles often refers to being thoroughly cross and out of sorts, sometimes in a mood of discouragement, sometimes with his whimsical grace and fancy. Others refer to it also. In his home, with those he cherished, breaks of temper seem to have been rare; but in his office, though he was much admired and much beloved, he was regarded with a good deal of awe.

And the jangled nerves brought hours of depression and temporary hopelessness. He sometimes refers to these, expressing them with his really wonderful gift of telling phraseology. "I did not mount my great heights of *abandon*; perhaps it is better described in your own sad words as a '*wise despair*'." Take, again, this passage of extraordinary self-analysis, written to Mrs. Bowles, and doubly striking from a man so schooled by persistent discipline to courage and hope:

Mary, don't let my fretful, downcast moods annoy you. They are unworthy of me and I ought to rise above them, and control them. But sometimes they master and overpower me. I want to give it all up sometimes. Nobody can understand the spell that is upon me. It cannot be described — it doesn't seem as if anybody else can ever feel it. Consider me if you can as a little child, sick and peevish, wanting love and indulgence and petting and rest and peace. There, this ought not to have been written. But it can't be unwritten, and it is too late to write anything else. It is morbid; but there's truth, sometimes the clearest, in our morbid reflections. Health is too often independence, selfish philosophy, and indifference.

Also, worn nerves bring not only general depression and discouragement, but a bitter sense of tasks unaccomplished and vast hopes unrealized. This impression of failure or of uncompleted effort was most keenly felt by Bowles. He was a man with more than the common human passion for success. He could not bear to have other men defeat him. He could not bear to have chance or cross-accident defeat him. To have his own nerves defeat him was humiliation hardly to be described. He loved power, he loved domination, he loved mastery. No one appreciated more broadly than he the immense power that is given to the modern newspaper, and it was for this reason, more than for any other, that he loved newspaper work. In his own office he was absolute master; not a tyrant certainly, but in a quiet, determined, final fashion the one sole authority on little and great affairs.

In this love of power lay unquestionably Bowles's weakness. The most marked failure of his life was his attempt to transfer his activity from the *Republican* to the *Boston Traveler*, in 1857. Various explanations were sought for this. Various elements no doubt entered into it. But a considerable element was the man's own autocratic and imperious disposition. Garrison's theory that he undertook the task "with a bumptiousness that at once made him the laughing-stock of his esteemed contemporaries" is much too harsh, but it suggests substantial truth, nevertheless.

So, in the conduct of his own paper, he was inclined to assert his personal views and feelings, for the pure pleasure of it. Independence in politics and religion is a difficult and dangerous path to follow, and an editor in absolute control is apt to mistake whim for pure reason and the rejection of others' judgment for the assertion of his own. If I quote Garrison's *Nation* review yet again, it is because there is a certain malicious pleasure in watching the editors of these two great journals, whose work was in some ways similar, criticise each other as they criticised all the rest of the world. Garrison, then, says, "The sort of independence which Mr. Bowles gradually achieved consisted in making a fetich of his journal"; and he again characterizes Bowles's effort as "the evasion of personal responsibility under the guise of a highly virtuous independence." When the critic of the *Nation* penned this and the other amenities I have before cited, he had just had before his eyes the following from one of Bowles's letters:

The *Nation* has become a permanent and proud addition to American journalism. Often conceited and priggish; coldly critical to a degree sometimes amusing, and often provoking; and singularly lacking, not only in a generous enthusiasm of its own but in any sympathy with that great American quality, by which alone we as a people are led on to our efforts and our triumphs in the whole arena of progress; the paper yet shows such vigor and integrity of thought, such moral independence of party, such elevation of tone, and such wide culture, as to demand our great respect and secure our hearty praise.

But if Bowles's criticism had some justice in it, so also had Garrison's. Bowles's own biographer admits that he was too ready to sacrifice friendship to what he considered duty, and that he freely found fault in his paper with those whom he loved and by whom he wished to be loved in private life. And have we not Bowles's own personal testimony on the subject, none the less forcible for being half jocose? "I mean to be as loyal as possible, and that isn't very loyal, for you know I do love to find fault and grumble, and thank God I can afford to." But who of us can really afford to grumble and find fault?

Yet what finer witness can there be to character than the great love that surrounded this man, in spite of his fault-finding? Those whom he attacked publicly resented it for a while, but once they met him they forgot it. He had the art of making men forget everything except his charm. All his life he fought Ben Butler. Yet whenever they met, they swapped jokes and stories. When Bowles was on his deathbed, he received from Butler a letter of sympathy and good wishes, and almost his last words were, "Write to General Butler, and say that while Mr. Bowles has always differed from him in politics, he has never failed to recognize his high qualities, and to appreciate his many personal attractions." Senator Dawes suffered repeatedly from the strictures of the *Republican*; yet he declared that he loved its editor more than any one outside of his own family. A member of the editorial staff, who had been a witness of many sharp rebuffs, confesses, "I almost worshipped him. There was more religion in my feeling toward him than in almost anything else in me." But most touching of all is the exclamation commonly heard among his humble neighbors in the city of Springfield, "I am so sorry Sam Bowles is going to die."

He was a striking and most sympathetic type of the journalist, and the journalist is interesting because he came into the world only a hundred years ago and seems likely to play an increasingly great part in it. Certainly no one who has followed our own Civil War in the newspapers can fail to feel the singular and important position they then occupied. If the war itself is to be regarded as a great tragic drama, the newspapers almost precisely perform the function of the Greek tragic chorus. They comment abstractly, yet with trembling eagerness, upon the conduct and motives of the actors; they intervene often indiscreetly and with doubly tragic consequence; they prophesy with pathetic or ludicrous incapacity of vision; above all they reflect from moment to moment, like a sensitized surface, the long, unwieldy, enormous ebb and flow of events and passions and desires of which no man can really divine the end.

15

Godkin of the *Post*

by HENRY F. PRINGLE

HENRY F. PRINGLE reported for the *New York Sun, Globe,* and *World* before becoming a free-lance writer and winner of a 1931 Pulitzer prize for his biography of Theodore Roosevelt. His article analyzing the work of E. L. Godkin appeared in *Scribner's Magazine,* December 1934.

~~~~~~

ON FRIDAYS, during the winter of 1886, the arrival of the noon train at Thomasville, Ga., was an event of importance. This was not due to the presence of noted travellers; it was because the week's copies of the *Nation* were on board. Thomasville was a winter resort and among the sojourners were ten or twelve faithful subscribers to the weekly journal of opinion founded by Edwin Lawrence Godkin. The historian James Ford Rhodes was one of them; two decades later he remembered sad occasions when the post was tardy, when the *Nation* did not arrive until late in the evening.

"It used to be said by certain scoffers," he wrote, "that if a dispute of political questions came up in the afternoon of one of those days, we readers were mum; but in the late evening, after having digested our political pabulum, we were ready to join issue with any antagonist."

Such was the influence wielded by the often bitter pen of E. L. Godkin, even after the *Nation* had become a weekly edition of the *New York Evening Post* and was less directly his personal organ. Ever since 1865, when the first issue appeared, Mr. Godkin had been doing the thinking for a large section of America's cultured minority. In 1874 James Russell Lowell protested from Paris, only half in jest, of his predicament when he found that the *Nation* was not on sale in the French capital. "All the time I was without it," he told Godkin, "my mind was in chaos and I didn't feel that I had a safe opinion to swear by."

Godkin, however, was far too opinionated an editor to suffer from any superfluity of praise. The extreme liberals disliked him because he

195

was, at heart, a conservative. The reactionaries criticised him for such liberalism as he showed. Never, though, was he guilty of restraint in the expression of his views. He loathed jingoism and fought it in the years between 1890 and the Spanish War, a decade during which the United States was throwing off its national inferiority complex by looking for war. He was an ardent "sound money" advocate when the farmers (how repetitious is history!) demanded inflation to lift the load of their debts.

Godkin was, I suppose, a typical Mugwump. The characterization has an antique flavor now, but in the '80's it was a fighting phrase. The politicians of both major parties viewed the Mugwumps with contempt and branded them idle theorists. The Mugwumps viewed themselves as independent spirits who were patently superior to the mass of their fellows. Larry Godkin was a typical Mugwump because he admitted the virtues of his tribe with complacency and boasted of their faults. He aroused bitter opposition in the hearts of the organization politicians — even such high-minded politicians as Theodore Roosevelt the First.

But Godkin, like T.R., stood for progress in politics. He was socially minded. He did not hold to that portion of the current American credo — current, alas, for many a decade after 1880 — which said that the Lord might bless the poor but He endorsed the rich. He stood somewhere left of the center on most questions. And if he looked at the extreme left with horror he was, at least, filled with scorn for conservatives who were unable to adjust themselves to changing conditions and times. The editor of the *Nation* would, I am confident, have written a pungent leader praising the defiance of that later and possibly greater Roosevelt who, on an Inauguration Day when the economic skies were black and stormy, cried defiance to the money changers and ordered them from the temples. He would hardly have been able, however, to accept Franklin Roosevelt's program for industrial or economic recovery. He would certainly have opposed the plans for cheaper money. The swing toward centralized government which accompanies the New Deal would have seemed unsound and dangerous.

II

The urge for self-expression, which makes preachers or actors or writers out of otherwise normal men, was in the blood of the Godkins.

The Reverend James Godkin was a Presbyterian clergyman. He was, even more, an Irishman who believed fervently in the Home Rule clause. He forfeited his pulpit because of that belief, but this cannot have been a serious sacrifice. The elder Godkin had been revealed, in 1848, as the author of numerous essays on the Irish question and he eagerly turned to writing when he lost his church. He became editor of the *Londonderry Standard* and then of the *Dublin Daily Express*. He published several books — rather ponderous works — on the Irish question.

Thus Edwin L. Godkin, born on October 2, 1831, at Moyne, in County Wicklow, grew up in a journalistic rather than a clerical atmosphere. His boyhood was spent in this mountainous part of Ireland. His environment included no flavor of the rigid propriety of the parsonage. Instead, the house was filled with Irish patriots. The boy heard his father discuss political questions with other home-rule enthusiasts. He heard violent, almost sanguinary, debates. Until young Larry was ten he was educated at home. Then he was sent to Silcoates, a small school, where he distinguished himself for scholarship. After three years he entered the classical department of the Royal Institute at Belfast and, in 1846, Queen's College.

Young men in Godkin's position were supposed to follow some profession and so he took up the law. It bored him, however. He did not look forward with anticipation to the life of a barrister. Journalism hardly ranked as a profession; it was, rather, a trade and a dubious one at that. But Godkin gladly accepted when an opportunity to become a journalist offered itself. He was, perhaps, the only person in the history of journalism to obtain a post as war correspondent by writing a letter to the editor. This was an epistle addressed to the *London Daily News* in 1853, as war clouds began to gather over the Crimea. Godkin, in the letter, defended the claim of the Greeks on Constantinople. "I was only twenty-two," he recalled many years later, "and knew nothing about either Greece, or the Greeks or Constantinople; but I was possessed of that common illusion of young men, that facility of composition indicates the existence of thought."

I doubt, though, that this modesty was wholly sincere. It was the expression of a mature man patronizing his own youth. In any event Knight Hunt, editor of the *Daily News,* was sufficiently impressed to invite Godkin to cover the Crimean War. He left for the near East in the late fall of 1853. The machine age had not yet transformed the art of war. It was still picturesque and glamorous, if one did not look too deeply beneath the surface. War was fought by professional soldiers, on a small scale but with great violence. The war correspondent of 1853, as in the Civil War and the War with Spain, lived in intimate contact with the troops. He often rode to battle with them. In Mr. Rollo Ogden's life of E. L. Godkin there is a charming photograph of the youthful correspondent. His costume almost defies description, consisting, as it did, of a strange high hat, skin-tight breeches and boots which reached above the knees. In this studio portrait, Godkin is resting his left hand on a huge sword while in his right is a notebook. He is magnificently bearded and his mustaches are luxuriant.

Godkin was, in fact, a forerunner of the Richard Harding Davis school. On one occasion, in Bucharest, a sentinel refused to honor his credentials and Godkin, fearfully insulted, drew his revolver. He might have used it had not the man backed down. But Godkin, unlike Davis, never succumbed to the lure of war. He thought it was stupid, savage, and unnecessary. The seeds of his hatred for the jingoes were sown while he watched this curious and foolish war in which Turks, Russians, Hungarians, and nearly all the other races of Europe leaped at each other's throats in an idiotic welter of blood. Godkin demonstrated too that he had courage and independence. He undertook to defend the Turks against the current conception that they were cowards. Their officers were bad, he admitted, but the men in the ranks fought fiercely. And the language in which Godkin described their character was forthright and without restraint. In one despatch to the *Daily News* he wrote:

The [Turkish] private soldier is, in general, an honest, good-hearted peasant, personally brave, as are all his race; his officer has in general been either a . . . coffee-server or pipe-bearer to some pacha, a wretch steeped in vice from his infancy, without honor or patriotism, who serves simply that he may plunder and embezzle. If you officered the British troops with the sweepings of the jails, selected the leading pimps, burglars, publicans, betting-house and brothel keepers of London, and made them captains, majors, and colonels . . . do you suppose they would receive charges of cavalry standing two deep or that 8000 of them would support the attacks of 40,000 during the long gloomy hours of a November morning?

The war over, Godkin turned homeward in 1856, to face the problem of a future career. The prospects were not too bright. No other wars were on the horizon. Besides, he had long been interested in the United States. He intended to go there as soon as possible, for a visit at least.

In November, 1856, he landed in New York. A Presidential election, the one in which James Buchanan emerged as victor, was but a few days away and Godkin was fascinated by the spectacle of the campaign. He went to a rally at the old Academy of Music and was, as he wrote, "astounded by the heat . . . and extravagance" of the speeches he heard. He differed from other notable visiting Englishmen — Dickens and Kipling for instance — in the measure of his understanding and sympathy. He did not consider Americans either crude or barbaric. From the start, he liked the people with whom he was destined to cast his lot and the nation to which, in due time, he was to subscribe allegiance.

Godkin arrived in the midst of stirring times. The Civil War was imminent. He again exhibited unusual qualities as a reporter and started, immediately after the election, on a journey through the South. His letters to the *London Daily News* were resumed during this trip. They were vivid, objective, concise. Godkin had only repugnance for the institution of slavery, but he made a sincere effort to understand the Southern viewpoint on the Negro. He was not an aloof commentator, giving ideas rather than facts. He mixed with Southerners, drank with them, lived with them. The poor whites of the South, he wrote, constituted the most wretched group of human beings he had seen in all his travels.

It is an attractive picture of a young journalist which arises from the letters he sent to the *Daily News*. Godkin was not afraid of hardship. He rode horseback through the swamps of Mississippi and Louisiana and on several occasions risked his life in pushing on from remote town to remote town. He witnessed the same crudities from which Dickens recoiled in disgust and which were to amuse a bewildered Kipling in the years ahead. But Godkin was a more robust individual. He saw the Southern planters as rather ignorant provincials clinging with desperation to an institution which was doomed and which was economically unsound. He thought that Northerners were often unfair in their abolitionist frenzies.

He was amused by a tendency of Americans in general, Bostonians and New Yorkers in particular, to indulge in wild gestures of enthusiasm when some celebrity, however obscure, arrived in their midst. From one article he wrote for the *Daily News* it appears that official welcomes for channel swimmers, aviators, prizefighters, and movie stars had a precedent well back in the nineteenth century. Godkin wrote:

No people was ever so devoured by that sort of hero-worship which expends itself in speeches, processions, fireworks, and poetry. . . . When they get hold of a celebrity, no matter how small, they never think of proportioning their praise to his deserts. When Kossuth came and Jenny Lind came, the excitement was of the maddest kind, and you may remember the wild extravagances that were committed in their honor. No other opportunity for an outbreak on so grand a scale offered itself until the Atlantic cable was laid, and then the tide reached a higher point than it had ever attained before. Cyrus Field was seized on as the specific object of the outburst, and there was nothing too wild or absurd to be said in his praise. He was compared to Moses, to Alexander the Great and Cyrus the Great.

The really important aspect of Godkin's visit to the United States lay in his friendship for the cause of the Union. When the Civil War came, this English-Irish writer was solidly on the side of the North and his letters to the *Daily News* played a very important part — no one can say how important — as counter-influence to the rising tide of prejudice in Great Britain. The sympathy of the English for the South is not hard to understand. This was the weaker side; the Southerners were the invaded people who were defending their homes. And there were more practical reasons for Southern support in England. Great Britain had sold vast quantities of guns and ammunition to the Confederacy. Unless the South won, no payment would be received. Besides, Great Britain's industries were vitally concerned with the South's cotton. The Northern blockade brought severe losses to Manchester and other textile centers.

As early as 1858, Godkin was presenting the Northern viewpoint in the columns of the *Daily News*. He criticised his native country for the *Trent* affair. His letters discounted the prevailing belief in England that the North was not fighting for the preservation of the Union and would, in due time, agree to a peace based on the creation of a new nation in the South. Of particular interest was the analysis he offered of the two armies. Godkin was well qualified to write on military strategy. He contrasted the American armies with those he had observed in Europe and drew the conclusion that it would be a long war. The Americans, he said, were amateur soldiers with amateur officers. They knew little about combat and, because of this ignorance, never realized when they were defeated; consequently battles raged for days. European troops were professionals. Their discipline was superior and so was their fighting. But a defeat shattered their morale. Together with every other intelligent observer, Godkin was horrified by the assassination of President Lincoln. He saw that it meant long years of disruption in the South, a period of bitterness, poverty, and heartache.

III

Meanwhile Godkin had decided that he would make his home in the United States. He had continued his law studies in New York, not because he was interested but because his journalistic future was still dubious. On February 6, 1858, he appeared in a minor law case and his attendance in one or two other court actions is noted. He made no apparent attempt to build a practice, however. In July, 1859, he was married to Miss Frances Elizabeth Foote of New Haven. A trip abroad consumed some time. Godkin was also fairly busy with his *Daily News* correspondence. But there were months of dreary discouragement. In February, 1864, he was editing a journal, hardly devoted to either culture or opinion, called the *Sanitary Commission Bulletin,* which, as he gloomily informed a friend, published "reports, articles on sanitary subjects and so forth." The salary was $100 a month and Godkin was able to live on it. But the work bored him.

Godkin had the yearnings of every young writer; he wanted an organ of his own, where he could express without restriction his views on politics, social matters, and foreign affairs. There was nothing unusual about the yearning. The remarkable thing is that Godkin, as early as 1863, had interested substantial business men in his project. One backer was on the verge of starting a magazine when, quite suddenly, he was called to California on business. He urged Godkin to follow him and even offered to found a newspaper with the Englishman as editor. Godkin declined on the ground — this was before California had publicized her climate — that he would not be able to endure so hot a place.

He was tired of his role as editor of a plumbing magazine and he debated returning to England. He would have done so had he not become so attached to the United States. In 1865 the clouds lifted. James Miller McKim of Philadelphia, an abolitionist, received word that Godkin had been attempting to raise funds for a weekly. He suggested that they work together and within a few months, being wealthy and acquainted with other men of wealth, he had raised $100,000. The stockholders were a varied group, for the most part liberals with a strong conservative slant. The prospectus proclaimed a journal "of politics, literature, science and art" which would hold forth on the topics of the day "with greater accuracy and moderation than are now to be found in the daily press." The *Nation*, as the new journal was christened, would stand for the "maintenance and diffusion of true democratic principles in society and government." It called for legislation which was "likely to promote a more equal distribution of the fruits of progress and civilization," but this did not mean that the *Nation* endorsed socialism or any other radical nonsense. Its abolitionist parentage was revealed in the third paragraph of the prospectus. The new weekly bespoke "earnest and persistent consideration of the condition of the laboring class at the South" and the removal of "all artificial distinctions" between the Negroes and the rest of the people. Among the announced contributors were Henry W. Longfellow, James Russell Lowell, Charles E. Norton, the Reverend Phillips Brooks, John G. Whittier, and Samuel Eliot.

The first issue greeted an eager, although small, public on July 6, 1865. "The week has been singularly barren of exciting events" was the first sentence written by Godkin for the *Nation*. He found enough to write about, however. The return of peace, Mr. Godkin felt, had given a new stimulus to the consideration of politics. "Orators and writers," he pointed out, "are entering the arena with a confidence which they never displayed as long as their arguments and predictions were liable to reversal or falsification at the hands of Lee or Grant."

Over half a century has passed since that first issue of the *Nation* came from the presses. It is a striking tribute to the talents of Godkin that its columns, examined today, seem fresh and wholly lack that depressing flavor of antiquity which normally marks the editorial offerings of yesteryear. It was a sprightly little magazine of thirty-two pages. The literary section began: "The publishing trade has rarely afforded less signs of action, even in the deepest depression of war times, than at present." This was followed by a review of two more volumes of Mr. Carlyle's *History of Frederick II of Prussia* whose style, said the reviewer, was "idiotic in the strict philosophical sense of the word." There were some notes on the show at the National Academy of Design and seven or eight pages of advertising. The paid notices were largely about books and security issues. But there was one advertisement setting forth the virtues of "J. W. Bradley's New Patent Duplex Elliptic (or Double) Hoop Skirt."

So the *Nation* started and began to circulate among America's fit, though few. Godkin found his path beset by difficulties. Some forty individuals had subscribed the $100,000 with which the *Nation* had been started. The editor learned, as editors nearly always do, that each stockholder had a different conception of the best editorial program. The free traders quarrelled with the protectionists. The abolitionists were chagrined when anything except appeals for the Negro was discussed. Finally, Godkin himself was subjected to absurd provincial criticism. He was an Englishman and therefore incompetent. The *Nation,* said the Anglophobes, had been financed with British gold and was seeking to undermine the sacred institutions of America.

At the end of the first year the capital had been drawn upon heavily. Godkin saw no prospect of further support from the same stockholders and so he reorganized the company. His new funds came from close friends. Thereafter his judgment was not questioned and for the next fifteen years the *Nation* prospered enough to pay its way.

IV

At best, however, the *Nation* was a precarious source of income. Godkin loved the pleasant things of life: good wines, a fine home, cultured friends, frequent trips abroad. As the editor of the *Nation* he received a salary of about $5000. But he was never certain how long it would last. The responsibilities of a weekly made it virtually impossible for him to get away. Too, Godkin feared that the magazine would suffer because he was getting on in years. ". . . at my age," he wrote, "I shall be fifty in October — my vivacity of mind and readiness for work must decline . . ."

Again, was this entirely sincere? Fifty years was not an extreme age. Godkin was to demonstrate full vigor for a good many years. The truth is that he wanted less work and more money. On May 25, 1881, it was announced that the *Nation* would thereafter constitute a weekly edition of the *New York Evening Post*, that journal of long and honourable heritage which had recently been acquired by Henry Villard. Godkin was to be one of three editors of the *Evening Post*. The others were Carl Schurz and Horace White. Until three years before, the paper had been under the editorship of William Cullen Bryant. Now it was to pass into even more able hands. For Villard was to give his editors complete control and to earn for himself, thereby, a distinguished place in the history of journalism. Villard, a German-American, had been a newspaper correspondent in the Civil War. Then he had demonstrated astonishing gifts as a builder of railroads in the northwest. He was about to complete the Northern Pacific in 1883. Mere financial success did not satisfy Villard, though. He had once known the smell of printer's ink and he could not do without it. So he bought the *Evening Post*.

Villard's only mistake was his belief that three editors so distinguished and talented as Godkin, Schurz, and White could work in harmony. It is hard to believe, in fact, that Godkin would have tolerated interference from anybody because, at fifty, the dictatorial side of his character had grown stronger. Of the three men, Schurz was probably the best known among the mass of the American people. He had long been in the public eye, most recently as United States Senator and as Secretary of the Interior. Horace White had been a Chicago journalist, a war correspondent, an aide to War Secretary Stanton. Schurz was the nominal editor-in-chief of the *Evening Post*, but the duties of the three men were based on their particular talents. Schurz was to write on national politics. White knew more about finance than the other two. Godkin's specialty lay in the editorial which attacked the evils of politics. The sachems of Tammany Hall were to feel the full force of such editorials.

The three men managed to work together for almost two years, but the friction was not far from the surface. They issued a distinguished newspaper which was liberal, well-written, complete. "My notion," wrote Godkin in 1883, "is . . . that the *Evening Post* ought to make a specialty of being the paper to which sober-minded people would look . . . instead of hollering and bellering and shouting platitudes like the *Herald* and *Times*."

The ultimate disagreement was not due to this conception, with which Schurz and White agreed. It was based on Godkin's belief that Schurz was, after all, a dry and humorless writer. The General, on his part, disapproved of Godkin's biting sarcasm. There was a degree of justice in the reaction of each to the other. Besides Schurz was far more of a liberal than the somewhat narrow Godkin. In July, 1883, a strike started among the railway telegraphers and Godkin, as Allan Nevins points out in his history of the *Evening Post,* adopted "a tone hostile to the strikers." He said that 30,000 or 40,000 men could not be allowed to interfere with transportation or communication. They should be made to perform their duties. Carl Schurz, away on vacation at the time, could not tolerate such a principle. He so informed Godkin.

Only one outcome was possible: one of the two men had to resign and Schurz, in that same month, abandoned his post as editor-in-chief. Godkin assumed command for the approaching presidential campaign of 1884. Day in and day out he thrust with his pen at James G. Blaine, the Republican nominee. Daily, too, his admiration for Grover Cleveland increased. Godkin was, however, shocked when the Halpin scandal occurred. He was so upset that he was unable to go to his office for several days and the reaction is important because it throws some light on Godkin's character. A liberal on political questions, the editor of the *Evening Post* had no small measure of the social snob in him. He detested public knowledge of private matters. Godkin was not a prude; he enjoyed to the full the hearty, somewhat ribald stories which, even in the '80's, permeated a newspaper office. But he felt that it was stupid for Cleveland to be caught in a low affair; a suave man, a sophisticated man, would have been careful to avoid detection.

Godkin soon regained his sense of proportion, however. He continued to support Cleveland. "Sex immorality," he wrote, "is not incompatible with the highest civic virtue." Had not great statesmen of the past, such as Cromwell and Benjamin Franklin, been less than chaste? This editorial was widely read; a sigh of relief went up from the respectable people who, until then, had been half afraid that a vote for Cleveland was a vote to undermine the sanctity of the home and American womanhood. Or, to be more realistic, they were apprehensive that it was a note endorsing the carelessness of a man who had been caught in an undignified scrape.

These were the days of personal journalism, when editors hurled epithets at each other and even, if the occasion required, pounded each other with canes. Godkin never indulged in physical combat with his rivals, but he did not hesitate to use the columns of the *Evening Post* to call them to account. "We must remind the *Tribune*," he would begin and then set forth the most recent asininities of that journal. But his chief abomination was Charles Dana. The editor of the *Sun* was a worthy foe. He shouted that the *Evening Post* was as heavy as it was dull. When the Brooklyn Bridge was about to open, the engineers tested its strength by having huge trucks bearing heavy weights trundle across it. A far more efficient test of the bridge's strength, said Mr. Dana, would be a wagon bearing a single copy of the *Evening Post*.

Mr. Godkin was a little too conscious of his own dignity and Dana knew this. Consequently he always referred to the editor of the *Evening Post* as "Larry," a contraction which Godkin abhorred. Godkin objected to crime news and kept his own journal as spotless as he could. He constantly berated Dana's *Sun* for sensationalism and analyzed, in one editorial, what he insisted was a typical issue of the *Sun*. On the first page were accounts of a minister on trial for immorality, a suicide and an assault case. Throughout the balance of the paper were to be found "a scandal about Lord Lonsdale and Miss Violet Cameron and a small item about another Lord Lonsdale and twenty-four chorus girls . . . half a column of the horse-whipping of a reporter by a girl, the discovery of her lover in jail by Miss Miller, the arrest of a small swindler and a few other trifles."

In April, 1890, Dana gloated over the fact that Godkin had been arrested for criminal libel, a perfectly grotesque action brought by one of the Tammany politicians being exposed in the *Evening Post*. Dana pretended to believe that this was proof of the unmitigated perfidy of "Larry" Godkin. On April 17 he wrote an editorial for the *Sun*:

> We sincerely hope that the prisoner told the truth when he declared to the Police Court Justice that he was not guilty of the despicable offense for which he was arraigned. . . . Under the well-known principle of law, Godkin's innocence must be presumed until his guilt is fully established by evidence. Candor compels us to say, however, that this presumption would weigh more in his case if his previous reputation for truthfulness and good faith was immaculate.

There are no such editorial battles in these too, too refined days. Mr. Ochs does not berate Mr. Roy Howard. Mr. Reid never castigates

Mr. Paul Block. The newspapers of 1932 sometimes emulate Mr. God-kin in more important matters, however. They crusade against evils in politics and industry. In 1884, the year after becoming editor of the *Evening Post*, Godkin began to attack Tammany Hall. "The three things a Tammany leader most dreaded," Godkin recalled, "were, in the ascending order of repulsiveness, the penitentiary, honest industry and biography."

Between 1884 and 1890, Godkin campaigned against Tammany without great success. On April 3, 1890, he used the weapon he considered most effective: biography. The *Evening Post* appeared on that day with nine columns setting forth the life stories of the leaders of the Wigwam. The first was a sketch of Hugh J. Grant, the Tammany Mayor, who had been a pawnbroker, an alderman, a member of the "Boodle Board" of 1884. The *Evening Post* told of his peculations as Sheriff of New York County, of his deals in public and private life. Next, Godkin took up Richard Croker. A biting sketch told of his start as a tough in the Fourth Avenue Tunnel Gang, of his days as a saloon keeper. Another worthy thus exposed to the glare of biography was "Patrick Divver, commonly called 'Paddy' [who] is the keeper of a sailor's boarding house and has interests in several liquor saloons." These sketches paved the way for the thunderings of the Reverend Charles F. Parkhurst and the overthrow of Tammany (temporary, of course) in 1894.

Godkin's hatred of Tammany was feeble, however, compared to his loathing for jingoism. "It is no longer sufficient for a people to be happy, peaceful, industrious, well-educated," he wrote. "It must have somebody afraid of it. What does a nation amount to if nobody is afraid of it?" He felt that all nations had become poisoned by the fervor for war. Godkin was heartbroken over the campaign against the Boers.

"To think of England, which I love and admire so much and which is so full of beauty, being filled with mourning at this season!" he wrote. "When I do speak of the war my language becomes unfit for publication. . . . Every one who believes in the divine government of the world must believe that God will eventually take up the case of fellows who set unnecessary wars on foot, and I hope he won't forgive them."

Even Grover Cleveland, whom Godkin admired more than any other man in public life, was not without guilt. He was appalled by Cleveland's sharp message on December 17, 1895, to Great Britain over the Venezuelan boundary dispute. This was made public on a Saturday morning when, according to custom at the *Evening Post*, most of the editorials were already in type. They were written on Friday and the editors took turns in coming to the office for an hour or so on Saturday, merely to watch possible later developments. On this Saturday Godkin was in charge. He hastily scribbled two paragraphs of savage condemnation. He continued to say, until the matter had been settled by arbitration, that a war on such an issue was close to criminal insanity. Naturally, as the tide ran more swiftly each month for a war with Spain, Godkin was again bitter. Even the sinking of the U.S.S. *Maine* could not persuade him that war was necessary. But the voice of Godkin was a lonely one and it was drowned out in the chorus of demands for war by Hearst and Pulitzer, Cabot Lodge and Theodore Roosevelt.

This was the last important issue on which Godkin fought. By the spring of 1899 his health was failing and he went to Europe for rest. He withdrew from active participation in the *Evening Post* in January, 1900, and he died on May 21, 1902. Godkin had long been an American citizen and he passionately loved the country of his adoption. But he loved England, too, and it was not unfitting that he should have been seized with his final illness there and that his grave is in an English churchyard.

V

During the last thirty years of his life Godkin was a great editor and a mediocre journalist. He was an educated man, a very intelligent and courageous man, who happened to be writing for a newspaper. As an editor he was unquestionably superior to Charles Dana of the *Sun* or Horace Greeley of the *Tribune*. He was the peer of Marse Henry Watterson of Kentucky; he certainly takes his place among the immortals of the American editorial page along with Frank Cobb of the *New York World*. Godkin's fame rests solely upon his talents as an editor. He held no public office. He wrote no important books.

But as a journalist Godkin was inferior to most of his contemporaries. Of the mechanics and problems of news gathering he knew nothing and cared less. The reporters of the *Evening Post* disliked him, and with reason. Sometimes, in the corridors of the editorial office, they met an aloof man with a gray beard and a flowing mustache who never deigned to recognize or to speak to them. They knew that he detested sensationalism in the news and would, had his associates not vetoed it, have barred every reference to crime from the paper. A contact with the reportorial staff was very rare. He saw the news writers only to obtain additional facts on some matter of economic or political importance. Godkin would question the reporter in a voice which still bore the traces of an English-Irish heritage. He dismissed the reporter curtly when the interview was over.

This disdain for news was a curious blind spot. It never occurred to him, apparently, that nine-tenths of his editorial judgments were based upon the fruits of reportorial energy. He read the news columns avidly. Without them he would have found it impossible to write the editorials — caustic or witty or argumentative as the case might be — which won so influential, if numerically small, a following for the *Evening Post*. Nor, earlier, would he have been able to publish the *Nation* had he not had the source material in the columns of the daily press.

Godkin particularly disliked the sentimental or the colorful in the news. On one occasion Lincoln Steffens, who was among the thwarted geniuses on the *Evening Post*, wrote an account of some German violinist who had died in poverty and whose body had been taken to the city morgue. It was a well-written article, restrained and dignified and moving. But when he read it, Godkin burst into a roar of rage and, on the following day, demanded an explanation from Henry J. Wright, the City Editor. Mr. Wright stood by his guns. He said the article was excellent, in every way worth publishing. Just then the Literary Editor of the *Nation*, W. P. Garrison, happened to enter the editorial sanctum and stoutly took the side of Steffens and Wright. Godkin swallowed his wrath, but with bad grace. He had been about to demand the dismissal of Lincoln Steffens.

Another time Norman Hapgood had been assigned to cover some congressional hearings regarding a bill for the regulation of interstate commerce. They were highly technical. Mr. Hapgood wrote several columns each day in clear, lucid English and when the hearings were over Joseph H. Choate, the attorney, called on the editor of the *Evening Post*. He wanted to know, he said, where the paper had found a legal expert able to write with such clarity and accuracy. Mr. Godkin summoned his City Editor. "Mr. Choate wants to know who wrote those interstate commerce articles," he said to Mr. Wright. "Will you please look it up and tell him?" But he turned to some papers while it was explained that Hapgood was the author, was not even a lawyer and merely an excellent newspaper man. Godkin was not listening. He never offered a word of praise.

All this was part of his aloof austerity. The same failing handicapped Godkin in the newspaper campaigns which he conducted. He was not close to his fellow men. He offered no program. He pointed to no Utopia. He knew, after all, rather little about the problems and aspirations of labor or the masses of the people and he wholly misunderstood the march of Bryan in 1896. Godkin's importance in American journalism cannot be adequately measured by the issues for which he stood and on which, more often than not, he was defeated. He was important because he was an able writer, was independent and courageous. He was an apostle of the vigilant press. But his first importance lies in the fact that under his regime, on the *Nation* and on the *Evening Post*, journalism was wholly divorced from commercialism. Few journals, daily or weekly, were thus free in Godkin's day. Few are so free today.

No one ever doubted that Godkin was supreme. No publisher, no advertising manager dared to suppose that his word was not final on any matter. On one occasion he had written an editorial certain to be offensive to a very large advertiser in the *Evening Post*. This time the advertising manager undertook to make a protest. He pointed out that dividends would be cut if the account was lost. But he made his plea without much enthusiasm and with no hope. The editorial appeared precisely as it had been written. The account was withdrawn, exactly as predicted. Godkin's contempt for the commercialized press was even greater than his contempt for a sensational press. When his freedom was questioned, he lost his temper completely and refused to give way an inch. It was very seldom questioned, for Godkin's wrath, once aroused, was as noisy as it was sincere. His curses rang through the offices of the *Evening Post*. Even the reporters, who disliked him, smiled as they bent over their tasks. For if Godkin was a free man they were free men, too.

And the *Evening Post*, under Godkin, was a free newspaper.

16

Kentucky Bourbon: Marse Henry Watterson

by HENRY F. PRINGLE

This characterization of Marse Henry Watterson of the *Louisville Courier-Journal* was written by HENRY PRINGLE for *Scribner's Magazine* in January 1935. The author was at one time a professor of journalism at Columbia University but now devotes full time to his writing.

HE WAS mellow and aged in the wood of long experience. We shall not see his like again and it is just as well. For Marse Henry Watterson, although he ranted against Wall Street and the extreme reactionaries, was a conservative at heart and he would, I am afraid, have viewed modern America with explosive alarm and disgust.

A panorama, broad and detailed, passed before his keen eyes. The editor of the *Louisville Courier-Journal* was, himself, a figure in many of its scenes. "I have read too much and seen too much," he wrote when, as old men do, he sat down to pen his memoirs. But Marse Henry did not mean this. Zest for living and for criticism was with him until he died. He had fought in the Civil War and then, as editor, had thundered against the obscenities of Reconstruction. He watched with misgivings the rise of the United States to industrial magnitude. He watched, too, the mirage of an imperialism smugly born of God; a God who smiled benevolently upon Senator Chauncey Depew, the export trade, and the United States Steel Corporation.

"I have lived a long life — rather a happy and a busy than a merry one," said the editor of the *Courier-Journal* toward the close. It was a life singularly without illusions. Marse Henry did not deceive himself about the wisdom of the people any more than did Abraham Lincoln who was, incidentally, the particular saint of this Kentucky colonel and Confederate army veteran. He did not deceive himself regarding the honesty of politicians or lawyers or journalists. "Great, great is flapdoodle," said Watterson, and he was in a position to know, for flapdoodle could sometimes be found in his editorial utterances.

An editor from the Civil War through the World War — with the Spanish War as comic-relief between — Marse Henry lived in the midst of change and admitted its inevitability. But he was not always in harmony with change. He opposed it violently when, as he saw it, the Constitution was in danger. William Jennings Bryan was a menace to the nation. Theodore Roosevelt, said Watterson, was not merely dangerous; he was insane. He sought to alter the existing form of American government, even to run for office again and again until, at last, he was King Roosevelt. In November, 1907, President Roosevelt suggested informally that corporations should be licensed by the federal government so that, when they broke the law, their operation could be halted.

Marse Henry was scandalized. In the first place, he wrote, Roosevelt was the last man who should wield such power. He was far "too impulsive." Besides, "the mere suggesting of substituting the will of the executive for the judgment of the courts is in the last degree radical and revolutionary."

It may be assumed that Watterson would not have looked with favor on the New Deal. He might, along with Carter Glass of Virginia, have refused to put "that black buzzard of the NRA" on his newspaper masthead. An individualist born, he always defended individualism; even when it failed to work. During the fifty years of his editorial dominance Watterson witnessed changes that were staggering but none so complete as those which followed March 4, 1933. "The moral alike for governments and men," he insisted, "is to keep to the middle of the road."

Thirteen Presidents came into power during the Watterson years and he knew all of them more or less intimately. To Lincoln, alone, he gave unstinted approval. Marse Henry quarrelled with most of the rest, whether Democrats or Republicans, because never would he subscribe to oaths of fealty. On a Sunday in November, 1908, he published an editorial commemorating the fortieth anniversary of the *Courier-Journal*. This was a splendid mixture of bombast and nostalgic memories. From the start, he wrote, "The *Courier-Journal* flew the flag of freedom. . . . It proposed to be its own master — to do its own leading — and, if die it must, to die fighting." He continued:

. . . The time will probably never come when The *Courier-Journal* will be exempt from the accusations of corrupt motives, which invariably assail it whatever it says or does. Originally it was represented . . . as a preacher of the Freedmen's Bureau, because it stood for the habilitation of the negroes of the South. . . . Then, because it fought Greenbackism, it was a hired minion of the Bloated Bondholders. Then, because of the support it gave Samuel J. Tilden, it was in the pay of the Sage of Gramercy Park. . . . Then it was rolling in wealth furnished by the Gold Bugs. And now, it is the attorney of the Brewers and Distillers, for no other reason than that it is opposed to a prohibition which does not prohibit, that it is opposed to paternal government and sumptuary invasions of personal liberty, and that it would save Kentucky from the ignominy of Maine and Georgia, where the liquor laws promote hypocrisy, favor lawlessness, and foster smuggling and adulteration. . . .

Clearly, Marse Henry was also a prophet. He did not live to witness all of the evils he predicted. It is pleasant to imagine that he may have known about the termination of the ignoble experiment after a decade and a half of error. Still, he cannot have been very much pleased as he watched the methods of the distillers immediately after repeal; the cutting of his beloved Bourbon whiskey, the exorbitant prices, the artificial flavors and colors, the bogus vintages. If he saw it all he must, I think, have called for some sheets of celestial copy paper and indicted a blast against the get-rich-quick liquor boys.

II

Henry Watterson passed through three phases of American journalism. First, as he analyzed it, there were "more or less servile party organs" in most of the large cities and in many small ones. Second came "the personal, one-man-controlled papers"; these, wrote Marse Henry with charming frankness, were "rather blatant and would-be independent." The final phase was the newspaper owned by a family or corporation. It was usually timid and dull; the interest of its owners was limited to revenue. Watterson and the *Courier-Journal* belonged, of course, to the personal, the "rather blatant" group. He crossed pens with nearly all of his contemporaries of the same school: Sam Bowles of the *Springfield Republican*, Murat Halstead of Cincinnati, Dana of the *Sun*, E. L. Godkin of the *New York Evening Post*, Frank Cobb of the *World* and the rest. But, though violent in language, Watterson was the soul of courtesy in his personal contacts. He was likely to grow very angry when some editorial underling of the *Courier-Journal* assumed the Wattersonian prerogative of criticizing a friend.

In the early '80s an item in the paper referred slightingly to White-law Reid of the *Tribune*, an editor with whom Watterson disagreed on nearly all subjects. When Marse Henry saw it, his letter of apology was prompt. "I'll abuse you, my dear Reid," he wrote, "as much as I please and whack-whaddle the *Tribune*, for truly it was never so exasperating or effective. But they shan't call you names in my presence."

And there was, of course, the famous occasion of the wager, "not of money but of wittles, with maybe a drop or two . . . to wash 'em down with," which Marse Henry made with the *New York World*. This was in November, 1909. Taft had been elected and Roosevelt was preparing to leave for Africa. On the surface all was harmony between T.R. and the man he had placed in the White House. Roosevelt was "through with politics." Taft was about "to carry out my policies." But Watterson, watching from his Kentucky editorial tower, was not convinced. He wrote a leader in which he said that Taft and Roosevelt would break, that a movement for the renomination of Roosevelt in 1912 had already started. Bunk! replied Frank Cobb in the *World*. "At present," Cobb added, "there is no more danger of a Republican split over Taft and Roosevelt than of the Colonel's [that is, Henry Watterson] voting the straight Republican ticket in 1912."

Watterson leaped to his ink-pots. Roosevelt was in "the high noon of life," he wrote; his return from Africa would be a great personal triumph, he was "a most astute politician," nothing "is so easy as the raising of a misunderstanding between friends." Anyway, he would bet that Taft and Roosevelt would be "at daggers' points" by December, 1911. He would gamble a dinner for twenty-four — among the guests to be the Chief Justice of the United States and the Vice-President — held at Washington, D.C.

"Bring on your feud or your food," said the *World*, accepting the challenge.

Two years passed. For months prior to December, 1911, it had been clear that Roosevelt and Taft were, in fact, "at daggers' points." Marse Henry wrote in triumph that the *World* must serve the wittles. "We pause," he concluded at the end of his lengthy editorial reviewing the case, "for breath and a reply." Despite the efforts of the *World*'s editors, all too willing to finance so delightful an occasion, the dinner was never held. Dates could not be agreed upon. Finally other interests became uppermost and it was dropped.

Stories like these and a hundred others made a legend of Marse Henry while he was still in the prime of life. He went everywhere and knew everybody. Although he called himself, with literary self-depreciation, "a rustic boulevardier," he was as much at home along the Champs Elysées as on Fifth Avenue. For decades he was the perfect knight of journalism. Editors throughout the country read the *Courier-Journal* and so did hundreds of thousands of people who never saw the Kentucky newspaper. Whenever a controversy was raging the Associated Press put his editorials on its wires as a matter of course. Callow cub reporters dreamed that some day they might achieve comparable eminence themselves. The young men who worked under Watterson found a cordial welcome when they sought posts in New York or other large cities.

Indeed, a Southern accent was a real asset to the newspaper man seeking a job. He could say with a soft Kentucky drawl that he had once worked in Louisville, whether he had or not. City editors concluded immediately that he was one of Marse Henry's boys and hired him on the spot.

III

As a youth, Henry Watterson was too versatile. The wonder is that he was not crushed to mediocrity under the burden of his many talents. "Among my ambitions to be a great historian, dramatist, soldier, and writer of romance," he remembered, "I also desired to be a great musician, especially a great pianist." When he was twelve years old and living in Washington he accompanied Adelina Patti (who was nine) on the piano at a charity affair. "The audience was enthusiastic . . . they fairly took the roof off," was his complacent recollection of the triumph.

In later years Watterson and Theodore Thomas, who was a master of the violin as well as orchestration, played duets together. But music was to remain an avocation, "a recourse and solace . . . during intervals of embittered journalism and unprosperous statesmanship." An illness crippled the muscles of one hand when Watterson was a young man and ended the possibility of his becoming a pianist. His other ambitions were, just as fortunately, thwarted also. He wrote some verses for *Harper's Weekly* and in due time congratulated himself that he had used a pen-name. He even completed a novel which a publisher-friend agreed to bring out and then changed his mind because it was so bad. ". . . so finally I gave up fiction," said Watterson, "and resigned myself to the humble category of the crushed tragi-comedians of literature who inevitably drift into journalism."

Politics or journalism was inescapable in view of Henry Watterson's parentage, habitat and environment. "I was born in a party camp and grew to manhood on a political battlefield," he wrote. But political office, although he held it briefly, was bondage to him. He had no taste for its compromises. He was far too outspoken to rise high in the councils of even his own Democracy. Such influence as he had, and it was a great deal, was that of a vigorous editor to whom the nation listened. So, occasionally, did the politicians.

Henry Watterson, like most of us, inherited his political gospels. His father, Harvey Magee Watterson, was a politician-journalist of Scotch ancestry who divided his time between being a Congressman and being an editor. Henry was born in Washington, D.C., on February 16, 1840, during one of his father's terms in the House. This birth at the national capital was accidental; the boy's native state was really Tennessee. The Wattersons had lived there for generations and were people of wealth and prominence. Henry grew up in Nashville and in Washington.

A sickly boy, he was petted a good deal and assured that he was extremely bright. Tutors guided him for a time and then he spent four years in a Philadelphia school. At sixteen he was back in Nashville for more work with tutors. At eighteen, doubtless something of a dilettante, Watterson set out to paint his name in golden letters on the literary sky. New York rather than Boston was, curiously enough, his goal. He went there and obtained, due to his knowledge of music, a post as critic on the *New York Times*. This was temporary, while the regular critic was absent on leave.

The New York venture was not too successful; editors did not quarrel for his services. Before long Watterson had returned to Washington where he obtained employment on a journal called the *Daily States*. It was an anomalous position due, as he later admitted, to the fact that he was "a very self-confident young man" and the son of an important father. But it marked the beginning of his journalistic education; at the hands of a remarkable woman, Jane Casneau, who was an editorial writer on the paper. This lady had defied her time and had lived with high adventure. She had married General George Casneau of Texas, an aide to Sam Houston. She was credited with having helped to bring on the Mexican War. Now, at fifty, she was virtually running the *Daily States* and she taught young Henry how to write. In view of the fact that such a woman was his mentor, Marse Henry might have been more cordial, in the years to come, toward the feminist movement. He might have talked less about "woman, the moral light of the universe" and the "crazyjanes" who dared to ask for opportunities equal to the ones guaranteed to men by law. But the mature Colonel Watterson was, after all, a Kentucky colonel and the Modern Woman was anathema to his breed.

The Watterson of 1860, not yet twenty-one, was a handsome dog. He was not tall, but he gave the impression of height because he was very slim. His hair was almost as long as that of Buffalo Bill and was worn in the same fashion. The final touch was a goatee. Watterson had good manners. He talked well. His music was further reason for his social acceptability. Every door in Washington swung outward and the ladies, it may be assumed, sighed softly in his presence. His life was just as full professionally. Watterson, both journalistically and socially, knew every one at the Capital. He did not approve of President Buchanan, but he saw him constantly. He covered the inauguration of Mr. Lincoln.

To Watterson the approaching war meant inner torment. A Democrat, he was none the less an ardent Union sympathizer who distrusted the secession leaders and believed that secession was wrong. As the storm grew closer he left Washington and returned to Tennessee. He would not fight, he told himself. Besides, the war could not last for long. The South was weak and the North was strong. Meanwhile he would bury himself in books and turn once more to his interrupted pursuit of literature. Alas for his hopes. He was a gregarious youth, as he was gregarious in old age. A sentence or two crept into his memoirs which told why emotion had overcome reason. "On reaching home," he wrote, "I found myself alone. The boys were all gone to the front." And the girls? "The girls were — well, they were all crazy." "My native country was about to be invaded," he added. "So, casting opinions to the winds, I went in, on feeling."

And yet the war touched Henry Watterson only lightly. He moved through its tragedies with a careless invulnerability; complete for his body, almost so for his mind. He pushed into western Kentucky with a Confederate force, fell ill, and returned to Nashville where he passed a winter doing newspaper chores. The city was captured by Union troops and Watterson slipped out of town. General Forrest "came thundering by . . . as I was making my way . . . afoot . . . and I leaped into an empty saddle." Soon he was on Forrest's staff and engaged in skirmishes which settled nothing much. The heartbreak of certain defeat for the South did not come to him. In all his writings I have been unable to find any awareness that civilization — gracious and lovely and his own — was being blown to atoms. All this was due, no doubt, to his divided loyalty, to the fact that he lived in a border state.

Watterson's sword was less important than his pen, even during the war. The Bank of Tennessee had bought a newspaper and Watterson was despatched to edit it, as a kind of quasi-official newspaper for the State of Tennessee. But he altered the plan. He renamed it the *Rebel* and he made it an army organ; a *Stars and Stripes* of the Confederacy. It made no pretense of telling the truth. Watterson would publish ostensible movements of Confederate troops with the hope that issues would fall into the hands of the Federals and mislead Union commanders. There was an "Agony Column" through which the Johnny Rebs could get into communication with each other.

The *Rebel* was a peripatetic newspaper. Watterson wanted to print it as near as possible to the scene of operations, so he loaded a press on a wagon and started off. When he had gathered enough news he would set the press in a field and run off the issue. He had a good deal of fun and one or two adventures. He was busily printing an issue, one day, when some Yankees appeared at the far end of the field. Watterson escaped in the wagon but the Damnyankees confiscated his plant and used his type for bullets. Another time his team ran away and very nearly catapulted him into a Union camp. He stopped them just in time.

On the whole, he was glad when the war was over. Watterson's real career was about to begin.

IV

The offices of the *Courier-Journal* in Louisville must have been a pleasant place. The paper was financially successful and Marse Henry

Watterson was a generous employer. Louisville was the principal city of Kentucky and despite the proximity of St. Louis and Cincinnati it received a fair share of the commerce bound for the South.

Although he was often away on his trips to Florida or Europe, Watterson was far from an editorial figurehead. He ran the paper himself, and never, happy man, was interfered with by the business office. For almost thirty years Marse Henry "put the paper to bed" in person; that is, he stayed at the shop until the final forms were locked. It was his custom to hurry to the composing room with the copy for his editorials — through swinging doors which were a menace to life and limb. Often he would plunge through them just as a burly pressman started the other way. But they were never changed.

Henry Watterson was only twenty-eight when the *Courier-Journal* published its first issue. When the war ended he had settled in a Cincinnati suburb and had risen to the post of editor on the *Cincinnati Evening Times*. He was a Southerner, however, and he wanted to live in the real South. So he went to Nashville, where, with the assistance of two army friends, he took over a broken-down paper and brought it close to prosperity within a year. Then followed an interlude of travel abroad. In 1867 the owner of the *Louisville Journal* stopped off in Nashville and offered Watterson a place as part owner and editor of his newspaper. At almost the same time Walter Haldeman, proprietor of a rival sheet called the *Courier*, tendered identical terms. It was obvious that Watterson could not be editor of two competing newspapers and his egotistical suggestion that they be merged was turned down. He chose the *Journal*, and, as he phrased it, "began to hammer at the *Courier*." This went on for six months.

"Mr. Haldeman," said Watterson as the circulation of the *Journal* increased further, "I am going to ruin you. . . . Let us put these two newspapers together . . . and, instead of cutting one another's throats, go after Cincinnati and St. Louis."

It was done, with Watterson, of course, as commander of the new project. A fortnight later the surprised citizens of Louisville found a combined newspaper on their doorsteps. Included in the merger was a third paper, the *Democrat*. From the fruit of the consolidation, Watterson remembered, "there issued . . . an aggressive self-confidence which affronted the *amour propre* of the sleepy villagers." Soon the villagers were to like it. The new paper was never dull. The new young editor, although a bumptious pup, invariably had something to say.

The horizons of America were dark as the presses of the *Courier-Journal* began to turn. Lincoln was dead. His successor in the White House was unjustly impeached and very nearly removed from office. The foes of reason were about to seize the government and wreak vengeance upon a defeated South. Graft was to appear in high places. The moral collapse which always follows war was everywhere apparent. For five years, it seemed, conditions grew steadily more grave. "On the whole," mourned Henry Watterson in a private letter in 1873, "things do not look as bright for our beloved country as they might."

Watterson was to wage a hundred fights but none so vital to the nation as his first one. Here was a Southern editor who was also a Confederate veteran, the son of slave owners and a Democrat. But he dared to speak on behalf of the Negro and his voice carried to the corners of the nation. Marse Henry was no foolish visionary, no pulpiteer arguing on the Boston Common. Slavery was wrong and indefensible, he said, "but the armed enforcement of freedom did not make a black man a white man." He argued for the rights given to the Negro by the amendments to the Constitution. He demanded that the so-called Black Laws be removed from the statute books in Kentucky and he succeeded in his plea. Meanwhile he was constantly berating the die-hards of the South as well as of the North. He was telling his fellow Kentuckians about Lincoln and his greatness. Watterson knew, to his credit, that the Bloody Shirt was being waved below the Mason and Dixon line as well as above it and whenever he spied its shameful folds he sent forth thunderbolts of scorn. The editorials which Watterson wrote between 1868 and 1876 were as courageous as they were wise.

Virtue was rewarded. The readers of the *Courier-Journal* increased and so, too, did the income of its editor-owner. During the war he had met the girl of his choice, a Miss Ewing who was the daughter of an eminent Tennessee family. They were married in 1865 and in the course of events had five children. Henry Watterson, the newspaper man, built himself a fine home, Mansfield, some twelve miles from Louisville, and soon to the countryside he was Marse Henry, the country gentleman. This was a charming home, generous and hospitable in the pattern of Southern homes. As Watterson grew older it was a house toward which gravitated the important people of the day.

They saw an old Southern gentleman with a fine shock of white hair, splendid white mustaches, eyes almost hidden by beetling brows. They found that he was a rare judge of wines and cooking; French cooking no less than Southern. They found that their host talked almost as well as he wrote. He would hold forth on politics, letters, music, or art; his white hair tossing as he waved his short arms or emphasized some point with his expressive hands.

Mansfield was the place to which Marse Henry always returned. He was, though, a restless individual. He wandered with his brood to far places; to Switzerland in the summer, to Florida in the winter. At Washington he was entertained by the Great, not infrequently at the White House itself. When in New York he associated with the moneyed men of the day. They were charming pirates, many of them, and Watterson seems to have been aware of their charm more than of their knavery. In any event, he lunched and dined with Jay Gould without a qualm and was offered part ownership of the *World* when Gould acquired the paper for his own peculiar purposes. Later, when Pulitzer bought the *World* from Gould, an offer was made to Watterson. If he would organize the editorial staff, Pulitzer said, he could have any fee in reason. "Go to the devil — you have not money enough," boasted the Kentuckian. He was taking things easy, he said. He did not intend to work so hard. Besides, he was going back to the wide verandahs of Mansfield.

Marse Henry was always planning to work less arduously. He retired from active management of the *Courier-Journal* several times. He announced that he would give the rest of his days to a biography of Lincoln. The book was never written. Watterson invariably assumed control of his newspaper again.

In 1876 he consented to complete an unfilled term in Congress, not because he had altered his convictions about political office but so that he could serve Samuel J. Tilden. Tilden was, save Lincoln, Watterson's only hero, pure and undefiled. When the lawyer was elected Governor of New York in 1874 the editor saw a man who could, at last, unite the Northern and Southern wings of the Democratic Party. He sounded his editorial trumpets promptly. Tilden owed his ultimate nomination very largely to his Kentucky friend. The result of the election was a harrowing blow, undoubtedly the most bitter disappointment of Marse Henry's long life. From Washington, where he was in the House of

Representatives, Watterson wrote despatches to the *Courier-Journal* in which he called attention to the "Hayes Conspiracy." He quite lost his head in his excitement. Tilden was to be counted out, he said. The conspirators planned to certify Hayes, "the defeated candidate." Was there, he asked, "no peaceful remedy"? The law was clear; Tilden had been elected.

"On the law the Democratic Party plants itself," he wrote, "and means to stand until it is driven off at the point of the bayonet. It is for our people to determine . . . whether this shall be done. If they will rise in their might . . . and will send a hundred thousand petitioners to Washington . . . there will be no usurpation and no civil war. The conspirators will be thwarted."

The nation trembled at these words. Timid souls everywhere said that peaceful petition was impossible when Kentuckians were involved. They saw visions of a hundred thousand Kentucky colonels, their white mustaches quivering with anger, advancing upon the National Capital with hoss-pistols and mint juleps in their hands. Marse Henry was roundly abused for inciting to riot and protested that his words had been misunderstood. This was a confession of sin, although it was true. Marse Henry would have dismissed an editorial writer who had similarly failed to make himself clear.

v

Eight more years of Republican rule — misrule to the Wattersonians — followed and when, in 1884, the star of Grover Cleveland began to rise, Marse Henry watched it with only mild approval. He said that Cleveland was without experience in national affairs and that the opposition of Tammany and other groups in the Democracy made his election doubtful. He supported Cleveland in the campaign, of course, but the new President and Watterson were never quite in harmony. Cleveland was a little too lethargic to suit the volatile Kentuckian, and to the President, no doubt, the editor was unsound.

Neither was fair to the other. Marse Henry believed in tariff revision and so did Cleveland. Marse Henry was a sound-money advocate and Cleveland, more than any other President, saved the nation from extreme inflation. Watterson had always been for sound money. He had denounced the Greenback enthusiasts of the South. When the shaggy head of William Jennings Bryan appeared over the Nebraska prairies it was Marse Henry who rained the most telling blows upon it. The United States, he told the Free Silver people, would never stand for their program: "They laugh best who laugh last. 'Free Silver' may be a good dog, but 'I told you so' is a better. Heed it, you jabberwocks, heed it! The tail may wag the dog in Persia, and India and China and Mexico and Peru, but it never has done it in the United States and it never will. Run, you jabberwocks, run!"

Mr. Watterson was abroad when Bryan threw a convention into hysterics and was nominated. But the shouts of 16 to 1 reached him across the seas and he sent a cable which became historic. "No compromise with dishonor," was his order to the *Courier-Journal*. Bryan must be defeated. Watterson did not return for the campaign, but he wrote a series of editorials and these reveal that Free Silver was only one aspect of his opposition to Bryanism. Marse Henry, always a conservative, felt that the platform was an appeal to class feeling. He became almost as much alarmed as did J. P. Morgan, the youthful Theodore Roosevelt, and Henry Cabot Lodge. He saw revolution in the immediate future unless Bryan was crushed.

It took courage for the *Courier-Journal* to fight Bryan and this time the readers of the paper did not follow their mentor. The paper lost half its circulation in a year. Watterson hurriedly returned to the United States and the task of rehabilitation was long and arduous. By 1900 — it is unpleasant to believe that expediency may have been a factor — Watterson was back in the fold. This time he supported Bryan. "He is four years older," was his grudging admission. "He must have learned something."

In 1908 Marse Henry was confessing that he had changed his mind. He had come to regard Bryan "as one of the simplest, purest and ablest of men" and his defeat by Taft as "a national misfortune." But even this was not the final judgment. In 1916 he was again berating Bryan, now Secretary of State in the Wilson Cabinet. ". . . his absurd career in the State Department," said Watterson, "is proof of what a blunderbuss of a President he would have made."

Far greater than Watterson's interest in Bryan was his absorbed fascination in Theodore Roosevelt. They disagreed as violently as two men could and yet preserved a mutual respect which sometimes warmed to affection. Roosevelt liked to boast of his Southern blood and did so whenever Watterson was at the White House. When Watterson's onslaughts were too violent Roosevelt ignored them, apparently on the ground that the Kentuckian was slightly mad. On his part, Marse Henry had no doubt whatever that Theodore was insane; he said so in the columns of the *Courier-Journal*.

Certainly the two men had little in common save vitality and a flair for talking steadily and charmingly. Perhaps this was more than most men have. "We are an expansionist," wrote Watterson in 1900 as Roosevelt was about to become Vice-President. "But we would expand on Jeffersonian lines . . . we would have the Constitution follow the flag." Roosevelt detested Jefferson and believed in having the Constitution follow T.R. Long afterwards, in 1919, Watterson wrote: ". . . the Monroe Doctrine was a fad. . . . We actually went to war with Mexico, having enjoyed two wars with England, and again and again threatened to annex the Dominion [of Canada]. Everything betwixt hell and Halifax was Yankee pre-empted. Truth to say, your Uncle Samuel was ever a jingo."

It was Roosevelt who had expanded the Monroe Doctrine and had, in his earlier outbursts of jingoism, advocated the annexation of Canada. The truth is, however, that Roosevelt the Imperialist did not bother Watterson very much. What really alarmed him was the President's progressive program. Thus in 1904: "We need a man in the Chief Magistracy who is a Magistrate and not a Mountebank. We need a just and sensible man, not a theorizing experimentalist." Then followed a plea for the election of Alton B. Parker and a bill of particulars against T.R. Roosevelt was "a self-confident, supercilious iconoclast" whose "judgment is faulty . . . spirit niggardly." He had started as a Free Trader and had become a High Protectionist. He had started as a civil service reformer and had become a spoilsman. In office he had been "brutal and reckless." The Panama revolution had been replete with "villainy from start to finish." Besides, although Marse Henry did not add it, T.R. was a Republican and Judge Parker a Democrat.

Watterson objected almost as much to Taft, as the Candidate of Roosevelt, although he had the grace to point out that the Republican nominee in 1908 was a man of irreproachable character. Logic was not invariably Marse Henry's strong point. Roosevelt was too radical. Taft was too conservative. The editor had, meanwhile, no use for the insurgents of Congress who were battering down the domination of

Speaker Cannon. By 1910 he had selected the tariff as the issue on which he would oppose Taft; with never a word in praise of the obvious fact that Taft was doing his level best to bring about reductions. "The President," he wrote, "is a good example of a man out of place, of a wheel out of line, of the great lawyer who makes a poor politician."

"Marse Henry's views," insisted Taft in a private letter, "do not have any interest for me. . . . I think he is as nearly unreliable . . . as any man outside of an asylum."

Thus Watterson had a unique distinction. The President intimated that he ought to be in the loony-bin himself. He wanted to put an ex-President there. The editorials in which Theodore Roosevelt's sanity was questioned are certainly among the most astonishing in the history of journalism. Roosevelt, with self-restraint quite unprecedented, took no notice of them. As early as 1907 Watterson was writing that the President would demand a third, a fourth, and a fifth term; after this would come "Life Tenure." Next, Watterson insisted that Roosevelt and Taft would quarrel. Marse Henry's acute alarm began when Roosevelt made his "Charter of Democracy" address at Columbus, Ohio, in February, 1912. This shocked his conservatism to its foundation.

"Not during the hysteria which deluged France in blood and terror," he shouted, "did one of the Mob-caps declaim his devotion to the people with deeper zealotry . . ." A few weeks later he wrote that T.R. was "as mad as a March hare" and suggested that his family lock him up before he did great harm. On April 27, 1912, he said: "If that one of the Caesars who goes by the name of Nero was insane, Theodore Roosevelt, aspiring to be an imitation Caesar, is insane. He carries all the marks typical of the perverted understanding; the devilish streak of wickedness, the ignoble malignancy, the logical intensity and inaccuracy of the lunatic."

A good deal more of the same thing followed. Marse Henry was still alarmed when 1916 arrived and the dwindling Bull Moosers were again filled with hope. He was, however, shocked when Roosevelt stepped back into the ranks of the G.O.P. and joined forces with the men who had robbed him, as he claimed, in 1912. This was an insult to all those who had followed T.R., he said.

But the rumpus was as impersonal as it was inflammatory. A day came when Marse Henry and Roosevelt were seated together at a banquet. "I think I am the bravest man that ever lived," said Roosevelt when he got up to speak, "for here I have been sitting for three hours by the side of Brutus — have repeatedly seen him clutch his knife — without the blink of an eye or the turn of a feature."

Marse Henry remembered the occasion when he wrote his auto-biography and told of his own, equally charming, reply in which he testified to the "perfect understanding" between himself and T.R. "His mind," Watterson added, a shade innocently, "was of that order which is prone to believe what it really wants to believe. He did not take much time to think."

Sometimes Marse Henry was also guilty of too rapid cerebration.

VI

It was Watterson's sad fate that no Democrat of whom he could entirely approve became President. In 1912 he preferred both Champ Clark and Oscar W. Underwood to Woodrow Wilson, who was "a schoolmaster and not a statesman." Marse Henry was again discovering Caesars behind every bush. Wilson, too, had designs on the Republic. ". . . beneath the veneering of scholarly polish," Watterson warned, "lay the coiled serpent of unscrupulous ambition." But he supported Wilson in 1916 as well as in 1912. Hughes was a great lawyer and would make a bad President, he said.

He did not believe that a vote for Wilson in 1916 was a vote for peace; on the contrary. He accused Hughes of being the candidate of the German-Americans and said that the Republican nominee "has uttered no word to deny that he is pro-German in his opinions and sympathies." Watterson was certain that the United States would enter the war and, unlike most of his countrymen who undoubtedly voted for Wilson and peace, he saw in President Wilson the best chance for successful prosecution of the struggle. He had been damning the Germans since 1914 and his endorsement was an effective answer to the arguments of Roosevelt and others that Wilson believed in peace at any cost.

"To Hell with the Hohenzollerns" was the cry of Marse Henry in 1914. This was the caption on an editorial which was among the shortest and best in the thousands he wrote. The sinking of the *Lusitania* gave inspiration for another attack which was reprinted everywhere: "The Heart of Christ — The Sword of the Lord and Gideon." Germany, he said, was "the nation of the black hand and the bloody heart." And yet Watterson counselled reason. "We must not act either in haste or passion"; in due time President Wilson would halt the German terror. He grew impatient, however, as the President continued to exchange diplomatic essays. When, at last, America went in he wrote two editorials which were a call for action. So moving were they and inspired that they received the Pulitzer award for that year. He was greatly pleased by the citation. "The boys in the city editor's room will find out that the old man is a journalist," he beamed.

Marse Henry was growing old; seventy-seven by now. A year later he transferred control of the *Courier-Journal* to Judge Robert Worth Bingham and called himself Editor-Emeritus. He did not, however, agree with the attitude of the paper on the League of Nations, nor with Wilson, nor with his close friend, Cobb of the *World*. It was inevitable, he said, that "Woodrow Wilson would be caught by such a whimsy as the League of Nations." The League tied the hands of the United States. Marse Henry would have none of it and he felt so strongly on the subject that even his connection as Editor-Emeritus of the *Courier-Journal* was severed. Besides, that oldest of apprehensions was bothering him again. They say, he whispered, that Woodrow wants a third term! Will you let him have it?

He drifted quietly toward the end; living most of the time at Mansfield, a sage who was greatly loved, who was clear-minded to the last. He died on December 21, 1921. Two years earlier he had finished his memoirs. They were rambling, discursive, without form. They were precisely the memoirs which should be permitted a journalist who all his life had been held to strict limitations of space and time. Marse Henry wondered, he wrote, why men lay awake at night and pondered the ingratitude of their stars or their countrymen. Webster and Clay had so pondered and what good did it do them now, "now that they lie beneath the mold, and that the drums and tramplings of nearly seventy years . . . have passed over their graves?" Marse Henry went on:

All of us, the least with the greatest, let us hope and believe shall attain immortal life at last. What was there for Webster, what was there for Clay to quibble about? . . . Yet they might have been so happy; so happy in their daily toil, with its lofty aims and fair surroundings; so happy in the sense of duty done; so happy, above all, in their own Heaven-sent genius, with its noble opportunities and splendid achievements. . . .

A few pages before he wrote Finis to his memoirs, Marse Henry added: "We know not whence we came or whither we go, but it is a fair guess that we shall in the end get better than we have known."

17

Henry W. Grady, Reporter

by RAYMOND B. NIXON

RAYMOND B. NIXON wrote the definitive biography of Henry W. Grady and summarized his research in this article for the *Journalism Quarterly*, December 1935. He is now a journalism professor at the University of Minnesota and the editor of *Journalism Quarterly*.

IN THE forty-six years that have elapsed since the death of Henry W. Grady, managing editor of the *Atlanta Constitution* from 1880 to 1889, the facts of his brief but remarkable career have become obscured by a haze of myth and legend. Although thousands of high-school orators still declaim his highly significant speech on "The New South," too often both declaimers and their hearers think of Grady as a political figure, when in truth one of the secrets of his hold upon the public was his steadfast refusal to run for office. Even those of us who recall that Grady was a journalist and not an office holder usually refer to him only as an editorial writer, when in fact he actually devoted much more of his time and talent to the news columns than to the editorial page. Most ironical of all, perhaps, is the fact that today his views on public questions are cited frequently by those who would make of him a reactionary, while in his own time Grady was as thoroughly progressive as any great leader could have been without cutting himself off from all influence over his own people.

The principal reason for these misconceptions is that Grady's life and work have never been the subject of a critical study. The usual source of information is Joel Chandler Harris's *Life of Henry W. Grady* (New York, 1890), a memorial volume which was compiled with such haste and by so many hands that it contains three different birthdates for its subject, not to mention more serious errors and the incompleteness of its slender biographical sketch. Because of the emotional stress under which Harris's book was brought together, it is necessarily too much a eulogy of the orator who died "literally loving a nation into peace" to be an adequate picture of the editor who, in the years immediately preceding his death, attracted to the weekly edition of the *Atlanta Constitution* the largest circulation of any newspaper of its type in the United States.[1]

It is to original sources that we must go if we wish to become acquainted with the real man. Fortunately, the long inaccessible scrapbooks, diaries, and personal correspondence of Grady have now been placed in the Library of Emory University, where fairly complete files of the newspapers on which he worked also are available. Here we come face to face with a genial, fun-loving and boldly enterprising young newspaperman who bears little resemblance, indeed, to the pompous figure of the Victorian monument in downtown Atlanta, or to the Grady of tradition, whom even the scholarly *Dictionary of American Biography* describes as "sentimental, pious, and . . . quite conventional." To a journalist the real Grady is far more interesting and important, if withal more human, than the somewhat legendary patron saint of Southern industrialists and prohibitionists.

The truth is that Grady was cast in the role of "national pacificator" less because of his ability as an orator than because of his accepted leadership as an editor. Senators, governors and congressmen represent only a state or a district, but the directing genius of "The South's Standard Newspaper" could and did speak for his entire section, irrespective of state lines.

The success of the *Atlanta Constitution* was due, furthermore, to the fact that it had in its managing editor a great reporter and a master news executive. Just as in his public policies Grady belongs to the New South rather than to the Old, so in his journalistic methods he exemplifies not the personal journalism which the Civil War rendered obsolete, but the modern era, with its emphasis upon the gathering and interpreting of news. The South, certainly, has never seen his like as one who "perceived instantly the multitudinous interesting things of life," and who could picture even the most difficult of subjects in colorful strokes that caught the popular fancy.

Grady's entry into journalism dates from two newsy letters which he contributed to the *Atlanta Constitution* while he was a student at the University of Virginia in 1868–69.[2] The sparkling style and humor of his articles so impressed the editor of the *Constitution* that, upon

Grady's return to Georgia, he was given the assignment of covering an excursion of Georgia editors over the state railroad. The inexperienced correspondent attracted immediate attention by his breezy writing and by the statement, in one of his dispatches, that "bribery was attempted on the press excursion." His boldness and originality scored especially with the editor of the *Rome Courier*, a tri-weekly paper in one of the Georgia towns visited by the excursionists, with the result that by September, 1869, Grady had been installed as the paper's associate editor. From Rome it was but a short step to Atlanta, where in 1872 he became editor and one-third owner of the *Atlanta Herald*.

The founder and senior editor of the *Herald* was Alex St. Clair Abrams, who for several years following the war had been connected with the *New York Herald*. Abrams was thoroughly saturated with the Bennetts' idea of what a newspaper should be, and from him Grady acquired his life-long conviction that it was the news, rather than the editorial page, which makes a great newspaper. The *Herald* was the liveliest paper Georgia had ever seen. It quickly eclipsed the *Constitution* in circulation and probably would have put the older journal out of business but for the fact that it lacked capital and was published on too ambitious a scale for the stringent financial period which followed the panic of 1873.

In July, 1876, after the death of the *Herald* and two other short-lived newspaper ventures in Atlanta, Grady turned down the editorship of the *Wilmington* (North Carolina) *Star* in order to follow a reporter's "hunch." Recalling, perhaps, that his friend St. Clair Abrams had been the Atlanta correspondent of the *New York Herald*, and that the *Herald* had not been carrying any special dispatches from Atlanta since Abrams' removal to Florida, Grady borrowed $50 and left suddenly for New York. Reaching the metropolis with $3.75 in his pocket, he registered at the Astor House, which was diagonally across the street from the *Herald* building. He did not know a soul in New York, but he had admired the Bennetts' paper from a distance for its enterprise in gathering the news, its political independence, and its friendliness toward the South, and he felt that he would receive a kindly hearing there. Going to the office of the managing editor, Thomas B. Connery, Grady obtained an audience and asked for the position as the *Herald*'s Georgia correspondent.

"Do you know anything about Georgia politics?" Connery asked.

"I know more about that than anything else," Grady replied.

"Then sit down," said the managing editor, "and write me an article on Georgia politics. I am going to be out of the office for a while."

With these words, the editor tossed Grady a pad of copy paper and left him alone to his task. Grady rapidly wrote out some 2,000 words on the Georgia political situation, and when Connery returned, the Atlantan was leaning back in his chair with his feet on the desk.

"What's the matter?" inquired the *Herald* executive.

"Nothing," said Grady, "except that I'm through."

"Very well. Leave your copy on the desk, and if it amounts to anything, you will hear from me."

Such an abrupt dismissal was rather disheartening. Grady feared that the article might not be published for several weeks, if at all, and he knew that his scant funds would last hardly a day.

"Early the next morning," Grady related, "before getting out of bed I rang for a hall-boy and ordered a copy of the *Herald*. I actually had not strength to get up and dress myself, until I could see whether my article had been used. I opened the *Herald* with a trembling hand, and when I saw my article, I fell back on the bed, buried my face in the pillow, and cried like a child."

Grady was at the *Herald* office that morning by 8 o'clock, several hours ahead of Connery, but he waited patiently until the managing editor arrived. The editor received him cordially. After complimenting him on his trial article, Connery told Grady that he could go back to Georgia and consider himself in the employ of the *Herald*.

A crucial test of Grady's reportorial ability came soon after his return to Atlanta. One afternoon he received a telegram from Connery asking him to ascertain whether a certain man was registered at any Atlanta hotel. Grady hastily examined all of the hotel registers in the city, but found no such name. He then sat down to determine why the *Herald* was so eager to find this particular person. In a recent issue of the *Herald* he found the answer. The stranger had been involved in some difficulties in Cuba, had fled from Havana, and had landed in Charleston two weeks previously. Reasoning that the fugitive would be more likely to go from Charleston to New Orleans than to Atlanta, Grady telegraphed at his own expense to a friend in New Orleans, asking him to search the hotel registers there. The reply came back promptly that the man was registered at the St. Charles hotel. Within three hours from the receipt of this query, therefore, Grady sent to the amazed Connery the information that he wanted. From that moment the *Herald*'s managing editor knew that he could depend upon his Georgia correspondent to get the news.[3]

Grady soon found, however, that the uncertain income from space writing for the *Herald* was insufficient to support his family. In October, 1876, he was about to go to Augusta, Georgia, to become editor of the *Constitutionalist* there, when he was offered a place as political reporter on the *Atlanta Constitution* at the same salary that he would have received in Augusta — $25 a week. Once again his love for reporting asserted itself, and he accepted the *Constitution* offer, retaining also his connection with the *Herald*.[4]

In November Grady was sent by both papers on his first big assignment of national significance — the investigation of the Florida election frauds, growing out of the bitterly fought Presidential contest between Rutherford B. Hayes, Republican, and Samuel J. Tilden, Democrat.

The accession of Hayes to the Presidency has been described as "the crowning crime of the tragic era" of Reconstruction.[5] On the night of the election, the victory of Tilden was celebrated everywhere, and on the next morning all of the New York newspapers except the *Herald* and the *Times* conceded the defeat of Hayes. The *Herald* asked: "Who is elected President? As we go to press the question is nearly as much of a mystery as it was Tuesday morning." [6] Just what happened in the *Times* office has been sharply disputed. The story now generally accepted by historians is that the *Times* presses were running with an edition virtually announcing the election of Tilden when a telegram was received from a prominent Democrat asking for election figures on South Carolina, Florida and Louisiana. Discovering that the votes of these three states would give Hayes a majority of one in the electoral college, the managing editor of the *Times*, which was supporting the Republicans, stopped the presses and claimed victory.

As soon as Zach Chandler, Republican national chairman, was apprised of the situation, he flashed telegrams to "good men and true" in South Carolina, Florida and Louisiana, telling each in turn that victory for the Republicans depended upon the vote in that state. Later in the day, Chairman Chandler boldly announced that Hayes had carried all three states and therefore had won the Presidency by a majority of one electoral vote.[7]

Although the Republicans, as a result of their Reconstruction program, still controlled the election machinery in South Carolina, Florida, and Louisiana, they were somewhat doubtful about Florida, where the powers of the state canvassing board were specified by law as purely ministerial. Because of the fears of his party's chieftains as to the outcome of the contest, the Secretary of War hurried federal troops to Tallahassee. Both Democrats and Republicans sent groups of "visiting statesmen" to look after their interests, and the New York newspapers assigned some of their best political writers to report the proceedings.

In his first dispatch after his arrival in Tallahassee, Grady gave a fascinating view of the scene which he found upon his arrival in the usually dreamy old Florida capital.[8]

The political situation here is fairly indescribable. Everything is overstrained and unnatural. It is all a whisper and a wink. There is nothing frank and easy. One is carried off into a remote corner to receive in utter secrecy the most casual information. There are lips to your ear all day long. Intrigue and suspicion exist in all things. The most atrocious rumors poison the air hour after hour. Every stranger here is something or other. This one (really a stationery drummer) is a New York detective; that one (really a corn doctor) is a professional mail robber; yonder fellow (really a young student making for the coast to fish) is a telegraph wire tapper, and that box he carries with him (really his tackle) is the dire machinery with which he is to break the wire and intercept messages. Venice in her palmiest days never had half so much of delightful mystery about her. "That barber," whispers one politician to another, "is our friend. He is with us. You may rely on this — sh-h-h-h!" And, with his finger to his lip and a suppressed wink trembling on his cautious left eyelid, he is off, leaving us to wonder what tonsorial art has to do with politics, and his friend to rejoice in the knowledge that he can at last secure a reliably Democratic shave. The truth of the matter is that both parties are at sea. Neither knows exactly what to do, and yet is bewildered by the fear that the other will do it first. . . .

"Grady was conspicuous everywhere" during the exciting days and weeks of the contest, according to an eye witness. His sense of humor usually placed him in "the center of a gaping, roaring circle, and he left a trail of mirth and comment in his wake," making friends on both sides of the controversy. Before the canvassing board itself he produced two essential witnesses, who, allegedly under inspiration from the Republicans, were stealing away when Grady discovered them. The son of an official who was in daily attendance upon the proceedings said that his father, in discussing each night around the family fireside the events of the day, "dwelt less and less upon the count, and more and more upon the presence in Tallahassee of a young Georgian representing the *New York Herald*, and his doings." [9]

The canvassing board's decision was announced about 5 o'clock one afternoon early in December. Despite amazing evidence of ballot-stuffing and other frauds, the result was a compromise by which the governorship and other state offices were given to the Democrats, and Florida's electoral votes were awarded to Hayes. Upon hearing the news, all of the newspaper correspondents except Grady rushed to the telegraph office, only to find that the wires had been cut, and that the nearest available telegraph station was at Drifton, thirty miles east of Tallahassee. There would be no train for many hours.

Grady, however, was equal to the emergency. Having learned earlier in the day that the wires were down, he had made his plans accordingly. As soon as the decision was announced, he stepped from the capitol into a light buggy drawn by a span of fast horses. While a Negro driver headed the horses toward Drifton Grady sat back and concentrated upon his story.

Although considerable time was lost when his driver fell asleep and allowed the horses to take the wrong road, Grady reached Drifton at 10 o'clock that night, ahead of every other correspondent. When the others did arrive, they discovered that their Georgia rival had taken possession of the office by buying the telegraph operator's entire library — a well-thumbed copy of Webster's blue-backed speller — and tearing from it enough matter to hold the wires until he could complete his story. Thus it happened that the *Atlanta Constitution* and the *New York Herald* were the only newspapers that printed the results of the Florida count in their early editions the next day. [10]

The controversy over the election continued until the eve of Hayes' inauguration. Grady stayed with the story nearly four months in all, remaining in Florida until January and then going to Washington.

Before leaving Tallahassee, Grady made for his own satisfaction an affidavit to the effect that Tilden had carried the state. Subsequent events proved that he was right. In the spring of 1878, while a bill was pending in Congress in an attempt to revive the question of Hayes' title to the Presidency, Grady returned to Florida. On this visit he obtained full confessions from the two principal manipulators of the frauds. His exclusive story occupied the most important news position in the *Herald* on April 24, and further details held the spotlight on April 25, 26 and 27. For this "scoop" James Gordon Bennett, Jr., sent him a check for $1,000.[11]

The *Constitution* also reported that Grady had received an offer from New York "so attractive that he could hardly refuse it," but refuse it he did.[12] His experience as a political reporter had given him a new sense of poise and confidence. He now had a job thoroughly to his liking.

In order that he might have more time as a free-lance, Grady gave up his $25-a-week salary on the *Constitution* to become a space writer. His "string" by 1878 included, besides the *Constitution* and the *Herald*, the *Philadelphia Times*, the *Cincinnati Enquirer*, the *Chicago Inter Ocean*, the *Detroit Free Press*, and the *Louisville Courier-Journal*. His income from these papers during 1879 totaled $3,843 — "a pretty good year's work," he wrote in his diary.

The problem of bringing about a better understanding between North and South engaged Grady's attention as a newspaperman long before he made any speeches on the subject. In fact, some of his best work along this line was done in 1877–81, while he was a roving correspondent. He traveled frequently to the North and wrote of that section and its leaders for the *Constitution*, the *Louisville Courier-Journal* and other Southern papers. To the Northern newspapers and magazines which he represented he continually was contributing interviews with leading Southerners, and feature stories on the progress and possibilities of the New South. In this way he helped to carry out the injunction of another great Georgian, L. Q. C. Lamar, who in his eulogy of Sumner, the dead Abolitionist, in 1874 had said, "My countrymen, let us know one another and we will love one another."

Grady's favorite form of reporting was the interview — "the neatest and handiest thing in journalism," he called it. The interview was a comparatively new device at this time, and some papers were endorsing it, others denouncing it. Grady, as "one of the chief sinners, if there be any sin in the practice," was its warm defender. In an article "On Interviewing," he wrote that "Socrates, a thoroughly respectable person, introduced the custom on the streets of Athens." Pointing out that the birth of the newspaper interview was an accident, due to the haste with which a *New York Herald* reporter wrote out a conversation with one of the participants in the raid at Harper's Ferry in 1859, Grady explained why he considered it so desirable:

The idea took like wild-fire. The system of interviewing gave more dignity to a report. It brought the person interviewed and the public face to face. It enabled the correspondent to preserve the flavor of the great man's individuality, and carry his subtle characteristics into print. By leading him from the single thread of a narrative into suggestive by-ways and turn-outs, all the minor lights and shades of information could be brought out.

. . . A skillful journalist, fully acquainted with the specific points upon which the public desires to hear from a noted person, and knowing by instinct what will be of interest, can, by leading him into the deviable lines of discussion, and picking out of him exactly what is wanted, get up a much more interesting paper, and convey to the public more information, than would come from the great man . . . alone and unaided.

The great objection to interviews is that many persons consider them an unreliable way of putting things. On the contrary, they are the most reliable way. . . . I have always found that public men prefer them to any other method of communicating with the public; and it is only the fewest of them that are ever denied. I have interviewed nearly every prominent man in the South and many of the greatest men in the North and West. I have published interviews covering from one to three columns, and giving their words and peculiar expressions. And I have never had one single man to seriously deny the authenticity or correctness of the interview.

I do not claim extra care or correctness. I simply use myself as an example to show that interviews are almost invariably correct and authentic. Of the thousands of important interviews with important people printed daily in the press, North and South, one can count on the fingers the whole number that have been impeached. . . . News-papers and rival correspondents frequently issue . . . denials, without the slightest sort of authority for them.

Trouble arises, Grady apprehended, when "some journalists publish an interview without having obtained permission to do so." But "no reputable journalist will do this sort of work," he added. "It is a violation of every suggestion of decency and propriety, and the man who filches a conversation in this way had much better steal the money out of his victim's pocket. It is the underhanded work that has given to journalists the name of ear-wigs and spies, and that has thrown suspicion on their work." [18]

The friendships which grew out of his interviews during these years with some 500 prominent persons, North and South, were invaluable to Grady throughout his career. Indeed, it is doubtful whether he ever would have become a part owner of the *Atlanta Constitution* if he had not gone in January, 1880, to Louisville, Kentucky, and "scooped the country" on the plans of the Louisville and Nashville Railroad for expansion to Atlanta and thence to the coast. Grady obtained the exclusive story from Victor Newcomb, the dynamic young President of the L. & N., who took a decided fancy to him. Newcomb invited Grady to accompany him on several trips. While the two were in New York in May, 1880, Grady made such a favorable impression upon Cyrus W. Field, the millionaire merchant and promoter of the first trans-Atlantic cable, that Field lent him $20,000 with which to buy a quarter interest in the *Constitution*.[14] Guided by Newcomb in a speculation, Grady profited enough out of a spectacular rise in L. & N. stock to pay back the entire loan within two years.

Although Grady became managing editor of the *Constitution* when he acquired an interest in the paper, he continued for at least two years to spend more of his time on the road than in the office. "I am on the wing all the time," he told a reporter of the *Charlotte Observer* in April, 1881. "I passed one-third of my time last year in a sleeper, and I haven't had an hour's rest in ten years." At this time he still had "co-equal supervision" of the *New York Herald*'s Southern correspondence, and was engaged in writing for the *Herald*, from advance sheets, a review of Jefferson Davis' long-anticipated book. Grady had come to North Carolina, accompanied by two artists, to prepare a series of illustrated articles for *Harper's* and the *New York Graphic*. "I suppose I have written more about the South," he said, "than any man living." [15]

After covering Atlanta's first International Cotton Exposition in the fall of 1881 for the Northern press, Grady gave up outside newspaper connections and devoted his attention to the *Constitution*. But even as managing editor he could never resist the desire to report a big news event. "There is no sense of editorial dignity about me," he explained. "I hold that the editor of a newspaper or anybody else about the establishment ought to do anything that comes to his hand, for news is the feature and opinions are of secondary importance. If I see a dog fight and think I can hit it off to suit the reader, I am going to do it." [16]

There are hundreds of instances, according to his associates, in which Grady the managing editor voluntarily assumed the duties of a reporter. [17]

As a managing editor, Grady believed that "newspapers, like men, proved themselves in emergencies." [18] While he insisted that his paper should be evenly good from day to day, he had boyish delight in the occasions that justified a "big spread." His mind and hand were never surer, Harris has testified, than "when the huge press of the *Constitution* was waiting his orders; when the forms were waiting to be closed; when the compositors were fretting and fuming over copy, and when, perhaps, an express train was waiting ten minutes over time to carry the *Constitution* to its subscribers. . . . He seemed to infuse something of his fire and enthusiasm into every member of his staff, and each man seemed to feel it was incumbent upon him to be at his best. . . ." Besides being "able to tell news when he saw it," writes still another associate, "he was equally able to tell in advance when it was going to happen, and he could usually manipulate things so as to make it happen." [19]

Grady's methods were Napoleonic. In a hotly contested election between Democrats and Independents in the fall of 1882, for example, the *Constitution* spent more than $2,000 in gathering the returns from two Congressional districts, mountainous and sparsely settled. Ordinarily the returns would have been days or weeks coming in. Grady determined to have the results the day after election. He chartered special engines, ran telephone and telegraph wires, engaged operators to stay up all night and established relays of horsemen in the mountains. One of the couriers rode forty-three miles over the mountains in four hours and ten minutes to bring returns from precincts that were shut off from railroad and telegraph. Within ten hours after the polls closed, the *Constitution* announced the full returns from the two districts. [20]

Grady realized the value not only of general news but of such special departments as society and sports. In those days of bare-knuckle prize fights, there was always a *Constitution* representative at the ringside, no matter where the fight might take place. Grady organized walking matches and bicycle races, charged admission and paid out the proceeds in prizes to the contestants. He was a baseball fan, and agitated the matter until Atlanta had a team in the Southern League. One day Captain Evan P. Howell, the editor and majority stockholder of the *Constitution*, complained about the telegraph tolls on baseball news. "If you don't stop it," he warned Grady, "I'm going to charge it up to you." "That's all right, charge it," the managing editor replied. "I'm going to have the baseball news just the same." [21]

The *Constitution* built up an extensive network of correspondents throughout the South, with Grady personally directing their work. On April 2, 1886, the paper boasted that it had used 12,000 words over the wire that day in addition to the 8,000 words received from the Associated Press. Its monthly bill for telegraphic service, the *Constitution* stated, was "as much as that of every other daily paper in Georgia, Alabama, Mississippi, North and South Carolina, and Florida combined."

When an earthquake shook the entire eastern seaboard of the United States on August 31, 1886, and news of Charleston's terrible disaster reached Atlanta, Grady was off on the first train for South Carolina. The regular train could go no farther than Augusta, but by carriage, boat, and special engine Grady reached Charleston at 10 o'clock on the night of September 2. He was the first newspaperman on the scene from the outside world. [22]

Riding over the city and interviewing authorities during the night and early morning after his arrival, Grady wrote and telegraphed to the *Constitution*, the *New York World*, the *Cincinnati Enquirer* and several other newspapers a story of more than 5,000 words on the earthquake. It was the most important event, to his mind, since the surrender of the Confederate army. He remained in Charleston several days, reporting not only the local details but obtaining from scientists throughout the country their opinions as to the probable cause and outcome of the tremor. Papers in Boston, New York, Philadelphia and Chicago later copied the opinions of their own scientists from the *Constitution*. [23]

The *Cincinnati Enquirer* editorially termed Grady's articles "the most brilliant and accurate description of the earthquake . . . that had appeared in print." The *New York World* said they "show in a strong light the value of the trained journalistic mind in grasping at once the salient points on a subject." [24]

Published in the *World* over his full name, the stories from Charleston placed Grady "suddenly and conspicuously before the whole American people." Just a few weeks later, he received an invitation to address the New England Society of New York. He was the first Southern man since the war to be so honored.

The national prominence gained by his speech on "The New South" in December, 1886, made it necessary for Grady to devote more and more of his time to his office and to the editorial page, and less to the outside exploits in which he so delighted. His correspondence was tremendous. Often he would have as many as fifty callers in a single morning.[25] He was the first national figure that the booming young city of Atlanta had produced, and every politician sought to hang on his coat-tail.

Office life did not agree with Grady. His uncommonly active mind and naturally nervous temperament required as a balance wheel the physical activity to which he had been accustomed. A comparison of photographs in the Emory collection shows that the trim, athletic figure of 1881 had become, by the latter part of 1887, unhealthily puffy and paunchy. "I went out for a half-hour today—the first time I had been on Whitehall in six months," he wrote to his mother in December, 1888. When pneumonia struck him on the trip to Boston a year later, his tired body had no strength to resist it.

Among the manuscripts found on the dead editor's desk was a sheet containing his last batch of editorial paragraphs. One of these perhaps reveals a deep longing of the great journalist whom fame and circumstance had thrust into an unsought arena. "A good reporter who subsides into an able editor," it said, "marks a loss to journalism." [26] Henry Grady was a good reporter.

NOTES

[1] *American Newspaper Directory*, 1889.
[2] *Atlanta Constitution*, May 28, June 19, 1869.
[3] Article by Amos J. Cummings, managing editor of the *New York Sun*, in Grady Scrapbooks. Clipping of Grady's first contribution to the *New York Herald*, July 25, 1876, also is preserved.
[4] Interview with Evan P. Howell, who employed Grady, in *Atlanta News*, Sept. 12, 1901; also, *Atlanta Constitution*, Oct. 19, 1876.
[5] Claude G. Bowers, *The Tragic Era* (Cambridge, 1929), p. 522.
[6] *New York Herald*, Nov. 8, 1876.
[7] Bowers, *op. cit.*, p. 523.
[8] *New York Herald*, Nov. 20, 1876.
[9] Article by W. T. Turnbull in *Atlanta Constitution*, Feb. 23, 1890.

[10] *Ibid.*

[11] Joel C. Harris. *Life of Henry W. Grady* (New York, 1890), p. 77.

[12] *Atlanta Constitution,* June 14, 1878.

[13] *Atlanta Constitution,* Aug. 16, 1879.

[14] Original documents in Grady Collection, Emory University.

[15] Clipping from *Charlotte Observer,* April, 1881, in Grady Scrapbooks.

[16] *New York Sun,* Dec. 24, 1889.

[17] Harris, *op. cit.,* p. 63.

[18] *Atlanta Constitution,* Sept. 5, 1886.

[19] Thomas H. Martin, *Atlanta and Its Builders* (New York, 1902), p. 652.

[20] *Atlanta Constitution,* Nov. 7, 8, 9, 1882.

[21] Article by "Bill Arp" in *Atlanta Constitution,* Dec. 29, 1889.

[22] *New York World,* Sept. 2, 1886.

[23] *Atlanta Constitution,* Sept. 5, 1886.

[24] *Ibid.,* Sept. 9, 1886.

[25] Information from J. R. Holliday, Atlanta, who was Grady's secretary in 1886–89.

[26] Grady Manuscripts, Emory University.

18

The Man Who Made the *Star*

by WILLIAM ALLEN WHITE

WILLIAM ALLEN WHITE of the *Emporia Gazette* was commissioned
by *Collier's* to write this article about William Rockhill Nelson in June 1915 just
after death took the founder of the *Kansas City Star*. The article thus has a
double journalistic importance in being the tribute of one distinguished editor
to another as well as in reflecting White's warmth and color.

IN THE beginning, thirty-five years ago when this generation was
young, Kansas City sprawled on a half dozen ugly yellow clay hills rising
from the west bank of the Missouri River, a "mean city," if ever there
was one. Mud streets, wooden sidewalks covered with wooden awnings
over the business thoroughfares that slouched or staggered toward the
river; cribbed vice reeking and stinking through all the north part of
the town, and the catfish aristocracy of the unreconstructed South
sulking on the hills about the town; a dozen railroads pouring thousands of Western immigrants into the Union Station every day —
vigorous, hustling young men and their wives and children pressing
into the great plains to take homesteads and grow up with the country; a few pioneering packing houses near the Kawsmouth beginning
to turn the great herds of the prairies into food; Northern hustlers
and Southern families dividing the town into factions; the larcenous
bark of the real estate vendor forever dinning into the consciousness
of visitors, and over all and through all the slambang a vast opium
eater's dream of power and glory and wealth and splendor that was
to come — such was the Kansas City of the late seventies.

Into this gorgeous nightmare of promise came William Rockhill
Nelson in 1880 to found the *Kansas City Star*. When he died, thirty-
five years later, April 13, 1915, to be exact — he left a newspaper which
is reckoned by men who know as one of the first dozen newspapers
in the world; an organ of public opinion that is the expression of the

243

universal world spirit of his age, translated through his personality into an intensely individual thing.

At first Kansas City had some trouble cataloguing Mr. Nelson. He was thirty-nine years old, with better than a fair education, and with more of the air of a man of the world than most men about him. He was nearly six feet tall and stout. He had a massive dignity that large men sometimes have. In the nature of the times, if he had been of another sort, people might have called him "Bill." For years thousands of people in Kansas City did refer to him as "Bill" Nelson, but no one called him "Bill." Sooner would one address a heroic statue of Buddha as "Bud." Time came when they referred to him as "Baron Bill" of Brush Creek, or as "The Baron of Brush Creek," for he was of the baronial type, but distinctly not of the "Bill" type. No man survived that day as Mister. The town had to do something with his name; so, early in his career in Kansas City, he became "Colonel." Not that he was ever a colonel of anything: he was just coloneliferous. When he came to Kansas City, in that early day a young man of thirty-nine, the strong, raw, noisy, lawless, conscienceless community, drunk and dressed up with optimism, spoke to something gay and adventurous in his nature, and on his part it was a case of love at first sight.

BACK OF HIM WAS BLOOD

He was a typical upper-class American then when the upper crust of our society was about where our middle class is to-day. Back of him was blood — good governing blood; his forbears' names are in city charters and regimental rosters of the Revolution; one was a judge, one a Congressman, one a Quaker pioneer, and one a two-fisted Irishman; his father was a prominent citizen of Indiana in the middle of the last century. There was no tradition of wealth behind him, but much tradition of responsibility. And the middle-aged person with a boy's head on his shoulders who came bolting into Kansas City in 1880 had in his head an assortment of varied memories. There were memories of days when he had been a rebellious young blade in Fort Wayne — too irrepressible for the public school and too energetic for Notre Dame, a Catholic school, where his father, an Episcopal vestryman, had sent the youth in the hope of curbing his insurgency; memories of a try at the law; an attempt at holding a petty office in the court; an adventure in the real estate business; an excursion into cotton planting and storekeeping in Georgia; a rather successful journey into practical politics, when he helped manage the Tilden campaign in Indiana, and a real fortune made and lost in railroad contracting and bridge building.

He was considerable of a man of the world for those hilarious days of the new Kansas City, and carried a certain consciousness of his distinction in his heart; and so, while he doubtless never resented the "Bill" business which would have been his natural portion, probably he also never exactly encouraged the familiarity of the fresh, crisp gentry of the place who but a few short years before had to be tied while they were collared and shod! So, because he would not get drunk with them, would not be bribed by them or bribe with them, would not share with them when they cut a melon in city graft, and would not brawl with them, but wore his clothes well, knew and observed the proprieties unconsciously, though not punctiliously, and preferred the society of his kind, he was knighted colonel, and from the first held in a sort of shivery respect.

When the *Star* was founded there were four other Kansas City daily papers. The *Times* and the *Journal* were the party thunderers, and there was a ragpicker or so and a plunderer in the field. The *Times*, being Democratic, represented the unconquered confederacy, made heroes of the James boys, regarded all Republicans as horse thieves, and frequently was called upon to punctuate its editorial utterances with a horse pistol. It was a fire-eating, blood-and-thunder, partisan sheet, of the type long since vanished from American journalism. The *Journal*, which was Republican in politics, sang softly as the organ of commerce and business progress, and spoke even in that remote day for the railroads and the banks. Its editor was in politics. He had a vision for the betterment of humanity — chiefly through prosperity — but something of the idealism of the fifties and sixties, something of what the war really meant, clung to him, and made the *Journal* rather more than respectable — a force for such righteousness as the times would permit.

Into this field came the *Star*. Mr. Nelson had tried his wings as an editor in Fort Wayne. He desired a wider field. He brought with him a few years' experience — and something better: a genuine passion for the newspaper business. In politics he was a mugwump, who had come into his independence by renouncing the Democratic party after it had refused to renominate Tilden in 1880. And a mugwump in that time and place was in a sore plight. Naturally he was taken for a blackmailer. Otherwise, why should he not line up with one of the parties?

THE STAR GAVE THE NEWS

And then another suspicious thing—the *Star* printed the news: all of it. In those days and in that part of the West money was used as naturally to suppress the news of unpleasant episodes—not of a political nature—as ligatures to suppress bleeding. It took the community some time to discover that the *Star* would not take money. It had but a meager telegraphic news service, and was filled with articles reprinted from other papers and from magazines and books. Once in those gala days when the old *Kansas City Times* was having the low resorts raided in order to catch certain prominent Kansas City Republican statesmen, the *Star* was running Emerson's Essays in short chunks scattered through the paper, and columns of book reviews, with editorials on Mr. Howells as a new force in American letters. It was awful. To be a gentleman; to be a mugwump; to refuse honest money for a peccadillo about professional ethics; to devote more space to Henry James than to Jesse in Jesse's home town, and still to be a big, laughing, fat, good-natured, rollicking, haw-hawing person who loved a drink, a steak, a story, and a fight—strong men shuddered and turned away from the spectacle. They couldn't be sure whether he was crazy or they were!

One of the earliest ructions the *Star* had was over the town "opera house." It was on the second floor over a store, and the *Star* called attention first to the fact that it was poorly built, and second to the fact that the narrow stairway from the single public exit made it a fire trap. The simple answer of Colonel Coates, the owner of the opera house and the leading citizen of the town, was that Colonel Nelson was a blackmailer. That answer sufficed for the public; it was used to blackmailers. But that answer did not satisfy Colonel Coates. And a few weeks later, after the article denouncing the editor of the *Star* as a blackmailer had appeared in another paper, Colonel Coates came to the *Star* office and said: "You were right, and I was wrong. The opera house is unsafe, and it is a fire trap." And the plans and specifications for the New Coates Opera House, which was the pride of Kansas City for a quarter of a century, were soon ready for the contractor.

THE STAR GOT THINGS DONE

This was probably the first notable demand the *Star* made for better living conditions in the new town. The later life of Mr. Nelson was a continuous battle for civic and State improvement. His life's aim resolved itself into a fight — there were so many fights, some of the battles waging simultaneously, that perhaps campaign is a better word than fight; so let us say that his latter activities resolved themselves into a campaign for the "more abundant life" of men and women in his city, in his State, in his sphere of influence throughout the Missouri Valley. It is therefore of interest to examine this campaign for a moment. Looking back over the *Star*'s files of that early day one is impressed with the fact that the motive in the contest was somewhat newspaper enterprise. It was one of the *Star*'s things. There was a certain pride of achievement in the accomplishment of the new opera house, which had youth and fire and pleasure in it. As the years go on, and we see in the *Star*'s files other struggles appearing day after day, we find that the motives behind these militant activities have been slowly growing into a policy. It is too much to presume that this policy was conceived in advance in Mr. Nelson's mind.

The human heart and head do not initiate omniscience — except in retrospect. It was gay old General Sherman who said it was unwise to give a reason for an action before doing it, because so many better reasons might turn up afterward.

THE GOOD OLD PATH

The career of the *Star* for thirty-five years seems to be going in a straight line to a definite end, from that first tiff over the rattletrap opera house down to the present fight for the city improvement bonds. And yet it is not the best praise of Mr. Nelson to declare that he looked ahead and saw all that was coming. But given a heart fundamentally honest, and a mind keen to express newspaper enterprise in the terms of public welfare, such a policy as the *Star*'s unwavering, consistent, indomitable policy is the natural result.

When the paper was but a year old it attacked the horse-car monopoly in a mayoralty campaign. The attack won; the *Star*'s candidate was elected over the opposition of the older papers — not because the *Star* was supporting him, but because the *Star* was able to state the situation clearly — to make the fight intelligently. The franchise that was granted in competition with the old horse-car monopoly developed into the cable system. And the cable system climbed over the yellow clay hills of Kansas City, dipped into the great ravines and dived across the valleys; and because Kansas City had a street-car system that permitted it to widen out and to become a city in its rough environment, it went ahead of Leavenworth, St. Joseph, and Omaha, and took first place as a Missouri River town beyond the Mississippi. Of course Mr. Nelson did not see this when he supported the anti-monopoly ticket. Business judgment, the bread-and-butter side of the problem, the business men and advertisers of that day were naturally with the order that was. They stood with the horse-car monopoly. But newspaper enterprise, plus fundamental honesty, gave Mr. Nelson vision to see that the *Star*'s interests were with the people's interests, and the people's interests were with the anti-monopoly crowd, so he went in. And he never had to apologize for that fight.

So it was with every battle in the thirty-five years' campaign. Time and time again he was whipped; the people couldn't see it the *Star*'s way. But never could they quote the *Star* of one campaign against the *Star* in another. Always Mr. Nelson took the honest side. The big, laughing, good-natured, kindly spoken man who came bursting into Kansas City with a newspaper that printed all the news, and yet never seemed to let its emotion express itself in black type or broken columns, but let its facts arouse their own emotions in the readers, had no gift of prophecy. His clairvoyance consisted in seeing from day to day and from year to year the essentially honest and workable plan for that day and for that year, and advocating it with all the enthusiasm of a nature built on almost grotesquely large lines, physically, mentally, morally; a nature vastly kind and intensely curious about a most interesting world; a nature literally bubbling with love of life and men and founded on a large and humorous charity that never remotely approached cynicism of any kind. It was this hulking, jovial, irrepressible soul, moving like a cumulus cloud through its earthly habitat, steadfastly, slowly, never turning, never breaking, never cyclonic, that reacted upon passing events about it, and made the policy of the *Star*.

And the policy of the *Star* gave color to the opinion and economic status of the people of the region known as the Missouri Valley.

Of course the town was many years getting into its consciousness the real meaning of the *Star* in its life. Yet to the few men who met Mr. Nelson even in those first years of his editorship his purpose seems to have been fairly clear. For when the circulation of the paper was growing beyond its press — a miserable little flat-bed press with a capacity of 3,000 an hour — the man to whom he turned for credit when he needed a modern press was Colonel Kersey Coates, whose "opera house" the *Star* had emptied. And Colonel Coates guaranteed the notes and the press came. It was first used on the *Star*'s fourth birthday. "And do you know," said Colonel Nelson many years after to a younger friend who had graduated from the *Star* and in his own office was putting in some new bit of machinery, "do you know I was so happy about that press that I couldn't sleep the first night it was in. I'd get up and look at the paper — gaze at it — it was a kind of holy picture to me, and then I'd go to bed and get up and look at it all over again — every page, every advertisement, and go back to bed." He laughed the great roaring, guttural laugh that came surging up from his pyramidal body into his massive face and threw back his fine gray head as he said: "And 'y gad I'm a good deal that way now; I never have got weaned from the *Star*. I'm likely to get up to-night and look at it and say: 'Well, now, ain't she a daisy!'"

To the hour of his death he kept his enthusiasm, his boyish joy in the passions of his youth. Age never changed his view of life. He was static in the eternal dynamics of his joyous growth.

One of the first jobs of the new press was to print a call for a mass meeting — that was something like a riot — to protest against the extension of a thirty-year street-car franchise without transfers. The city council had passed the franchise. The mass meeting gave the mayor reasons for vetoing it. The press was not paid for. The expenses of the *Star* with the old press had not been met by its income. Mr. Nelson's notes were baled in a considerable stack in the Armour bank, and the Armour bank was the political bank of the town in those days. And the politics of the town was for the franchise. But that did not affect the *Star*'s policy. And the franchise was lost.

"No," he said again to his young friend, new to proprietorship, in discussing the mass-meeting incident. "It wasn't so much courage; I have no more courage than the rest of them. But I saw those scoundrels [he said damned scoundrels, but we'll forget that] putting all kinds of pressure on the mayor — from all the so-called respectable and business element — to tie the people up in a knot, and I had faith that the people would not stand it, and then," he laughed, "you know all the other papers were in the scheme, and there was too much competition in that line — so I took the chance." And he won, and the people began to have faith in the *Star* and to expect its leadership.

And here is a curious element of his strength. It was faith in the *Star*, not faith in Mr. Nelson, that inspired the people. The town was growing. Excepting a few thousand people who remembered him when he first came to town, no one knew the editor of the *Star*. He did not attend the riotous mass meeting that upheld the mayor in his veto. He had served on no committees. He had never appeared on a speaking program at a dinner or a meeting, and all his life Mr. Nelson shunned crowds. He went from his house to his office and back again in the first years of his editorship alone; later he rode in a carriage, still later in a coupé, and finally in a limousine. Being born to a social purple, he had no social ambitions. While the editor of a paper in St. Louis was so eaten up with social vanity that he printed the names of the occupants of the reserved seats at a circus to get his name in the society columns of his own paper, Mr. Nelson's name rarely appeared in the *Star* — except at the top of its editorial columns. Through his entire career Mr. Nelson cultivated a sort of elaborate anonymity. So, in the contest for good government, he desired to establish faith, not in himself, but faith in the *Star*. Therefore he would run for no office, nor would he permit his name to be considered for an office. "An editor," he declared, "should be a kind of political monk; he must take a monastic vow against holding office. For if he doesn't — as sure as God made little apples — they'll get him. If he has a blind side — society or business or politics — they'll get him. These rascals [omitting the damn for brevity] down there at the courthouse and the city hall and down at Jefferson City, if they knew I'd take any office [again we cut out the qualifying adjective] from dog catcher to President, would be around with their peacock feathers fanning me to sleep."

"BUT NEVER NEUTRAL"

He felt keenly that the *Star* should receive every ounce of credit it could have without bragging. But W. R. Nelson in his eyes was a person whose inconsequential attitude would have delighted the heart of Mr. Toots. He was accessible enough. Always his office door was open. The humblest citizen of Kansas City could and did come to him. But because he preserved his obscurity; because he never served on a committee, or caroused around at uplift meetings in person, few of his own social and financial cult or class knew him. In all the half a million people within twenty miles of the *Star* office, not over a thousand would have known Mr. Nelson if he had appeared on the street. He could have walked into any of a dozen political gatherings he denounced without being identified by the men whose activities he was deploring. So in his later life as in his earlier life, the avenues of sinister approach to him were few.

As the years went by, and the *Star*, which was always independent but never neutral, came to have the character of a real personality in its sphere of influence, the personality of its editor was forgotten for the most part by its readers. And that is a curious thing: for the personality of the editor of the *Star* was infinitely more vivid than was the personality of the *Star*. Some men — even some men with elements of greatness in them — repress the outward expression of themselves. They are gray and leaden and puzzling. Mr. Nelson was one of those men who exude character. To begin with, he looked different from the ordinary run of men. He was big — monumental, with a general Himalayan effect as he loomed behind a desk. He had a great voice; in his emotional moments — which were not infrequent — this great voice rattled like artillery. He loved figures of speech; had a thousand homely similes and often spoke in parables. Moreover he was always doing things that were interesting — outside of his professional career. Stories of his sayings and doings sprang up in his pathway and became legends. Always there were stories of his vast charities; his patience with rascals or fools — or both. He despised a fool and hated a rascal and was forever lending them a humorous tolerance — but never in the *Star*. There the fool and the rascal had scant welcome. But in his private relations with men he was given to a sort of Browningesque forgiveness of the unforgiveable, and tolerance of the intolerable.

Perhaps one reason for this seeming duality of characters arose in the fact that he never wrote for the *Star*. Certainly no other editor ever pressed his own dominant personality into a paper more completely than Mr. Nelson put his vigorous personality into the *Star*. But the equation of his personality never got into the *Star* through any peculiarity of his literary style. One comes to know Henry Watterson, now the Last of the Mohicans, and one used to know Charles Dana and Horace Greeley, and one recognized Joseph Medill and the editorial giants of the elder days by what they wrote; by the way they turned phrases; by the quirks of their rhetorical self-illumination.

WAS HE A WRITER?

Mr. Nelson thought he was not a writer. He never put his pencil to paper. He called one of his editors or reporters — he referred to all of his writers as reporters — talked the matter in hand over, and the article, whether it was a news story or an editorial, appeared to run through the mental machinery of the writer. Often some phrase or some group of phrases in the strong, homely, figurative language of Mr. Nelson persisted. If it did persist, it was the meat of the article. But often no phrase of his was preserved in articles that pioneered out into new and daring policies.

Yet the article was more truly his than if he had polished every phrase. It was his vision, his courage, his conception of justice. And the irony of it all is that readers often will read personality only from phrases, from literary style; they do not seem to get personality — not, at least, those intimate traits and those delicious human foibles that make a human being well-beloved — through an exhibition of the major virtues. So even to the millions who came to know and follow the *Star*, the man who made it great by sheer force of his own masterful greatness lived and died a stranger to them. If they met the ruddy-faced, square-shouldered, great-bodied, short-legged, bronze-featured man in the street, if they heard his rumbling, good-natured voice, if they met the radiant sunset of a smile that often glowed in his kindly face, doubtless they would turn their heads and say: "There goes some one!" But only a few of his million readers would have identified him with the upstanding, enterprising, wholesome, good-natured newspaper that brought them daily much of their mental and moral and spiritual pabulum.

CAPTURING KANSAS

Before the *Star* was ten years old it had the lead over all papers in its field. It captured Kansas City in five years, and had taken Kansas in two years more. Because it had gone into city politics, and had taken the honest side intelligently and with incidental courage, Kansas City people trusted the *Star*; and because it was interesting, because it had a distinctly literary flavor and avoided sensationalism, Kansas took the *Star* for her bosom pin. In the first two decades of the *Star*'s existence it did not take any considerable part in Kansas politics. Indeed, from 1880 until 1900 there was no black and white of wrong and right in Kansas politics. The Republicans were sordid and narrow, and the Democrats and their heirs and assigns, the Populists, were broad and incompetent. So the *Star* printed the news and scorned the devil, who was rather well intrenched on both sides of every question in Kansas in those days. Nationally, Mr. Nelson supported President Cleveland in office and out, through thick and thin. And the things he stood for the *Star* upheld. Low tariffs, a gold standard, civil service, the overthrow of the plutocracy — these were the fundamentals of the *Star*'s politics and policies so far as they affected matters national. But in the first twenty years of its life the *Star* paid relatively little attention to any political matters outside of those in Kansas City.

In city matters Mr. Nelson's vision of righteousness was unfolding rapidly. It was no longer newspaper enterprise that moved him. He was consumed by a fire to serve. In 1892 he went after election thieves mercilessly — even election thieves who had helped to elect the men whom the *Star* had supported. The thieves went to the penitentiary. The next year a fight for cheaper gas consumed Mr. Nelson's interest, and he hired experts, paying them the fancy price that experts demand; he coached his reporters and writers in the cost and price of gas, and made the whole city see what a just price was. Kansas City people knew as much about gas as they knew about arithmetic. And he won his fight. In the winter following the *Star* began to promote organized charity. The editor talked with his young men, sent them out to investigate cases, assigned his editorial writers to reportorial beats so that they would put some well-directed emotion into their editorials; the *Star* gave, and it demanded that others give. It attacked poorly built tenements; it went after loan sharks. Like a great watchdog, it shook shyster lawyers who were bleeding the poor. For years this continued demand for equitable treatment for poverty was a moving passion in Mr. Nelson's heart. As a result appeared the free legal-aid bureau, the municipal farm, the welfare board, the divorce proctor, and, interlocked with these things, came the demand for a park and boulevard system.

Curiously enough, the park and boulevard system of Kansas City is the obvious monument to Mr. Nelson's thirty-five years of activity. And this is because it is a material thing. He literally gave color to the life and thought and aspiration of ten millions of people living between the Missouri River and the Rio Grande in the formative years of their growth as commonwealths — part of the national commonwealth. He and they together were dreaming States and building them, each reacting upon the other. The aspirations of the people were caught by his sensitive brain, and he gave these aspirations back in the *Star* policies. Kansas, western Missouri, Oklahoma, northern Texas, New Mexico, and Colorado form a fairly homogeneous section of our population. That section has grown up on the *Star*. Its religion, its conceptions of art, its politics, its business, its economic scale of living, reflect the influence of the indomitable mind of the man behind the *Star*, just as he gathered and voiced the latent visions of these people and gave them conscious form. These things are of the spirit. But half a hundred miles of paving amid trees and grass and flowers and pergolas, and several thousand acres of flowers and grass and trees in parks — these are material. And so the park and boulevard system of Kansas City stands as Mr. Nelson's monument because it is of the earth — earthy.

Yet, after all, these things of earth and wood and stone are accurate symbols of what Mr. Nelson stood for. These boulevards and these parks, from one end of Kansas City to the other, furnish the setting for tens of thousands of homes of a character almost unique for urban populations. They are, first of all, homes in detached houses. In front of each home is a plot of grass, some shrubs, and a few trees. The house is generally a two-story-and-a-half house, built most frequently of brick or stone. Its cost runs somewhere from five to twelve thousand dollars. A considerable majority of the houses in Kansas City built in the last twenty years are of this character. The apartment and the flat are the exception in Kansas City. Generally speaking, the flat and the apartment are found in the business district, or near it, and they were built in the old days before the park and boulevard system came, and offered cheap real estate, plenty of breathing space, and the opportunity to build the ideal middle-class home. Kansas City, like Los Angeles, is a distinctive middle-class American town. The upper class and the lower class are in the minority. The section of the country in which the *Star* finds its circulation — a section almost as large as Europe without Russia — is a middle-class section. No one is very rich there and few are afflicted with biting poverty. Democracy in government comes nearer finding a realization, and economic equality is more nearly approximated than in any other similar area in the world. And the park and boulevard system of Kansas City, for which Mr. Nelson in his studied anonymity through the *Star*, fought so valiantly and so well — the park and boulevard system of the commercial capital of this kingdom of the Southwest — is as suitable a monument as any material characterization might be of all that the man stood for.

The fight through the Missouri Legislatures and the Missouri courts for the park and boulevard system ended in 1895. Then the parks and boulevards began to grow in Kansas City. And the *Star* found itself in a bitter, almost daily, war with speculating real estate owners. It was no new controversy. From the first year of the *Star*'s existence until the day its founder died he had fought just one kind of a battle: the fight between property and men. He took the side of men. With the owner of the fire-trap theatre, with the franchise grabbers, with the election crooks who sought to perpetuate graft, with the waterworks company seeking to prevent municipal ownership, with the gas company for dollar gas — all the differences had been upon the fundamental issue between the rights of men to service that would broaden the lives of the many and the rights of property to profits that would enhance the lives of a few. It was the middle-class fight. And Kansas City emerged a middle-class town.

But all this battling, which may have begun with newspaper enterprise for its impulse, was telling upon the editor of the *Star*. He was thriving on it as a publisher, growing with it as an editor, and broadening and deepening with it as a man. He came West a practical business man, who had made and lost a fortune, who had the essential democracy of the American aristocrat of the latter half of the nineteenth century, who had the ideals of the governing classes, and he came West to grow up with the country.

And every day of his life he did grow up with the country — spiritually. Growth was the motive of his life. He socialized himself as completely as it is possible for a man to socialize himself and live practically in modern civilization. He lived a soldier's life — a soldier of the common good, and he had to be forever casting off unnecessary equipment. His paper dropped whisky advertising. It turned away quacks and clairvoyants. It barred fake land sales and get-rich-quick schemes of all kinds. Many harmful patent medicines went by the board.

HE WAS PROUD OF HIS ENEMIES

Scare headlines never were allowed in the *Star*, nor was appeal ever permitted to the prejudice and passion of the ignorant through red type, flaming letters, and gaudy pictures. The first page of the little four-page sheet issued in 1880 with no box-car letters, and with no screaming heads, is enough like the first page of the *Star* to-day to be the second edition of the same issue. The decent form and the frank statement of the middle-class ideal are the only things in all the *Star's* mental and physical environment that have not changed. And all the while the devil has posted a competitor beside the *Star* who practiced every carnal art known to the yellow trade. One paper after another has entered the evening field with its big scare heads, with its crass appeal to the mob, with dirty advertising, with emotional sob squads like howling dervishes of journalism tearing up the earth around the *Star*; with mud slingers attacking Mr. Nelson savagely, accusing him of personal immorality and sculduggery; calling him a blackmailer, a grafter, a thief — and organizing the criminal section of the community against him. Yet never one word has he replied. Not once in thirty-five years has the *Star* mentioned the name of one of its slanderous competitors, nor replied even by inference to any of their charges.

And the other crowd, the wealthy privilege reapers, have attacked Mr. Nelson and the *Star* in their own way. They have organized advertising boycotts. They have tried to undermine his credit. They have organized with the crooks in politics and have fostered an anti-*Star* party in Kansas City, sometimes operating under one national party name and sometimes under another. They have manned the courts against him, have got behind fake libel suits, have even haled him into court for contempt, and then their weapons bent or blunted, and were ineffective. Once in a libel suit within the last decade or so, when the attorney for the plaintiff was the attorney for one of the great public-service corporations with which the *Star* had been fighting for a bone of privilege, it was announced that they were going to give Mr. Nelson a grilling on the stand and make him tell of all the boodle and graft and corruption he had shared. When he went on the stand he said: "Now I don't want my attorneys to object to any possible questions the plaintiff's attorney may ask. My life is an open book. Go ahead with your questions," and no question was asked outside of the issue, and no attorney ever gave a witness such distinguished consideration as that corporation counsel prosecuting a measly little libel suit gave to Mr. Nelson.

As the years went by he came to know the works and ways of the plunderbund of common interests that preys on every community, large or small; that unites always the very rich and the criminals in a community to maintain the order that is; to stop progress, because progress means a wider distribution of the fruits of civilization. And when the *Star* began a fight it knew its enemies. And for all his wide tolerance of the weaknesses of men, for all his forgiving nature which made him forget easily, no wings of a pale sainthood sprouted under Mr. Nelson's suspenders. He was as proud of his enemies as Cornelia was of her jewels. And he liked to keep them and count them over.

Once the president of a scurrilous newspaper that had dogged Mr. Nelson's heels for years, accusing him of all the crimes of the calendar, became manager of a theatre — the Willis Wood — a beautiful playhouse and popular. The time came for the *Star* to increase its rates. Notice was served on all the *Star*'s patrons, and they agreed to the raise — all but the Willis Wood. It refused to pay its bill. Naturally its advertising was refused. It was told that it could have advertising over the counter at the counter rate. It came in a few times, paid the counter rate, and then formally notified the *Star* that it would use the *Star* no longer as an advertising medium. In a few weeks the manager of the theatre saw that he could not get along without the *Star*. He brought his advertising back. It was refused. Mr. Nelson declared that the Willis Wood had gone out voluntarily; it could stay out.

As the winter grew old it was apparent that the Willis Wood was losing money. Its owners tried to get the *Star* to take the theatre's advertising. Delegations of business men came and pleaded. Mr. Nelson was obdurate. Finally came R. A. Long, one of the most benevolent of the rich men of Kansas City. A kindly, churchly, soft-spoken, meek man was Mr. Long. He sat before the pyramidal hulk of the *Star*'s editor and begged that the *Star* would take the advertising of the failing theatre. He knew, did Mr. Long, that the manager of the theatre, as president of the scurrilous newspaper, had attacked Mr. Nelson unmercifully; had accused him of dastardly crimes; had assailed his honor and integrity, without a word of defense or reply from the *Star*. And Mr. Long recited these things and begged the editor to take a high and charitable view of the man who now was pleading for his financial life. Mr. Nelson's theory was that the community was better off if the manager of the theatre and the newspaper company didn't have any further financial life. Finally Mr. Long said: "Now, Mr. Nelson [he said Colonel, of course, as the world did], "now, Colonel, wouldn't you feel better if to-night you could think that in all this town you had not one enemy when you turn on your pillow to rest?"

Quickly as a flash the deep roaring voice came thundering out of the mountainous pyramid with the implacable face at the apex:

"No — no, no, by God. If I thought that I wouldn't sleep a wink."

WHAT NELSON LOVED

He loved his enemies — so dearly that he wouldn't part with a real choice one for money. For money had little meaning to Mr. Nelson. He made it easily and valued it lightly. His estate seems to be worth five or six million dollars — perhaps more. He trusteed it for his wife and child for life, and gave it all to the city to found an art gallery for the people. In handling money he invested it, but not upon a speculative basis. When he built a house for rent — and he built many hundreds — he used two by sixes instead of two by four for the studding and rafters. He put out scores of miles of stone fences around his renting property, and covered the fences with roses and honeysuckles — and kept them growing. He loved beauty. He founded and maintained for twenty years an art gallery, where good copies of famous pictures could be seen seven days and nights in the week. He sent a shipload of food to the starving Cubans, not as a newspaper enterprise, but to feed the hungry. The only newspaper enterprise he knew was to get all of the news and print it wholesomely. If Providence let unpleasant things happen, it was his business to tell of it, but not to gloat over it, not to stick a banal snout in it and whiff it for his readers.

FIGHTING THE GOOD FIGHT

When he bought the old Kansas City *Times,* after one owner following another had been sinking money in it, and the paper mills controlled the property, the first step he took in the trade was to find out how much money the last owner — a lame man — had sunk in it, and he made that sum the first consideration in the trade. Thus, when the attorney for the paper mills opened the trade by reciting what good neighbors he and Mr. Nelson had been in the past, the big man listened for a time and then rumbled from his big chest:

"That's all right — now let's quit being so damn neighborly and make a trade here that won't rob a cripple."

He did not spell his success in terms of money. He cheapened nothing he did by estimating it in dollars and cents. When he cut liquor advertising from the *Star* he adjusted no halo on his head. Instead he laughed and said: "Now I've got that foot loose!" He counted his freedom the gain, and never thought of the hundreds of thousands of dollars he had lost. He saw the need of free swimming pools, playgrounds, and a convention hall for his town, and they grew out of the columns of the *Star* like magic palaces. That was in the late years of the last century.

But it was with the rise of the progressive movement of the first decade of this century that the *Star*'s real power outside of Kansas City took root and grew and fruited into a slow revolution in the whole idea of State and city government in the *Star*'s territory. In campaign after campaign in three and four and sometimes five States the *Star* was waging battles for free government. The initiative and referendum came in Missouri, Arkansas, Oklahoma, Nebraska, and Colorado. Commission government with the initiative and referendum and recall for city officers came in all these States and Kansas. Direct popular government is a weapon of the people of the Missouri Valley. So is the primary. The relation of the State to the citizen has been revolutionized in the *Star*'s territory. Bank deposits are guaranteed. Investments are certified by the State. The issues of stocks and bonds of public utilities are supervised by the State; rates of public utilities are being made by the State for consumers of the products of public utilities. Higher technical and professional education is supplied free by the State; the State schools furnish expert aid to the State in its scientific activities. Preventive medicine has become a State industry that touches every citizen. The Board of Health has almost as much power as the Governor. Mothers' pensions are provided by the county and the hours and wages of women and children are controlled by the State. And in all the *Star*'s territory, excepting half a dozen large cities, the sale of liquor is prohibited either by State-wide prohibition or by local option.

During the dozen years while the fight was active for these revolutionary changes in the State governments of the Missouri Valley, Mr. Nelson's reporters were really lieutenants, emissaries, and proconsuls rather than mere writers. They made the news as they went, and like a general in his tent, the big white-haired, ruddy-faced, bull-voiced old soldier of righteousness sat and swore sweetly in mellow joy at the news from the front. He knew every politician in half a dozen States in every party who was true; and the *Star* branded the traitors and the crooks — not by calling names but by printing roll calls. And slowly the firing ceased, and at the beginning of the second decade of the century it was evident that the campaign was over — and won. But the fighting blood still pumped in the brave old heart. He mapped out a new campaign.

When the Progressive party was organized Mr. Nelson followed Colonel Roosevelt, and accepted the Progressive platform as good so far as it went. But he was going farther. Mr. Nelson believed that the courts are bulwarks of privilege, and that high-priced lawyers are the big guns of privilege behind the bulwarks. So he started his campaign for socialized justice. For a public defender, for a commission to throw out vicious litigation, and merely technical causes. If the rich and the poor were real equals in court, had exactly the same kinds of attorneys, as they have the same kinds of judges, or outside of the courts, have the same kinds of school teachers, or the same kinds of preachers, Mr. Nelson believed that privilege would be forced out of the courts. He was perfectly willing to recall judges and decisions if the Bull Moosers desired to recall them to put the fear of the Lord, which is the beginning of wisdom, into the courts. But the recall was a popgun, he thought. The 42-centimeter gun was free justice. Of course it is revolutionary. When it comes, as it will, it will destroy the vicious power of the dollar in the courts, as corrupt practices acts are destroying the vicious power of the dollar in elections and in legislatures, and as the free public schools and universities are destroying the vicious power of caste in social life.

A great vision that for a daily newspaper; for a man to begin striving for at seventy. And yet he rose and went to battle as gayly and as vigorously as he began his first newspaper contest for a modern theatre building in Kansas City. He had come a long, long way in those thirty years, and always in the flush of youth; always with a great laugh that sounded like a cataclysm, always with belief that the particular segment of the millennium he sought was just around the corner. Life never hardened the arteries of his faith, never bleached his hope, never sterilized his wide, humorous charity. For he had never cheapened life by using it for sordid ends nor selfish purposes. His human meannesses and hates and foibles — and never was a man further from anemic sainthood than Mr. Nelson — were not the meannesses and hates and foibles of a prig or an academician or a maiden aunt. When he admitted a person to the intimacy of his enmity, he admitted him as a public nuisance, not in private spite. Mr. Nelson socialized even his enemies. He loved and hated as a public spirit, and with high voltage.

HOW HE MET DEATH

So when he was stricken in death, he met death as an incident of life. For ten days or such a matter his doctor had been sustaining Mr. Nelson's life by an artificial stimulant; by a saline solution. He found it out, and his scorn at living as a sham roused his rage. He called the doctor into the room, and when they were alone, got the truth. He was an old man, as men go — seventy-four years and more. And life was full and fresh and joyous as he was living it. But he would have no life that was not genuine.

"So," he demanded, "I should have been dead the fifth of March?"

The doctor acknowledged the truth.

"And you have kept life going by this — this saline solution, when I had no physical life in me — no real right to live?" he asked.

That also was declared to be about the truth.

"Doctor," cried the patient angrily, "I have taken you into my family; I have given you my confidence as a personal friend; I have trusted you as a square man — and now — this is the way you treat me — this is my reward — that you cheat death from day to day and keep me lying here a dead man by rights." And then came the last cussing out that ever rose from that hearty old breast.

When the doctor had left, Mr. Nelson said very gently to those about him whom he loved: "Well — if this is the end, I am willing to go!"

But he stalked up to death a gentleman unafraid, like his "peers, the heroes of old." He went girding up his loins, alone and with the courage a man feels alone, to enlist for the next battle of the eternal war!

VI

MASS CIRCULATION: THE PRESS GIANTS

~~~~~~

THE massing of urban population and the rise of great business corporations brought increased circulation and advertising revenue to newspapers in the period between the Spanish-American War and World War I and gave social and economic stimulus to the heightened tempo of American metropolitan journalism. The growth of newspaper chains and the entrance of the newspaper into the field of corporate finance brought consolidations and mergers, which struck down the less solvent papers and tended to centralize control of the American press in fewer hands. Press associations and rapidly expanding news and feature syndicates helped bring in an era of mass production of newspaper copy with its attendant standardization of products.

The trend toward high-pressure metropolitan journalism was given considerable impetus in the 1880s when Joseph Pulitzer and William Randolph Hearst developed strong, crusading dailies in St. Louis and San Francisco. Will Irwin, veteran San Francisco and New York newspaperman, tells the Pulitzer-Hearst story in his article, "Yellow Journalism." Hearst, it needs to be remembered, was the pupil; Pulitzer the master. But so apt a pupil did Hearst become that when he bought the New York Journal *in 1895 and began his famous circulation battle with Pulitzer's* New York World, *the ensuing competition assumed such proportions that it severely taxed Pulitzer's journalistic genius and stamina and caused both publishers for a time to attempt to outdo each other in the use of lurid, ultra-sensational newspaper techniques.*

Various phases of Pulitzer's brilliant, eccentric personality, his nervous "drive," his devotion to the World, *and his concern that it be kept an instrument for maintaining social justice in its community, have been dealt with by numerous writers. Former* World *staff member Don Seitz in his "Portrait of an Editor" presents all these aspects in well-rounded and readable fashion. The Seitz article deals chiefly with Pulitzer's New York period, but it was the success of the community-conscious, crusading* St. Louis Post-Dispatch *which set the pattern that was to make the morning* World *one of the country's great liberal dailies.*

While Pulitzer was building his reputation with two newspapers, Hearst was acquiring dozens of them. Starting with the San Francisco Examiner *and the* New York Journal *he went on to become the biggest chain publisher in the United States. Even before his death in 1951 Hearst had become a legendary figure. For some sixty years his eccentricities as publisher, political aspirant, art collector, and multimillionaire playboy shocked and thrilled generations of Americans. George P. West analyzes him in the light of his hereditary and regional limitations, but West's analysis was done in the 1930s and the Hearst empire underwent important changes in the next two decades. Edwin Emery's "Tentative Appraisal" provides background for a more complete and up-to-date estimate of the contradictory character of one of America's most powerful and perverse publishers.*

Second only to Hearst in number of papers acquired as a chain publisher, Edward W. Scripps has achieved greater journalistic "immortality" because of the liberal, constructive policies which he outlined for his newspapers. Relatively little has been written about "the damned old crank," as Scripps called himself, for he avoided the limelight and was disinclined to talk with interviewers. He is presented here through two articles, one a review of his career which appeared in Editor & Publisher *at the time of his death, the other a recent analysis by Kenneth Stewart and John Tebbel of his place in American journalism.*

No one has disposed of Frank A. Munsey, "the great consolidator," with more good-natured irony than has Robert Duffus in his "Mr. Munsey." After reading the article one understands why Munsey was better fitted to run grocery stores and publish magazines than to put out newspapers.

While Munsey was experimenting with some of his early theories of consolidation and while Pulitzer and Hearst were using the impending Spanish-American War to build circulations for the World *and*

Journal *running past the million mark, there occurred in New York what might be termed "the newspaper paradox of the nineties." Adolph Ochs bought the faltering* New York Times *and quietly set about building it into America's most comprehensive and influential newspaper. What manner of man it was who did this is engagingly set forth by Benjamin Stolberg in his "The Man behind the* Times." *Author Stolberg admires Mr. Ochs, but he is too perceptive to let the man be confused with the legend.*

These men were among the leaders who directed the fortunes of America's influential newspapers in the post World War I era. It was an era of change and progress as was the post Civil War period. Following World War I, newspaper revenues soared with the current of national prosperity. Not only did advertising shoot up to new levels, but circulations were sent spiraling by a war-bred avidity for up-to-the-minute news and entertainment. Tabloids — newspapers of smaller format, using many pictures and emotionalized news — were introduced to tickle the appetites of New York readers and spread in less sensational form to other cities. The nonmetropolitan or country press, led by such able editors as William Allen White of the Emporia Gazette, *retained its important position in community life. State and national organizations of weekly and daily newspaper publishers and editors made their contributions. So increasingly did schools and departments of journalism, whose rapid growth in American colleges and universities provided a wealth of professionally trained young men and women for both city and country papers. But perhaps the most socially significant development was the association of newspaper editorial workers with the labor movement, through the organization of the American Newspaper Guild in the depths of the depression of the 1930s.*

During the depression years and the accompanying socio-economic revolution called the New Deal, there was, however, extensive criticism of some segments of the press, arising out of dissatisfaction with the growing trend toward concentration of newspaper ownership in fewer hands and a consequent lessening of variety of opinion and news presentation. The Hearst press and the Chicago Tribune *were particular targets for critics of irresponsible handling of the news and obvious political partisanship. The* Tribune, *which had achieved national reputation and a strong local position under the editorship of Joseph Medill, now reflected the personal philosophies of Colonel Robert R. McCor-*

mick. Still a solid, dominating force in Chicago journalism and still capable of exerting a crusading influence reminiscent of the days of Medill and his managing editor James Keeley, the Tribune *under the McCormick regime became a bitterly controversial newspaper. In this volume the selection from* Time *magazine, which appeared in 1947 upon the occasion of the hundredth anniversary of the* Tribune's *founding, presents a distillation of the anti-McCormick point of view.*

Balancing the controversial colonel in the 1940s and 1950s were other publishers more sensitive to their responsibilities in presenting impartial and well-rounded news. Men like Arthur Hays Sulzberger of the New York Times, *Barry Bingham of the* Louisville Courier-Journal, *and Joseph Pulitzer, Jr., of the* St. Louis Post-Dispatch *kept old traditions alive, and other publishers and editors likewise sought to build stronger, better newspapers. Their success depended upon the men and women in the ranks of journalism who, through their professional organizations and individually, were striving to overcome deficiencies and maintain the economic stability of a press which was buffeted in depression years, squeezed in new periods of war and inflation, and harassed with radio-television competition.*

If we look back to the few hand-printed sheets of America's first newspaper in 1690, the present status of the American newspaper — whatever its faults — is indeed impressive. Nearly 1800 dailies with a combined circulation of 54 million copies and some 10,000 weeklies testify to the strength of the American press and to its continuing potential for constructive service as the primary agency for dissemination of news and opinion.

19

Yellow Journalism

by WILL IRWIN

WILL IRWIN was one of America's great reporters at the turn of the century, when the modern newspaper was emerging. He reviewed changes in journalistic techniques in a series of articles for *Collier's*, and his study of yellow journalism appeared in the issue of February 18, 1911.

THE seeds of yellow journalism, so called for want of a better name, sprouted at St. Louis and San Francisco during the eighties; they came to fruition in New York, thrashing-floor for changes in journalism, during the early nineties. In the decade which preceded the full flowering of Hearst and Pulitzer, however, a change in the spirit of newspaper publication had crept in by way of the business office — a change which prepared the ground for this new seed. From a rather humble professional enterprise, the newspaper had become a great "business proposition," holding infinite possibilities of profit.

Dana, Medill, Greeley, Godkin, even Bennett, adopted their vocation from that mixture of motive and chance which leads a man into any profession; they certainly reckoned the chance of getting rich very slightly among possibilities. But the field for newspaper circulation grew, as I have shown; and with it grew the perfection of swift mechanical processes. By 1891 a quadruple Hoe press would print, fold, cut, paste, and count 72,000 eight-page papers an hour. The linotype, or mechanical typesetting machine, climax of delicate mechanism, was not yet perfected; that was to come just after the yellows made their start. Our publishers had facilities, therefore, to handle any imaginable increase in circulation. It was necessary only to enlarge basement spaces and increase the number of presses. And now big retail business discovered the newspaper as a salesman. Yankee advertising had been a jest of Europe for a half-century long, before experience proved that for most commodities advertisement in a regular and respectable periodical pays better, dollar for dollar, than advertisement by circular or sign-board.

THE NEW SALESMANSHIP

In the same period the retail dry goods business, consistently an advertiser since the first newspapers, began to concentrate in department stores and to drag into these great emporiums other forms of retail business, such as hardware, jewelry, and groceries. With their bargain days, their special offerings, designed to attract customers to the store, their advertising became a matter of news. They did not now announce, as in 1810: "We offer prints and calicoes at lowest prices," but: "Special today: A hundred dozen pairs of ladies' lisle hose, worth 75 cents, at 49 cents." For this form of publicity the newspaper was the only possible medium except privately distributed circulars; and a circular, as experience has shown, is usually thrown into the ash-can, while a newspaper notice, surrounded by matter which commands some respect, is kept and read. Newspaper and periodical advertising grew from tiny beginnings to a great force of distribution. Where the senior Bennett's old *Herald* got its advertising revenue by hundreds of dollars, the junior Bennett's *Herald* of the eighties got it by tens of thousands. There came, then, a gradual shift of power from the editorial rooms to the business office.

The stalwart old-time newspaper proprietor, who had entered the editorial game for love of it, still held his paper to editorial ideals, though he grew rich incidentally. McCullagh of the *St. Louis Globe-Democrat*, it is remembered now in these changed days, would not let a business office man come on to the editorial floor, lest his staff become commercialized. There remained, however, a multitude of lesser souls who yielded to the temptation of the flesh-pots and trained their eyes solely on commercial possibilities. Their advertising solicitors raked the city for copy; the less scrupulous coerced advertisers by a species of blackmail — "You advertise with us and we'll leave you alone." Above all — and this is where the commercial movement ties up with "yellow" journalism — they were ripe and ready for any method which would serve to extend circulation and therefore make their advertising space more valuable.

During the seventies, a young German-American, a pest to his fellows with his truculence, a blessing to his employers with his news sense and his vigorous writing, shuttled back and forth between the German and English newspapers of St. Louis. Joseph Pulitzer had been a soldier of bad fortune for some years before he entered journalism; he had served as coachman, as waiter, as common laborer, as private in the burial squad which laid away the dead after the St. Louis cholera epidemic; and he had learned the common man's attitude toward life and the news. His fellows of the police stations in his early journalistic days remember him as a restless, inquiring youth, ready to try almost any experiment with life, if he might learn thereby what was inside the sealed envelope: above all, as a man with his own opinions, ready to back them with fist and tongue. He rose; he did his turn at Washington, where his writing attracted the attention of Dana; and he might have taken service with the *New York Sun*. He preferred the power of the game to its art, however; and in 1878 he raised money to acquire the *St. Louis Post-Dispatch*, an obscure paper, dying of inanition.*

WHAT PULITZER FOUND

It is not true, as some assume, that Pulitzer founded yellow journalism then and there. What he did discover — and that is only one element in yellow journalism — was the means of fighting popular causes by the news. The process was not wholly original with him; the *New York Times* had smashed the Tweed Ring by publishing plain accounts of their corrupt transactions. Perhaps, however, Pulitzer was first to go out systematically and find evil before evil obtruded itself on public notice. He had a conservative community to serve. In such an atmosphere certain set and old injustices always flourish for lack of popular opposition. Pulitzer scratched this surface and showed what lay beneath. He made himself the bugaboo of the big cinch; he made his organ such a champion of popular rights that to this day the humble citizen of St. Louis who has a grievance tends to write to the *P.-D.* before he employs a lawyer. That was the kind of journalism which Pulitzer brought to the hospitable-minded metropolis when, in the middle eighties, he bought the *New York World*.

THE BEGINNINGS OF HEARST

The yellow streak was working from quite another beginning at the other end of the continent. William Randolph Hearst, only son of

* EDITORS' NOTE: Actually Pulitzer merged two papers, the *Post* and the *Dispatch*.

rich and able parents, had come out of Harvard. His father, Senator George Hearst, a rough, hustling mining millionaire and politician, had bought the *San Francisco Examiner* as a kind of a flyer in connection with his political and commercial schemes. The son had taken a fancy to journalism, and had his eye already on the *Examiner*. Even in college he made a daily study and comparison of the current newspapers. The *Examiner*, as he found it, was an old, conservative paper, weak in the spine through many changes of political ownership.

Unbiased and unblinded, as though this were the first and only publication in the world, Hearst set out to find how he could make it the greatest, the controlling newspaper of the Pacific Coast region. His father's old employees, and especially one "Petey" Bigelow, a wild genius of a reporter who flourished in San Francisco at that period, took him in hand and taught him all they knew. He listened to their advice — and rejected it, mainly. Not until he discovered that S. S. Chamberlain was willing to take a position on the far coast of the United States did Hearst find the man to show him the way.

Chamberlain had seen service with both Bennett and Pulitzer; for the former, he had edited the *Paris Herald*; and he had started *Le Matin*. He came to the *Examiner*, therefore, schooled in the most sensational journalism which had appeared up to that time. He was — and is — a master of popular psychology, a seer at perceiving the subtle values in public taste. Through all the subsequent years of the yellow craze he remained a rock of real news-journalism in the Hearst organization. To Hearst, experimenting blindly with what the public wanted, this exponent of sensationalism was a godsend. Under his tutelage the young millionaire began to make a noise. He attacked the Southern Pacific, the eternal corporation bugaboo of California — did it with such success that, during his first long absence from California, Collis P. Huntington compounded with his resident manager and bought the paper off for a thousand dollars a month. A schooner went ashore on Brandt Rock, a dangerous reef outside the harbor mouth. Hearst equipped a tug under command of "Petey" Bigelow and rescued the survivors — on behalf of the *Examiner*. He sent up balloons to distribute prizes to the populace — on behalf of the *Examiner*. Whenever, in all his radius of interest, occurred a disaster or a startling crime, he despatched to the scene a special train loaded to the window with

Examiner writers and illustrators. The public park of San Francisco wanted a specimen of the fast-dying Californian grizzly. Hearst set hunters to work; they trapped the biggest bear to be had; "Monarch, the *Examiner's* Grizzly," made space for weeks. This caught the fickle and unaccountable public fancy, and Hearst pushed the movement along by adopting the bear as the *Examiner* trademark. James Swinnerton, in the first flush of his powers as a rough-and-ready cartoonist, drew bears for a year, until people tired of the feature.

Whenever the other newspapers produced a man suited to his purposes, Hearst bought him over at his own figures. So he got E. H. Hamilton, one of the great American reporters; Homer Davenport, destined as a cartoonist to play his part in political history; Arthur McEwen, second only to Brisbane as a writer of editorials in the Hearst manner. Chamberlain conceived the idea that the city hospital was badly managed. He picked a little slip of a girl from among his cub reporters, and assigned her to the investigation. She invented her own method — she "fainted" on the street and was carried to the hospital for treatment. She turned out a story * "with a sob for the unfortunate in every line." That was the professional beginning of "Annie Laurie" or Winifred Black, and of a departure in newspaper writing. For she came to have many imitators; but none other could ever so well stir up the primitive emotions of sympathy and pity; she was a "sob squad" all by herself. Indeed, in the discovery of this sympathetic "woman writing," Hearst broke through the crust into the thing he was after. His greatest single hit, before he left San Francisco for wider fields, was the "Little Jim Ward" — simply a movement to establish a ward for incurables in the local children's hospital. "Little Jim" was a helpless cripple whom Annie Laurie discovered and whom she used as an example. Every day for weeks the women of San Francisco exchanged tears across the back fences over "Little Jim."

Hearst was experimenting every week, every day; trying a hundred expensive departures, only to abandon ninety-nine for the sake of the one which "panned out." This week, he arranged the heads in certain symmetrical patterns — for "make-up" or the physical appearance of the paper, was always a hobby with him. Next week, he tried the effect

* I find that I must ask the reader to accept one piece of professional argot. A "story," in the newspaper sense, is any contribution, from a market report to a leading editorial. What the English purist calls a "story" the newspaper man calls a "fiction story."

of veiled salaciousness. Another, he got such sensation as he could out of Sunday's sermons to see if his readers "really cared for religion in the news." And he experimented always with one object in view — to find what the public wanted, how he might sell the greatest number of copies.

Consciously or unconsciously, Hearst and Chamberlain were working on a principle whose formation was as original to our Occidental journalism as Bennett's discovery of news. He who serves the intellectual and artistic demands of the populace must give them in some measure what they want. If he proceeds from the very highest ethical and artistic ideals, he must make concessions, or they will not listen. But having established a common ground with his public, he may give them a little better than they want, so leading them up by the slow process of education to his own better ideals; or he may give them a great deal worse. The gentlemen who conduct our theatrical affairs, for example, have of late given the public worse than it wants, so that when some sound, sincere, and artistic piece of work like "The Three of Us," "The Great Divide," or "Paid in Full" slips past them to success, they stand amazed. When Hearst began, the spirit of the old-age editor still guided newspaper publication; the great majority of editors, no matter how strong their desire for circulation, still served news and editorial in fashion much more intellectual than the public wanted, still appealed to the mind rather than the heart. Hearst's task was to cheapen the product until it sold at the coin of the gutter and the streets.

So he came generally to reject all news stories which did not contain that thrill of sensation loved by the man on the street and the woman in the kitchen; no paper ever published fewer news items to the issue. He trained his men to look for the one sensational, picturesque fact in every occurrence which came to the desk, and to twist that fact to the fore. "What we're after," said Arthur McEwen, "is the 'gee-whiz' emotion." Pressed for further explanation, he said: "We run our paper so that when the reader opens it he says: 'Gee-whiz!' An issue is a failure which doesn't make him say that." The basic human passions — "Love for the woman, power for the man" — Hearst was after them. A story to be available for his purposes must have romance, sympathy, hate, gain, in the first sentence, the first line, the first paragraph.

Necessarily, since he was reaching out to grip and to hold the populace, his editorial policy leaned to the people's side. He began as a Democrat, that being then the party of the under dog. At once he ran clear beyond Democracy until he impinged on Socialism. He adopted the union labor cause, even at the cost of an expensive mechanical department in his own newspaper. For years, or until rows and bickerings over the political support of union labor broke the alliance, this was a foundation-stone of Hearst editorial policy. Here convenience wed sincerity, doubtless; those who knew Hearst best in this early era declare that under his cold exterior he kept a real sympathy for the submerged man and woman, a real feeling of his own mission to plead their cause.

When he took the *Examiner* it was dying. In 1888, when Chamberlain came, he had brought it to 30,000 circulation. By 1893 he had 72,000; and he held a secure lead over the other San Francisco newspapers. That lead he never lost; year in and year out, except for the set-back of the great disaster in 1906, the *Examiner* has returned its $30,000 to $40,000 a month to keep the other Hearst papers floating.

This journalism he brought to New York when he bought the *Journal* in 1895. It was not yet quite what we call yellow, though it approximated that happy condition. For real yellow journalism had beaten him by a few months. Joseph Pulitzer had been fighting his way on the *New York World* with the sensational, militant style which he perfected in St. Louis. He took personal charge of the *World* in 1884. Within two years he had attacked so many things which the other newspapers had not perceived as copy, or had not dared to touch, that he was disputing circulation with Bennett the Younger and Dana. By the end of the decade the *World* was altogether the most reckless, the most sensational, and the most widely discussed newspaper in New York. He has been several men, all extraordinary, in the course of his career, this Pulitzer; nothing so impresses one who regards him in the light of a historic character as the manner in which his able, penetrating, highly energized mind has shifted its point of view. In that stage he was a creature of infinite recklessness and incredible suspicion. By mental habit he scratched every fair surface to find the inner corrupt motive. Journalism, it appears, bounded his ambition; that was one secret of his extraordinary freedom from control. Had he cared for political position, for pure financial power, the history of American journalism in the past twenty years might have been very different.

Within that narrow limit he, like the silent, cold, light-eyed young man experimenting out on the Pacific Coast, had the passion for leadership. "If you should put Hearst in a monastery," said one of his early associates, "he would become abbot or die." The gods cut Pulitzer off the same stripe.

The Sunday supplement was by this time an integral part of metropolitan journalism. As early as the Civil War period, the newspapers had been giving space on Sunday mornings to entertaining matter bearing only indirect relation to the news. When, with the development of the rotary press, they were able to print large issues by eight-page sections, the most advanced journals began to add one of these sections on Sunday mornings as a kind of catch-all for routine semi-news matter, like notes of the fraternal orders and women's clubs, and mild write-ups of picturesque features of city life, together with such embellishment of fiction and beauty hints as they could afford. S. S. Mc-Clure, breaking into the world of print at about that time, made a fortune from his idea of selling the best current literature to newspapers for simultaneous publication on Sunday mornings, the famous McClure Syndicate.

PULITZER FINDS THE MAN

Pulitzer, like the rest, published a supplement. Although by 1891 he had brought his Sunday circulation up to 300,000 copies, the *World* did not show so great a proportionate increase over daily circulation as the *Herald* or the *Sun*; and Pulitzer worried and tinkered over it. In 1891, H. H. Kohlsaat, then part owner of the *Chicago Inter Ocean*, saw in Paris the rotary color presses of the *Petit Journal*. Printing in colors, be it known to the layman, had hitherto been done almost exclusively on slow, flat-bed presses, fed by hand, not from a roll or web. It had been thought impossible to the swift rotary press. When Kohlsaat returned to Chicago, he had Scott build him a color rotary on the European model. This would not handle whole sections, but only small inserts; Kohlsaat used it mainly for premium World's Fair views and the like. Pulitzer, alert to anything new, sent a man to see this press. The report was favorable. He consulted the Hoes, who informed him that they were already manufacturing color rotaries for small sheets. As a costly experiment, he ordered a rotary, turning out full-size pages in three colors and black. With this the *World* printed colored cartoons and beauty pictures on the outside pages of one Sunday section.

The process was costly and infinitely troublesome; and the dash of color had no visible effect upon the Sunday circulation. At the end of the year the heads of the department sent a round-robin to Pulitzer, who was fighting blindness in Europe, begging him to drop it. "The very building groaned," says an old executive of the *World*, "when the boss cabled back ordering us to put a new man in charge of that section, and use the color pages for funny pictures, like *Puck* and *Judge*."

Already, Pulitzer had found his editor for the Sunday supplement. Morrill Goddard, a young city editor "with a dynamo inside," had developed a faculty for getting "features" out of the news. Against his earnest protests, Pulitzer sent him over to the Sunday supplement. Once established at his new desk, Goddard, like Hearst, set out, naked-eyed, to find what the common mind wanted. An instinct quite extraordinary, considering that Goddard is a ripe scholar, led him to it; within the year he was running in that supplement what we now call "yellow journalism" as distinguished from "sensational journalism."

Pictures first — for ten grasp with the eye to one with the mind. He brought the size of pictures up from one column to two, to five; and, finally, the first "seven-column cut" made its appearance in his Sunday *World*. Then reading matter so easy, with the startling points so often emphasized, that the weariest mechanic, sitting in his socks on Sunday morning, could not fail to get a thrill of interest. "Economy of attention" — that, unconsciously to him probably, made up his whole formula. Nothing which called for any close attention; something which first caught the eye and then startled, tickled, and interested without wear on brain tissue. For subject-matter he clung close to the news, choosing and expanding the bizarre, the startling, the emotional, though the item occupied only a line in the daily paper. When such subject matter failed, he was capable of making history yellow. Did a treatise on *The Man in the Iron Mask* appear, Goddard, taking the publication of this book as an excuse, would rush into print a page of the *Iron Mask*, with nightmare pictures, three inches of "snappy" introduction "playing up" the mystery, and two or three "box freaks" distributed among the pictures, giving learned opinions by great historians. So he

275

played on still another popular weakness; he made his readers believe that they were on the royal road to learning.

One of Goddard's old associates has given his formula for a page in a yellow Sunday supplement. "Suppose it's Halley's comet," he says. "Well, first you have a half-page of decoration showing the comet, with historical pictures of previous appearances thrown in. If you can work a pretty girl into the decoration, so much the better. If not, get some good nightmare idea like the inhabitants of Mars watching it pass. Then you want a quarter of a page of big-type heads — snappy. Then four inches of story, written right off the bat. Then a picture of Professor Halley down here and another of Professor Lowell up there, and a two-column boxed freak containing a scientific opinion, which nobody will understand, just to give it class."

THE "SECTIONAL VIEW"

From the smallest opening, Goddard would develop a road to popular interest. He and Andrew E. Murphy, his assistant, used to walk home to their lodgings in Washington Square, talking newspaper as they went. "Have you noticed," said Murphy one night, "how the crowd stops to watch the picture in that drug-store window? It's nothing but a cheap chromo. What's the reason?" This was indeed the crudest kind of chromo — it represented "sponge fishing on the Florida coast." Goddard studied it a long time. "I have it," he said that night. "It's a sectional view. You can watch the ships above and the shark eating the diver below at the same time. Let's try it." And the Sunday magazine of the *New York World* had a "sectional view," first of its kind, in the next issue. This bit of prospecting opened a paying streak. A hundred others ended in blind pockets, and Goddard abandoned them at once.

And just when the comic section and the Sunday magazine of the *World* were beginning to bear fruit in increased circulation, Hearst bought the *New York Journal* and broke into the metropolis — "with all the discreet secrecy" some one has said, "of a wooden legged burglar having a fit on a tin roof." He brought his Chamberlains and McEwens, his Hamiltons and Winifred Blacks; brought his own sensational, ruthless style of journalism; brought also the Hearst millions and the steady profits of the *Examiner*. He began to win over the Pulitzer men by offers of increased salary; Goddard was one of the first whom he lured away. Forthwith, the yellow supplement burst out on the *Journal*. A carnival of bids and counter-bids for men followed. Newspaper salaries, in the sensational division, went up never to fall back to their old level; newspaper desks became tenancies of a day.

Some one met "Cosey" Noble, Hearst man, in a restaurant. "What are you doing now, Noble?" he asked. "When I left the office," Noble replied, "I was city editor."

BRISBANE GOES TO THE JOURNAL

Arthur Brisbane, a graduate of the *New York Sun*, was then a kind of factotum on the *World*. He admired the Goddard discoveries in journalism, and had maintained, against Pulitzer's own pride of invention, that the supplement, and not the colored comics, was responsible for the steady rise of Sunday circulation. When Goddard went over to Hearst, Pulitzer made Brisbane his Sunday editor. At once this section went still further in audacity, so that Goddard, to maintain the pace, had to outdo even himself. The Sunday *World* had 450,000 circulation when Hearst appeared. By 1897 Brisbane had raised it to 600,000. And now the yellow flood flowed over from the Sunday magazine to the daily paper. "What are you fellows doing?" asked Pulitzer and Hearst, in effect, of the managing editors and city editors. "The Sunday is going ahead; you are standing still." Having no great discovery of their own to stimulate circulation, the editors of the daily paper imitated the Sunday supplement. Into their own product they brought this fake, shallow, supersensational method, this predigested information, this striving for hitting effect at any cost.

Sensational newspapers tremble always with office politics. In 1897, after the club boycott on yellow journalism, Brisbane found his position on the *World* fading away from him. Hearst, meantime, had established a circulation for his morning *Journal* (later called the *American*), and was making inroads on the *World* with his Sunday paper; but the evening paper lagged at little more than 100,000 a day. Brisbane, who had already received bids from across the street, approached Hearst with a proposition. "I'll take charge of your evening paper at a hundred dollars a week," he said, in effect. "But I'll expect a dollar a week raise for every thousand I add to the circulation." Hearst accepted.

Brisbane, with a free hand, started to make an evening newspaper

on the plan of a yellow supplement. He invented the job-type head —
half the front page devoted to two or three smashing words, blaring
forth sensation. He went further and devised that trick headline wherein
the first and third lines, in immense type, proclaim a sensation, while
the interlarded second line, in small type, reduces the whole head to
a commonplace meaning ("WAR Will Probably be DECLARED,"
for example). Then fortune filled his sails. He took the evening *Journal*
late in 1897. On February 14, 1898, the *Maine* was blown up in Havana
Harbor. There followed six months of rumors of war, preparation for
war, and, finally, war. Never had sensational editor such an opportunity. In heads which occupied sometimes three-quarters of the page,
the *Journal* blazoned forth the latest rumors. In smashing, one-sentence-
to-the-paragraph Brisbane editorials, it bellowed at the Government
the mob demand for vengeance on Spain. In one year the *Journal*
touched the million mark; and Brisbane was earning, by his agreement,
$50,000 per annum. It is said that the agreement was in form of a
short note, and that Hearst might have broken it had he gone to law.
But he paid gladly, personal liberality being one of his virtues. And
liberality was wisdom, for Brisbane has been a gold-mine to his
employer.

There followed the climax of the yellow craze, an episode in social
history which we may yet come to regard with as much amazement
as the tulip craze in Holland or the Mississippi Bubble. Now did the
World and *Journal* go insane with violent scareheads, worded to get
the last drop of sensation from the "story" and throw it to the fore;
now did they make fact out of hint, history out of rumor; now did
they create, for their believing readers, a picture of a world all flash
and sensation; now did they change their bill day by day like a vaude-
ville house, striving always for some new and startling method of
attracting a crowd. Now they hunted down the criminal with blaring
horns, so playing on the mob weakness for the thief chase; now, with
the criminal caught and condemned and sentenced, they howled for
his reprieve, glorified him in hysterics, so availing themselves of the
old mob sympathy for the victim of the law, mob hatred for the
executioner. Now they dressed out the most silly and frivolous discussion of the day with symposiums of solemn opinion from prominent citizens; now they went a step further in audacity and headed
an interview from Bishop Potter or Chauncey M. Depew "By Bishop

Potter" or "By Chauncey M. Depew," as though these eminent citizens were real contributors. Now they discovered the snob in all humanity and turned reporters, artists, and — after the half-tones became possible — photographers loose on "Society." The Four Hundred of New York, largely a newspaper myth, was the target for this army. Their doings, with the follies emphasized, bedecked column after column, daily and Sunday, of hysterical slush. Life, as it percolated through the *World* and *Journal*, became melodrama, the song of the spheres a screech.

PULITZER SHIFTS GROUND

Suddenly the *World* dropped the whole game; changed almost in a week from yellow to merely sensational. This came almost coincidentally with those three months in a dark room from which Pulitzer emerged almost totally blind. There are those who believe that Pulitzer, had he retained his sight, would have drawn a string of yellow newspapers across the country as Hearst has done. I prefer to think, as do his best old counselors, that Pulitzer perceived the end of this madness; that he came to one of his sudden transformations in point of view. This blind man sees further into his times than any other American journalist; he must have known that it could not last. Change he did in the spring of 1901, so that now the worst one can say of the evening *World* is to call it a little sensational and rather silly, while his morning *World* is possibly the freest and most truthful popular newspaper in New York.

Hearst went on; as he grew great in influence and money he spread out to Chicago, to Boston, to Los Angeles, carrying his journalism in a form modified for the environment. Only his *New York Journal* and his Chicago papers were ever supremely yellow; but in these, for a few years after Pulitzer dropped out, his office staffs, and especially the lesser reporters, went on to the very madness of journalism. At its best the form stretched truth to the bursting point; for it consisted in warping facts to suit a distorted, melodramatic point of view. From this to outright falsehood was but a step, taken without perception by men no longer capable of seeing the truth. The fact became but a peg whereon to hang the lie. Did the police find a poor, tired, sodden servant girl dead by her own hand near the park lake? — "Mystery of the Park — Pretty Girl Richly Dressed — Believed to be Member of

Prominent Family." Did the reporters need an interview to dress out any large general story? If the "prominent citizen" refused the interview, the reporter wrote it just the same. Often he did not even attempt to see the "prominent citizen." The method for avoiding the trouble which naturally followed was one of the Hearst arts.

"RIOT AT MORGUE!"

After the *Slocum* disaster I, as reporter for a conservative New York newspaper, had the mournful assignment of watching that temporary morgue where the police and divers were laying out the bodies. A new consignment had just arrived when I started back for the office. The crowd outside, mainly relatives of the dead, had grown impatient with delay, and one little German shook his fist at the police. For a minute the crowd pushed and jostled; then the doors flew open and they filed soberly in. When I reached the newspaper offices, an extra was pouring out from the *Journal* basement — "Riot at Morgue — Frantic Mob Charges Police!" This all over the front page in red letters three inches high. Later in that summer, the hypothetical Black Hand kidnaped one Tony Manino, six years old. Since this was an Italian case, the reporters could do no work of their own on it; we merely loitered about the police station or the house, getting our news second-hand. Of course, with its appeal to emotion and mystery, this was a great yellow feature; the *Journal* went daft with it. And day by day the cubs and younglings of the *Journal* seized at every absurd rumor and shot it over the telephone as fact. "I heard a kid kind of yelling in one of the tenements and I followed it up. Nothing doing," a detective would remark. A rush to the telephone by the *Journal* delegation; in an hour we would have it in an extra, something like this: "Hears Tony Manino Weeping for His Mother." I mention these instances as typical, not exceptional, in the height of the yellow insanity.

THE "PRETTY GIRL" PICTURE

As for photographs — what offenses were committed in their name! For people who will yield up the news gladly are conservative about giving up pictures; and pictures the yellows must have, especially for "pretty girl stories." There was a time when they used the various poses of photographic models for the "pretty girl" whose picture was unobtainable. This growing monotonous, they placed orders with photographic agencies for photographs of foreign women in private life — people who would never know that their pictures were serving in America for the "Pretty Girl Who Whipped Burglar" or the "Prominent Society Leader of Evanston."

So much for its vices, of which its falsity was chief and its rowdy denial of the right of privacy in news-getting only second. Let me not omit its virtues, which loom larger now that the madness is over. Publishers, in relation to the public, may be divided roughly into two classes. On one side are the instinctive worshipers of wealth and money, the men hypnotized by success and its rewards. The other and smaller class — which includes, it happens, most of our greatest editors — go just as far to the other extreme in suspecting the rich and great. To this class belonged both Pulitzer and Hearst in their most active days. Question not too far the motives of great, strenuous spirits like these two. Such must find outlets for their energies without conscious direction toward an end; "the job" itself is their objective. Yet each — Hearst probably the more definitely — had somewhere down among his tangled motives a genuine sympathy for the under dog in the industrial fight. This sympathy, and the convenience which traveled parallel with it, made and kept them advocates of the common man at a period when he needed an advocate. Nothing made Pulitzer so indignant as "corporate iniquity"; and, as for Hearst, this may suffice to illustrate: the common schools have always been his hobby, and his editorial associates have seen him walking the floor with indignation at some injury to the system.

SOME YELLOW VIRTUES

I have shown how Pulitzer brought to New York, as the nucleus of yellow journalism, the method of finding and fighting public evils through the news. This method the yellow newspapers perfected with their growth in general efficiency. They learned how to fight; they taught the method to other newspapers. Their period of greatest power was also the period of unchecked corporation abuses, of alliance between bad ward politics and bad high finance. The ten-cent magazine, with its healthful "muck-raking," had not yet arrived. These blatant voices, husky with much bawling, were almost the only voices raised, for a decade long, against such principles as Mark Hanna typified.

Again, like the French philosopher, they "brought philosophy from the library and the cloister to dwell in the kitchen and the workshop." A parade of learning, of scientific and philosophical knowledge, was always among their little tricks. They gave it to their readers predigested, the sensational detail to the fore, with an eye always on "economy of attention"; but they did hammer the big principles home, I believe, to people who could have accepted them in no other form. Their "stories" were an edge of interest for the wedge of knowledge. So always philosophies first reach the bottom of popular intelligence. Had we an accurate and critical record of early Christianity, we should find, probably, that after its first pure flow the people in general accepted its picturesque superstitions before they grasped its spirit; and the Darwinian theories had been mentor to the laboratories for a quarter century before the mob believed that Darwin taught anything except the bizarre idea — which he never did teach — of man's descent from the monkey.

"THIS MAN BRISBANE"

In this last activity of yellow journalism, Brisbane stands supreme. The country has forgotten, if it ever knew, his influence in making sensational journalism yellow journalism. We think of him as the writer of those "heart-to-heart" editorials which even the judicious sometimes admire. With the hindsight so much better than foresight, the men who built with Hearst in his building days at San Francisco see what a chance they missed when they walked on the edge of Brisbane's methods. For Hearst said again and again: "I wish I could get the same 'snap' into my editorials that you fellows get into the news columns." Arthur McEwen tried the hardest and came nearest to grasping what Hearst wanted. The truth is, McEwen had too much of what the prize-ring calls "class." His talents as journalist and writer were basically too high and sound.

Now arrived Brisbane; he became the genius of the evening *Journal*, deepest yellow of all newspapers. He was a man after Hearst's own kidney. He, too, had a sympathy with popular causes underneath an amazing ruthlessness of method and a talent for insincere sincerities. He found how to get "snap" into the editorial page, how to talk politics and philosophy in the language of truckmen and lumbermen. Day by day for ten years he has shouted at the populace the moral philosophies of Kant and Hegel, the social and scientific philosophies of Spencer and Huxley, in lurid words of one syllable. On alternate days he has shouted, just as powerfully, the inconsistencies which suited Hearst's convenience of the day, the fallacies which would boost circulation, pull in advertising, kill rivals. No man can be so sincere or so plausibly insincere as Brisbane. To analyze his best flights, to show how artfully he conceals the one necessary flaw in an otherwise perfect chain of logic, is an exercise which I recommend to our university classes in forensics.

His violence of language and expression, which has led to so many assaults on the Hearst newspapers, is, in fact, a trick of method. At the risk of mental snobbery, it must be said that the comparatively uneducated class to which he appeals is weak in fine intellectual distinctions. Not only is black black and white white to them, but gray and cream and pearl are white, and brown and purple are black. "I've done hard work in the ditches," says one of the great, sane editorial writers of his time, "and let me tell you when a ditch-digger calls a man an unlimited whelp he doesn't mean what you and I mean. He may mean a slightly disagreeable person or a real scoundrel. In short, he has no language to express disapproval except the most violent. So, when Brisbane called McKinley 'the most hated creature on the American continent,' he shocked the educated, but he conveyed to his readers, in the only kind of language which they understood, merely general disapproval of McKinley."

As a writer, with these editorials, as an editor, with thorough grasp of what his kind of reader wanted, he came to typify yellow journalism in its last period of real power. The profession of journalism rightly calls him the one widely influential editorial writer in these declining days of the daily editorial page. Such Hearst newspapers as use his work publish a million and a half copies for at least five million readers. In the nature of Hearst circulation, he reaches that class least infused with the modern intellectual spirit of inquiry, least apt to study their facts before forming their theories — the class most ready to accept the powerfully expressed opinions of another and superior being. We cannot view American civilization without reckoning in this young exponent of means which justify ends, any more than we can view it without reckoning in his employer and discoverer — Hearst.

20

The Portrait of an Editor:
Joseph Pulitzer

by DON C. SEITZ

Joseph Pulitzer's official biographer, Don C. Seitz, rose to the management of the *New York World* and was intimately acquainted with the great publisher. This article appeared in the *Atlantic Monthly* in 1924, year of publication of Seitz's *Joseph Pulitzer: His Life and Letters.*

Joseph Pulitzer was tall — six feet two and a half inches in height — but of a presence so commanding as to make his stature seem even greater. His hair was black and his beard a reddish brown. A forehead that well bespoke the intellect behind it shaded a nose of the sort Napoleon admired; his chin was small but powerful and of the nutcracker variety, such as the portrait of Mr. Punch affects. To conceal this he always went bearded after he was thirty. His complexion was as delicate and beautiful as that of a tender child. His hands were those of genius, with long, slender fingers, full of warmth and magnetism. The eyes before they became clouded were of a grayish blue. Always weak, they never lent much expression to the face, yet his visage was animated and attractive. Temperamentally, his was the type of the poet and musician; yet, while adoring music, he professed to care little for verse and rarely read it. However, he appreciated the singers in his native tongue and, I have often thought, really repressed his poetic instinct for fear it might be considered a weakness.

The nose vexed him. If there had been any way of modifying its prominence, he would have greatly rejoiced. But it was the delight of cartoonists, chief of whom was his friend, Joseph Keppler. When idling together in the cafés of St. Louis, Keppler would rack his brains for an idea and, failing to find one, would remark: "Well, Joey, there's only one thing left to do. I'll go back to the office and draw your nose" — which he invariably did to the great disgust of the subject.

His days after his withdrawal from active work were monotonously regular: morning hours spent with his secretaries over the papers and mail, a drive before luncheon, then an hour of reading and repose, after which he rode in a carriage or on horseback, saw visitors from five o'clock to six, went to bed for a brief rest, dressed for a seven-thirty dinner, left the table about nine, listened to a little music, and was read to sleep by one of his secretaries.

Just as old King Frederick William of Prussia, father of Frederick the Great, was always hunting Europe over for tall men to recruit his Potsdam Grenadiers, Mr. Pulitzer, who resembled his Majesty in many ways, was forever hunting readers and secretaries. Ballard Smith, while London correspondent, and after him Frederick A. Duneka, David Graham Phillips, and James M. Tuohy, all English representatives in the order named, were on perpetual assignment. The secretaries in office were frequently set to finding other secretaries, and George Ledlie, his general and personal representative, had a permanent commission to find "the right man." Alfred Butes, a clever young Englishman, came closest to filling all the requirements. He had been in Africa with General Francis de Winton, was an accomplished stenographer, wrote an excellent hand and, above all, was most discreet. He penetrated more deeply in his employer's confidence than any of the other young gentlemen; indeed, he was destined to become a trustee of the vast estate and to receive a handsome legacy, although he forfeited these honors in 1907 to join Lord Northcliffe in a secretarial capacity.

The duties of the secretaries were very exacting, and the position was irksome except to men of sympathetic temperament and to lovers of good living. Most of the secretaries were English, although occasional Americans served with individual success. But the life palled on these lighter temperaments and they required frequent furloughs.

Mealtimes were play hours. At the table, liberty of speech was the rule and the guests and secretaries had full freedom to express themselves without regard to the feelings of the host. Sometimes the fire became pretty hot and Mr. Pulitzer would retreat to have his dessert and coffee alone. Violent disputes about music, literature, politics, history, and art were the rule, with not infrequent assaults upon his own opinion and the ways of the *World*, tempered by anecdotes and good stories. He loved table-talk of this sort. "Tell me a good story" was his most frequent greeting to a guest. It was hard to set him to "reminiscing"; but when he did venture back over the traveled road, the tale was worth hearing.

He was always interesting, seldom companionable, taking all he could from the minds of others, but rarely giving much back, his method being to dispute and to reap the benefits of an aroused defense. Thus he became a great hunter for facts. Often at luncheon or dinner, when a free-for-all conversation took place, some remark would arouse a dispute over accuracy of statement. If the question could not be settled by someone at the board, he would command a charge on all the reference books at hand and there was no rest until the doubt was cleared up. The waiters were often prohibited from serving more food until this happened. The facts found, he would listen intently to their reading and they remained in his mind forever. The best of dinners would be much improved for him if there had been added a satisfying fact-hunt. He would puff his cigar, pat the pile of reference books lovingly with his graceful hands, and smile in deep content.

Mr. Pulitzer read omnivorously. He was always buying books. One of his great griefs over the fire that destroyed his Fifty-fifth Street mansion was the total loss of his library. He was not a "collector" in any sense, but loved his volumes for what they contained. Like most of us who were fed educationally on Homer in our youth, Mr. Pulitzer reserved the *Odyssey* as a treasure to be enjoyed in riper years. He had long looked forward to the celebrated episode of the wooden horse. Coming to the event, he found it described in seven rather dull lines. "I was so d——d mad," he remarked, "that I could have kicked Homer!"

His speeches during the Greeley campaign were all made in German, his familiar tongue. When he came to stump for Tilden, he employed English. This was not an easy task, for he thought in German and had to translate as he talked. To facilitate clearness of expression he laboriously wrote out his addresses in English and committed them to memory. When he spoke in later years, after coming to New York, he had acquired the habit of thinking in English, and when asked to make an address in German during the Nicoll campaign, found it very difficult. In his after years of retirement he took up German again and used it faultlessly, cultivating the language, through skilled readers, from the best books in German literature.

He loved art and music, a taste reflected in the great benefactions made in his will to the Philharmonic Society and the Metropolitan Museum of Art. When sight grew dim, as with most blind people, music became a solace. The piano appealed to him especially and he heard great players whenever possible. Now and then Paderewski would pay him a visit and there would be a carnival of piano playing. The strings were next. His winters on the Riviera were made happy by the splendid orchestra maintained at Monte Carlo by the Prince of Monaco. He frequented the opera, but the social noises usually drove him home early. The group of secretaries always included one excellent pianist whose duties were by no means light and whose slightest error in technique met with instant and fierce rebuke.

Like Napoleon his omnivorousness and great curiosity gave him a tremendous appetite. He was most insistent about his meals; ate often and heavily, frequently awakening in the night to satisfy his hunger with an extra meal. He was fond of luxury — always craved and secured the best. This was from no vainglory of extravagance, but was an inborn instinct, which he almost always managed to gratify even when poor. The best vintages came to his table, the finest moselles, champagnes, and burgundies; yet he drank little, rarely more than a single glass. He loved to be warm, to sleep well, to be comfortably housed, and to have at his command good books. In his later years he spent at least twelve hours of the day in bed. His afternoon nap was the trial of his valet and the terror of fellow travelers. Rooms had to be kept vacant above, below, and on either side of him at hotels; and the White Star Line, upon whose steamers he usually made his European voyages, kept his good will for many years by maintaining a huge drugget, made of manila rope, which was spread upon the deck so that the footsteps of the idlers on the promenade deck could not jar his slumbers in the stateroom below.

This desire for silence became almost a mania. The great house, Chatwold, at Bar Harbor, had added to it in 1895 a huge granite pile, called by some of the humorous inmates the "Tower of Silence." It was provided with specially constructed walls and partitions designed, unsuccessfully, to shut out all noise. The new city mansion, on East Seventy-third Street, New York, built in 1902, failed to provide soundproof quarters in spite of much planning by the architects, McKim, Mead & White. Indeed, his own rooms seemed to be haunted by noises, among them a strange knocking that nearly drove him frantic. After experts had failed, I discovered the trouble. In building the house, a living spring which could not be suppressed was found in the cellar. It was fed into a sump-pit; this in turn was emptied by an automatic pump, operated by electricity, which started when the water reached a certain level. By a rare fatality the pump had been placed so that the drum of the heating system acted as a sounding board and spread the incidental vibrations through the house, centring most loudly in Mr. Pulitzer's bedroom. The pump was shifted under the sidewalk, but he abandoned the room and built a single story annex in the yard, with double walls packed with mineral wool. The windows were guarded by triple glass; ventilation was by the fireplace chimney. He was sure that the jar of early morning whistles found its way to his ears by this opening. Silk threads were stretched across it to break the sound. Three doors were hung in the short passage from the main house, the floor of which was on ball bearings to prevent vibrations. The room was so still as to be uncanny.

Behind the "Tower of Silence" at Chatwold was a little balcony overhanging a rock-lined canyon through which Bear brook went babbling to the sea. This was his favorite resting-place. Here he would sit in the cool of the morning, or in the grateful shade of the afternoon, listening to the surf breaking almost under his feet, and gaining a tranquillity denied him elsewhere in the clatter of life.

The entourage came at times to be skeptical about Mr. Pulitzer's sensitiveness to noises, but rarely dared to experiment. Once, when the *Liberty* was in dock at Marseilles, a local carriage was hired by Norman G. Thwaites, then secretary, for a morning's ride. Mr. Pulitzer joined him with Harold S. Pollard, his reader and companion. Hardly had the equipage reached the park when a wheel began squeaking outrageously. Mr. Thwaites nerved himself for an explosion. None came. Instead Mr. Pulitzer remarked sweetly: "There must be a great many birds in this park, Thwaites." Thwaites had not seen any but he agreed that it was quite possible as there were plenty of trees.

"*Tweet-tweet, tweet-tweet,*" went the wretched axle. "Really, now," said he, "can't you hear them singing? It is very delightful."

His olfactory nerves, like the nerves of his ears were abnormally sensitive. Perfumes he especially abhorred. On one occasion while at Cap Martin, a luckless British medico, who had come from London to be surgeon of the *Liberty,* for the first time in his life loaded his pocket handkerchief with patchouly. By mischance a whiff of this reached Mr. Pulitzer before the candidate was presented and roused him to fury. The doctor was taken below by a valet and deodorized before the patient could be examined; but the incident so unsettled the professional man that he declined the berth.

His love of chess was cherished as long as his fading sight made playing possible. He had a special set of chessmen made, of large size, to render them plainer to his fading vision. In time it became impossible to employ even these. During the early days of his exile, when at Beaulieu, Arthur Brisbane sought to allay the tedium by reviving Mr. Pulitzer's interest in the seductive game of draw poker with a pack of very large cards. All went well until Arthur's winnings at a sitting ran up to five hundred dollars. Mr. Pulitzer paid up but discontinued the diversion. Long afterward Joseph Junior chanced to remark that he had taken up the game for amusement — carefully adding that the "limit" was always twenty-five cents, and that he found it entertaining. "I don't know about that, Joseph," remarked his father, doubtfully. "I am afraid you will find it a rather dangerous accomplishment."

He loved horses and rode with the grace and freedom of one born to the saddle. Always in good weather, at home or abroad, an afternoon ride was the rule. As he became more blind, the pace was always a sharp trot or a canter but his seat was secure and his mastery of his steed perfect. Good horses were always plentiful before the automobile drove them out of use. At one time the Chatwold stables contained twenty-six animals. He was slow in taking to the motor car, but once converted took to it amazingly. Indeed, he liked speed. To be in motion was his incessant delight. For this reason he made long and seemingly purposeless journeys. Life soon became dreary if he settled down for a time. The thought of moving cheered him up and in motion he was serenely amiable.

He was singularly delicate about being fully clad and could not bear to have any part of his person exposed to the gaze of another. His sensitiveness in this particular developed in an amusing way at Cap Martin in the spring of 1910 when, after much negotiation, the great Rodin was commissioned to execute a bust. Rodin insisted that

Mr. Pulitzer in posing should lay bare his shoulders in order that the poise of the head might be correctly revealed. To this Mr. Pulitzer objected strenuously. Rodin was obdurate but it was not until he threatened to throw up the commission and return to Paris that his subject surrendered, and then only on condition that none but his immediate attendants should be admitted to the studio. This was agreed to and the work went on, the model proving very petulant and unruly and refusing to talk to Rodin, who naturally wished to put his sitter at ease and to get at least a glimpse of his mind. The contract was for busts in bronze and in marble. The bronze is a mere head with no attempt to indicate the shoulders. The marble goes further — and here Rodin had his revenge; for he laid a bit of ruching across the chest, playfully suggestive of a chemise!

As Mr. Pulitzer was troubled with asthma, his yacht, the *Liberty*, was often set in motion for no other object than to create a breeze which would pour fresh air into his gasping nostrils. "Find a breeze" was his most frequent sailing-order. He was a reckless navigator, defying harbor rules, and often taking great risks from storm and tide. Odd as it may seem, he knew nothing of the latter phenomena and had to be argued with when told it was a factor to be reckoned with when the *Liberty* had to wait outside a harbor.

Although long blind for all practical purposes, complete loss of sight had apparently come by 1910. One evening while the *Liberty* lay at anchor in Mentone, the marvelous moon of the Mediterranean came up in its fullest splendor. Mr. Pollard, the companion, thinking Mr. Pulitzer might get a glimpse of its glory, led him to the bow of the yacht and placed him where he could see to the best advantage. Mr. Pulitzer strained his eyes long in the given direction, but said sadly at last: "No use, my boy, I can't make it out."

Miss Dorothy Whitney, now Mrs. Willard D. Straight, was one of his last memories before his eyes grew dim. "You know," he once said, "before I lost my eyes I used to walk around and talk politics with Whitney. He was so very interesting. This young lady, then a little girl, would climb upon my knees and pull my whiskers. So she stays in my memory as among the last of those whom I could see. I shall always be interested in her."

As Ponce de Leon sought the Fountain of Youth, Mr. Pulitzer was forever seeking the fountain of health. Consulting doctors became a passion with him. The most distinguished practitioners in Europe passed in review, taking fees and leaving no cures behind. The entourage came to believe that seeing doctors was more of a pastime than a hope, especially after the distinguished von Nordheim, who journeyed from Vienna to Wiesbaden, was turned away with the excuse that his prospective patient was "too ill" to see him.

The search for the attendant doctor was always on, even with a satisfactory man in the entourage. He always wanted to be sure that another could be had if the incumbent should weary of his job.

This letter to the late James M. Tuohy, the *World*'s London correspondent, written March 9, 1910, from the Villa Arethuse, Cap Martin, by Mr. Pulitzer's secretary, Norman G. Thwaites, shows the system:

MY DEAR MR. TUOHY:

Mr. Pulitzer asks me to write to you at once that it may catch you before you start on your holiday. He has been ill in bed for two weeks with severe bronchial cold, reviving his old whooping cough, and is now amazingly weak and sleepless. As soon as he is able to be moved, he is planning a month's trip on the yacht, probably into the East and the Red Sea.

The point is this: utterly disregarding all qualifications heretofore specified as to agreeability, conversation, knowledge of history, editorial ability, and so on, can you set in immediate motion a search for a first-rate, practical physician who would be willing to go off immediately for a month on the yacht? Mr. Pulitzer underlines three times the point that *you can drop all former requirements as to personal qualifications*, concentrating on experienced, reliable, first-class professional ability. The man need not be a specialist so long as he is able to study and diagnose Mr. Pulitzer's peculiar history and condition of nervousness, insomnia, and recently recurring complications of whooping cough.

You can also dismiss the idea of permanency. Mr. Pulitzer's present plan is leave here about March 15, and to be gone till about the first of May, calling very probably at Constantinople, Athens, Egypt, and the Red Sea. The man will have nothing to do except to enjoy himself, and, apart from the study of Mr. Pulitzer's case, it ought to be an exceedingly pleasant trip for anyone.

Needless to say the man must be sea-sick-proof!!!

Mr. Pulitzer says emphatically he does not wish this matter to interfere with your holiday or to spoil it. It must not interfere with that.

You will see that it is quite different from anything he has asked for before in that it distinctly eliminates the point of intellectual companionship, and asks merely for a first-rate doctor. Mr. Pulitzer says he may stutter or be a hunchback, but of course not preferably so. This ought to make the search much easier. Mr. Pulitzer has really been very ill and ought not to go off without a serious-minded, capable physician, in whom he and Mrs. Pulitzer can have some confidence. I am sure you can understand why the present author-physician fails to inspire that feeling.

Hoping that someone may be found as soon as possible as it is entirely desirable that Mr. Pulitzer should get away at once, and with best wishes to yourself,

Yours sincerely,
NORMAN G. THWAITES

When John S. Sargent was approached to paint Mr. Pulitzer's portrait, in 1909, a shy secretary intimated that Sargent's specialty lay in divining the innermost weaknesses and powers of his sitters and putting them on canvas. Mr. Pulitzer grimly warned the painter not to spare him. "That is what I want," he said. "I want to be remembered just as I really am, with all my strain and suffering there." The picture shows the blind man seated, holding a riding crop in the one hand and resting the other lightly against his cheek — a favorite attitude. The pain and suffering of years shows on his face, blended with high intellect, energy of character, and fierceness of temper.

Mr. Pulitzer's habits of thought and his later invalidism kept him aloof from affairs. Where a Horace Greeley became personally one of the shapers of a cause, Mr. Pulitzer after the early days of his *World* ownership was in but slight touch with individuals in politics and affairs. He did not wish to be in intimate touch with or in the confidence of political leaders. I recall once mentioning the visit of an eminent Democrat to the *World* editorial rooms. His instant comment was: "I don't like that. I don't want those fellows calling at the office."

He did not care to have an inside share in moulding matters, wishing all his efforts to appear openly on the editorial pages of his newspapers. He lived most of his life apart from other men, having a feeling that his was the fate of the true journalist, that he must devote — and limit — his interest to his paper.

Discussing some passing matter, I once used the phrase "your friends." "My friends," interrupted Mr. Pulitzer ironically; "I have no friends. You fellows in the office will not let me have any."

This was in a great measure true. But the "fellows in the office" did not have any either, and he knew it and delighted in the singleness of their devotion to the *World*. There was no list of "sacred cows" in the place, nor any *index expurgatorious*. The facts had to warrant the story. That was the only rule.

Mr. Pulitzer cared little for the evening or Sunday editions of the *World*, beyond expecting them to prosper, which both did amazingly. His interest and affection centred in the six-day morning issue, which he regarded as his paper. The others were mere commercial enterprises, but the morning *World* contained his soul — and that of the establishment. He lavished money on it, leaving the evening edition to get along with a slender force, though one of much talent. In time it developed almost complete independence of him and his ideas and became what it is to-day.

The *World* was managed by its managers and edited by its editors. Mr. Pulitzer suggested freely, but ordered little. Final judgment was always with the office. He once advised me, when business manager, that I could do anything on behalf of the paper except hunt for the North Pole, or back the invention of a flying machine, both ideas seeming chimerical to him. Within less than a decade after this adjuration Peary reached the Pole and the Wrights had conquered the air. Mr. Pulitzer was still alive. Indeed, it was the *World*'s award of $10,000 to Glenn Curtiss for flying from Albany to New York that enabled that aviator and inventor to establish the great business which now bears his name.

His initiative, strange as it may appear, was not extraordinary, and he frequently showed a hesitancy that verged upon timidity in adopting policies urged upon him by the juniors. His strength lay in stimulation. Here he had few superiors. He was a man of enormous impulses curbed by great reactions, who safeguarded himself from the effects of either by carefully warning his aids not to be swept off their feet by any order he might issue; all directions from headquarters were to be tempered by judgment or fuller information which he might not possess. If a very radical ukase came, the office custom was to reply, fixing a delayed day and hour for the execution. Usually a restraining telegram came above five minutes before the appointed moment. Under his policy the virtues of the *World* were easily his own, while the mistakes and conflicts became readily the property of others.

Extravagant as he was in verbal expression, Mr. Pulitzer valued judgment that waited on facts. In one of the changes of a generation in the office, when the old heads vanished almost altogether, he caused each of the younger moulders of opinion to be given a beautiful set of gilded scales from Tiffany's — the hint was quite plain.

It was his habit always to require two men on the same job and then to let them fight it out, though often to his own discomfiture and despair. The office theory was that he liked competition and sought to gain advantage by the strivings of the one man to outdo the other. If this is correct, it never worked; either hopeless deadlocks followed or the men divided their domain and lived peacefully. There was probably something in the theory, but more in the habit of precaution which he developed early in life. He always wanted to have a second resource in hand if one chanced to fail him, and to avoid being held up by any journalist who might think himself super-valuable.

The new men on the paper were always under scrutiny and the old ones never free from the test. One day at the lunch table at Bar Harbor, in October 1899, the company was discussing the achievements of an able reporter, Charles W. Tyler, who had just done a very good piece of work. Mr. Pulitzer was complimenting Tyler highly. Professor Thomas Davidson spoke up: "I cannot understand why it is, Mr. Pulitzer, that you always speak so kindly of reporters and so severely of all editors." "Well," he replied, "I suppose it is because every reporter is a hope, and every editor is a disappointment."

His blindness caused him to test men severely. He could learn the shape of an article by touch, but the qualities of a man could be ascertained only by intellectual pressure, and this he applied so searchingly as to seem merciless. Yet it can be truthfully recorded that no survivor ever failed at his task.

To one of the young men, who afterward rose to high rank on the *World*, Mr. Pulitzer remarked: "I wish I could take your brain apart and look into it."

"I don't," the youngster said; "I am afraid you would mix up the parts and never get them in place again."

Usually each fall, after election, the *World*'s circulation dropped. Mr. Pulitzer would credit the slump to the errors of the editors during the campaign, and a shake-up almost always followed. One year there was no election, with the same result. Much puzzled, he called on me for a solution of the mystery. I proved that it was due to the shortening of the daylight hours, showing that the paper always grew in the lengthening days. Appeased, he left the staff in peace on this one count at any rate.

"Forever unsatisfied" described his temperament. He was forever unsatisfied, not so much with the results as with the thought that if a further effort had been made, a sterner command or greater encouragement given, more would have been accomplished. Curiously enough, he was most pestiferous in his urgings and drivings when all was going at its best. In times of trouble he rested his lash. Men were left unhampered in their responsibilities, seldom chided when they failed, if there was evidence that they had tried to succeed, and richly rewarded if they triumphed.

Another high quality he had: to use poker parlance — he never would "call" anyone. From the same characteristic no one could "call" him. Men who tried it were usually sorry. He had an amazing patience with human frailty and an unfailing belief in the merits of mankind.

All newspapers have periods of "flattening out," when the entire editorial force needs reinvigorating. During one of these spells on the *World*, Mr. Pulitzer was sojourning at Lakewood, New Jersey. Much disturbed, he wished to know the cause of the dullness. The business manager thought the boys were track-sore and suggested a "shake-up" —meaning a shifting of jobs, familiar to all pressworkers in the metropolis, invented, it is believed, by the younger James Gordon Bennett, who sometimes made weird transpositions in his endeavors to stimulate the staff. Mr. Pulitzer liked this kind of experiment, but this time it did not appeal to him.

"I don't think that's the reason," he said. "I think it's because nobody on the staff gets drunk. Brad [Bradford Merrill, then editorial manager] never gets drunk; Burton [city editor] lives in Flatbush — he never gets drunk; Van Hamm [managing editor] sleeps out in New Jersey — he never gets drunk; Lyman [night managing editor] he's always sober. You live in Brooklyn and never get drunk. When I was there some of them got drunk, and we made a great paper. Take the next train back to the city, find somebody who gets drunk, and hire him at once."

Returning on this strange errand, when crossing Park Row, the business manager ran into a very brilliant writer whom he had long known as a friend of the flowing bowl. He looked down-at-the-heel and depressed.

"What are you doing?" he was asked.

"Nothing," was the glum response.

"I thought you were on the *American*? What's the trouble?"

"Same old thing," was the dolorous response. "I can't let the hard stuff alone."

So he was still eligible. "Good!" cried the business manager. "I have a life job for you."

With that he dragged him into the office and nailed him to the pay roll. Supplementing this the Flatbush city editor was given two weeks' board at the Waldorf-Astoria — to get some acquaintance with New York. Curiously enough, the paper responded to the prescription and became lively again.

While severely critical of the *World* and its makers, Mr. Pulitzer could not brook the least disapproval of either from others. One day at Bar Harbor, after a period of very acrimonious faultfinding, he wound up with this blanket condemnation of the shop: "It had no head, no sense, no brains."

This passed in silence, but later in the day he broached a suggestion to which I replied that the idea had been tried by the *Herald* without success.

"Why do you mention the *Herald*?" he interrupted sharply. "They have no head, no sense, no brains!"

"Neither have we," I replied.

He reached his long arm forward and, grasping my throat, choked it vigorously and remarked reprovingly:

"Stop that! You are altogether too critical and unjust to the office!"

To compress cables and telegrams a considerable code was developed through the years, which included the names of men in the office, rivals in the profession, and others who had to do with business or politics. For himself he selected the cipher word "Andes," modestly taking the name of the second highest altitude on the earth's surface. He commonly went by the code name in office conversation. Mr. William H. Merrill, his chief editorial writer, was "Cantabo"; his treasurer, J. Angus Shaw, was "Solid" — a neat compliment; S. S. Carvalho was designated by a single syllable, "Los"; John Norris became "Anfracto"; C. M. Van Hamm, "Gyrate," illustrating perhaps the vicissitudes of a managing editor; Florence D. White was "Volema" on the wire. I was honored with three stage-names — "Gulch," "Mastodon," and

"Quixotic"; Dumont Clarke, his vice-president, was "Coin," a commodity with which he had much to do; Colonel George B. M. Harvey was "Sawpit"; James Gordon Bennett came over the cable as "Gaiter," and William R. Hearst as "Gush." For William J. Bryan, two code designations were used: "Guilder" and "Maxilla," the latter possibly a delicate reference to jaw. Pomeroy Burton became "Gumbo," perhaps as he himself said because he was "so often in the soup." The code amused Mr. Pulitzer and he was forever tinkering it.

His telegrams and cables usually came unsigned save for a final word — "Sedentary" — which meant that a prompt reply was required. This usually went back in a single word — "Semaphore" — meaning "message received and understood." When in good humor and pleased he would sign personal messages "J.P.," but when his wrath was high they came signed "Joseph Pulitzer." That meant trouble. In my eighteen years of association I received three bearing the ominous full signature!

Like most successful men, he had his superstitions, and one of these was a reverence for the figure ten. He was born on the tenth of April, reached St. Louis on the tenth of October, consolidated the *Post* with the *Dispatch* on the tenth of December, 1878, and bought the *World* on the tenth of May, 1883. He made the superstition something of a fad and used the numerals always when he could. In buying his first New York house, he selected No. 10 East Fifty-fifth Street — the two fives adding another ten. Lastly he cut the price of his morning newspaper from two cents to one, on February 10, 1896, and began the interesting duel with the millions of the Hearst estate. The result of the latter experiment was not to his liking and he lost interest in the superstition in his later years. But the dates remain milestones to be remembered in considering his extraordinary career.

Perhaps his birth on the eve of the great revolutionary period of 1848, had something to do with the fact that all his life he was a passionate devotee of Liberty — liberty of action, of opinion, of government. He opposed all sumptuary legislation, all tax-law inequities, all political bossism whether of the party or its leaders, and above all war!

When some new delight came his way, he liked to pass it on to those he wished to reward or encourage. Coming from the mild and humid central Mississippi Valley, he found the New York winter chill and took to a furlined overcoat for protection. This was before the days of heated street cars or comfortable subways, and the heavy garment gave him great content. Soon the men of mark on the *World* were garbed in fur with the compliments of the owner. When his eyes grew troublesome, he secured needed shade from the flexible brim of a Panama hat. Presto, all the favorites were likewise bedecked. He had great regard for the tall silk hat and always wore one on occasions that seemed important. When the *World* passed its 100,000 mark every employee received a silk hat with Mr. Pulitzer's best wishes. He usually closed all arguments with a bet when the talk grew too strenuous, and the wager took the form of a hat — frequently *five* hats. I had a controversy once that lasted five months over the "return" rules of the *New York American*. He refused to believe my statements, but finally incontestable proof of their accuracy found him at Corfu. He cabled me to buy the hats, but stipulated that one of them must be a "crush" for the opera, knowing that I detested both. This and other winnings kept me in headgear for about twenty years at Mr. Pulitzer's expense.

The considerable fortune left by Mr. Pulitzer was enhanced by the profitable outcome of wise investments in American securities listed on the New York Stock Exchange. They were not made primarily with this intent, but to protect the *World*. When the paper began piling up money, with his customary caution he looked ahead for lean years. He wished to be securely beyond the need of borrowing from banks. So he picked out what appeared to be the soundest easily marketed securities on the list. The paper never needed his aid and the investments grew with the years and the increasing prosperity of the country. When his property was listed, but one worthless item was found, a twenty-share certificate in some long-forgotten effort to build a railroad in Missouri. Every other item had held or increased its value. Some had repaid him more than three-hundred fold!

He bought stocks in large lots — 2000, 3000, and 5000 shares, always in even numbers so that the holdings might easily be carried in his memory. Some of these vast blocks were made up of Delaware, Lackawanna & Western, Lake Shore, Central Railroad of New Jersey, and like gilt-edges. They were bought at the instance of the late Dumont Clarke, president of the American Exchange National Bank, and long vice-president of the Press Publishing Company, though having no relation to the production of the *World*. To Mr. Clarke's sound judgment Mr. Pulitzer added his own with highly satisfactory results. Mr.

Pulitzer had himself a fear of the influence of his growing wealth upon his views and their consequent reflection in the paper. In 1907 he sent for Frank I. Cobb, his chief editorial writer. It was during the tremors that preceded the "Roosevelt" panic. The editor was addressed in this wise: "Boy, I am, as you probably know, a large owner of stocks. Some of them are bound to be affected by public actions. I am not sure of myself when I see my interests in danger. I might give way some day to such a feeling and send you an order that would mean a change in the paper's policy. I want you to make me a promise. If I ever do such a thing swear you will ignore my wishes."

The promise was made, but no such order ever came. It would have passed unheeded had it come, so thorough was the singleness of purpose which characterized the paper. Once in a while the traffic manager of the Western Union would claim a large share of words because the owner of the *World* was one of its chief stockholders. Such visits usually increased the trade of its Postal rival. Mr. Pulitzer never mentioned his holding in the concern to anyone in the shop.

He never embarked in any enterprise for making money, confining himself entirely to the investment of earnings from his newspapers in sound securities. Yet of his talents in a financial way, Lord Rothschild once said, "If Pulitzer would devote himself entirely to finance, he could be the richest man on the globe."

His personal expenditures were enormous, probably exceeding, outside of royalty, those of any man of his time. The *Liberty* was always in commission and her operating cost, with repairs, ran close to $200,000 a year. In addition to this he maintained costly residences at Bar Harbor, Jekyl Island, Georgia, and in New York, to which was added the finest villa to be had at Cap Martin. Probably the bill totaled $350,000 a year, but it barely dented the great income from newspapers and investments. There was always a large annual surplus.

Although one of the masters of the art of attracting attention, he was singularly shy himself. He did not like to be pointed out publicly, or to be personally a centre of interest. Once at Bar Harbor I had told Mrs. Pulitzer a merry tale about him, the joke of which was on the other fellow. She repeated it to her husband. "What's this story you have been telling Mrs. Pulitzer?" he queried at luncheon. I replied that it was a good one. He was silent for a moment, then said gently: "Don't tell stories about me. Keep them until I am dead."

21

Hearst: A Psychological Note

by GEORGE P. WEST

A former West Coast newspaperman and author, GEORGE P. WEST, wrote this psychological analysis of William Randolph Hearst for the *American Mercury* in November 1930, in the heyday of the most amazing newspaper publisher that America has ever seen, or is likely to see.

I

CALIFORNIA that cradled him has received Hearst in the evening of his life, a career has come full-circle, and at San Simeon on the shore of the Pacific the strangest and perhaps the most significant figure of our times holds court in a Cecil de Mille magnificence with movie actors as his courtiers.

A towering vanity, fed for thirty years on dreams of the White House and the power of a Caesar, rests at last on a veritable movie-set of Moorish palaces, rising above the sea to command his four hundred square miles, and on the flattery of that Hollywood circle which is both the creature and the wish-fulfillment of the mob on which Hearst has played all his life. And while he putters about among his ship-loads of transplanted marbles, or presides, pale and silent, amid the revelry of these puppets, his newspapers that once harried the captains of finance and industry until they trembled in their beds now lead the chorus in hymns to Mammon and genuflections before his high priests.

Plagued by business worries inherent in his huge and scattered enterprises, served by a pack of uneasy executives whom he distrusts and among whom his suspicion and sudden tempers breed a neurosis of fear and jealousy, looking hopefully but unassured for help from his sons, Hearst begins at last to take on a human quality and a dignity that he has hitherto lacked. It is the dignity of tragedy, or of near-tragedy, for he touches at times a true magnificence, and his failure and defeat are those of no ordinary man.

And it is failure, make no mistake about that. The illusion was complete; the man had visions, saw himself noble and exalted, craved not merely power but the love and respect of his fellows; and if at sixty-seven he is without honor except the fawning of those who fatten on his favors, from the newest movie star to John Hylan and Calvin Coolidge, it is because the fates at his birth gave him a twisted and partial vision, left something out of him, blinded him to values and proportions that move even the mob when it turns thumbs up or down.

Dusty files tell the story of his hope. It was 1906, and he was running against Charles Evans Hughes for Governor of New York, when Arthur Brisbane wrote of him in the pages of the *North American Review*. It was a hostile and incredulous audience, and Brisbane knew it when he deliberately penned these words: "There is no doubt that Hearst will be elected President of the United States if he lives. He is the most popular man in the United States today."

Did Hearst believe it? Of course he did, and if he read the editorial in the same issue he probably laughed when the editor, frightened by his temerity in admitting the Brisbane piece, demolished him as a demagogue and added that, "as a journalist, he is a blazing disgrace to his craft."

It was in the same year that Lincoln Steffens broke through Hearst's guard and listened as the silent finger-drumming man talked of Caesar, Napoleon, Washington, Jefferson, and Lincoln, frankly admitted his ambition, and argued that Caesar was a popular reformer who was killed by members of the Old Gang. He had the dream, and he labored prodigiously to make it come true. With his rich man's contempt for any means save money, he multiplied his newspapers, infested the labor movement and the Democratic party with his paid agents, built a new party that he owned body and breeches, made a war with Spain, harried the trusts not only in cartoons and editorials but in lawsuits as the people's tribune, bought stolen papers to expose and destroy Archbold, Foraker and Bailey, forced a revision of the Hay-Pauncefote treaty to allow fortifying the Panama Canal, used Ambrose Bierce to whip Collis P. Huntington in Congress, controlled Tammany for a season, and as recently as 1922 forced his name on the party slate as Democratic candidate for United States Senator from New York.

It is merely a detail that it was Alfred E. Smith who forced it off and returned again and once again to deliver the *coup de grâce*, giving the quietus to his political career in blistering sentences that only Hearst could draw from the amiable Al. It is merely a detail, for the end was predestined.

But it is irony that his final defeat should come at the hands of Smith and Jimmy Walker, boys from those sidewalks of New York where Hearst's *Journal* had been supreme, while the stuffed shirts and the plutocracy that were his chosen target for thirty years stood aside, or even commiserated with him in the person of his dear friend Judge Gary, head of the largest of all the octopi.

II

On the hills above San Francisco Bay there lived for a few years a jovial and impoverished poet. Cashiered from a British warship for fighting a duel, Daniel O'Connell came to San Francisco from the China station, ornamented the Bohemian Club bar, and lived on the bounty of friends at Sausalito. When he died there they erected a beautiful granite seat, in a sweeping semi-circle, on the spot where he had sat looking out on the passing ships and the distant city, and in the granite they carved the verses of his last graceful lyric. Strangers pause and read it, women sit in the sun with their children, and Daniel O'Connell's memory is fragrant. Not a stone's-throw away, where the hill slopes sheer to the water, well-kept live-oaks, their trunks neatly whitewashed, march down the hill to great stone bastions and retaining-walls, and from this silent and deserted spot signs warn off the trespasser with threats of jail.

It is the site of Hearst's boyhood Summer home, a three-story frame building, torn down in 1921. Here he played as a child, and here he lived during the years when he was getting his stride as publisher of the *Examiner*. Nowhere is there a reminder of him, and about the place are no stories, save the whispered apocrypha of some newspaper veteran, grown garrulous late at night in a speakeasy. Only a real estate agent, passing the place, tells strangers parrot-wise: "This is where Hearst sowed his wild oats." It is a vague and slightly sinister phrase, carrying a forgotten bad odor, and the town forgets.

A bad odor. Yet it hangs about a man who has done a thousand gracious and generous things (for those he could control), whose wealth and power have been poured out time and time again to aid the humane and libertarian movements of his time, whose personal modesty is extreme, who is adored by the handful of satellites who have walked with him down the years.

Hearst was born in San Francisco in 1863. He attended the public schools there, and except for a few years at a school in New Hampshire, where he could not get along, and at Harvard, from which he was expelled, he lived in San Francisco until he was thirty-two. He learned his trade there, amazed his teachers with new tricks, and wrote a brilliant chapter in newspaper history, and it was a San Francisco staff that he took with him to man the *Journal* when he invaded New York in 1895.

The revenues from his California paper pulled him out of many a hole, and today he publishes five dailies in the State, two each in San Francisco and Los Angeles and one in Oakland. And for the past ten years he has spent by far the greater proportion of the time at his California ranch at San Simeon, on the coast midway between San Francisco and Los Angeles. He is one of the largest land-owners in the State, by far its largest publisher, and all his background is there. His eldest son is publisher of the parent *Examiner*, his next son is a graduate of the University at Berkeley, and both married California girls.

In his heredity Hearst is so completely Californian that a novelist wishing to catch up the State's history in an individual could not have invented a better case. George Hearst left his father's Missouri farm to join the gold rush and spent the fifties as a miner in the foothills of the Sierras, a tall, bold adventurer with the strong aquiline nose of the Southern mountaineer. He was of the Southern faction by birth and temperament, and when, loaded with millions, he married a genteel girl of Virginia-Missouri stock and built his mansion in San Francisco, he had little in common with the men from Yankeeland who lorded it over the State as owners of the new railroad.

He was intransigent in his loyalty to the old traditions of the mining camps. He would not buy himself a dress suit, not even for his wife's finest parties in Washington, where he went as Senator. He rebuffed dandies and pretentious people addicted to decorum and dignity, and he spent his happiest hours to the last among old mining cronies at the bar of the What Cheer House. By them he was adored. Mrs. Hearst took care of all that social nonsense, and he gave his amiable consent to her ideas and doings without for a moment committing himself.

The young Hearst, an only child, inherited this maverick streak from his father, although it took different forms, and he was a notorious dandy until political ambition put him into a cowboy hat. He added to his father's contempt for decorum a great shyness that concealed an enormous will to power. If psychology were a science, it might be possible to say what gave the lad his inferiority complex, his towering will under some pressure that made him uneasy, bashful, with a passion for creating discomfort and astonishment in those whom he tried to ignore and despise. Awkward, lymphatic, with big hands and feet, perhaps it was a mere matter of glands. From the first he was uncomfortable with his equals. A San Francisco contemporary remembers how Will Hearst as a small boy would collect two or three ragamuffins of his own age, lavish candy and soda-pop on them, and take them to the best seats at the theatre. He had a genuine kinship with the lowly.

Neat explanations of the mysteries of personality are the order of the day, and, more than half convinced, I present Hearst as in part at least a product of the California frontier and the Missouri-Far West stock and tradition, born into a more effete world, an organized world in which he became merely one more millionaire. So in journalism he found his métier, and he invented yellow journalism as a substitute for the racy, anarchic, flamboyant life of the mining-camps.

The difference was that he was never disciplined. He missed the earlier years when his father was the poor prospector, learning respect for others and winning their respect in turn by observing the code. The young Hearst commanded a substitute for respect from the first, by the sheer brutal power of the money jingled by a rich man's only child. He could not adapt himself to boarding-school, where a crude money patronage failed him, and he came home undismayed, just as later he left Harvard undismayed. He would show them, and he did.

At Harvard he had been fascinated by Pulitzer's *New York World*, and after his expulsion he went to New York and met some of the men who were hatching yellow journalism. Thus he met Sam Chamberlain, handsome, debonair, resourceful, who had been James Gordon Bennett's secretary, editor of the *Evening Telegram*, editor of *Le Matin* in Paris. Chamberlain came to San Francisco as Hearst's editor as soon as the young man had persuaded his father to give him the *Examiner*, then a feeble afternoon sheet maintained by George Hearst as an organ of the Democracy that had sent him to the Senate. And Chamberlain taught Hearst more than Harvard.

The *Examiner*, made into a morning paper, jumped from almost nothing to 30,000 circulation within a year. Soon it was at more than double that figure. Hearst gathered about him a brilliant staff.

III

To talk with one of the survivors of that crew is to get the flavor of a happy and extravagant world, now gone forever. The *Examiner* office was a madhouse inhabited by talented and erratic young men, drunk with life in a city that never existed before or since.

They had a mad boss, one who flung away money, lived like a ruler of the late Empire at his house above the water at Sausalito, and cheered them on as they made newspaper history.

When Senator Hearst died, in 1891, the star reporter selected to write the story of the funeral was overcome by the strong waters which the occasion seemed to prescribe, and failed to show up. Chamberlain thereupon turned the job over to Eddie Morphy, a graduate of Dublin University but just arrived from New York, the dust of the train still upon him, who sat down and swiftly dashed off a moving account of the obsequies as older members of the staff stood by and provided him now and then with some ineluctable fact.

It was the same Eddie Morphy (now editor of the weekly *Argonaut* in San Francisco), under orders to fill a Sunday page with seven parallel columns of town characters, who, stumped for material for the last column, invented the orphaned McGinty boys and wrote a story, "The Last of the McGintys," that brought tears to the eyes of Hearst's mother, living then on the top floor of the old Palace, so that she sent over five clinking twenty-dollar gold-pieces for the McGintys, into which the dismayed Morphy and his colleagues made heavy inroads for refreshments as they scoured Telegraph Hill for two ragamuffins who would look McGintyish in the pictures that were now demanded. And Morphy remembers a tall, solemn, long-nosed young man in a dog-cart, waited grimly outside a crab-seller's on the Sausalito water-front until the recreant reporter had to emerge at last and submit to being taken back to the *Examiner* office and locked in a room with whiskey and sandwiches until he had completed a dissertation on California wild-flowers. Wildflowers! The paradox meets you on every page of the man's life.

Ambrose Bierce celebrated his withdrawal from the Hearst payroll after twenty years by writing some fugitive memories and judgments of the man, to be included in the complete edition of his works. He remembered that "at one time on the *Examiner* it was customary when a reporter had a disagreeable assignment for him to go away for a few days, then return and plead intoxication." He relates that the excuse remained valid until one day Hearst met a man, cold sober, who was reported off on a spree. "On the scamp's assurance that he had honestly intended to be drunk, but lacked the price, Mr. Hearst gave him enough money to reestablish his character for veracity and passed on."

Bierce recalled, too, his first meeting with Hearst. A tall young man appeared at the door of his lodgings in Oakland one evening and mentioned the *Examiner*. "You come from Mr. Hearst, then?" Bierce queried. His account continues:

"That unearthly child lifted its blue eyes and cooed 'I am Mr. Hearst,' in a voice like the fragrance of violets made audible, and backed a little away. Twenty years of what his newspapers call 'wage slavery' ensued, and although I had many a fight with his editors for my right to my self-respect, I cannot say that I ever found Mr. Hearst's chain a very heavy burden." But, he concludes finally, "I am not sorry that, discovering no preservative allowable under the Pure Food Law that would allow him to keep his word overnight, I withdrew."

Yet he kept a certain admiration for the man, felt the paradox. He tells how a celebrated quatrain he had written, predicting the assassination of McKinley, was seized upon by Hearst's enemies and used as the heaviest gun in a campaign that almost destroyed him after the shot at Buffalo. Hearst, he says, never mentioned the matter to him, and Bierce adds: "I fancy there must be a human side to a man like that, even if he is a mischievous demagogue." And again: "Never just, Mr. Hearst is always generous. . . . In San Francisco and New York his habit of having the cleverest obtainable men advanced the salaries of all such men more than 50%. Indubitably he did get the brightest men."

306

Once, says Bierce, he caught a manager stealing, discharged him, then reappointed him. Bierce expressed his surprise:

"'Oh, that's all right,' Mr. Hearst explained. 'I have a new understanding with him. He is to steal only small sums, hereafter; the large ones are to come to me.' In this incident we observe two dominant features in his character — his indifference to money and his marvelous sense of humor. . . . The money to which he is indifferent includes that of others, and he smiles at his own expense."

Bierce's contempt extended to Hearst's writing. "As to Mr. Hearst's public writings, I fancy there are none. He could not write an advertisement for a lost dog. The articles that he signs, the speeches that he makes, well, if a man of brains is one who knows how to use the brains of others, this amusing demagogue is nobody's dunce." I think Bierce's prejudice here carries him too far. Hearst's editors are convincing in their denials, and since Bierce wrote in 1913 there have come to light a number of confidential telegrams from Hearst to his editors, sent from distant roadsides where no staff was available, that disclose a capacity for very clear and trenchant expression.

Bierce closes his remarks with the following: "With many amiable and alluring qualities, among which is, or used to be, a personal modesty amounting to bashfulness, the man has not a friend in the world. Nor does he merit one, for either congenitally or by induced perversity, he is inaccessible to the concepton of an unselfish attachment or a disinterested motive. Silent and smiling, he moves among men, the loneliest man. Nobody but God loves him, and he knows it."

As to this, I asked one of Hearst's oldest employees if he had ever followed another man's lead, sincerely, and with admiration or affection. The reply was an emphatic affirmative. I was told that he worshipped William Jennings Bryan in the 1896 days, and that he had once ordered $5,000 worth of orchids for Mrs. Bryan!

IV

The eight San Francisco years were only a rehearsal for what began in New York when Hearst bought the *Journal* in 1895. The best men of the San Francisco staff were brought east, with Chamberlain in charge and Arthur McEwen as editorial writer, and then Hearst began that brutal use of money that has provided his sole access to talent ever since.

With more than $7,000,000 at his disposal from the settlement of his father's estate and his doting mother's generosity, Pulitzer's *World* was at his mercy. Sam S. Carvalho came over in April, 1896. Morrill Goddard, Pulitzer's brilliant Sunday editor, was bought the same year, and moved in with his entire staff. It was Goddard, a scholarly, retiring Maine Yankee, who invented the truly Hearstien and wholly diabolic use of type and "art" to amaze the vulgar with huge lay-outs illustrating the more erotic scenes of history and the more exotic discoveries of explorers and scientists.

It remained for Arthur Brisbane, lured away from Pulitzer in 1897, to achieve headlines half a page deep and similar audacities, while Brisbane's own scholar's baggage matched Goddard's as he rewrote Marx and Voltaire (in those earlier years) in short crisp sentences for the editorial page. To supplement such staff reporters as Karl Decker, James Creelman and Alfred Henry Lewis, Hearst raided the magazines and his money poured into the pockets of all the best writing-men of the day.

The lives these men lived and the extravagant things they did make a saga of American journalism. It is a masterpiece of the picaresque and the disreputable, with Hearst's pale face and long awkward figure dominant at the center. He drove them, inspired them, bribed them with huge salaries and complete freedom to go off on sensational sprees, to indulge their temperaments, and to resign periodically, provided only they came back and continued to boom circulation. He was a prodigious worker himself, and he demanded demoniac energy in his men.

Thus he developed what he called the New Journalism. Not content to wait for News, they made it. In San Francisco they captured a grizzly bear and presented it to Golden Gate Park, dispatched a special train to dig transcontinental passengers out of the Sierra snows, and sent Annie Laurie as a fainting street girl to the Emergency Hospital to expose its cruelties and lecheries. In New York they solved murder mysteries, sued the coal, ice, and milk trusts, sold coal for a few cents a bucket, and finally brought on the Spanish-American War by sending Karl Decker to Cuba to rescue the imprisoned Señorita Cisneros from an Havana prison and by a dozen other such inflammatory devices.

All this was amusing enough, but history must deal with the question whether we did not have here, in the work of these brilliant young men with their crossed fingers, the birth of a technique, almost a cult of hokum that has infected the nation with its most salient vice. Critics of democracy in the Machine Age will say it was inevitable. But Hearst started it on the grand scale, and he accelerated it through the success of his journalism until it captured three American newspapers out of four and stamped the journalistic tribe with that appalling cynicism which is its curse today. For the nation there could be no more deadly channel of contagion than its press. Robert Louis Stevenson speaks in "The Wreckers" of a newspaper editor in San Francisco of the late seventies who was "a dull, sober, Christian gentleman singularly intent on imparting the truth." Not all of them were sober. But they were respectful in a degree to the manners of a gentleman. Even the blacklegs who then abounded gave lip-service to decency, knew their betters, lacked the courage of their raffish impulses.

It is impossible to conceive the New York tabloids with their frank appeal to the illiterate, to what William Allen White has called "the new, raw, happy, moron Middle Class," in the days before Hearst. Certain recent advertising campaigns, the racket system, the very mood of our bright young men of business, can be traced to an essential spiritual identity with the callow diabolism of Hearst's yellow journalism. Back of it all was an unscrupulous contempt — for codes, for principles, for the truth, for the public good.

Hearst was perhaps the first man to exploit the discovery that the minority of honorable and intelligent men can be disregarded in a time and country given to mass production and the rise to power of the lower classes. In his own tastes he *was* the lower classes, and he will not be understood by those who miss his personal preference for the gaudy features that sold his papers along the Fourteenth streets of the land, and who suppose that he consciously and sardonically stooped to a plane below that on which he lived. There was never a really successful demagogue who was not sincere. Always the lower reaches of the theatre have provided Hearst with such substitutes for cronies as his walled-in personality has allowed him, and without wealth he might have been a clogdancer, or, in these later days, a saxophone player.

His assault on good taste and veracity disguised itself during those early years as the high spirits of young men intent on raising cain for its own sake, and it had an attraction because it was done so gayly and hit so many hypocrisies and stupidities. But essentially it was, as Milt Gross would say, a business, and it hardened quickly into the ugliness of a calculated technique for exploiting the sex-cravings, the envy, the savage tribalism, or any other convenient half-cocked emotion of the mob. "What we are after," said the brilliant Arthur McEwen, "is the gee-whiz emotion." But the gee-whiz emotion was the best of it, and often it was something baser than any open-mouthed oafish amazement at which they aimed. They aimed with a special leer at the crowd's moral indignation, as when Winifred Black, sent crusading against Mormonism in Utah, wrote (for the oriental Mr. Hearst!) under a flaming headline: "Protect the Home! Crush the Harem!" It was all immensely audacious and clever, and hugely successful in getting circulation. And it has filled our newspaper offices, the Hearst offices in particular, with swarms of callow and blighted young cynics, men whose outlook is expressed by their sweeping verdict that everything is the bunk.

Stultified and all but concealed by that blight loom forty years of journalistic achievement without a parallel in brilliance. From Ambrose Bierce to Bernard Shaw Mr. Hearst has printed for the enlightenment of his vast popular audience a hundred words of intelligent exposition and analysis — of "good stuff" in the language of the trade — where his nearest competitor has printed ten. The record of the good things he has fought for, of battles won against greed or stupidity, is a perfectly amazing one. From the day when he plumped for Bryan in 1896 against the warnings of all his staff to his stubborn resistance to the war-fever in 1917, he has been utterly impervious to fear in following the lead of his own baffling prejudices, whims, or convictions. We can only guess at our debt to him for whatever toleration and freedom we enjoy at the hands of the urban masses and their leaders.

Isn't it at least of some significance that the most backward parts of the country are those in which the Hearst newspapers have not penetrated? Arthur Brisbane is tedious enough these days in his endless repetitions of the creed of the realty boards, but in his time he has been the greatest journalistic propagator of a realistic and rational view of the universe and the most effective agitator against the Yankee notion that God is a rich banker and poverty a sin.

Hearst is still capable of sacrificing revenue by a sustained attack on the power companies and an exposure of their propaganda, but the impulse grows feeble and a majority of his newspapers are in the hands of men who decline to get their feet wet. They are, indeed, usually members of the inner circle of the business *cabala* that controls the flow of gravy and tells the lunch clubs what to think. And they use the Hearst newspapers with great effect to propagate the current American faith that there is no sin, sickness, or death for those who trail along with the big fellows, but always the chance of winning places nearer the head of the trough. Hearst's three California papers of largest circulation have remained eloquently silent all through the years in which the Mooney-Billings convictions have been exposed as the most grotesque and venal miscarriage of justice in American history. What there is left of the man's liberalism is so erratic that it seems as cynical and calculated as his periodical "moral" campaigns to keep the church people in line. Even when his personal sympathy is engaged for a liberal cause he will allow a local editor with the mind of a police sergeant to fly in the face of it.

v

The truth is that the man himself is in conflict. In the interview of 1906 he told Lincoln Steffens that his papers did not suit him and that he would probably have produced a journal nearer his desire if he had not expanded so rapidly. There is no question about it, Hearst is almost always better than his agents. In 1906 he had papers in Chicago, Boston, and Los Angeles as well as New York and San Francisco. Today he publishes twenty-four newspapers and nine magazines, and owns half a dozen wire and news reel services extending all over the world. In the earlier years there is every evidence that he took a fierce pride in his outlandish but brilliant performances. Then ambition stung him, his papers became merely means to an end, and circulation began to mean votes. He invaded Chicago at the request of Bryan, who wanted a mid-Western organ in 1900. His political ambition became an obsession. He even changed his dress. In the *North American Review* article of 1906 Brisbane gave him away: "More than six feet two, very broad, with big hands and big feet, a strong neck. . . . His hair is light in color and his eyes blue-gray, with a singular capacity for concentration. Of late his dress has been the usual uniform of

American statesmanship, combining the long-tailed frock coat and the cow-boy's soft slouch hat."

But political ambition here gave the impetus to an expansion that probably would have occurred in any event as this restless and enormously able and energetic man tried in vain to satisfy his ego. Always a spendthrift (he lost $7,000,000 in the movies and his San Simeon place has cost him millions more), he has never laid up a large surplus, and for years he has been bedeviled now and again for ready money. His enterprises are vulnerable in proportion as they are huge and scattered, and this weakness is the key not only to the growing conservatism of his papers but to the general deterioration that comes of standardization on a mediocre plane. He keeps shoddy go-getters in power because he needs the money and has no illusions about the taste and intelligence of the business clan through which a paper's revenues are funneled.

In later years he has permitted cautious advisers to persuade him, against his inclination, to take the safe course, as when he withheld support from La Follette in 1924. A withdrawal from personal editing that began when his role as statesman absorbed him has continued ever since, confirmed now by the impossibility of running twenty-four papers as he ran the *Examiner* and the *Journal*. Today he sees his papers objectively and impersonally, as business properties, and turns his back in cynical and amused indifference when his executives resort to shoddy methods to get and keep advertising, as when a dramatic critic is also held responsible for theatre advertising or the automobile pages are filled with the Elks Club sapience of high-pressure gentlemen from Detroit.

Aggravating his failure here is his dislike of personal contacts and his cold suspicion of men. Friendship, the hearty chemical expansiveness and sympathy that draw men to a leader, is beyond him, and he employs men whom he half despises and then watches them, sets them against one another, keeps them frightened by sudden shifts and demotions. There were years when he gave his trust wholeheartedly to men who grossly betrayed it, and doubtless these betrayals destroyed his faith, always shy. It could function in one office, where daily contacts reassured him, but in administering his vast string he has not known how to control men except by inciting in them the hope of large rewards — he is said to pay a hundred men more than $30,000 a year apiece — or by instilling the fear of instant and humiliating dismissal or demotion. A very few break through this distrust and are let alone, and doubtless many more would win his confidence if the system he has adopted did not restrict his list largely to those who deserve no better treatment.

With the standardizing of the Hearst papers and business-office control has come greater decorum and better manners. Outrage has gone from them along with the old brilliance, and an old lady who saw Hearst with horns in the nineties would be surprised on examining one of his sheets today to find nothing to alarm her. This is particularly true of his morning papers, for on the evening side he meets the challenge of the tabloids with whole pages of pictures designed as of old to titillate the oaf and the ogre. All his papers still bristle with bright features, and in the morning field, God help us, Hearst is today the most liberal and enlightened publisher of anything like his range in the United States. Yet to compare even the best of his papers with the *New York Times* or the *Baltimore Sun*, is to realize that on the technical and craft side of the business he has left no solid and lasting achievement. A study of the *Times* discloses not a single feature, typographical or editorial, for which he can claim the credit.

The Hearst sheets, indeed, remain shoddy in the extreme. From the beginning they have scorned the cardinal principle of good newspaper work — a respect for the objective fact which the good reporter shares with the scientist. Hearst bought all his talent, and the fact discloses him as a business man and not an editor. For the latter's greatest pride is the discovery and development of talent. It requires a genuine interest in others and a generous respect for them that Hearst's nature could not compass. Ambrose Bierce's experience was exceptional and perhaps unique. Others have had to swallow their integrity and write instantly what Hearst wanted written. He has a pet phrase that exposes his attitude toward the business eloquently. He will telegraph an editor: "Please *make* an editorial." In that hideous phrase taken from manual industry is all his contempt for the professional or craft status of journalism, and for the integrity of the men who work for him. Writing is merely a commodity that he can buy, as he buys paper and ink.

He will turn on even a high executive ferociously, and in public, and he will discharge a dramatic editor, as he recently did in San Francisco, instantly, by peremptory telegram, for not praising extravagantly enough a motion picture in which he is interested. It is the other side of his high salaries and quixotic indulgence—this tyranny that fills a Hearst office with fear, and turns an executive staff too often into a pack of snarling, back-biting intriguers. As for the underlings, they are despised menials, and they know it.

There enters here a decisive new factor in journalism, introduced by Hearst, although it was inevitable. Time was when every editorial staff numbered men whose talents were essential to the paper's success. Their skill at good writing, of features, comment, news stories of love and humor and tragedy, even obituaries, was the paper's strength, and they were respected by everyone in the shop from the publisher down. Such men have been scrapped by the syndicated feature, dating from Hearst's discovery early in the century that his high-priced New York menagerie of artists and writers could be used for all his papers with as good effect as if the stuff were prepared in the home office of each. It was a routine discovery in mass production, and it has revolutionized and all but ruined the newspaper trade. Said Brisbane to a young reporter many years ago:

When I was a young man on the old *Morning Sun*, a reporter went out and talked with the people he was to write about, and came back and wrote his own story. He had plenty of time and he was encouraged to write into his story whatever quality of emotion the situation held— humor, pathos, romance, and so forth. Young men got excellent training and the news columns sparkled with good writing. Now we find that it is cheaper and more efficient to give our readers their daily ration of humor, pathos, love-interest and what-not in the form of syndicated features. And the news, for the most part, is cut down to mere bulletins, the facts gathered by a leg-man and telephoned in to a rewrite desk.

So the star reporter takes his place with the dodo. Often he was a boozy and irresponsible wretch, ungrateful and as inconstant as a spoiled child, and the uneasy suspicion presses on me that Hearst's latter-day contempt for the species and their craft is a reaction from knowing them too well in the days when he would jump into a hack with them and dash to the scene of the crime.

VI

When John K. Winkler's book on Hearst appeared in 1928, the old guard of Hearst idolators were delighted. It had been out some time

when one of them asked Hearst if he had read it and, receiving a negative reply, commended it to him. But he shook his head.

"If it doesn't tell the truth, it will make me mad," he said, "and if
it tells the truth, it will make me sad."

Pondering this story, I believe at least in his sadness. It is the under-
tone of many stories that drift these days from San Simeon, stories
indicating a humorous, philosophical, almost humble mood. Hearst,
defeated and facing the end, becomes at last a human being. "I am
afraid," wrote James Branch Cabell recently, "that human nature, since
it is alike the offspring and begetter of all failure, cannot ever deal in
utter justice with the flamboyantly successful." Perhaps Hearst was
never that, but many men feared and resented his power, while he
himself deafened us to his virtues by blaring them into our ears through
the noisiest megaphone ever devised by one man for his own glorifica-
tion. Since he gave up the White House, that clamor of self-praise has
died away, and the man gradually emerges. Perhaps in time he will
even discard the frock coat and the cow-boy hat. And when the history of our times is written he will go down as not merely a very
extraordinary man, of prodigious energy and surpassing boldness, but
even as an engaging, yes, a tragic figure. And to achieve that status is
the best that any man can hope in this world dedicated to human frustration.

Already the archives are full of records like that of Bierce, by men
who disliked Hearst and resented him; for the uses of understanding
we need a chronicle and commentary by one who loved the man.
None? There are a few, and among them none so well qualified as
Mrs. Bonfils, who, under the names of Winifred Sweet, Winifred
Black and Annie Laurie has filled his newspapers with spirited copy
for forty years. She worships Hearst and she should, for their relations
have been starred through the years by his distinguished kindness.
Many pertinent things could be said by one able to get by that primary
dislike which marks the general run of his critics.

I have remarked that in his personal tastes the old Hearst *was* the
lower classes. Well, so was Charles II and many another whom the
world acclaims. And there is something kingly in the disdain with
which he has gone his private way. There is much to be said for the
gay crowd of movie players that gathers about his lavish board at San

Simeon. Hidden by snobbery is the plain truth that these are amusing young people, without pretension or self-righteousness, and far better company than the aging statesmen and moneybags with whom a more orthodox publisher spends his declining years. I'd rather, for instance, spend a week-end with Hearst at San Simeon than with the saintly Cyrus H. K. Curtis in the comely but depressing suburbs of Philadelphia.

I wish Annie Laurie would let herself go. She would not convince me, but her record would be an important item in a solution of the riddle that Hearst remains.

22

William Randolph Hearst:
A Tentative Appraisal

by EDWIN EMERY

EDWIN EMERY, journalism professor at the University of Minnesota, wrote this appraisal of the Hearst career in the month of the chain publisher's death. In it he reviewed the evidence concerning Hearst's place in American journalism. The article appeared in the *Journalism Quarterly*, fall 1951.

THE distinguished American historian Frederic Logan Paxson, of the Universities of Wisconsin and California, once told a graduate seminar that he willingly would abandon all his other work if William Randolph Hearst only would call him to San Simeon and tell him that the files were open for a legitimate historical study of the Hearst career.

Professor Paxson never was invited to San Simeon; nor in Hearst's lifetime was any other scholar permitted access to the publisher's private papers and the records of the Hearst empire. This didn't stop people from writing about Hearst. But either they wrote briefly after gleaning what they could from the public record — a necessarily fragmentary knowledge — or they patched together facts and rumors to produce book-length studies which fell far short of achieving either reasonable balance or real worth. Some persons, of course, attacked Hearst in vehement fashion without bothering to study the evidence at all.

As a result, the official Hearst biography released by International News Service when the publisher's 64-year newspaper career closed in mid-August 1951 noted in its second paragraph: "And as he fashioned his vast enterprises, there grew progressively in the public mind a picture of the builder himself. It was a strange portrait, obscured by myth and legend, confused by controversy and distortion."

The purpose of this brief essay is scarcely to clear away all those

317

confusions and obscurities. It is only, first, to review the nature of what has been written about Hearst, and then to suggest some basic approaches to "the problem of Hearst" which should be borne in mind by those attempting to come to some judgments about him.

Hearst is not the only famous American newspaper publisher for whom no adequate biography exists. But considering the complex nature of the man's personality, the social and political impact of his many ventures, and the length and extent of his career, he probably is the most difficult man of journalism to study and to estimate. The lack of any successful attempts at definitive studies of the man and his newspapers, or of even easily accessible summary studies of any length, is therefore especially unfortunate.

Four biographers have tried their hand with Hearst. Mrs. Fremont Older's authorized account, *William Randolph Hearst: American* (1936), gets the student nowhere. John K. Winkler's *W. R. Hearst, An American Phenomenon* (1928) is generally favorable, but inconclusive and unsatisfying, and outdated. Ferdinand Lundberg's *Imperial Hearst* (1936) turns the spotlight on the publisher's financial affairs and sources of wealth, but gives Hearst the worst of it at every turn in unobjective fashion. Best of the lot (although also approaching the outdated label) is the book written by Oliver Carlson and Ernest Sutherland Bates, *Hearst, Lord of San Simeon* (1936), a strongly critical but better balanced study in contrast with the others.*

From the biographies the student might turn to a collection of Hearst newspaper editorials published at the turn of the century, and to the voluminous selected writings of Hearst himself. He has the observations of Will Irwin, printed in *Collier's* in 1911; the comments of Oswald Garrison Villard and other press critics; the biographies and reminiscences of other newspapermen; and, of course, the accounts in the various journalism histories. For documentation of the sensationalism of Hearst's *New York Journal* in the nineties he has Willard G. Bleyer's painstaking analysis in *Main Currents in the History of American Journalism.* For documentation of the *Journal*'s activity in the Spanish-American War period he has Marcus M. Wilkerson's *Public Opinion and the Spanish-American War* and Joseph E. Wisan's *The Cuban Crisis as Reflected in the New York Press.* Finally there are

* In 1952, after this article was written, John Tebbel repaired this lack with his capable journalistic summary of the Hearst story, *The Life and Good Times of William Randolph Hearst.*

318

the magazine articles and newspaper stories, published at intervals during the long Hearst career and listed in journalism bibliographies. These are not as valuable in Hearst's case as they sometimes prove to be in journalism history, but the latest of them represent the only recently published sources of information available.

The mid-thirties brought several magazine pieces about Hearst. One, which turned out to be an overly-optimistic analysis of the Hearst financial picture, was published in *Fortune* in October 1935. *Editor & Publisher* recorded the fiftieth anniversary of Hearst's newspaper publishing career in March 1937. Forrest Davis did his "Mr. Hearst Steps Down" for the *Saturday Evening Post* in August 1938, summarizing the financial facts at a moment when the Hearst goose seemed cooked, and depicting life at San Simeon.[1] *Collier's* added "Good That Hearst Did" in April 1939, and *Time* gleefully and bitterly wrote the publisher off in March 1939 with "Dusk at Santa Monica."

The facts were, Hearst was neither dead nor broke. But no one corrected the published record until August 1951 when at last "the Chief" was gone. Only occasional reports in *Editor & Publisher* testified to the Hearst empire's comeback and to the continued powerful, if diminished, position of the aging publisher.

What appeared in the first month after Hearst's death offers some updating and critical evaluation. The best work was done by two strongly contrasting publications. The *New York Times* for August 15 delved into the publisher's 88-year life and into the finances of the Hearst corporate maze in excellent fashion. The issue of *Life* for August 27 accompanied a pictorial story with a penetrating editorial analyzing the qualities of "Hearst Journalism." As an antidote for the flood of vaguely worded statements which appeared in the wake of Hearst's death, *Life's* editorial was badly needed. A. J. Liebling, of course, dissected the New York newspapers' coverage of Hearst's death for the *New Yorker* of September 8. *Editor & Publisher's* coverage, while voluminous, was disappointing. The newspaper world's trade journal no more came to grips with the problem of Hearst than did the Hearst organization's own official biography carried by INS and published in the chain's newspapers.

The result is that the student wishing to read beyond the journalism history book accounts of Hearst's career has a most difficult time obtaining even a balanced diet of factual information. He finds plenty of stories about Hearst's fabulous private life, his pre-capitalistic attitudes toward money and power, his incredible San Simeon. But interpretations of Hearst's journalism are less productive, and the student is hard pressed to come up with even some of the answers to the questions which present themselves when the name Hearst is mentioned.

These questions all revolve about the major one: Where does Hearst rank as a journalistic leader and as a contributor to the advancement of the newspaper profession? Many shades of answers might be obtained from the literature about Hearst, depending upon the weight given to one or another source.

The points most often listed in support of the thesis that Hearst made notable contributions to American journalism are these:

1. Hearst built the world's largest publishing empire, in terms of numbers of newspapers and their combined circulations. At the peak, in 1935, Hearst printed papers in 19 cities. They included 26 dailies, with 13.6 percent of the total daily newspaper circulation in the country, and 17 Sunday editions, with 24 percent of the country's Sunday circulation.[2] In addition he controlled the King Features syndicate, largest of its kind; the money-coining *American Weekly*; International News Service, Universal Service, and International News Photos; 13 magazines, 8 radio stations, and 2 motion picture companies. This, then, spells a success which must be recognized.

2. Hearst's methods and innovations in newswriting and news-handling — particularly in makeup and headline and picture display — and his utilization of new mechanical processes were highly important. Hearst journalism changed the character of American journalism, and therefore it must be recognized.

3. Hearst newspapers were edited to appeal to the mass of readers, and encouraged millions to increase their reading habits. Because of this, and because of Hearst's editorial policies and his own political activities, Hearst newspapers exercised a powerful influence in American life which must be recognized.

4. Hearst was in many ways a constructive force — stalwart in his Americanism; a believer in popular education and in the extension of the power of the people; and during different phases of his long career an advocate of many progressive solutions to national problems. These included advocacy of popular election of senators, the initiative and referendum, a graduated income tax, widespread public ownership (in

1900 Hearst wanted to nationalize the coal mines, railroads and tele-graph lines which were the symbols of the new industrial era), break-ing up of monopolies and trusts, and strong encouragement of the economic and political powers of labor unions.

All this, the argument runs, cannot be washed out. It is in the record for all to see.

Counter-arguments to these points are also to be found in the record. They should be prefaced, however, with this general observation:

The building of a great publishing empire does not in itself assure Hearst a high standing in his profession. The newspapers which the craft recognizes as great are those which demonstrate their integrity and zealousness in the telling of the news, and which at the same time possess the social conscience which is acquired by their recognition of the needs of society, and by a proper and reasonable adjustment to society's desires. Honesty and comprehensive coverage of the news is of course the first essential. The second is a demonstration of what Professor Leon N. Flint so aptly called "The Conscience of the News-paper." The great newspapers — whether conservative or liberal, Re-publican or Democrat in their political beliefs — are those which are aroused whenever basic principles of human liberty and progress are at stake in a given situation, and which are constantly on guard against intolerance and unfairness. Operating within a consistent social frame-work, they do their best to be the kind of progressive community leaders America expects.

Keeping these two tests of the greatness of a newspaper in mind, then, here are the rebuttals to the specific points listed in Hearst's favor:

1. The Hearst empire, for all its onetime size, was not the roaring success which the accumulated figures would indicate. Hearst began to borrow from banks as early as 1924. In the early 1930s he had his newspapers publicize and sell a 50-million-dollar stock issue to keep themselves afloat. Here, of course, the intricate nature of the Hearst corporate structures makes a clear answer to the causes of this eco-nomic decline impossible. The publisher had a very large income from inherited mining properties and other business investments which could be poured into his journalistic ventures — and was. He also spent fabulous sums — an estimated 40 million dollars on art treasures and oddities, untold millions for his personal life — and sank more than 50 million dollars in real estate holdings which by depression time

became enormous liabilities. Some of this spending represents a drain on the journalistic properties; how much, no one knows. But it is known that great sums were lost, as well as made, in journalism. Hearst's efforts to win a foothold in Atlanta alone were calculated by him to have cost 21 million dollars before he gave up.[3]

After the liquidation process had commenced in 1937, groups of trustees largely were responsible for the business decisions once made solely by the Chief. By 1951 Hearst papers were appearing in only a dozen cities, with 16 dailies and 13 Sunday editions on the list. Their combined circulations still were larger than those of the 26 dailies and 17 Sunday editions published in 19 cities in 1935. But Hearst had lost ground in his percentage of the country's total circulation. The average Hearst daily circulation at the time of his death was 5,264,420, or 9.8 percent of the total daily circulation; Sunday Hearst circulation was 8,357,795, or 18 percent of the national Sunday total.[4] These represent substantial drops in Hearst circulation influence from the 1935 figures of 13.6 percent daily and 24 percent Sunday previously cited.

The remainder of the empire had melted, too. Universal Service was gone; only eight magazines and three radio stations remained; the *American Weekly* was being hard-pressed in the Sunday supplement field. On the non-journalism side, many of the art treasures had been auctioned off in Gimbel's basement; Hearst's 40 million dollars in New York real estate holdings had been largely liquidated; and even many of San Simeon's acres had been sold.

Despite the successful consolidation of the Hearst holdings and the regaining of some measure of the owner's power after 1947, danger signals continued to fly. Recent annual statements of Hearst newspaper operations show that they are earning less profit than the average for newspapers their size for which financial reports are available.[5] In the first half of 1951, Hearst Consolidated, which controls the bigger newspapers in the chain, reported profits of but $1,322,700 as against $3,599,800 for the same period a year ago, and the corporation's Class A stock dividends went to $8.75 in arrears. This scarcely bears out the picture of success which is claimed for Hearst.

2. Undoubtedly Hearst editing and printing methods made their impress on American journalism. Particularly Hearst's sponsoring of mechanical innovations, and the Hearst format techniques, spurred others on. But these were contributions which are largely technical

in their nature, and in the judgment of most newspapermen they were more than matched on the negative side by Hearst proclivities for sensational treatment of news.

3. Undoubtedly, too, Hearst drew many new readers of newspapers to his fold. But what was the end result? Pulitzer defended sensationalism in the *World* by arguing that it attracted readers who then would be exposed to the columns of his carefully-planned high-quality editorial page. The same could not be said of the Hearst newspapers, as will be explained later in detail.

Nor did Hearst exercise the powerful influence in American life which his great circulations might indicate. Among the men whom he wanted to see become president of the United States were William Jennings Bryan, Champ Clark, Hiram W. Johnson, William Gibbs McAdoo, John Nance Garner, Alf Landon, General Douglas MacArthur and William Randolph Hearst. Among the men whom he fought while they were in the White House were William McKinley, Theodore Roosevelt, William Howard Taft, Woodrow Wilson, Franklin D. Roosevelt and Harry Truman. Hearst got on the bandwagons of Warren Harding, Calvin Coolidge and Herbert Hoover in the 1920s largely because he disapproved of their Democratic opponents. He rode the Wilson bandwagon in 1912, and the Roosevelt bandwagon in 1932, but promptly got off in high dudgeon both times.

Hearst himself served two terms in Congress from a Democratic district in New York City from 1903 to 1907. His high point was the casting of 200 votes for him in the Democratic national convention of 1904 (Judge Alton B. Parker, the presidential nominee, got 658). In 1905, running as an independent for mayor of New York, he lost by some 3,500 votes as the result of Tammany's counting him out at the ballot boxes. The next year Charles Evans Hughes defeated him by 60,000 votes for the governorship of New York, and the Hearst political star had set. He lost decisively in the 1909 New York mayoralty race, and in 1922, when he wanted to run for senator, Al Smith refused to let him on the Democratic ticket, making a bitter speech attacking Hearst's isolationist record in World War I.

4. What then of Hearst as a constructive social force? Certainly he was an advocate of Americanism. But to many his continued espousal of nationalistic policies, in a time which demanded American cooperation in international security efforts, was the most distressing feature

of his newspapers. Certainly, too, Hearst newspapers have given stalwart support to public education and to the idea of public ownership of utilities. But they have backslid on many of the other progressive features of the Hearst editorial platform as written before World War I.

Curiously enough, the official Hearst obituary contained several paragraphs describing the aid Hearst gave in swinging Garner delegates to the Franklin Roosevelt banner in the 1932 Democratic convention. Although this settled an old score with Al Smith, why anyone felt that Hearst still would want to receive credit in 1951 for helping to make Roosevelt president is not clear — unless perhaps there were some persons with long memories in the Hearst organization.

For the Hearst policy editorials, as published in the *San Francisco Examiner* in 1933, went like this:

Franklin Roosevelt's inauguration brings hope to the American people. . . . Curiously enough, though the G.O.P. in the last campaign sought to spread the propaganda that Roosevelt's election would be bad for business, business and financial leadership today are looking forward to receiving genuine stimulus from the new presidential program. (March 4)

President Roosevelt's remarkable skill in making up his mind quickly on critical problems and his ability to persuade his countrymen to follow under his banner are unseen assets which will go far toward turning the scales toward a new and more stable prosperity. (March 17)

President Roosevelt's message to Congress on unemployment relief (WPA) emphasizes the humane theme which dominates his entire reconstruction program. . . . (March 26)

Again in the crisis President Roosevelt has displayed courage and initiative. His decision to suspend exports of gold . . . is a victory for the Hearst newspapers. (April 20)

It is good news that the "New Deal" is drafting a so-called "National Industry Recovery Act," which embodies several basic policies long advocated by the Hearst newspapers. (May 6)

By 1935 the tune had changed. It was the "Raw Deal" and the "National Run Around" in both news and editorial columns. The Supreme Court decision outlawing NRA was greeted with an American flag and the headline, "Thank God for the Supreme Court!" And the Hearst editorial stand was now:

Which? American Democracy or Personal Dictatorship? The latest decisions of the Supreme Court should arouse all loyal American citizens to a full realization of how entirely this so-called Democratic administration at Washington has abandoned Democratic principles and how utterly it has discarded the fundamental Democratic policy, and the fundamental American constitutional principle of strict limitation of Federal powers. . . . (June 2)

There are other examples in the 1935 issues of the *Examiner* of the extent to which the earlier beliefs of Hearst had changed. The publisher who had once been perhaps the most aggressive in supporting the power of labor unions said now:

The Wagner Labor Bill . . . is one of the most vicious pieces of class legislation that could be conceived — un-American to the core, violative of every constitutional principle and contrary to the whole spirit of American life. Congress in passing it is betraying the country. (May 29)[6]

The publisher who had fought so long against monopolies and trusts said now:

The Wheeler-Rayburn Bill, decreeing death to the holding companies, is PURE VENOM distilled by a PERSONAL and MALIGNANT OBSESSION, without a pretense of economic or legal justification. (June 21)

The publisher who believed that he understood the common people, and was understood by them, had extensive front-page coverage of WPA activities in 1936 with headlines like this one: "Taxpayers Feed 20,000 Reds on N.Y. Relief Rolls." And his newspapers warned that the Social Security Act was "A Pay Cut for You! . . . Governor Landon, when elected, will repeal this so-called security act."

What has happened since 1936 is familiar. Hearst newspapers have opposed the basic foreign policy adopted by the American people during and after World War II, and they have followed the 1935 line rather than that of 1933 in opposing domestic reform. Politically they descended to a ridiculously synthetic, but fully-publicized, boom for General Douglas MacArthur for president in 1948, giving every appearance that they believed he was a major contender for the Republican nomination that year (MacArthur received 11 votes in the convention, all from Wisconsin).

Hearst newspapers have used their news columns in behalf of their publisher's private beliefs, attaching labels to the ideas which he opposes, creating stories in behalf of their causes, and distorting the news picture in many ways. *Life* put it neatly when it said in its editorial on "Hearst Journalism": "Hearst Journalism never overburdened its readers with information of any kind — for information may sometimes be dull and dullness is a sin — but it was especially lean on any information from the other side of the fence." [7]

On the modern record, then, Hearst newspapers have no claim — not even the superficial claim of success and power — to ranking as great newspapers. Their record in handling the news is bad, and their quick switches in thinking about basic social issues nullify their editorial leadership, to say the least.

In considering the place of their publisher, however, one must look back to the earlier years of the Hearst career to see whether or not historical perspective gives him a higher ranking among American journalistic leaders.

The crucial question for anyone seeking to evaluate Hearst's place in American journalism thus becomes: Was Hearst in his early days a sincere and effective champion of the common man? Upon the answer quite likely depends whatever measure of journalistic esteem Hearst might permanently retain, other than that won by his technical achievements in publishing. Yet in the literature about him the answers vary widely.

Will Irwin, writing about Hearst in 1911, says that his editorial policies might well represent a marriage of convenience and sincerity, but adds that "those who knew Hearst best in this early era declare that under his cold exterior he kept a real sympathy for the submerged man and woman, a real feeling of his own mission to plead their cause." [8]

Time magazine said bitterly in 1939:

No other press lord ever wielded his power with less sense of responsibility; no other press ever matched the Hearst press for flamboyance, perversity and incitement of mass hysteria. Hearst never believed in anything much, not even Hearst, and his appeal was not to men's minds but to those infantile emotions which he never conquered in himself: arrogance, hatred, frustration, fear. [9]

To help avoid the dangers of hindsight coloring attitudes toward the early Hearst, the question might be put another way as a historical guessing exercise: If Hearst had died in 1915, rather than in 1951, what would have been the estimate of his contribution to journalism then?

Posing the question this way seems to be a means of getting at the problem. In many respects there do appear to be two Hearsts. One is the young publisher who invaded New York with his *Journal*, backed William Jennings Bryan for president in a year when the best people were terrified by the menace of populism, adopted a platform more radical than that of many progressives of his time, and centered his editorial appeal on a frank espousal of the gaining of political power by the working man.

The other Hearst is the older publisher of the past 30 years — thwarted in satisfying his own political ambitions; increasingly plagued with financial problems; consistently nationalist in his outlook and therefore increasingly isolationist in contrast to the changing currents of American thinking about world affairs; finally reviled as the enemy of the common people he had once sought to lead.

At once the question arises: Were there two Hearsts? Or is it simply that there were two social situations, in only one of which Hearst seemed to be a progressive force?

Unquestionably Hearst was profoundly affected by the bitter personal attacks made upon him during World War I, and by the consequent dashing of his lingering hopes of gaining political power. Like many another isolationist who stubbornly opposed the main trends of American foreign policy, he came to fight his enemies on domestic issues which the hated internationalists also happened to espouse. But basically it had to be the same Hearst for the entire 64 years. Whether for convenience's sake or in all sincerity, he traveled the main stream in the 1890s and early 1900s, seemingly accepting the necessity for social change, and recognizing the desirability of economic and political readjustments. Later, in many respects, Hearst was left behind in a new social situation to which he was unable or unwilling to adjust.

Nevertheless, judging solely on his socio-political record, a Hearst who had chanced to die in 1915 would seem to rank close to the Pulitzers and the Scrippses in his journalistic leadership. Yet there would be good reason not to accord him that position. Hearst journalism then was powerful; its master advocated progressive beliefs; his newspapers were widely read and were financially successful. But Hearst journalism then also was degrading in its use of techniques to reach the reader, no matter what; its master lacked in final analysis the responsible feeling a worthy publisher must have for his public mission; and, above all, Hearst journalism lacked depth.

Many things may be meant by the phrase, "Hearst journalism lacked depth": Depth of intellectual appeal; depth of sincerity; depth of understanding of social issues; depth of responsible conception of its public trust. No matter which of these objections was the one held by an individual, however, it would rule Hearst out as a journalistic leader of real force. And while Hearst had his loyal followers, there were many instinctive doubters.

The Norman Thomas of 1951 says (in the *Reporter* of September 18) that the Norman Thomas of 1905 admired Hearst's political stands but quite distrusted the publisher and believed him to be thoroughly cynical. Assuming that the Norman Thomas of 1951 can recall his opinions of 1905 objectively, why did he believe that Hearst lacked depth of character?

One answer lies in the kind of newspaper Hearst published. Its appeal was pitched to a low level, whether in the news columns or on the editorial page. Arthur Brisbane, writing in the *Cosmopolitan* in September 1898 about "The Modern Newspaper in War Time,"[10] unblushingly explained how the *Journal* went about its job of capitalizing on the just-ended Spanish-American War. Brisbane was so certain of his reading audience that he included this paragraph in his widely-circulated magazine piece: "Before the type size reached its maximum, 'War Sure' could be put in one line across a page, and it was put in one line and howled through the streets by patriotic newsboys many and many a time. As war was sure, it did no harm."

And of course there was the immortal explanation of the Hearst news technique given by Arthur McEwen, another Hearst stalwart: "News is anything that makes the reader say 'gee, whiz!' That is what we're after, the gee-whiz emotion."

The Hearst editorial page followed the same approaches. It spoke in one-syllable words. It talked about human virtues, religion, science and love more easily than it talked about significant current issues. It had no men of the intellectual caliber of William H. Merrill and Frank Cobb of the *World*, or Charles R. Miller of the *Times*. It did have Arthur Brisbane and Arthur McEwen, among others.

Hearst preferred the cartoonist and headline writer to the editorial thinker. As evidence of this, the testimony of Willis J. Abbot about life on the *New York Journal* of the late 1890s may be quoted. Abbot, who later became editor of the *Christian Science Monitor*, records the following in his autobiography about his introduction to Hearstian methods:

> Within an hour after meeting him [Hearst], I was engaged as "Editor-in-chief" of the *New York Journal*. The resonant title was most grateful to my still youthful and ingenuous mind. . . . It took months of cruel disillusionment to reveal to me the two facts that despite a liberal conferring of titles, Mr. Hearst was the only editor-in-chief of any of his papers, and that of all his newspaper pages the editorial page of which I had charge was the one on which he looked with most tolerant contempt.[11]

Abbot continues by asserting that for three weeks he conducted the editorial page of the *Journal* without a single scrap of instructions from Hearst or any other editor. (Shades of Joseph Pulitzer and his rigorous training of Frank Cobb!) Abbot adds, however, that about 1910 Hearst took up the writing of editorials himself in earnest, and in good style, and thereafter held the page in slightly higher esteem. In Abbot's judgment, except for Hearst's own occasional contributions, the average Hearst editorial page in 1930 showed "no progress in quality or character from what it was in the 1890s."

Here then is the second major reason for Norman Thomas' instinctive distrust of Hearst. The editorial page lacked depth of intellectual appeal, and therefore to Thomas it lacked depth of sincerity and understanding. He was joined by many others in this judgment of Hearst the publisher in his early career. Hearst entertained, yes; he struck some high notes in popular appeal, yes; he performed some worthy services, yes; but in the end it all added up to a most disappointing performance.

Indeed, when one looks through the records of journalistic achievement, where does he find the name of Hearst, or of his newspapers? There are no high awards, no selections of Hearst papers on any lists of outstanding newspapers of the country; instead there are dead cats for the Hearst trophy shelf. There is no James Reston, no Bert Andrews, no James Pope coming to the front from Hearst papers. This is not to deny that there have been many competent newsmen among the thousands of Hearst staffers, but the high expression of leadership does not come from them.

It would not be right, however, to dismiss Hearst and his journalistic career as something to be buried and forgotten — nor could anyone do so if he wished. There is a final estimate to be agreed upon, whenever fresh studies of the man and his newspapers bring a better understanding of the complex "problem of Hearst." In the meantime, only tentative conclusions such as these can be advanced in the effort to interpret the impact of the Lord of San Simeon and to come to some judgments about him.

NOTES

[1] Reprinted in *Post Biographies of Famous Journalists,* edited by John E. Drewry (Athens: University of Georgia Press, 1942).

[2] William Weinfeld, "The Growth of Daily Newspaper Chains in the United States, 1926–1935," *Journalism Quarterly,* Dec. 1936.

[3] A direct quotation reported by Jim Brown in *Editor & Publisher,* Aug. 18, 1951, p. 13.

[4] Hearst circulation figures are those reported by International News Service, Aug. 14, 1951.

[5] According to studies made by Dr. J. Edward Gerald, University of Minnesota School of Journalism.

[6] The Wagner bill, of course, ensured permanent protection for the American Newspaper Guild's organizing activities, begun in 1933, and a source of trouble for Hearst newspapers particularly.

[7] *Life,* Aug. 27, 1951, p. 22.

[8] *Collier's Weekly,* Feb. 18, 1911; reprinted in this volume and in *Readings in the History of American Journalism* (mimeographed), edited by Edwin H. Ford (Minneapolis: University of Minnesota, 1939).

[9] *Time,* March 13, 1939, p. 49.

[10] Also reprinted in Ford, *op. cit.*

[11] Willis J. Abbot, *Watching the World Go By* (Boston: Little, Brown and Company, 1933), pp. 134–35.

23

Edward W. Scripps

What the newspaper profession knew about the limelight-shunning Edward Wyllis Scripps at the time of the great liberal publisher's death is reflected in this article from *Editor & Publisher*, which appeared unsigned in the issue of March 20, 1926. The closing paragraphs have been omitted.

AROUND the year 1876 a tall, gangling youth, born on a farm at Rushville, Ill., stood one evening on the sidewalk of a fashionable residence street in London, England. An awning had been stretched from the entrance of a palace to the curb, and carriages were dashing up, discharging gentlemen in long black cloaks and top hats, with ladies on their arms dressed like flowers of the field.

"I looked in through the opening doorway and was warmed by the color and gaiety of these people," said Edward W. Scripps, years later. "They were having a good time and I was having a hard time, trying to get started on a literary career in London. Suddenly, I glanced about me, at my companions on the sidewalk. There was a bootblack, an old hag under a shawl, a porter in livery, a dumb-faced man, a strange appearing young woman. I stood with them on the outside of the brightly illuminated house. It was there and then that I decided that for me it was better to go under the awning than stand looking at others pass through. Some cannot do it — must always stand on the side-line. I felt that I had the energy to lift myself to economic independence and that man's first duty was to provide his creature comforts. They are greatly exaggerated in most men's minds, the bright lights in the fashionable house may be false beacons, but a man who does not do his best to establish his family beyond the dangers of necessity and get what comfort belongs to him is unnatural."

That may be as good a place as another to start an obituary of E. W. Scripps. In 1841 his father, James M. Scripps, emigrated to America from England, where his ancestors had lived for generations,

331

originally named "Crips." James M. Scripps settled in the frontier town of Cleveland, three years later marrying Miss Julia Osborne, a school teacher and woman of high natural intellectual attainments, as his second wife. The couple soon went west to Rushville, Ill., 160 miles from Chicago, settling on a farm.

In all, James M. Scripps was father of thirteen children, the eldest, born of his first wife in England, being James E. Scripps, who founded the *Detroit News*. The inspiration of the family was a grandfather who was once editor of the *London Literary Gazette*. John Locke Scripps, E.W.'s father's cousin, years before had gone to Chicago and had become part owner and editor of the then struggling *Chicago Tribune*. Journalism seemed to be a family trait.

E. W. Scripps received his education in the public schools, but was greatly influenced by his talented mother. After he had decided that a literary career was not for him, he returned to Detroit where he had previously worked in various capacities on his brother's paper, the *News*. He solicited subscriptions, organized country circulation, worked in the counting room, reported fires and murders, took a hand at copy editing, learned the run of the work in a few months. His first salary was $4 per week. In a month he had organized some newspaper routes that brought him $40 a week.

The Scripps family owned the *News*, Ellen and George Scripps being associated with James, and E.W. being allowed one share of stock.

They did most of the work, James managing, editing, selling the papers to the newsboys over the counter; Ellen, a sister, rewriting and condensing; George keeping the books; all working long hours and with rigid economy.

The *News* was the first paper of its kind. It was just about one-sixth the size of the other papers. Other papers at that time were sold for 5 cents on the streets, or $10 to $12 a year.

In spite of the general prediction of its failure by publishers and business men, the success of the *News* was certain from the start.

The *News* gathered a small group of brilliant writers, who, when given this opportunity to write freely, took an entirely new line in journalism. The *News* was soon regarded as a roaring lion. Its reputation spread nationally.

E. W. Scripps, then 24, was eager to carry the experiment further. He persuaded the Scripps family to back a paper in Cleveland with $10,000, putting him in charge. So in 1878 the *Cleveland Penny Press* was founded, the first penny paper in the country.

Two years after the *Press* was founded, Scripps started the *St. Louis Chronicle*, but it did not have the same response that the *Press* had received.

However, the *Cincinnati Post* was a success from the start, although for years it had a struggle. A paper started at Buffalo was unsuccessful. But ultimately the string grew, developed in the Middle West, passing on to the Pacific Coast, then into the South and finally into the East.

E. W. Scripps founded and until his retirement controlled the United Press Associations, now with world-wide service, and the Newspaper Enterprise Association, now NEA Service, Inc., serving many hundreds of newspapers. He also created Science Service, the object being to disseminate to the public authentic news of scientific developments.

On October 5, 1885, E. W. Scripps married Miss Nackie Holtsinger, daughter of Rev. S. W. Holtsinger, West Chester, Ohio. They had four sons and two daughters, of whom Robert Paine Scripps, now controlling head of the newspaper organization, and two sisters survive. Mrs. E. W. Scripps lives at Miramar, the 10,000-acre Scripps ranch in Southern California.

As each of the sons matured E. W. Scripps began personally to train them to succeed him. One son died in infancy. John Paul Scripps was schooled as an editor and was appointed editor-in-chief of the Scripps-McRae League. His untimely death occurred in 1914. It was a terrific blow to his parents. James G. Scripps, the eldest son, was trained for business management and succeeded Milton A. McRae in control of the business, but at the height of his power he, too, died, in 1921. Robert P. Scripps, talented as an editor, devoted student of his father, a writer and as well a business man, survives as head of the organization, in association with Roy W. Howard.*

After these two young men had come into formal control of the huge business, then operating under the title Scripps-Howard Newspapers, the aged publisher, who was putting off to sea in his yacht *Ohio* to "play dead" and give his successors free rein, placed in their hands a remarkable letter. It read as follows:

* EDITORS' NOTE: Robert P. Scripps died March 3, 1938.

MY DEAR SON:

A little over four years ago I turned over to you and Mr. Roy W. Howard the control of all my newspapers and news-gathering and news-disseminating agencies, directing you to act as editor-in-chief.

I executed a power-of-attorney, appointing you to take full charge of my estate.

I advised you to "go slow" in the matter of exercising control over the editorial direction of the institution until you should have become thoroughly acquainted with the personnel, and until you should have had time to mature your own convictions with regard to public policies.

Under your and Howard's direction of the institution, its property value has greatly increased.

I am now past 70, and have decided it will be better not only that I should cease active control, but also cease to have any influence over your activities.

It is my opinion that the value of the properties over which you exercise control might well increase manyfold if your chief aim were merely to cause increase in wealth.

However, I repeat now what I told you when I first launched you in your career: That I would prefer that you should succeed in being in all things a gentleman, according to the real meaning of the word, than that you should vastly increase the money value of my estate. Being a gentleman, you cannot fail to devote your whole mind and energy to the service of the plain people who constitute the vast majority of the people of the United States.

I have so arranged my affairs that beyond all doubt you will control my estate after my death, and hence control all of those newspapers which I had previously controlled (and perhaps many more) besides those news-gathering and news-disseminating associations which I built up.

I have turned over to you a property so large and so well organized that not only can you afford to do your full duty as a public servant, but you are, and can be, continually, entirely free from any temptation to cater to any class of your fellow citizens for profit.

You have not had nor should you at any time ever have any ambition to secure political or social eminence. I belong to two past generations. You belong to the present and future generations. I cannot consider that you have any inclination or that you are going to be subject to any temptation to do anything other than your full duty toward the public of this and future generations.

Roy W. Howard entered the Scripps-McRae organization as news editor of the *Cincinnati Post*, selected by the late John Vandercook. He was 22 years of age and had been a reporter for the *Indianapolis*

News, sporting editor of *Indianapolis Star*, and assistant telegraph editor of *St. Louis Post-Dispatch*. Howard was a dynamo of energy and soon landed in New York as correspondent of the Scripps-McRae League newspapers. Thereafter Scripps merged the Publishers' Press and the Scripps-McRae Press Association, creating the United Press Associations, with John Vandercook, formerly London correspondent, latterly editor of the *Cincinnati Post*, as general manager. Vandercook brought into the organization as his aid Roy W. Howard, and when Vandercook died, two years later, Howard succeeded him. His meteoric rise is well-known in newspaper circles of this day.

No story of Scripps' life and no estimate of his nature would be complete without a complete understanding of the influence upon him of Miss Ellen Scripps, his sister, now in her 90th year, a resident of La Jolla, only a few miles from the Miramar ranch. It was an idyllic relationship between brother and sister, starting at Detroit when Scripps was opening his career and his sister was a proof-reader on the *Detroit News*.

Through the years and all the amazing vicissitudes of the founding of the huge newspaper and service organization this demure little woman, sitting quietly by her window, was the chief counsel of the publisher. Without her approval or knowledge he made no major move. He told many men that she was the guide of his fortunes.

In her youth Miss Scripps was an advocate of woman's suffrage, gracefully accepting the ridicule that then went with such theories. She preached prohibition in the seventies. In later life she gave a park to San Diego and a community welfare building. She passionately believed in the principle of free speech and free press. The Scripps editorial policies were to her an open book. Her most conspicuous public benefaction was the foundation, always with her brother at her side, of the Scripps Institute of Biological Research and the Scripps Memorial Hospital.

Last week's news was touching to those who have long known the relationship of E. W. and Ellen Scripps, that throughout his voyaging around the world the aged man had not failed to write a daily letter to his sister.

Another life-long close relationship was that between Mr. Scripps and Robert F. Paine, who joined the *Cleveland Press* in the early days, a mere boy, to become its editor and to participate and often lead in all of the Scripps journalistic ventures. Milton A. McRae was E. W. Scripps' partner for nearly 40 years, a man of remarkable business ability, almost the exact opposite of Scripps in temperament. Others of the "old guard" were Harry N. Rickey, William B. Colver, Willis Thornton, J. C. Harper, B. H. Canfield, W. H. Porterfield, A. O. Andersson, N. D. Cochran, Hamilton B. Clark, Marlen Pew, Arthur Hopkins, Charles Mosher, E. H. Wells, Ed Chase, John Vandercook and a sprinkling of men of the type of E. E. Martin who remain in executive positions in the organization.

Throughout his career Scripps ran militant newspapers, a direct reflection of his free mind and amazing energy. He fought corrupt municipal bossism for many years, wherever it plagued the people of cities catered to by his newspapers. Yet he was once heard to say that a benevolent boss was the very best government a community could have, the danger being that the benevolent boss would sometime have to die.

He held that a man who had not realized his ambition by forty, would never do so, and every five years there was an almost complete readjustment of the executives in his organization. For many years, through various plans, certain of his employes were helped to share profits. It is said that more than fifty of them have either retired rich, or are still in office possessed of substantial fortunes. The profit-sharing plan of the present day makes it possible for an employe to invest his savings in Scripps securities without the risks that were taken in the earlier days when stock would be sold and "carried" in a new venture which might or might not succeed. The present profit-sharing is in securities of newspapers in a number of cities, thereby reducing risk to the average profitableness of a group of properties.

Mr. Scripps once wrote the following in a letter:

The incentive to work amongst the editors and business managers of my papers lies not in their hope for promotion or increase of wage; each one desires to be a better business manager or better editor than any other business manager or editor in the concern, or a better editor or business manager than any other editor or business manager employed by the owners of contemporary newspapers.

Even in the field of high finance, where only millionaires and multi-millionaires flourish, men do not work hard and feverishly for the simple purpose of getting more dollars for themselves. The dollars are only the markers of the game, and, as the game is purely finance, each is struggling to make a bigger pile of dollars than some competitor in the field of honors. As soon as one millionaire has passed his first rival, he seeks for another who has a still larger pile of dollars, and tries to make his pile as big or bigger. And the great desire that masters each of them is that his pile will be bigger than any other one man's pile of dollars.

The first issue of the *Cleveland Press*, then the *Penny Press*, was dated Saturday, Nov. 2, 1878. One of the paragraphs from this first issue, written and edited by E. W. Scripps, read:

"What are your politics?" asked a certain Cleveland gentleman today of the editor of The Penny Press. The gentleman was told to look for his answer in the paper. Here it is: We have no politics, that is in the sense of the word as commonly used. We are not Republican, not Democratic, not Greenback, and not Prohibitionist.

We simply intend to support good men and condemn bad ones, support good measures and condemn bad ones, no matter what party they belong to. We shall tell no lies about persons or policies, for love, malice or money. It is no part of a newspaper's business to array itself on the side of this or that party, or fight, lie and wrangle for it. The newspaper should simply present all the facts the editor is capable of obtaining, concerning men and measures, before the bar of the public, and then, after having discharged its duty as a witness, be satisfied to leave the jury in the case — the public — to find the verdicts.

The payroll of the *Penny Press* when E. W. Scripps put it upon the streets in 1878 was: E. W. Scripps $12; John S. Sweeney $12; H. C. Farnum (commission guaranteed) $20; John A. Spencer, editorial writer, $18; Tom Renshaw $18; Peter T. Forsyth $15; Maurice Perkins, "who has some fame as a humorist, and whom I wanted so badly he was able to hold me up for $15," as Scripps wrote later.

Mr. Scripps enjoyed a joke, had a glowing sense of humor. One of his pet stories involved Hamilton B. Clark, who had been at one time his private secretary and finally became president of the United Press.

Dominoes was Mr. Scripps' favorite game, and he enjoyed winning. After Clark had retired from the presidency of the United Press and active participation in the concern's activities, he played several games of dominoes with the Chief at the ranch one day, and beat him easily.

"I don't know how the devil you improved your game so much, Ham," Mr. Scripps said. "You never used to beat me."

"Ham" came right back: "Oh, that was different. I was working for you then and couldn't afford to beat you, but I could have done it then just as easily as I have now."

Mr. Scripps smoked cigars made especially for him out of the mildest available tobacco. He would consume 40 or more in a day when working at his desk.

It is not true, as has been reported in the stories of his death, that he was greatly affected by noise. The decks of the *Ohio* were not padded and the crew did not speak in whispers. Mr. Scripps got great enjoyment from a storm at sea.

His reading was wide in its scope, from the heaviest scientific works to detective stories, mystery tales and love stories. He played bridge at times, but he preferred dominoes.

"There was method in his long absences from his newspapers," said N. D. Cochran, this week. "He wanted a long range view that enabled him to see the high spots without bothering with petty details. Most of all he wanted to have the soul he had put into his creation kept alive long after his death. During his several retirements he played dead, and then came back to see what had happened. Finally he was satisfied that it was safe to stay dead, so he turned all his properties over to his son Robert P. Scripps, and Roy W. Howard. He felt that his life's work was done, and he was ready for the end."

There are scores of incidents in the life of E. W. Scripps which are told and retold in his organization and the following may bear significantly on his character and methods:

In the early days at Cleveland he was arrested by a policeman for speeding his horse and buggy through the Public Square and was fined in police court. He ordered the police reporter to "give me a good write-up, for I was at fault and speeding must be controlled."

When the McNamara brothers were arrested and their case was tried in Los Angeles Scripps counselled with Clarence Darrow and Lincoln Steffens. He talked about the "belligerent rights" of men fighting in a labor union against consolidated capital. He was bitter against the crime, but could understand the motive. He aided Darrow when he was arrested for alleged jury bribery. Darrow was acquitted. During the Cincinnati riots in the early days of the *Post*, Scripps went to and from his office in a cab, with an armed man on the driver's seat.

Once the police of San Diego stopped I.W.W. speakers from talking on the streets and Scripps, living 27 miles away, thought it an interference with the right of free speech. He opened a building lot he owned in the city as a free speech ground, and with a sign bade all comers to bring their soap boxes in on private land and say what they had to say about politics and social-economic reforms. A gang of court-house bums were stirred up by some local patriot to go out to Scripps' ranch and "tar and feather" him. Some friend heard of the proposed outrage and warned him. He armed the servants, largely Japanese, with a strange assortment of weapons, old rifles and shotguns for which there was ammunition, and a few butcher knives from the kitchen, and led them out to the gate of the ranch. "These fellows are coming here to whip me," he said. "There will be more of them than there are of us, and they will be well armed, but we will butcher every one that steps on this land until they butcher us." The servants stood pat. They waited a long time, but the mob did not appear, and it was later learned that the leader had turned back when he learned from a man who had passed the ranch in an automobile that Scripps and his servants were ready to make the tar party a bloody business.

Around 1910 Scripps conceived the idea of a tabloid daily for Chicago. N. D. Cochran, who had made a great success of the *Toledo News-Bee* and was close in Scripps' counsels, was selected as editor and publisher. The tabloid was called the *Day-Book* and about half the size of the present tabloid papers. The chief principle was that the paper was to be non-advertising, solely devoted to reader interest. At the then price of newsprint 30,000 circulation would have been profitable, as the *Day-Book* was operated economically. The experiment was still in process when the war broke and Mr. Scripps ordered Mr. Cochran to join him at Washington and suspend publication.

In 1909 Scripps said to a caller: "I have really only been engaged in newspaper work for eight years. My occupation now is much more farmer than publisher. I give most of my time to other matters — reading is my chief pursuit."

When America entered the World War Scripps went to Washington. He had been in retirement, he had believed permanently, but he reassumed active command of his organization. He counselled with President Wilson and various cabinet members and accepted many commitments to support the administration's war program with all the resources of his vast publicity machine. He had been told by physicians that if he worked he would not live five years, but he did work, expecting, however, that his sons, trained to succeed him, would relieve him. When they succeeded in taking the work from him, the old man again retired. Robert P. Scripps was removed from an army camp too ill to do military service and was honorably discharged from the army.

Scripps believed that the present generation should pay for the war and particularly that those best able to pay should carry the burden. He advocated before a Senate committee high sur-taxes for his own wealthy class.

At Miramar, the California ranch, one would usually find, in addition to Scripps' lieutenants, scientists making studies under direction of the publisher, perhaps some reformer come to "talk it out," a painter or sculptor at work on a commission, an old employe on tour and calling to see the "boss," on occasion a sea captain or a Naval or Army officer, magazine men begging Scripps to give interviews, which he never did, the author of some book that had attracted Scripps' interest, a cattle breeder or a forester come for opinion, a host of persons casually calling because of the fame of the man and his estate. The dining room seemed like that of a hotel and was operated a la carte without set hours for serving. Few would see Scripps, but any worthy stranger would find a welcome.

24

The Legacy of Scripps

by KENNETH STEWART and JOHN TEBBEL

KENNETH STEWART and JOHN TEBBEL, journalism professors at the University of Michigan and New York University, analyzed "The Legacy of Scripps" for the April 1952 *Nieman Reports*. The article was based on chapters in their *Makers of Modern Journalism* (copyright 1952 by Prentice-Hall, Inc., New York), pages 257–94. It is reprinted by permission of the publisher and the authors.

THE history of American Journalism throbs with rich tradition, heart-warming legend, and lofty purpose. Sometimes the glories of the past have been kept glowing; sometimes allowed to languish; sometimes fanned into new life; sometimes dissipated, traduced, and transmuted.

The spirit of Scripps is one of the richest legacies of the lot. Today the *Detroit News* and the Booth Newspapers in Michigan; the Scripps League of Newspapers in the Northwest; the John P. Scripps papers on the Pacific Coast, and, most importantly, the Scripps-Howard cross-country chain, with its allied interests, the United Press and three feature syndicates, all stem from the same family source. The towering genius in the journalistic clan that sparked these widespread enterprises was Edward Wyllis Scripps.

The promising young men he found as editors and business managers of his new papers were each entitled to purchase 10 per cent of the stock, if and when the paper began making reliable profits, and at the incorporating price, which usually was the actual amount of money invested in the property up to that time. Usually they did not have the money to pay for their stock, so the central office of the concern loaned it to them at 6 per cent interest.

These papers were typically rowdy, rambunctious little sheets, published on a shoestring in shabby quarters. Scripps was sad to see that as they grew prosperous they became conventional — perhaps cautious — and less concerned with the problems of working-class readers. He tried to stop this trend but, in most cases, succeeded only in modifying it or slowing it up.

Although he emphasized each paper's autonomy, E.W. did his utmost to train his editors to feel and think as he did. Each new editor went through a rugged period — often a month — as the Old Man's guest at Miramar. Every morning he listened to the Old Man talk. He returned to his paper inspired and stimulated and whether or not his own stamina or the circumstances surrounding his paper enabled him to carry out E.W.'s principles, he never forgot what the Old Man said.

From his retirement, E. W. Scripps wrote to his son, Bob, in 1924:

It is my opinion that the value of the properties over which you exercise control might well increase manyfold if your chief aim were merely to cause increase in wealth.

However, I repeat now what I told you when I first launched you in your career: That I would prefer that you should succeed in being in all things a gentleman, according to the real meaning of the word, than that you should vastly increase the money value of my estate. Being a gentleman, you cannot fail to devote your whole mind and energy to the service of the plain people who constitute the vast majority of the people of the United States. . . . You are, and can be, continually, entirely free from any temptation to cater to any class of your fellow citizens for profit. You have not had nor should you at any time ever have any ambition to secure political or social eminence.

E.W.'s will left to Robert Paine Scripps, the only surviving son, controlling interest in papers in fifteen states, the United Press Associations, the Newspaper Enterprise Association, Acme Newsphotos, United Features Syndicate, newspaper mechanical and supply properties. With Robert Scripps at the editorial helm, business management had been entrusted to Roy W. Howard.

To an extraordinary degree E. W. Scripps left his heirs free to make what they would of the papers he built; the trust instruments gave great power and discretion to the trustees.

Back in the days when E. W. Scripps was courting Nackie Holtsinger in the Ohio countryside near Cincinnati, a tollgate stretched across the road at Gano between his boarding house and Nackie's home. In his impatience to see her, Ed usually jumped his horse over the gate or the hedge alongside or turned off into the field. He paid little heed to the Scottish family of Wilsons who lived in the cottage there, even though daughter Elizabeth had been Nackie's schoolmate.

Some years later, Scripps learned that Roy Howard, by then a reporter on the Scripps *Cincinnati Post,* was the son of Elizabeth, the tollgate keeper's daughter, and of William Howard, her Irish railroad-brakeman husband. This information, with its sentimental association, aroused in Scripps an interest in the young reporter that, in Scripps' own view, opened opportunities for Howard and greatly influenced his whole career.

All this time Howard's path had not directly crossed that of Scripps. When they finally did meet at Miramar, Scripps found him

. . . a striking individual, very small in stature, a large speaking countenance and eyes that appeared to be windows for a rather unusual intellect. His manner was forceful, and the reverse from modest. Gall was written all over his face. It was in every tone and every word he voiced. There was ambition, self-respect and forcefulness oozing out of every pore of his body. . . . However, so completely and exuberantly frank was he that it was impossible for me to feel any resentment on account of his cheek.

That was in February 1908. Two months later, upon the death of the UP's first president, John Vandercook, the directors of the UP appointed Howard to the vacancy on a temporary basis. Having other candidates in mind himself, Scripps was surprised when he found himself being urged to let Howard have the job permanently.

"Certainly at this critical point in his career," Scripps observed, "he owed everything to the fact that he was the tollgate keeper's grandson. My fancy was tickled with the idea."

However, as Scripps took pains to point out, Howard, the upstart, made good. As general manager and president of the United Press, which was rapidly expanding into an important newsgathering and distribution agency, Howard hobnobbed with the world's great, with premiers, foreign secretaries, generals, and leaders in every field.

In making Howard first business director of the Scripps-McRae interests and then chairman of the board in 1920, E. W. Scripps was paving the way for his even bigger plans, as was evidenced when the name of the organization was changed to Scripps-Howard in 1922.

Howard concentrated upon the newspaper chain and particularly upon getting it a foothold in New York, a city that Scripps always shunned and Howard always fancied. Within less than a year after the Old Man's death, Roy Howard gained his metropolitan outlet by buying the *New York Telegram* from William T. Dewart, Frank A.

Munsey's executor. Howard imported some of the chain's brightest talent from Cleveland and other Scripps-Howard centers to breathe life into the spineless old sheet, but for complete acceptance it needed the prestige of a local name and reputation.

Howard's eyes were still on the *World* and at a chance shipboard meeting between Howard and Ralph Pulitzer in 1929, Pulitzer agreed that if he ever sold his papers he would talk with Howard first. Thus newspaper history found Howard and the Pulitzers, in February 1931, persuading the Surrogate in New York to let them break old Joseph Pulitzer's will, which had enjoined the sons to "preserve, perfect, and perpetuate" the Pulitzer papers. Caught off guard, the *World*'s staff made a frantic and futile eleventh-hour effort to raise enough money to buy and keep alive the beloved "newspaperman's newspaper" on which they were so proud to work. But the *Morning World* was abandoned, the *Evening World* incorporated into the *World-Telegram*, and Howard's New York venture had its base.

The national depression in which the *World* died had moved the Scripps-Howard papers to criticism of President Hoover, whose election they had favored in 1928. They called for a sweeping redistribution of wealth and aid to the unemployed.

Howard, savoring politics, worked to get Newton D. Baker, Scripps-Howard general counsel, nominated on the Democratic ticket, but that failing, the chain's editors voted at their customary policy conference in French Lick, Indiana, to support the party's nominee, Franklin D. Roosevelt, since the Democratic platform opposed prohibition.

Within a year after Hoover's defeat by Franklin D. Roosevelt, the Scripps-Howard papers were acclaiming the "New Deal revolution," flaying "government by money changers," and warning against the "Bourbon diehards" who would attempt to "stigmatize" Roosevelt's program as "socialistic." The Scripps-Howard editors, again in 1936, voted to support Roosevelt against Landon.

The *World-Telegram*'s first great crusade, the New York mayoralty election of 1933, routed Tammany and swept the Fusion candidate, Fiorello H. LaGuardia, into office.

It was becoming increasingly apparent, however, that Howard's sympathies and aspirations did not coincide with those of the chain's founder, although he continued to regard himself as a liberal. As New Deal legislation regulating big business hit home to him and his friends,

344

Howard became restive and irritated. In 1935 he wrote to Roosevelt that large-scale industry was harnessed by taxation, which it considered "revengeful," and suggested "a breathing spell and a recess from further experimentation until the country can recover from its losses." The Scripps-Howard papers followed up the letter by attacks on "silly public works," on the Works Project Administration, on the Wagner wages-and-hour act, and other Administration measures.

In 1937 Howard lost the services of his old friend Lowell Mellett, editor of the Scripps-Howard *Washington News*, who saw the New Deal as the expression of the old Scripps progressivism. In the early twenties Mellett had written a series of articles denouncing "government by courts," and the papers had urged limitation of the power of the Supreme Court. Now, however, the Scripps-Howard papers, along with most of the rest of the nation's press, vigorously opposed Roosevelt's plan to reorganize the Court, and Mellett quit the *News* rather than go along with the attacks upon Roosevelt's "court-packing scheme." Other old Scripps men who felt that Roosevelt was closer to the spirit of Scripps than was Howard — men like Max Stern, Robert Horton, Herbert Little, George West — also left the organization. Some of them, along with Mellett, went into the developing government information service.

In Howard's view the Supreme Court move "signalized the New Deal's abandonment of its original liberalism in favor of modified state socialism, government by bureaucracy and a bastardized brood of political isms."

Roy Howard was as unlike E. W. Scripps, in appearance and in attitude, as Bob Scripps was like his father. Bob, just over six feet tall, had a commanding presence but was quiet and sensitive, allowing executives wide latitude and keeping in the background at Miramar or at his home in Connecticut except for visits to New York to confer with Howard. Forrest Davis's biographical sketch, written for the *Saturday Evening Post* in 1937, described Scripps as "king with final power of yea and veto," Howard as "prime minister, ruling boldly, conspicuously, restlessly, but only with Scripps's consent."

Less and less was heard of Scripps, who had retreated to Miramar. In 1938, stricken with a hemorrhage, he died as his father had, on his yacht at sea, in Magdalena Bay, off Lower California, at the age of forty-two.

The Scripps trust agreement provided that Howard, William W. Hawkins, United Press veteran and vice-chairman of the Scripps-Howard board, and George B. ("Deac") Parker, editor-in-chief of the chain, would succeed Robert Scripps as trustees, each to be succeeded in turn by the sons of Robert Scripps as they reached the age of twenty-five.

None of the founder's grandchildren was yet old enough to take over, and so, in 1938, Roy Howard became the sole ruler of the empire that he had dominated for some time. But he was always careful to point out that neither he nor any other single individual controlled the editorial policies of Scripps-Howard. Those policies, he insisted, were a composite of the opinions of its general editorial board, appointed under the trusteeship.

It was no longer an expanding empire numerically, several of its papers having been abandoned in the thirties, including the one-time hard-hitting crusaders like the papers in Akron and Toledo. Economics had forced papers everywhere by then to contract and concentrate.

The dramatic story of two of Howard's columnists, of their relation to one another and to Roy Howard, throws considerable light upon both the transmutations of Scripps-Howard policies and upon the conflicts and concerns of the turbulent thirties.

Heywood Cox Broun, big of body and of heart, had been a sports writer, dramatic critic, and humorous stylist for the old *World* until his easy-going nature was stirred to indignant protest against what he saw as the rank injustice of the Sacco-Vanzetti case in Boston. There, he felt, an innocent shoemaker and fish peddler were being railroaded to execution for a payroll robbery merely because they were philosophical anarchists and convenient scapegoats. He hammered so hard on the case in his *World* column that Ralph Pulitzer asked him to desist and when Broun refused, Pulitzer fired him.

Roy Howard promptly got Broun to go over to the *Telegram* on his own terms as to freedom of expression and salary.

Westbrook Pegler, son of a Hearst newspaperman in Chicago who had grown up in the old rough-and-tumble "Front Page" tradition, wrote so sharply and provocatively on the sports page that Howard hired him away from the *Chicago Tribune* to do a general interest column and gave him the same freedom he gave Broun.

The clashing viewpoints and divergent moods of Broun's "It Seems to Me" and Pegler's "Fair Enough," across the page from one another, made exciting reading. Broun, sharp with some capitalists, with enemies of the New Deal and of the Newspaper Guild, was humanitarian and warm in spirit. Pegler was misanthropic and bitter.

When Broun's contract expired it was not renewed and Broun transferred to the *New York Post*. Broun's first column in the *Post*, and the last one he ever wrote, was a call to President Roosevelt to accept the nomination for a third term. On December 15, 1939, Broun died of pneumonia.

When the time came to renew Pegler's contract in 1944, Howard asked Pegler to agree to certain stipulations. Although Howard shared Pegler's point of view, the criticism of the columnist that impressed him most as a publisher was that Pegler had become "the stuck whistle of American journalism." Howard, reminding Pegler that it was felicity in sports writing and the light touch that won him his first popularity, wanted to specify in the contract that Pegler would confine his attacks on the Roosevelts and labor racketeers to three days a week. Pegler replied that he could not "be funny a la carte" and, ten days before the old contract expired, he reported to Howard that he had signed up with Hearst's King Features Syndicate where he could write as he pleased six days a week (it was abundantly clear by now that what pleased Pegler also pleased Hearst).

In a public statement Howard said: "The impact of Mr. Pegler's writing upon the opinion content of any newspaper is very great — so great in fact that the editorial voice of Scripps-Howard could only continue audible by resort to a stridency which we do not care to employ."

At the end of 1946, Robert Paine Scripps, Jr., two years past the stated age of twenty-five but delayed in assuming his responsibility by war service, replaced Hawkins (who meanwhile had married the widow of the senior Robert Scripps) as trustee of the Scripps-Howard institution. Born in Washington, D.C., young Bob Scripps was educated at home until he attended Webb School at Claremont, California. Then he took some agricultural courses at the University of California at Davis. He worked for a short time in the business office of the trust before entering the Army, where he rose from private to sergeant, finally commanding a regimental reconnaissance platoon for the 161st infantry in the Philippines. After the war he became a farmer, raising alfalfa, sheep and cotton on a substantial property that he co-owned with his uncle in Fort Stockton, Texas. Bob Scripps, a shrewd business-man, conscientiously attended to his duties as a trustee even when it interfered with his farming, but made no secret of the fact that he was completely uninterested in newspapering, either on the editorial or business side.

A month later, the second son, Charles Edward Scripps, reached twenty-five and Deac Parker stepped down. Chairman of the trust and now titular head of Scripps-Howard, Charles had attended Webb, and William and Mary and Pomona Colleges. He worked briefly on the editorial side of the *Cleveland Press* under Louis Seltzer, one of the chain's editors cast most closely in the Scripps mold, and then served in the Coast Guard. Charles displayed more interest, however, in the mechanics of publication than he did in ideas or politics.

In 1949, the year that Deac Parker died, Charles Scripps became chairman of the trust and titular head of Scripps-Howard. Walker Stone succeeded Parker as head of the Washington bureau, which was, in practice, the fountainhead from which the concern's national and international policies emanated, but no successor was named to Parker's more important post as editor-in-chief, to which he had been appointed by Robert Paine Scripps. Old Man Scripps had always warned against the concentration of editorial and business control in the hands of one man.

In January of the following year, the *New York World-Telegram*, bellwether of the flock that now included nineteen newspapers pub-lished under the slogan, "Give the people light and they will find the way," bought the sinking *New York Sun* from Thomas Dewart, son of the man from whom Howard had acquired the *Telegram*. The big, bulky *World-Telegram and Sun* that resulted took pride in the fact that it now united under one roof three great traditions of American journalism, combining the ideals of Pulitzer, Scripps, and Dana, but the caustic *New Yorker* gibed that these three great names were now buried in one grave.

Of the deal, the rival and aggressively liberal *New York Post* said:

Thus, in death, New York's intransigent organ of conservative Re-publicanism is mated with the daily that once drew its inspiration from the fighting liberal tradition of the old *World*. Yet the union is not entirely incongruous. The latterday editorial pages of the *Sun* and

World-Telegram have been wedded in most causes. Together they hated Roosevelt and together they embraced all the great Old Guard causes. It might be said that the *World-Telegram*'s hardening conservatism destroyed the *Sun*'s last reason for existence.

Local autonomy still allows wide variation among the other member papers — in Cleveland, Cincinnati, and Columbus, Ohio; in Houston, Fort Worth, and El Paso, Texas; in Covington, Kentucky; in Evansville, Indiana; in San Francisco, Washington, Indianapolis, Knoxville, Memphis, Birmingham, and Denver — and many of them continue vigorous crusades against municipal corruption along the old Scripps lines.

Samuel H. Scripps was slated to succeed Roy Howard as trustee on his twenty-fifth birthday, October 30, 1952, thus restoring the family to full nominal control of the properties. His interests were in the arts, and, when he elected not to take up his option, the succession fell to the fourth and last son, E. W. Scripps II, a former student at the University of Nevada who had worked for the United Press and served in the Navy, a personable youth with a reporter's approach to life.

Of the two granddaughters of E. W. Scripps, the younger — Nackey Scripps Gallowhur, wife of a New York chemical company executive — has turned more toward horses and painting than toward newspapers, and the other — Margaret Scripps McCabe, wife of the editor of her grandfather's disquisitions — was a good newspaperwoman before her marriage but is now fully occupied with her family. She is as deeply concerned as her husband over the turn the papers have taken.

Will the return of the Scripps family to full control of their properties swing the papers back toward the courageous championship of the common man that gave them their original character? Only time will tell.

As for Howard himself, although he had relinquished his trusteeship on his seventieth birthday, he was still strongly in the saddle as editor and president of the *New York World-Telegram and Sun*, and his son, Jack, was firmly established as president of the E. W. Scripps Company.

25

Mr. Munsey

by ROBERT L. DUFFUS

ROBERT L. DUFFUS was a newspaperman at the time Frank Munsey was becoming known as the "butcher of American newspapers." His comments on Mr. Munsey were published in the *American Mercury*, July 1924. The author of twenty books, Mr. Duffus is now on the staff of the *New York Times*.

I FIND difficulty in writing about Mr. Munsey's beginnings because it is so hard to think of him as anything but the completed Mr. Munsey. He must have crawled before he toddled, and toddled before he ran; his nose, like the noses of all normal infants, must sometimes have needed wiping; and there must have been aunts who poked jocose fingers into his youthful midriff and called him Ootsie-Tootsums and other absurd names; but the thought of these occurrences merely induces in a modern observer a shuddering sense of *lèse majesté*. I am not indulging in unseemly levity. Mr. Munsey is an artist in deportment. He plays so well the part of the present Mr. Munsey that one can hardly believe he ever played other parts.

Yet the records testify that he obeyed the laws of growth like the rest of mankind; he did not fall out of a star or spring full-panoplied from an ocean wave, but was formed slowly in the womb of New England Puritanism. His energy is the accumulation of three centuries of ferocious combat with stubborn elements; the guiding principles of his career have resulted from the simple transfer of old-fashioned piety from the religious to the economic sphere. Or one may think of him, not inconsistently, as one of those mountaineers, full of the simple virtues of camp and field, who at intervals in human history sweep down from the hills to fall upon the cities of the plain.

Thanks to Mr. Munsey's foresight in publishing "A Munsey-Hopkins Genealogy," by Dr. D. O. S. Lowell, of the Roxbury Latin School, even his more remote origins are now open to respectful scrutiny. The Munsey family, according to Dr. Lowell, first came to notice in Normandy. Ancestral Munseys, appearing variously on the roll of Battle Abbey as Mounchesny, Monceus, Mouncey and Monceals, assisted William the Conqueror in combining the best features of the Norman and Anglo-Saxon civilizations. The first known Munsey in America was at Ipswich, Massachusetts, about 1659. Stephen Hopkins, an ancestor of Mr. Munsey's on the maternal side, "was one of the twelve *Mayflower* passengers who had a title (Mr.) prefixed" to their names. Mr. Munsey's mother could count four *Mayflower* passengers in one line of descent among her ancestors and eight in another.

But more important than colonial or Norman blood in determining Mr. Munsey's course in life were the circumstances of his childhood. His father, though a man of "strong qualities and rugged honesty," was a failure in worldly affairs; his mother, like many other women in a similar situation, transferred her ambitions from her husband to her children. "The greatest regret of my life, since my income began to mount," wrote Mr. Munsey, in a sincere and plainspoken preface to Dr. Lowell's book, "has been that my mother was not with me to make free use of it. It would have enabled her to do the things and have the things that her fine, true nature craved. . . . My father . . . came on the stage of young manhood when Maine was a semi-wilderness. There were few openings for advancement in the rural sections. Saving up money as capital with which to make a start in life was a slow business. How far my father had progressed in this respect when he married I do not know, but I do know that marriage put an end to it."

When it came Mr. Munsey's turn to adventure into the world he traveled light: he never married.

II

Frank Andrew Munsey, one of six children, was born at Mercer, Maine, on August 21, 1854. Six months later the family moved to Gardiner, Maine, and three years later to a farm near Bowdoin. "Here," says Dr. Lowell, "Frank Andrew lived until he was fourteen years of age, doing real work on the farm, laying the foundations for the future, and forming the habits which have characterized his life." Later the family lived in Litchfield, Livermore Falls and Lisbon Falls. At

Lisbon Falls Mr. Munsey worked in a grocery store, where he picked up local color which was to serve him in a later essay in juvenile fiction. He was, as a boyfriend describes him, a staid, thoughtful boy, not brilliant but pretty good in mathematics. He was "a splendid penman," and "his habits were faultless; he didn't even smoke."

But the stored energy of the long line of frustrated Munseys and Hopkinses was at work in the boy; and joined to it was his principal characteristic, a will almost ferocious in its intensity. In the eyes of a country lad a telegraph operator was mysterious and romantic; Mr. Munsey therefore learned telegraphy and was sent to take charge of the Western Union office at Augusta, the State capital. But it was not long before the Augusta telegraph office, like the Lisbon Falls grocery store, was to him, in his own words, like "the cage to a tiger yearning for the boundless freedom of the jungle." He picked up an acquaintance with James G. Blaine and other prominent citizens, but this merely added to his discontent. "Their lives had scope," he said many years later, "mine had none. I chafed bitterly under the limited possibilities of my environment, where energy and ambition counted for so little. My very soul cried out for an opportunity to carve out for myself a bigger life. . . . But the opening did not come my way. There were always sons or relatives, or people of political influence, who stood before me in line for the place. I was pretty nearly as good a business man, at that age even, as I am now, and the tantalizing part of it was I knew it."

Mr. Munsey went into the publishing business (and incidentally into the literary business) by accident. "Railroading, steel, manufacturing, shipping, banking, or any other of the great staple industries" would have suited him just as well. But Fate, with an ironic glint in her eye, shoved him into the ink pot. After his arrival in Augusta he had procured a position in a local publishing house for one of his boyhood friends. As time passed and this friend inconsiderately prospered and was offered a job in New York "at a handsome advance in salary," Mr. Munsey saw that he had made a mistake: he should have taken the position himself. The incident turned his thoughts toward publishing, of which he presently acquired just enough knowledge, as he has said, "to be dangerous."

He worked out plans for a boy's weekly magazine, which was to be called *Munsey's Golden Argosy*. He had saved $500 out of his salary as a telegraph operator, an Augusta broker agreed to put in $2500, and his friend in New York offered to go into partnership with $1000 more. He landed in New York on September 23, 1882, with $500 worth of manuscript and $40 in cash. Benjamin Franklin entering Philadelphia with a bun under each arm was hardly a more modest figure.

III

When Mr. Munsey arrived in New York he was a tall, blond young man of twenty-eight, with eyes and features which, if his earlier photographs do not lie, were singularly and deceptively mild. He threw himself into a decade of appalling struggles and toils, besieging a Troy more stoutly defended than Homer's and emerged at the end wealthy, successful, arrogant — in short, the Mr. Munsey now known to fame. I doubt that anyone can read the story of those ten years without thinking more charitably, or at least more philosophically, of him. For if he is inclined to be uppity in his old age he is merely giving back without excessive interest what was inflicted upon him in his youth.

He found that the publication he had planned, illustrated and printed on good paper, was impossible. Next his broker friend in Augusta abandoned him. A New York publisher agreed to get out the magazine, making Mr. Munsey editor; three months later the publisher failed. Mr. Munsey offered to settle the debts by taking over the bankrupt enterprise. He borrowed $300, and with that as his capital jumped into the maelstrom. He has written most appealingly of what followed. He lived through "four years of toil and disappointment, with never a vacation, never a day for play, and rarely a night at the theatre." "With a determination to keep the *Argosy* alive at all hazards, a determination that amounted almost to an insane passion," he says, "I went on and on." He undertook a circulation campaign "that in its intensity and ferocity crowded a life's work into a few months." He wrote "The Boy Broker" — "6000 words a week dragged out of me, dragged out at night after the awful activities of the day, a complete switch from red-hot activities to the world of fancy, where by sheer will force I centred my thoughts on creative work and compelled myself to produce the copy. What a Winter, what awful chances and what a strain on human vitality and endurance!" Sometimes he couldn't go out to dinner unless the mail brought a subscription check to pay for it.

He was indefatigable. The possessing and dominating instincts grew stronger within him. Neither then nor afterwards would he tolerate a partner or an equal in any enterprise of his. He was "editor, advertising manager, office boy and chief contributor." He had twenty salesmen on the road east of the Mississippi before he had a stenographer or a bookkeeper in his New York office. He borrowed $95,000 and spent every cent on advertising. He gave away eleven million, five hundred thousand copies. "The Boy Broker," written at night, added 20,000 to the circulation. "Five years of poverty," he says, "five years of awful struggle and now the earth was mine — rich at last, richer than I had ever dreamed of." But his expenses, alas, outran his mounting income. "Merciful Heavens! how the bills fell due, how the notes fell due! The cry from in town and out of town, from men on the road and from all the four corners of the earth, and in a thousand voices, was money, money, money! The whole world had gone money mad." In later years Mr. Munsey has had much to say about money; is perhaps even more conscious of money than most rich men; one begins to see why.

For six years longer the battle went on. At 115,000 circulation the *Golden Argosy* wavered and stuck. In 1889 Mr. Munsey started *Munsey's Weekly*, which "lasted two and a half years and lost over $100,000." In 1891, he transformed the weekly into a monthly and ran it for two years at twenty-five cents a copy, losing money all the while. Why was it, he asked himself, that "out of eighty millions of people there were not over 250,000 magazine buyers? Was the Sunday paper crushing the life out of the monthlies as well as the weeklies?" For two years, while the dollars drained out of his pockets and his credit stretched nearer and nearer the breaking point, he meditated. Finally he decided that "if a magazine should be published at ten cents and made light, bright and timely it might be a different story." Mr. Munsey arrived at this conclusion just as John Brisbane Walker and S. S. McClure arrived independently at a somewhat similar one. Neither Mr. Walker nor Mr. McClure, however, ventured upon ten cents. *McClure's* came out at fifteen cents in May, 1893, and the *Cosmopolitan* at twelve and a half cents (it was later raised to fifteen) in July.

Mr. Munsey was assured that his scheme was impossible. The news company which had been handling his magazines refused to take the ten cent *Munsey's* at a price which would pay expenses. But the Munsey-Hopkins will power did not weaken. He persuaded a paper manufacturer, even in that year of hard times, to grant him credit. He advertised, also on credit. He called upon the ultimate consumer to come to his rescue. The response was instantaneous. No chewing gum or collar ever leaped to fame more swiftly than Munsey's new magazine. The circulation had been about 20,000; it went to 40,000 in October, 1893; to 60,000 in November; to 100,000 in December; to 150,000 in January, 1894; to 200,000 in February; to 250,000 in April. By March, 1895, it was 500,000; by December, 1899, it was 650,000; in 1903 it was 700,000; in 1908 it had reached 800,000. By this time Mr. Munsey was publishing not only *Munsey's* and the *Argosy* but also the *All-Story* and the *Scrap-Book,* with a combined circulation of more than two million copies, or, as he proudly put it, "a thousand tons of magazines." A thousand tons of magazines is not to be despised. And Mr. Munsey had really and truly achieved this miracle single-handed. "The magazine," he said, "came through because I came through, lived because I lived, was the vehicle merely of what I did."

At forty, twelve years after his arrival in New York, Mr. Munsey had turned the corner. He could now go out to lunch without waiting for the postman to bring a subscription check. He could and did mingle in the "great, big world." The Munsey-Hopkins lineage was vindicated; the blood of those farmers and craftsmen who had toiled so long and patiently and obscurely now flowed in the veins of one of the rulers of America. The poor boy had become rich and famous.

IV

The reader who will turn back to the files of *Munsey's Magazine* in the early nineties will not only find that publication considerably better than the *Munsey's* of today, but better than anything that Mr. Munsey is publishing today. The breath of life was in it as never in any Munsey newspaper. It was literally "light, bright and timely," but it was not trivial. Month after month it gave space to articles on modern art, with excellent accompanying illustrations. It had a literary department, which kept up in chatty fashion with the fiction of the day. It had a theatrical department, baited with photographs of stage beauties; it gave two or three pages monthly to well-chosen light verse; it made obeisance at the feet of the captains of industry, who had not then been taught their places; and it took up current events in a serious way. Its fiction sometimes reached a pretty high level. Indeed, Mr. Robert H. Davis, who took over the function of selection after Mr. Munsey turned his attention to more austere concerns, would have made *Munsey's* the best fiction magazine in the country if Mr. Munsey had been willing to pay what good fiction cost. As it was, Mr. Davis developed swarms of promising young writers, who were snapped up by more generous publishers as soon as their talents became known.

In the early days Mr. Munsey himself wrote a great deal. We find him, for example, expatiating on horsemanship, and later on the automobile, and hanging wreaths on successful business men and politicians. Even then he could hardly say too much in praise of "the intelligent and wealthy portion of the community, who as a rule do things well." Was he not practically one of them? Were not his magazines "earning more money than any other publishing proposition of any kind whatsoever in America?" But Mr. Munsey was not a mere article writer. He also wrote fiction. He wrote "Afloat in a Great City"; "The Boy Broker"; "A Tragedy of Errors"; "Under Fire"; and "Derringforth." Of these the first two and the fourth were boys' stories, intended for publication in the originally juvenile *Argosy*; the others were for readers who were supposed to have grown up. Yet, as may easily be seen, the thread of a common philosophy and a common literary method ran through them all.

"In a good story," wrote Mr. Munsey, in his preface to "The Boy Broker" (that midnight tour de force), "plot and action are but the setting to the gem — the means of conveying a lesson in disguise in such a way that the reader will not suspect he is being taught." The hero of this narrative, Herbert Randolph, goes to New York as Mr. Munsey did, "to become what is known as a successful man, to make a name for himself — a name that would extend to his native State and make his parents proud of their brilliant son." Arrived in New York, he makes the acquaintance of a rough but honest newsboy, finds a job in a broker's office, falls in love with "the light-hearted merry daughter of the senior partner," and gets into a peck of trouble through the wicked machinations of a boy who had sought a position in Mr. Goldwin's office for the purpose of robbing it. He is kidnapped, rescued by his newsboy friend, and turned out on the streets to hunt a job. By dint of good fortune and energy he emerges from these disasters, is vindicated of the false charges against him, gets rich and marries the light-hearted merry daughter previously mentioned.

Fred Worthington's experiences in "Under Fire" are even more appalling and his ultimate triumph even more dramatic. Fred is the son of the village shoemaker and works in Mr. Rexford's grocery store. He aspires to the hand of the daughter of the village doctor, which naturally leads an unscrupulous rival first to try to have him knocked on the head by a thug, then to lure him into a billiard den and get him drunk, next to spread lying stories about his alleged dishonesty, and finally to set the grocery store on fire in the hope that Fred will be convicted of the crime. Mr. Munsey goes so far as to let Fred be tried for arson, but he comes out all right in the end, marries the girl and gets rich. All Mr. Munsey's heroes get rich.

Let us now turn to "Derringforth," a romance for adults, which represents the author's later period. "Derringforth" was published serially in *Munsey's Magazine* between March, 1893, and July, 1894, and was later issued in two volumes, cloth-bound and neatly boxed, for the small sum of a dollar and a half. It did not increase the magazine's circulation until Mr. Munsey lowered the price to ten cents; on the other hand, it did not prevent the magazine from going to 250,000 after Mr. Munsey had lowered the price. "It had been love since infancy. There is nothing sweeter than such love." What member of the younger generation would suspect Mr. Munsey of such sentiment? Yet it is his. "Derringforth" is a robust, well-tailored novel. Its hero is Phil Derringforth, "tall and straight, with soldierly bearing and fine presence"; its heroine Marion Kingsley, who was "tall and willowy" and "played the violin with considerable skill." "Her eyes," Mr. Munsey tells us, "were intelligent and pleasing. The lines of her face were good and her coloring was exquisite. . . . She showed the effect of careful training. She knew nothing of the lighter novels. Her reading had been confined to standard authors."

"Derringforth" has no less than four villains, all of them bent on destroying the hero's happiness if not his life. There is "J. Harrington Van Slump, a sleek old man of full three score, very bald but otherwise well preserved"; there is Martin Strum, a vicious money lender; there is a false friend, Burrock; there is a jealous rival, Stanley Vedder. But the tragedy, for it is a tragedy, turns less on the efforts of these undesirable characters than on the foolish ambition of Marion's mother, who wishes to expose her daughter to the perils and fascinations of a year in fashionable society before allowing her to become engaged. There is also a missing letter, which causes an immense amount of havoc. Derringforth wins and loses fortunes against enormous odds in Wall Street (this at twenty-four), and wipes out his enemies, only, in the end, to marry the wrong girl and expire in the last chapter. All of Marion's admirers, in the meantime, have disposed of themselves by marrying some one else or breaking their necks by falling off horses. The reader drops a furtive tear as Derringforth, the Old Guide beside him, slips silently into eternity; while Marion, her lesson learned at last, faces the Dawn of Another Day.

Mr. Munsey's plots are put together like a Ford automobile. One may make fun of them if one likes, but they run. The indomitable Munsey-Hopkins will power exhibits itself in all of them. "I wrote and re-wrote the early chapters many times," he says of "Afloat in a Great City." "It was midnight toil — work done by candle light after long days at the office. I wrote that story with a special purpose. I wanted something to advertise and put my faith to the test by plunging on it to the extent of ten thousand dollars." Let the literary snob who sneers at Mr. Munsey's art ask himself whether he would have sufficient confidence in his own wares to do the same.

One thought may already have occurred to the reader, as it has occurred to me. When Mr. Munsey failed to go into the motion picture field he missed a gigantic opportunity. He had, when he wrote "Derringforth," the magic touch that makes kitchen and parlor one.

v

It would be unfair to Mr. Munsey and his art to leave this phase of our subject without touching upon his philosophy as revealed in his works of the imagination. A few excerpts, will, however, have to serve:

No true success can be obtained except by operating on the solid principles of truth and honesty.

In this country there is always a chance for an honest, ambitious and determined boy to succeed by careful thought, patient endurance, and hard work.

Why do boys go to destruction by visiting iniquitous dens, by keeping low and vulgar company, by drinking, smoking and gambling . . . when they might be refined, respected and supremely happy?

Billiards is a fascinating game and from the very fact of its fascination it is extremely dangerous to boys.

A cruel world this seems sometimes when one reflects how unevenly the joys and sorrows, and luxuries and misery are distributed among brothers and sisters, neighbors and countrymen.

God's tender care for the human race is thoughtfully manifested in the faculty He has given women of finding relief in tears from an overburdened soul.

Happiness always follows a generous act.

He was wholly wrapped up in his business. He could not look beyond that and had no feeling for others. . . . I often pity such men, for though they may have wealth in abundance they know not how to enjoy it. . . . They have starved their nobler nature that is nourished on higher things, until it is dwarfed and shriveled, and the baleful results of such an unnatural mode of life are pictured in their countenances.

To these sentences from his earlier works may be added two or three of a later date:

The literary profession is a business like everything else.

The wages of labor will never come down until the supply exceeds the demand.

We must have a substratum of plain labor. Modern life and modern civilization cannot exist without it.

Nothing succeeds without ownership interest in the management.

Mr. Munsey went through the muckraking craze almost unmoved. "The people of this country," he wrote in 1913, taking a retrospective squint at the period then just past, "have come to realize that prosperity rests in upbuilding, not in destruction. That these muckraking articles, taking them as a whole, did some good as well as a lot of harm, there can be no question. But *Munsey's Magazine* never went in for them. Its whole attitude has been for constructive work, for upbuilding." Mr. Munsey would not bite the economic system that fed him.

Magazines whose editors were less tenderly solicitous passed *Munsey's* in the race for popular favor. Little by little the Munsey publications, although they continued prosperous, ceased to be significant. But by this time Mr. Munsey was tired of the magazine game, and scenting new battles and greater conquests, turned his attention to daily journalism.

Like Jim Hill, Mr. Harriman, Napoleon Bonaparte, and the former emperor of Germany, Mr. Munsey had early been brought to believe in amalgamation. He arrived at this position logically — indeed, it is the only one at which a successful, large-scale business man logically can arrive. He was impressed by the folly of small-scale production. "We have passed by the period, and passed it forever," he said, in discussing the affairs of his magazine, "when small volume and big profits will rule in the business world." He reasoned exactly as Havemeyer did when he took a profit of one-eighth of a cent a pound on sugar; exactly as Ford did when he sold cars at less than cost, knowing that increased sales and the resulting economies of quantity production would repay the temporary losses many times over. He came to believe in amalgamating not only industries but also political parties. Finally he felt himself called upon to amalgamate newspapers, of which, he thought, there were "fully sixty per cent" more than there ought to be. He said:

Suppose the God-given genius of some of these really great men who now control a single great metropolitan journal were utilized to govern the policies of a hundred or of a thousand newspapers, what a tremendous power that would be! There is no form of industry that lends itself to combination more naturally and readily than newspaper building. . . . With a central ownership big enough and strong enough to encompass the whole country our newspapers can afford to be independent, fearless and honest. . . . A million dollars a year for the general editorial department for a chain of a thousand newspapers will mean only a thousand dollars to each newspaper.

Inasmuch as at the time this remark was made there were not more than twenty-five hundred daily newspapers of all descriptions in the United States (there are fewer now, thanks partly to Mr. Munsey) this conception was sufficiently grandiose. Compared with Mr. Munsey, Messrs. Hearst and Scripps were men devoid of imagination, unable to see beyond their own noses. Such was the dream. What is the reality? The question was thus answered by Mr. Philip Schuyler in the *Editor & Publisher* a few months ago:

In 1920 Munsey said his investment in the *New York Herald*, the *Sun* and the *Telegram* amounted to $11,500,000. His total investments in newspaper properties he then announced as more than $16,000,000. Since that year he has paid the reported sum of $2,000,000 for the

Globe and well in excess of $2,000,000 for the *Evening Mail*, bringing the total investment up to more than $20,000,000. He bought the *New York Star* and the *New York Continent* in 1890 and sold them in the same year. He paid a half million for the *New York Daily News* in 1901 and sold it in 1904 for little more than junk. He paid $600,000 for the *Boston Journal* in 1902 and put a million more in it before he sold it for a song. In 1908 he tossed a million into the *Philadelphia Times*, which he bought in 1901 for $200,000 and sold sixteen years later for $500,000.

Of sixteen newspapers (counting the Paris edition of the *New York Herald*) upon which at one time or another Mr. Munsey has laid hands, he has either killed or sold all but the *Evening Sun* and the *Evening Telegram*. At this moment both of these newspapers are probably earning him a handsome profit, for the circulation he has bought and jammed into them is considerable. But they have no general or permanent significance. They merely reflect Mr. Munsey, and when he is dead they will reflect someone else. He has acquired no following in daily journalism; he has created nothing. Indeed, he is not so much a force as a portent of journalism. He has demonstrated that newspapers are not institutions, like schools and churches, but commodities, like motor cars. He has legitimatized journalistic murder. He has invented a new and effective method of doing away with free speech. Perhaps this consoles him for his inability to own and edit one thousand "independent, fearless and honest" American newspapers.

26

The Man Behind the *Times*

by BENJAMIN STOLBERG

Adolph Ochs was at the peak of his career as the rejuvenator of the *New York Times* when this article appeared in the *Atlantic Monthly* for December 1926. The author, BENJAMIN STOLBERG, was a journalist and lecturer in the fields of economics and sociology.

T HE sole trouble virtue demands," said Hume, "is that of just calculation and the steady preference of the greater happiness." "Success" says Mr. Adolph S. Ochs, the managing owner of the *New York Times*, "is simply won by the practice of the ordinary virtues." Clearly the famous utilitarian and the eminent publisher agree. But while Hume's naiveté is complex and artful, Mr. Ochs's is palpably ingenuous. He just naturally believes what Hume was forced to conclude from sheer skepticism. And between skepticism and animal faith the advantage is all with faith.

Being *ex animo* certain, Mr. Ochs does not hesitate to share the secret of his simple success. "I really can see no excuse," he insists, "for any healthy young man, born of self-respecting parents, not to succeed in the fullest sense of the term. It took no genius to build the *Times*; just hard work, common sense, self-reliance, and honesty." After faithfully exercising these "ordinary virtues," Mr. Ochs was able to celebrate, last August 18, the thirtieth anniversary of his ownership of the *New York Times* by making on his editorial page some highly satisfactory observations. "When [the *Times*] passed into the ownership and control of the present management [its] daily circulation . . . had dropped to 9000. The regular employees numbered 300, and the annual gross income was $500,000. At the present time the *New York Times* has an average daily circulation of 370,000 and 625,000 on Sunday; has over 3000 regular employees, and has an annual gross income of about $25,000,000." Such phenomenal success has so absolutely convinced Mr. Ochs that the exercise of the "ordinary virtues" is the best policy that he is willing to bet on them. He would gladly organize a Company to Assure Success.

My Company to Assure Success would ask of its policy-holders nothing out of the ordinary, no special brilliance, no abnormal talents, no inordinate industry even. In passing upon applicants for success it would, however, inquire rather carefully into a youth's antecedents and parents, for the first thing is to be well born. Satisfied on this point, the Company would investigate the youth's record to date, and if he was found to have done moderately well at school, if he had established a reasonably good reputation in character, and if he possessed good health — good health is essential — then he would be eligible. In issuing this policy, about all the rules and conditions would be: "You must strive faithfully to live up to the precepts taught you as a child by your mother. You must be industrious, temperate, and honest. You must give diligent attention to your business, lead a clean, honorable life, and deserve as well as try to succeed."

Mr. Ochs's friends smile indulgently. His critics smile cynically. Both miss the point. It is not his naiveté, but the obsession of his naiveté, which matters — an obsession which is completely hidden even from himself by a rare personal charm. It is his absolute faith in the "ordinary virtues" which conquered for him the world of his choice. And though Mr. Ochs is "no genius," he touches genius in the psychological unawareness with which his virtues function, in the unconscious virtuosity with which he orchestrates them. There is something organic, rather than moral, about Mr. Ochs's decencies.

His virtues fall into the rhythm of his age. He is keenly aware of its instruments and never dubious of its fundamentals. His high courage never challenges the established order, though it is often extremely daring in its uses. His high sense of honor merely bespeaks his rights and duties as a free man in established opinion. His uncanny shrewdness is never ulterior, for his mental processes function as though they were dipped in a utilitarian solution whose chemistry he does not know. Mr. Ochs is not merely an honest, but a congenital conformist. He is the living norm of the median culture of American life. In turn his times have rewarded him with the highest protective coloration. It is this protection which enabled him to build our only national newspaper.

Mr. Ochs can "go to bed" with his paper and rest calmly between its lines in the unconscious certainty that his personality will color every word in each of the eight columns of the thirty to forty pages of the daily *Times*. In the *Mid-Week Pictorial*, in the *Annalist*, in *Current History*, Mr. Ochs stops for a moment to review synoptically the fugitive news of the day. And on Sunday he dresses up in two-hundred-odd pages of the most perfect typography, in exquisite roto-gravure, in the beautiful half-tones of the Magazine Section and Book Review, in dignified special features. The Sunday *Times* is really Mr. Ochs's temple, in which he does homage to the American environment which blessed his "ordinary virtues" so prodigally. Mr. Ochs's career reaffirms the Aristotelian dictum that man is an institutional case — in proportion to his success. The *Times* reflects our complex institutional culture in faithful perfection. No wonder the best journalistic crafts-men have drifted to Mr. Ochs as their publisher. Louis Wiley is by all odds the most competent American newspaper manager. Carr V. Van Anda and Frederick T. Birchall are beyond the shadow of a doubt the greatest American news gatherers. Rollo Ogden is a dis-tinguished newspaper editor. The heads of the various departments are among the leading national experts. It is around the simple magnet of Mr. Ochs's sensibility to the world as it is that these men have built the most highly technical compass to follow the phenomenology of its news.

II

Obviously Mr. Ochs's conscious reasons for his success, though absolutely sincere, do not explain. The only way to analyze his intrinsic processes, which alone are significant, is by reading critically the *Times*. It is only by looking behind its news and advertising and editorial policy, in their trinitarian balance, that we can discover the real Mr. Ochs.

The main reason for Mr. Ochs's success as a newsman is in fact very simple. He caught the idea of mass production at just the right time in the New York newspaper field. In this respect the success of the *Times* is the success of Ivory Soap, which is ninety-nine and a fraction of a per cent pure, and whose fractional impurity cannot be humanly helped. The *Times* is as much of a *news*paper as its management can humanly make it. It has no leg shows, side shows, or circuses. It employs no middle-aged, rundown newspaper men to grind out advice to the lovelorn. It peddles no funny sheets, Krazy Kats, Nize Babies, or humor by Andy Gump, Mutt and Jeff, and F.P.A. Mr. Ochs held to the conviction that the job of a newspaper is to print *news* even in the early days of his management of the *Times*, when it seemed that such a high-minded policy in the midst of the yellow war between Hearst and Pulitzer, complicated by the younger Bennett's brilliant manufacture of news, was heading him straight for bankruptcy. And as one reads the *Times* at the breakfast table, with the certainty that without it one would miss literally most of the news, one cannot help but appreciate that Mr. Ochs's simple courage is a national asset.

Today Mr. Ochs proudly justifies his original judgment. "When I first came to New York," he told me, "I had hopes that there might be at least 30,000 intelligent, serious, high-grade people who would appreciate this kind of newspaper. But of course I never dared to hope for all this" — and his large blue eyes slowly swept his magnificent office, and their gaze trailed out of the window and rested in wistful gratefulness on the imperial city which his humble decency conquered.

Mr. Ochs is both right and wrong. His strength lies in just this happy mixture of rightness and wrongness, in the oversimplification of his reasons for his motives, an inadequacy which saves these motives from the inhibitions of self-analysis. Mr. Ochs found not merely 30,000 but an average week-day and Sunday circulation of over 400,000. He never found 30,000 readers of the type he had in mind. An astute observer on the *Times* staff "guessed" that "probably no more than 10,000 people are capable of keeping up with the excellence of the *Times*." The other 390,000 buy it because of the ineradicable characteristic of "respectability" to appear more intelligent than it is. It is the intelligent minority, from the most reactionary to the most radical, which finds it necessary to read all about the Dawes Plan, the Chinese Consortium; which has to wade through the full speeches of high-placed politicians; which wants to know how Article X in the League Covenant and Article XXVII in the Mexican Constitution are working out. The rest buy the *Times* because the best have read it. "The *Times* is the sort of newspaper," Mr. Ochs once innocently said, "which no one needs to be ashamed to be seen reading." This, rather than its excellence, is its main selling asset.

If one reads the Hall-Mills murder case in the Hearst press one is frankly interested in murder. But if one reads almost twice as much about it in the *Times* — where one could if one wished also read the latest news of the World Court or the Williamstown Institute — then one has a sociological interest in crime. If one reads in the gutter tabloids all the details of the mob hysteria at Sheik Valentino's death, one is just another member of the mob. But if one reads about it in the *Times,* then one is a student of the hysteria. It is in the *Times* that we can all worship the Idols of the Cave without being caught in our idolatry.

Yet in the long run the "respectable" majority is bound to fall way behind the intelligent minority. This gap the *Times* bridges by its very encyclopaedism, which covers all special interests, and appeals to each reader both professionally and avocationally. The financier, the industrialist, the big and the lesser business man, the student of social politics, the professional man, can all follow in the *Times* the news of their own worlds, the news of each other's world, and their own fancy in the news of the world in general. The *Times* has a composite reader. And "all the news that's fit to print" is simply the news which appeals to the best composite reader, who thereby is naturally raised into an "intelligent, serious, high-grade" fellow.

It is because Mr. Ochs in his own person represents the median of our national culture that he is by all odds the best judge on his staff as to what news is "fit to print." And he is peculiarly gifted in presenting the social panorama by the very fact that his own fabulous news sense is entirely unhampered by an interpretative censor. He reads reams of details on Stalin's victory over Zinovieff; on General Pilsudski's senseless revolution in Poland; on the British general strike; on the reaction in Italy and Spain; on the political assassinations in Greece and Turkey; on the troubles of the Catholic Church in Mexico and its triumph in Chicago; on politics in Washington, London, and Paris; on the doings of big business and labor. But the inner drift of this panorama fortunately escapes him, which accounts for his success in *impersonal* journalism. The great value of the *Times* lies in the fact that it is the best commercial photographer of the world's happenings.

The very volume and expense of this policy require a high expertness of the gathering of news, a delicate efficiency in management, in presentation, in the whole complex business administration of the modern newspaper. In the technique of newspaper building and owning Mr. Ochs has no rival. In this technique, in fact, he is not merely instinctively shrewd, but philosophical, articulate, and expert. His occasional talks on the industrial arts of newspaper management, especially on advertising policy, are pearls of wisdom compared to the usually fatuous professionalism of the "high-power" executive and the pseudo-scientific lingo of the university business schools. The *Times* of course has to pay the price of encyclopaedism by being often dreadfully overwritten, with long paragraphs connected by motley conjunctions. And its tendency toward anonymity, and the somewhat Philistine flavor of its respectability, do not help its style. But its mechanical composition is flawless. Its craftsmanship has been especially perfected since 1914. The World War and the consequent world unrest, our own rapid transition from debtor nation to world empire, the generally accelerated kaleidoscope of latter-day social events, constantly require a technical vigilance which gives infinite scope to Mr. Ochs's training and talents as an administrative journalist. The *Times* has risen to its present position as the world's greatest newspaper organization in the period of the world's greatest unrest. And naturally this has only served to strengthen Mr. Ochs's belief that this is a pretty nice world after all.

No newspaper is freer from outside control. Mr. Ochs is inordinately proud, as he has every right to be, that the *Times* has no Ivory Towers, no Sacred Cows. The high-placed in any field are to him not Sacred Cows but high-bred Holsteins, provided they live up to their breeding. Hence his resentment flares up the more sternly when they indicate a meretricious desire for preferential grazing ground in his columns.

There is no doubt that the *Times* is given to the Idols of Authority. But in the nature of the case the views and deeds of those in authority *are* news — very important news — always were, and always will be. What Messrs. Coolidge and Baldwin and Trotsky think of politics; what Messrs. Green and Weisbord think of the Passaic strike; what Messrs. Hoover and Gary think of business; or even what Mr. Tunney thinks of the uppercut, or Miss Ederle thinks of the Australian crawl, *is* important. The radical paper is a failure as a *news*paper because it is iconoclastic. The function of the radical press is not so much to print news as to propagate social conditions in which its prejudices will become news. The only successful Socialist newspapers in this country, the *Jewish Daily Forward* and the *Milwaukee Leader*, are successful because Socialism is in authority on the East Side of New York and in Milwaukee, and they have news to report.

Mr. Ochs's respect for authority is natural, free, and independent. In fact the *Times* respects authority far less in the field of social and economic politics than in the intellectual professions, where none but ideological radicals could possibly accuse it of ulterior motives. It finds it often necessary to disagree with powerful politicians and the leaders in vested life. But the bigwigs in science, education, letters, and arts it respects indiscriminately. When the evolutionary controversy was at its height the *Times* did not invite Professor Morgan of Columbia or Professor Carlson of the University of Chicago or an expert of equally high standing to clarify the issue. It permitted itself to be used by notorious publicity seekers in high academic positions, whose views on evolution are more or less of a joke among professional scientists. And because of its very exhaustiveness the *Times* printed more nonsense on this subject than any other paper in the country.

III

The advertising policy of the *Times* is both sensitively honorable and technically extremely high. It exercises both an alert and a relevant censorship. Once or twice a week the *Times* shrewdly advertises "its regret for the necessity of the omission of eight (or six or seven) columns of advertising" on account of the pressure of news, never failing to explain how the individual advertiser may avoid such annoyance in the future.

In the early history of Mr. Ochs's ownership a very large advertiser asked for certain considerations which then were not considered peculiarly offensive. A correspondence ensued. Mr. Ochs finally wrote: "You must excuse me from discussing with you the policy of the *New York Times*. . . . The *Times*, as long as it is under its present management, will endeavor to get along without your business." Later on, the *Times* lost an advertiser whose business was worth over $1,000,000 because of a misunderstanding in which Mr. Ochs preferred to grant the benefit of the doubt to his own sense of freedom. The honor roll of such instances is the best testimony to the meticulousness of his independence. His independence of the advertiser is really due largely to his fine sense of workmanship, which is merely the other side of his shield of honor. The advertiser who is cheap enough to want

368

to influence a newspaper's policy will sooner or later deface its advertising space; and in the long run this kind of independence secured for the *Times* the "quality" market, which forces the individual advertiser to conform to its standards in spite of its touch of insouciance.

Mr. Ochs won the high-quality market of advertising in very much the same way in which he won the high-grade reader. Just as the news policy of the *Times* appeals to the rank and file of its readers through their imitativeness of the intelligent minority, so the advertising in the *Times* is framed to appeal to the great middle class through an upper minority of taste.

IV

Mr. Ochs is convinced that his is the freest editorial page in the world. "I never in my life asked any man to write one word in which he did not believe." And there are certainly few papers, if any, in which a more fastidious regard is paid to the writer's conscience. But it is an old ethical truism that respect for personality in itself is one of the strongest of influences. Mr. Munsey, who was in the habit of tearing up editorials of which he disapproved in the face of their writers, had to write the editorials nearest his heart with his own pen. At any rate to write, day in and day out, editorials for the *Times* without due regard for Mr. Ochs's opinions is inconceivable, for the sufficient reason that Mr. Ochs *is* the *Times*. There is no newspaper which, in the long run, would keep on buying articles wholesale which it would reject retail — as special articles. And on the *Times* this is especially true, for Mr. Ochs knows what he wants by just being himself.

Yet every personality fights shy as much as possible of the influence of another even in agreement, which probably accounts for the unusually large number of noncontroversial or even idyllic topics on the editorial pages of the *Times*. Whatever differences of personality, if not in fundamental opinion, there may be between Mr. Ochs and his editorial writers are at least in part amiably sublimated in polite reflections. A recent, quite typical, *Times* editorial page has five editorials out of eight on the following subjects: A Fine Officer Gone; English and American Litterers; The Discoverer of Oxygen; The Arts in the West; A Great Maltese Writer. The other three editorials were of the usual liberal-conservative "broadcloth" variety. They were undoubtedly written by men who did not object to them. And they certainly expressed Mr. Ochs's views to a nicety.

What is far more interesting is the psychological mechanism of Mr. Ochs's influence, not on the peripheral, but on the central opinions of the editorial writer. The *Times* staff member who writes its editorials on Russia, one of the most delicately ironic of American essayists, is a liberal with an early Socialist background. Were he an editor on a liberal paper, it is quite likely that his indictment of Communism would be of the conventional semisympathetic "objective" variety. On the *Times*, where his liberalism is under a steady tug to the Right, Bolshevism has resuscitated his earlier Socialist feelings in all their anti-Communist bitterness. And so one can read once or twice a week in a *Times* editorial that curious Social-Democratic argument according to which the Russian experiment is the exact opposite of Socialism and is betraying it by its rapid drift toward capitalism. All kinds of economic statistics and Russian government edicts are cited to prove this strange illusion. Mr. Ochs, whose common sense tells him that the trouble with Bolshevism, in the light of American democracy, lies not in its Socialist failure, but, *exceptis excipiendis*, in its Socialist success, is of course very much pleased to learn that even radicals have no use for it, and he is even more pleased to learn that Russia is gradually returning to the capitalist economy. Furthermore, his sense of news scents Russian recognition in the comparatively near future, and he appreciates editorials which both indict Bolshevism and yet analyze changes in Russia which will render her worthy of our recognition. Mr. Ochs is pleased. The writer enjoys his militant opinion. And the *Times* editorial public is pleased for Mr. Ochs's reasons. His feelings and public opinion are usually in tune.

Mr. Ochs's very sensibility to public opinion shields him from the public view. Nothing delights him more than his own low visibility in his paper, which sees everything. It is this paradox which gives his modesty a curiously elated and childlike joy. His modesty is proud of his handiwork. This ambivalence of pride and simplicity is one of his greatest charms. Mr. Ochs is indeed one of those fortunate mortals whose virtues never cheat him of the pleasures of their corresponding vices. With excellent taste he realizes that to be behind the *Times* gives him a great deal more self-feeling than he would get were he in front of it. A born newsman, he knows instinctively that there is no publicity which compares with genuine modesty – if one is powerful. The editors and managers of the *Times,* being important people, take their legitimate place in the public view. Mr. Wiley is socially prominent. Dr. Finley seems to serve on every board. Messrs. Ogden and Van Anda are nationally known journalists. And for whom do they work? For Mr. Ochs.

V

The adjustment between Mr. Ochs and his environment is so perfect that it is a beautifully simple matter to trace the morphology of this adaptation. Mr. Ochs is an abnormally normal heir of his background, and a perfectly well behaved child of the age. It is this adjustment which gave him that marvelous power of prestidigitation with his "ordinary virtues" which makes the *Times* look like a miracle of "genius" while in fact it is merely the reward of a long training in these virtues.

Adolph S. Ochs was born on March 12, 1858, in Cincinnati. He was born strategically, not merely of "self-respecting," but of just the right combination of parents for his subsequent career. His father, Julius Ochs, came to this country from Bavaria in 1846, one of the very first refugee immigrants of the revolutionary movement which broke out two years later. When the Civil War was declared Julius Ochs joined the Union Army. His revolutionary youth in Germany and the Civil War completely exhausted whatever pugnacity there may have been in his gentle nature. In 1865, when little Adolph was seven, Julius Ochs moved his family to Knoxville, Tennessee, then a city of less than ten thousand. There he settled down to a life of good citizenship, and the citizens of Knoxville rewarded him with the justiceship of the peace. In 1872 he experienced a slight liberal resurgence and served as a delegate to the Liberal Convention in Cincinnati which nominated Greeley for President. But after that he lived in complete peace. He accepted the universe of the small-town Southern community. He joined the Royal Arch Masons, the American Legion of Honor, the B'nai B'rith, the Royal Arcanum, the Schiller Lodge, and one or two other orders which in those days had a libertarian complexion so sadly lacking in their present-day tawdry counterparts. He served as a lay reform rabbi of the small Jewish community, and as the religious teacher of its youth.

371

One of our most noted contemporary sociologists lived as a boy just around the corner from the Ochs home. "As I look back," he told me, "I appreciate that Julius Ochs was probably one of the most cultivated men in the whole Reconstruction South. His wide reading, his whimsical knowledge, above all his exquisite kindness in the smallest things, still linger with me." "My father," says Mr. Ochs, "was a very lovable and a most versatile man, but he was not built for success." Mr. Ochs could not have possibly issued a "success policy" to his father. His were not the ordinary but the ineffable virtues.

It is from the atmosphere of his father that the son inherited his own deep respect for personality, his abiding kindliness. The wages on the *Times* are the highest. Discharges for reasons of economy and except for real cause are unknown. The *Times* really succeeds remarkably well for such a large institution in being a "happy family." Its welfare department, its old age and sickness pensions, have nothing about them of that meretricious counter-reformation with which so many employers are meeting social unrest. Mr. Ochs's annual Christmas campaign for the Hundred Neediest Cases, whatever its economic wisdom, is so free of all "scientific" social work that it is very much like the delicate charity of Julius Ochs. And it is no doubt in the same spirit that the *Times* always keeps on its payroll one or two broken-down newspaper men who have seen better days.

But the qualities which assured his success Mr. Ochs undoubtedly got from his mother. It is not platitude but a profound personal experience which makes Mr. Ochs advise the young man about to take out a "success policy": "You must strive faithfully to live up to the precepts taught you as a child by your mother." Bertha Levy Ochs was an active, dominant, extraordinarily effective personality, and it was she who built the common virtues into young Adolph with a master hand.

At the age of fifteen, in the revolutionary year of '48, she made a daring revolutionary gesture one evening in Heidelberg. The next morning she caught the sailing vessel for America. She joined an uncle in New Orleans and grew up in the traditions of the conservative South, which proved very congenial to her essentially conservative nature. During the Civil War her ardent sympathies were with the Confederacy. While her husband was stationed as a captain in the Union Army in Cincinnati, she would wheel across the bridge to

Covington a baby carriage packed with quinine destined for the Confederate Army, while little Adolph sat in blissful and round-eyed innocence on top of this contraband, as unaware of social conflict then as he has remained ever since. "Yes," Mr. Ochs reminisces with affectionate disapproval, "Mother gave Father a lot of trouble in those days." And, indeed, for a Southern belle and a mother in Israel to defy her husband and an entire army was no mean assertion in early militant feminism.

Bertha Ochs began the task of training little Adolph in her own habits of thrift, industry, honesty, and responsibility when he was a mere child. Under her combination of ethical and vocational guidance he became a prodigy in the common virtues and their application. At the age of eleven he began delivering newspapers for the *Knoxville Chronicle* at four o'clock every morning. At the age of fifteen he rose to printer's devil. Two years later he became a practical printer on the *Louisville Courier-Journal*. Then he returned to Knoxville as a compositor on the *Daily Tribune*. There he rose in rapid succession to assistant foreman in the composingroom, to star reporter, and finally to the position of business manager. At the age of nineteen he became the manager of the *Chattanooga Daily Dispatch*. In 1878 the *Dispatch* failed and Mr. Ochs became the receiver. He liquidated its debts and a few months later, at the age of twenty, he consolidated it with the *Chattanooga Times*, of which he gained control with two hundred and fifty borrowed dollars. He still owns the *Chattanooga Times*.

During these nine formative years from eleven to twenty, which constituted a perfect apprenticeship for Mr. Ochs's subsequent career, his mother constantly extended her personality through him. Gradually young Adolph took over one family responsibility after another under her guidance. Julius Ochs became the nominal treasurer of the *Chattanooga Times*. But most of the father's life was spent in teaching, in charity, in living up to his own conceptions of good citizenship. It was Adolph who sent two younger brothers through college, foregoing such an education himself, and this left him an indelible wistfulness for formal education and no doubt accounts for the *Times*'s vast admiration for professors.

This intimate tutelage over his brothers goes back as far as 1872, when Adolph was fourteen, George eleven, and Milton eight. Though Adolph was going to school and getting up at four in the morning to deliver his newspapers, he found that his evenings were being wasted. And so he organized a company with George and Milton to sell refreshments at Staub's Opera House. And here is the contract, in its original spelling, written on the stationery of Julius Ochs, Justice of the Peace and Notary Public, and "witnessed" by the tiny tot sisters.

State of Ten   Knoxville Tenn
Knox Cy

This day of Nov. 1/72, We Adolph, George and Milton Ochs, do hereby agree to become partners, In selling refreshment at Staub Opera house, in the city of Knoxville Tenn, for the term of one year ending Nov 1/73 under the firm name of Ochs Bros, It is agreed that the sum invested by Julius Ochs be paid to the said Julius Ochs from the sale of the goods, It is also hereby agreed, that Adolph Ochs give his attention to the finicial matters and to the selling and buying goods, And that George and Milton Ochs, tend to the selling of goods through the Opera House, and it is also hereby agreed That each shall have an equal share in the Business and that the Profits be divided

Signed by
Adolph S. Ochs (s)
witnessed by   George W. Ochs (s)
Bertha Ochs (s)   Milton Ochs (s)
Nannie Ochs (s)

This partnership has held good for fifty-four years. George and Milton are still working for Adolph. George W. Ochs Oakes is now the editor of *Current History*. Milton B. Ochs is the managing editor of the *Chattanooga Times*.

VI

The story of the *New York Times* under Mr. Ochs is very simply told. In the spring of 1896 he came to New York in response to a wire from a friend who was unofficially authorized to offer him the management of the *New York Mercury*, which somewhat resembled the present-day *Morning Telegraph*. Mr. Ochs was but mildly interested. And while he hesitated Henry Alloway, the Wall Street reporter of the *New York Times*, informed him that the *Times* could be purchased, as it was in extreme financial difficulties. Mr. Ochs became interested, and after a few weeks of negotiation he acquired the newspaper by a contract that gave him the controlling interest when he had for three consecutive years earned its expenses. The series of financial transactions which he manoeuvred for the control of the reorgan-

374

ized company was so skillful that all he ever had to invest for his majority interest was $75,000.

On August 18, 1896, he took charge. The old staff was kept on. Mr. Ochs religiously lived up to his ideas of news. In two years he was nearly "broke." His friends advised him to raise the price of the paper from three cents to five. Then he took a desperate chance, which was a stroke of genius. He cut the price to one cent. Circulation went up, advertising came in. In 1900 the *Times* evenly turned the corner of the century. In 1901–2 it made $153,000.

Luck helped. The younger Bennett threw away his chances on the *Herald*. He was too erratic to follow his marvelous nose for news — news which he created when nothing spectacular happened. Greeley was primarily interested in Fourier and Owen. Godkin tried valiantly to live up to the political ideals of Cobden and Bright. Dana was busy with style and wit. Later on, Munsey began his career of murdering newspapers. The *Press*, the morning *Sun*, and finally the *Herald*, were killed. And the *Times* prospered. To-day its profits are around $4,000,000 a year, of which almost ninety-seven per cent are ploughed back into the business. It is the world's richest newspaper; and, I think, also its best — as a *news*paper.

In 1918 the *Times* was awarded the first Pulitzer Gold Medal in Journalism. Mr. Ochs is a member of the Executive Committee of the Associated Press. His power over public information is incalculable. He is a Commander of the Legion of Honor, an honorary Master of Yale, a Doctor of Laws of Columbia, and a Doctor of Letters of New York and Chattanooga Universities. But he himself is essentially the same simple boy who fifty-seven years ago ran a newspaper route in Knoxville. All this success was implicit in his mother's encouragement of the "ordinary virtues." To doubt this success is to doubt her. And to it he clings with childlike simplicity. In his ingenuousness are all the resources of his personality.

VII

Mr. Ochs is honest enough to suit the most sensitive honorableness. He could not sincerely manage the *Times* differently. The tower of the *Times* leans backward in meticulous propriety. By his own works Mr. Ochs has proven to himself the social value of impersonal journalism. But deep in him there is a balked censor which hesitatingly points to Garrison, Greeley, Bowles, Godkin, Villard, to the "crusaders" of personal journalism. Mr. Ochs represses this censor; for he finely perceives that there is something very precious in the "follies" of these crusaders, while his "common sense" indicts these follies as querulous and absurd. Hence his extraordinary touchiness to all but conservative criticism. Hence the subtle defensive and protesting note about his success. "I would trust these crusaders with my last will and testament, but with an idea I would not trust them around the corner," he told me. Their ideas disturb his childlike fixation in the ordinary virtues.

The critic of the *Times* interprets this protest as a sense of guilt. It is the reverse. It betokens not a guilty but a baffled conscience, which is a very delicate conscience. Mr. Ochs cannot bear to have his simple recipe of life doubted, because that is all he believes in. And when he defends his deep-felt conviction that the *Times* is merely the logical reward of simple integrity a childlike hurt steals into his luminous eyes which is irresistibly human.

Possibly it would have been better if the spirit of Julius Ochs had now and then interfered with the success of the *Times*.

27

The Colonel's Century: *Time* Looks at Robert R. McCormick

Colonel Robert R. McCormick, publisher of the *Chicago Tribune*, has shared with William Randolph Hearst much of the criticism directed against the modern American press. In June 1947, on the occasion of the hundredth anniversary of the *Tribune*'s founding, the following unsigned article appeared in *Time* magazine. Used by permission, copyright Time Inc. 1947.

Just to reassure himself, City Editor William Donald Maxwell got the fireworks company on the phone. "Tell me," he pleaded, anxiously chomping a long cigar. "I don't care if you're spending five thousand bucks or 15 thousand. But are you sure this is going to be the damnedest fireworks show *any*body ever saw, *any*place?"

"Yessir," came the answer. "Damnedest fireworks show *any*body ever saw, *any*place."

Don Maxwell knew it had better be. His awesome and exacting employer, Colonel Robert Rutherford McCormick, was sparing neither money, manpower nor gunpowder to make his *Chicago Tribune*'s 100th birthday celebration next week the most colossal show since the Chicago fire.

The Colonel had invited 5,000 carefully screened leading citizens to sip punch and nibble cake with him at a reception in Tribune Tower, his 36-story, $8,000,000 Gothic pile at 435 North Michigan Avenue. He had bought a $20,000 hour on 240 stations of the Mutual network (in which the *Trib* owns a fifth interest and a key outlet, WGN) to salute his paper and himself. And he had commanded his battery of giant presses to spin out a centennial edition that would make his newsboys stagger.

For next Tuesday night, on the flat Lake Michigan waterfront, he had decreed a grand finale: a covey of acrobats performing like June bugs, surfboarders jumping through flaming hoops, the "damnedest

377

fireworks show" with two Niagara Falls, Hiroshima (in natural color), pinwheel portraits of Abraham Lincoln, Dick Tracy and Orphan Annie, and tableaux from the *Tribune*'s history. The Colonel expects fully 400,000 readers to turn out for the show and sing *Happy Birthday*.

PYROTECHNICIAN

The fire-breathing monster which calls itself the "World's Greatest Newspaper" (and which Oswald Garrison Villard nominated as the world's worst) is accustomed to writing its history in fireworks. Of the 1,700 dailies in the U.S., the *Chicago Tribune*, an organ of tremendous vigor and imposing technical virtuosity, is easily the loudest and perhaps the most widely feared and hated. It is also the biggest (circ. 1,040,000 daily, 1,500,000 Sunday) among papers of standard size; its flashy offspring, the tabloid *New York Daily News*, is the biggest of all. Between them, parent and child rake in profits as high as $13 million a year, and Tribune Co. stock is worth $42,000 a share.

All through the five-state empire, which Colonel McCormick likes to call "Chicagoland" (the late Frank Knox, "afternoon colonel" of the rival *Chicago Daily News*, liked to call it "Scatterville"), the trumpeting *Tribune* is the autocrat of town and country breakfast tables. Its strident voice of command, always heard if not always heeded, is shrewdly pitched to pierce the eardrums and excite the ancient prejudices and suspicions of the Midwest heartland. In fighting the draft, heckling the war effort and filibustering against U.S. participation in the postwar world, the *Tribune* has coldly appropriated to its own uses the Midwest's vestigial isolationism and the regional inferiority complex that shows itself in a belligerent assertion of superiority. There is more to this process than mere toadying to local tastes: Colonel McCormick feels the same way.

The *Trib* still sees silk-hatted Wall Street bankers lurking around every State Street corner, and redcoats behind every red oak tree. (In 1943, its publisher solemnly told a Detroit audience that after World War I he had helped the U.S. General Staff work out plans to repel an invasion from Canada by 300,000 British regulars.) But even when it is up to no good, Colonel McCormick's xenophobic "World's Greatest Newspaper" is one of the last, anachronistic citadels of muscular personal journalism.

ROBERT R. MC CORMICK

BERTIE V. DANTE

Like William Randolph Hearst, the *Tribune*'s Robert Rutherford McCormick is more easily caricatured than portrayed. The sharpest shaft ever aimed at him — that he possessed "the greatest mind of the 14th Century" — did Bertie, as well as Dante, a disservice.* So have the oversimplified pictures of McCormick as a feudal lord of the manor, aping the English aristocrats he professes to detest; as a fascist menace; as "Col. McCosmic," the frustrated military strategist; as a crackpot Midas.

A realistic portrait would show a tall (6 ft. 4 in.), ruddy, 200-lb. man of 66 who can still get into his World War I uniform. The haughty eyes, ice-water blue, would window an inordinately shy, insufferably proud, incredibly prejudiced mind, acutely aware of its heritage.

It is in some ways a brilliant mind, with some appalling blind spots. The Colonel is well-read in history, at least in the names and dates of battles, but has learned from it only his single-track, narrow-gauge approach to world affairs. The people he despises most are amateur military strategists, and none more than that fellow amateur, Franklin Roosevelt.

WHAT HATH HE WROUGHT

The Colonel is not sure that his own equal in military knowledge has existed since Hannibal. In February 1942, when a onetime *Tribune* employee asked him how he could campaign so hatefully against the Administration when the nation was at war, McCormick wrote him in reply:

What the most powerful propaganda organization in the world has misled you into believing was a campaign of hatred, has really been a constructive campaign without which this country would be lost.

You do not know it, but the fact is that I introduced the R.O.T.C. into the schools; that I introduced machine guns into the army; that I introduced mechanization; I introduced automatic rifles; I was the first ground officer to go up in the air and observe artillery fire. Now I have succeeded in making that the regular practice in the army. . . .

On the other hand I was unsuccessful in obtaining the fortification of Guam. . . . I was unable to persuade the navy and the administration that airplanes could destroy battleships.

* Also slighted: Chaucer, Petrarch, Boccaccio, John Wycliffe.

379

I did get the Marines out of Shanghai, but was unsuccessful in trying to get the army out of the Philippines. . . .

The opposition resorts to such tactics as charging me with hatred and so forth, but in view of the accomplishment I can bear up under it.

Chicago Poet Carl Sandburg's admiring comment was: "And on the seventh day he rested."

POOR LITTLE RHODE ISLAND

The Colonel once imperiously read Rhode Island out of the Union for packing its supreme court with Democrats, and ordered a star (Rhode Island's, that is) taken out of the flag in the *Tribune* lobby. When a deskman suggested that defacing the flag might be illegal, the Colonel had him call the *Tribune*'s attorneys, and stood by for their ruling. Out of the receiver came the lawyer's anguished squawk, loud enough for the Colonel to hear: "Now who in hell wants to cut a star out of the flag?"

McCormick starts each year with a baronial New Year's reception at the office. It is a command performance: his employees file past their morning-coated boss (a police dog mounts guard at his side), shake his hand, then pass on to the cigars and the punch bowl. Watching the show, his cousin, the late Captain Joseph Medill Patterson of the *New York Daily News*, once drily observed: "Bertie certainly likes to crack the whip and watch the serfs march by."

FARM TO MARKET

The Colonel rises at 9 A.M. in his 35-room Georgian mansion (begun by grandfather Joe Medill the year Bertie was born) at Cantigny,* his 1,000-acre farm near Wheaton, Ill. Over a frugal breakfast of coffee and juice, he scans the *Trib*'s fat, one-star final and Marshall Field's skinnier *Sun*, tearing out clippings. He scribbles swift notes on them and stuffs them into his pocket for delivery to his editors. For an hour he strolls Cantigny's gardens and rolling fields (now mostly idle). He has given up riding: "Can't get a groom, dammit," he complains. "There just aren't any good grooms any more."

At 11, one of his two chauffeur-bodyguards brings one of his Buicks around to the door for the 29-mile drive into town (via an arterial gallingly named Roosevelt Road). After one recent commuting trip

* Originally named Red Oaks, renamed by the Colonel after the first real battle of World War I in which U.S. troops (including McCormick) participated.

on which he noted that the crows seemed to be getting out of hand, he was moved to take over the *Tribune* farm column for a short essay on weapons: "The firearms manufacturers," he wrote, "have been dead from the neck up for about 40 years. . . . The crow easily gets away from anything the old-fashioned shotgun can throw at him. There is needed a crow gun to decimate this pest. . . ."

In McCormick's cavernous, walnut-paneled 24th floor office, guarded by two secretaries and one of the *Trib*'s 45 pistol-packing cops, the daily schedule ticks off with military precision. First come Leon Stolz with his squad of editorial writers, and Carey Orr with his crew of highly skilled cartoonists, to hear the orders of the day. The discussion often goes into luncheon at the 19th floor Overset Club, the executives' dining room.

Sometimes a big advertiser is asked to lunch (for buttering), or a politician (for fence-mending). Like many big dailies, particularly in well-bossed cities, the *Tribune* has found it convenient to live with its local administration. For years the Colonel, a rampant Republican, lived in harmony with Democratic Mayor Ed Kelly and his machine.

But the Overset Club can seldom toast an unqualified political victory these days. Against McCormick's advice, Chicago and Illinois went for F.D.R. all four terms. Today, as the state's No. 1 GOPoohbah, the undaunted Colonel is embarrassing his party's national leadership with lavish gifts of his time, thought and peremptory advice. He is scheming to capture the state delegation to Philadelphia in 1948, if not the convention itself. He has already cut down most presidential timber, thinks General MacArthur "the only successful man in public life today."

WHAT'S THE NEWS?

Back from his light lunch, McCormick phones Managing Editor J. Loy ("Pat") Maloney. They talk over the news and the Colonel's slants on the news. The rest of the afternoon the Colonel reads his mail, takes tea and toast, researches his weekly radiorations on forgotten U.S. heroes, sends off memos (signed "R. R. McC.") down his chain of command, and summons department heads to the sanctum. They have learned that it is well to lay a problem crisply on the line, get his decision, which is almost invariably prompt, and get out fast.

"You can't hold his interest if you change the subject on him," says one executive. "Got too much on his mind — logs in the rivers, paper at the mills, the new presses. . . ." He is also getting a little hard of hearing; the man who stays too long finds the boss drifting off into a Yogi-like silence. His men are careful not to smoke in his presence.

Visitors to McCormick's office find him sitting in lonely magnificence behind a great marble desk that dwarfs grandfather Medill's plain wooden one, standing near by. When they get up to leave, they find no exit. Sometimes McCormick lets them stand there, in mounting confusion; then, with a glacial chuckle, he taps a kickplate in the baseboard and a panel in the wall springs open. He is enough of a gadget-lover to wear a watch on each wrist. One is a fancy computing chronometer. "Tells what day it is, too," he says. "Very convenient when traveling."

He knocks off around 5:30, heading for Wheaton or his old and elegant Astor Street town house, where Winston Churchill was a prewar guest. Before bedtime (11:30) he gives the early editions a hawk-like once-over.

A virtual social recluse for several years after his first wife died, McCormick has mellowed and relaxed since December 1944, when he married his neighbor and onetime tenant, gay and gracious Mrs. Maryland Mathison Hooper. Last year he joined the Wheaton First Presbyterian Church, and plunged into an enthusiastic study of Presbyterian theology. Nowadays at Cantigny there are movies and a buffet on Friday nights, and the Colonel and his lady take frequent flying jaunts in his well-appointed Lockheed Lodestar. At his party last Christmas night (complete with boar's head and singers from WGN), he unbent so far as to lead the family in carols around the piano.

ABE AND JOE

McCormick comes by his strongest opinions honestly, by bequest from the man he probably reveres most, his grandfather. Famed *Tribune* Editor Joseph Medill never had any use for Easterners, Englishmen or kowtowing to anybody. A founder of the Republican Party, he once told Abraham Lincoln: "Take your goddamned feet off my desk, Abe!" Years later, he went to Washington to protest the high Illinois quota in a Civil War draft call. "You, Medill," the President scolded him, "are acting like a coward." After all, said Mr. Lincoln (as Joe Medill told it), the *Tribune* had helped promote the war. "Go home," he commanded, "and send us those men."

Robert McCormick was born in downtown Chicago 33 years after the *Tribune*, and almost within earshot of its presses. He has remarked that more people visit his birthplace than Lincoln's; the room is now the upstairs bar at the Key Club, one of Chicago's better eating places. He was a reserved boy; some of his relatives guess that strong-willed Kate Medill McCormick lavished most of her affection on Medill, her charming first-born son. A lonely second son, Bertie grew into a proud and lonely rock of a man. In preparation for Groton and Yale, he went to school in France and England. He was too young for it to do him any permanent harm, as it does the more mature Rhodes Scholars who, he firmly believes, turn into British spies. At Groton he was one form behind F.D.R. who, he recalls, "was not regarded as one of the most promising boys. If he had not become President, I doubt if I would have remembered the man at all."

At first the snobbish Eastern "Grotties" gave Bertie the country-cousin treatment; he has never forgiven the East for that. When he went home and complained, his father assured him that he came from a fine old Virginia family. Says the Colonel: "I just put my nose a little higher than the rest of the boys, and I got along fine." He went on to Yale, later studied law and decided to become a judge. ("They had a lot of Yale men on the Supreme Court then, and we got the idea that it was the thing to do.") At that moment in history Cousin Joe Patterson, lately out of Yale, was writing socialist plays. Joe's sister, Eleanor ("Cissie") Patterson, now boss of Washington's rancorous *Times-Herald*,* was cutting capers (as Countess Gizycka) in Continental society. Then death came to Joe's father, the editor of the *Tribune*. Says McCormick: "There was no one else to take over the paper, so that 'elected' us to the newspaper business."

ONE WHO SURVIVED

Monthly, from 1914 on, the cousins took turns editing the *Tribune*. In off months, Bertie tended to the business side, and Joe, a born Sunday section-hand, began weaving his magic with comic strips. Because

---

* EDITORS' NOTE: Mrs. Patterson died in July 1948 and willed the paper to seven of its executives. They sold the *Times-Herald* to Colonel McCormick in July 1949, and he took personal command of it in 1951. The death of Joseph M. Patterson in 1946 left the *New York Daily News* under the control of a board of directors, whose most influential member was McCormick. He did not take an active interest in the paper's operations, however, leaving it in the hands of its executives.

the two often disagreed, readers of their editorials were frequently confused. In France, in 1918, they hit on a better plan. McCormick had had his day of battle (at Cantigny) and was on his way home. "I construed my orders very liberally," he says. "Douglas MacArthur, a good friend of mine, was chief of staff of Joe's division and gave me a permit to go see him."

On a dunghill back of a farmhouse at Mareuil-en-Dôle, the cousins held the famous conversation that sired the fabulous *New York Daily News*. Excited by the success of Lord Northcliffe's tabloid *London Mirror*, Patterson talked McCormick into joining him in a Manhattan picture paper.

After a colicky start, their brainchild shot into the black in its second year. While Patterson ran the New York invasion, the Colonel proceeded to knock Hearst out of the Chicago morning field in a circulation war organized by the late rough-and-tumble Max Annenberg, whom the *Trib* had hired away from Hearst. As a sure source of newsprint, Bertie also built the gargantuan trees-to-*Tribunes* production line that now grinds out 300,000 tons of Canadian paper a year, insuring both papers against shortages.

MASTER'S VOICE

The uses to which McCormick has put that newsprint have horrified critics of the U.S. press. On its 75th anniversary the "W.G.N." crowed that "Homer would have liked to work on the *Tribune*. . . . So would Horace . . . Balzac, Addison, Samuel Johnson, Dickens, Hardy, Kipling and Mark Twain." In the paper's "golden era" they might have, if they were hard up; they would have found Ring Lardner, Charles MacArthur, Percy Hammond and Burton Rascoe at nearby desks. But they would not have liked the period between wars. By then, McCormick was spreading his direction from the editorial page to every page, and the *Tribune* was shamelessly but cleverly angling and twisting the news to suit his fears and whims.

It was a hectic era that found Colonel McCormick touting Fascism (a 1927 editorial: "Dictatorships frequently are constructive. That is the case with Mussolini." 1928: ". . . we can use that sort of government here"). He pooh-poohed the bomber (1926: ". . . the outlook for bombing plane versus battleship does not favor the plane"). In a careless moment, he even nominated Roosevelt II (1929: "In this role he might . . . from the White House restore the rich heritage of constitutional order . . .").

But it was on the flaming issue of war and peace that McCormick won his reputation as the most bitterly hated press lord of his time. Beginning in 1939, daily and Sunday, the *Trib*'s eight-column banner lines screamed McCormick's ideas on the approaching conflict:

WAR BLAMED ON U.S. ENVOYS

HALIFAX STEERS F.D.R. BILL

HOUSE PASSES DICTATOR BILL

FIGHT JAPS. BRITONS TO U.S.

It was that kind of talk that goaded Marshall Field III (whose grandfather had staked McCormick's grandfather when he bought the *Tribune*) into starting the *Chicago Sun*, three days before Pearl Harbor exploded the issue of isolationism *v.* interventionism.

FIRST WITH THE MOST

Today, after shattering his lances on the *Trib*'s tough hide for 5½ years, White Knight Marshall Field, at a cost of about $10,000,000, has proved one thing, if nothing else: that it takes more than good intentions, an unlimited bankroll and an Associated Press franchise to make good in the newspaper business. What it takes, the Colonel has got.

The big reason for his *Tribune*'s success is that McCormick has simply made it indispensable. No paper in all Chicagoland can match its overwhelming coverage of the news. When a big story breaks, the *Trib* can throw a score of men on it to outreport and outwrite the opposition. In sports, in comics, women's pages, signed columns and display ads it offers all things to all people. It is the housewife's guide, the politician's breakfast food, a bible to hundreds of small-town editorial writers. A classless paper, it is read on the commuter trains from swank Lake Forest, and on the dirty "El" cars taking workers to the stockyards. (The Colonel once banned foreign titles from his pages, still insists on simplified spelling, *i.e.*, "frate" for freight.)

Two years ago Louisville Publisher Mark Ethridge made a realistic appraisal: "I have always felt that those who said [the *Tribune*'s] great hold came from comic strips and other features were wrong: it possesses an animal vigor. . . ." Out of the side of its mouth, the *Tribune* proudly accepted the tribute: "Comes the dawn. It ain't Orphan Annie. It's the hair on our chest." The editorial staff has a talent for translating the Colonel's often pompous edicts into gutty, readable prose.

ARMS AND THE MEN

The *Tribune* is a tightly run command, but it is no one-man show. McCormick's army of talent is extraordinarily well paid, headed by high-powered brass:

Chesser Campbell, 49, the *Tribune*'s $100,000-a-year advertising manager, is a Phi Beta Kappa from the University of Michigan, who started with McCormick's old, expatriate *Paris Tribune* in 1921. One measure of his success: last year the *Trib* led the world in advertising lineage.

Louis Rose, 66, tiny, tough-talking director of Circulation ($110,-000 a year), is an ex-newsboy, disciple and brother-in-law of the late Max Annenberg. He is the only executive who can stop the presses (with a buzzer that blows a siren in the press room). "Louie" Rose cruises his newsstands at night in a new, $5,000 Packard. His boss bought it, found the roof too low for the high McCormick head, told Rose: "If you like it I'll give it to you." Rose liked it.

Arthur H. Schmon, 52, mustached president of McCormick's Ontario Paper Co. and head of its timberlands, paper mills and ships, bosses more people (7,850) than the *Tribune* and *Daily News* employ together (3,200 apiece). He was the Colonel's World War I adjutant, named a son Robert McCormick Schmon, is probably closest to the boss of all executives (none of them calls him "Mac," and few presume to call him "Bert").

Elbert M. Antrim, 61, rosy-cheeked business manager, watches the *Tribune*'s fat till.

Pat Maloney, 55, head of the 420-man news department, transmutes the boss's notions into type. He is a Phi Bete from Dartmouth, flew with Rickenbacker in World War I, graduated in reporting from the cooperative City News Bureau, from which he hires up to 18 bright young newsmen a year.

Arch Ward, 50, is a $50,000-a-year sports editor who looks more like a mousy small-town merchant. But his merchandise is one secret of the *Tribune*'s success: a whole generation of readers has grown up thinking of the *Trib* in terms of his staff's well-done sports reporting and his own huge promotions (the Golden Gloves, Silver Skates, all-star football and baseball games). His "In the Wake of the News" column was once Ring Lardner's.

THE HIRED MEN

From top officers to plain foot soldiers, the *Tribune*'s staff is an efficient, well-equipped army of professionals who march on full stomachs. People of good will sometimes wonder how men of all political and sociological stripes can work for McCormick without forfeiting their journalistic souls. The answer is that *Trib* men are not required to put their hearts into every cause for which they bear arms. The conscientious objectors are not assigned to combat duty on McCormick campaigns — although those who join the crusades get ahead faster.

The airy, relaxed, two-story local room is a good place to work, where the Colonel is felt (he has a rule against feet on desks) but rarely seen. The "R. R. McC." memos and verbal orders are polite and direct. "There's a lot of rain," he will tell his farm editor. "Maybe we ought to tell people how to plant beans." The C.I.O. Newspaper Guild has made no headway on the *Trib*: it has little to offer newsmen who get good salaries, free dental service, big bonuses, home loans, chests of silver when they marry, and even a "drunk bank" for the man who wakes up broke after a binge.

The shock troops of the 13-man Washington bureau are so well conditioned by the time they go to an assignment in the capital that they need no telling how to slant their stuff. They get a constant stream of impatient queries from the Colonel (sample: "What's happened to Robert M. La Follette?"), are the best-paid ($137 minimum) staff in the capital. Walter Trohan now directs them; 70-year-old Arthur Sears Henning, a sort of commander emeritus, gets $30,000 a year for life, whether he works or not.

For all its array of talent in depth, the only Pulitzer Prize the *Tribune* ever got went to old-school Cartoonist John T. McCutcheon. It gets awards of a different sort: next to the Hearst papers, it was voted "least fair and reliable" in a 1936 poll of Washington correspondents; "the newspaper . . . most flagrant in angling or weighting the news" in a 1944 poll. Its publisher was named No. 1 in a U.S. "hall of fame" five years ago — by Rabble-Rouser Gerald L. K. Smith.

The *Tribune* has had to live down scandals that would have crippled most papers. There was, for example, the murder of Reporter Jake

Lingle, who, it turned out, was so tied up with his underworld news sources that he had piled up a fortune of $150,000. Prosecutor C. Wayland ("Curly") Brooks got a conviction against the murderer, an obscure gangster. Later, with the *Tribune*'s blessing, Brooks was elected to the U.S. Senate. Even more embarrassing to Military Expert McCormick was the Battle of Midway story that irresponsibly gave away the vital war secret that the U.S. had cracked the Jap code.

IN HIS STEPS

The eccentric newspaper genius who has made the *Tribune* what it is today is wholly dedicated to his job. He considers his top aides his best friends, and he is suspicious of overtures from anyone else. He once told his attorney, Weymouth Kirkland: "The minute I become friendly with a man, he wants me to keep his divorce out of the paper or something." When he dies, the Colonel will leave his empire in the hands of a junta of its officers. He has no son and heir, but he has a favorite niece, blonde Ruth McCormick ("Bazy") Miller, 26 (daughter of the Colonel's late brother Medill and Ruth Hanna McCormick), who is learning the business with her husband by running a small-town daily in La Salle, Ill.

At his 65th birthday party, the Colonel asked Bazy Miller to stand up in front of his 170 guests. "Bazy," he rumbled, "tradition has an important part in every organization. And when, 15 or 20 years from now, I am no longer [here], Ruth Elizabeth — Bazy — will be carrying on the tradition of Joseph Medill, an invaluable thing to all of you." *

By the Colonel's own estimates, that will not be until 1960 or 1965. So he is by no means ready to drop the reins; he has nothing but pity for his Yale classmates "who went into the big Eastern banks, retired at 60 and now have nothing to do." He has plenty to do. The country is still to be saved; the Midwest has still to be rescued from the East, and the U.S. from the British Empire.

Last week an interviewer asked him if he hoped one day to be President of the U.S. The Colonel shot him a withering look. "Out of the question," he snapped. "No big publisher has ever held high public office." As any fool could see, if a man had a commanding view from the Tribune Tower, what would he want with the White House?

* EDITORS' NOTE: Mrs. Miller served as editor of the *Washington Times-Herald* from July 1949 to April 1951, but resigned after a disagreement with McCormick.

INDEX